BEYOND I

HARRY VERHOEVEN
ANATOL LIEVEN
(*Editors*)

Beyond Liberal Order

*States, Societies and Markets in the
Global Indian Ocean*

HURST & COMPANY, LONDON

First published in the United Kingdom in 2021 by
C. Hurst & Co. (Publishers) Ltd.,
New Wing, Somerset House, Strand, London, WC2R 1LA
© Harry Verhoeven, Anatol Lieven and the Contributors, 2021
All rights reserved.
Printed in Great Britain by Bell and Bain Ltd, Glasgow.

The right of Harry Verhoeven, Anatol Lieven and the
Contributors to be identified as the authors of this
publication is asserted by them in accordance with the
Copyright, Designs and Patents Act, 1988.

A Cataloguing-in-Publication data record for this book
is available from the British Library.

ISBN: 9781787385436

www.hurstpublishers.com

CONTENTS

CONTENTS

ACKNOWLEDGEMENTS

This book emerged, like many of the most promising journeys, from a set of sprawling conversations that ranged from the virtues of the double harmonic scale and Nyonya cooking to the role of Australian commanders and Colombian, Eritrean and Sudanese mercenaries in the Yemen Civil War. These exchanges began in 2015—after we both relocated to the small peninsula-state of Qatar where it was impossible not to be struck by how a country that until a generation ago was cast as one of the Middle East's most introverted societies was furiously reimagining its past and future in the world. As the launch pad of Qatar Airways' global conquest, the host of endless art exhibitions and the 2022 FIFA World Cup, and the base for broadcasting Al-Jazeera's citadel storming bulletins, it is much more than just a shoreline where the ripple effects of transnationalization wash up with unpredictable consequences. It is a city where the pulse of globalization—in all its promises and its dark-sides—can be felt and from whence the process is being further accelerated: where gastronomical traditions are being fused and reinvented by some of the world's most creative cooks; where the biggest military base in the Middle East sustains what remains of the Pax Americana; and where exiles from civil wars the world over pray next to each other and discuss the future of democracy and justice. Qatar is at the heart of dazzling financial circuits, whether sovereign wealth buying up London and Paris, sprawling charity networks that sustain Islamic proselytization in Java and the African Sahel, or remittances pushing back poverty in the remotest corners of the Philippine Archipelago and the Somali territories.

ACKNOWLEDGEMENTS

With circa 90% of the population consisting of foreigners, the country's extraordinary demographics are sometimes described as a microcosm that reflects the linguistic, cultural and economic cosmopolitanism of the Indian Ocean World—at once hierarchical and segmented but also equalizing and opportunity creating. Doha constitutes a central node that is at once revitalizing deep, multilayered patterns of imbrication between Africa, Arabia and Asia *and* experimenting with globe-spanning ambitions and new forms of connectivity through polyglot worldmaking: it is simultaneously an experiment enabled by various episodes of liberal international order and a challenge to the way that concept is usually thought of and analytically deployed by scholars of international relations. While the International Hydrographic Organization does not consider Qatar part of the oceanic rim, it embodies, in many ways, what this edited volume articulates as the "Global Indian Ocean": a context from where we can rethink notions of hegemony and the geography of processes of (dis)integration through the mobility of capital, ideas, identities and people that this book is centrally concerned with.

We have been extremely fortunate to have such a stimulating setting shape the contours of this intellectual project. We have also been able to count on the generous support of many in bringing together our own transnational web of scholars to reflect on questions of political order, social stratification and modes of belonging. Inevitably, we can only thank some of them here; nonetheless, the editors and contributing authors are all deeply grateful for the privileged opportunities granted to us and for the challenges and suggestions that have been shared with our team over the course of half a decade.

The Qatar National Research Fund provided important resources to host an international conference and a follow-up workshop that explored our core interest in thinking through and thinking beyond liberal order through a heterogeneity of geographies. Salim Al-Qassmi opened doors in Oman as did Valerie Hänsch, Tamer Abdel Kreem and the team at the Centre for African Studies in Maputo and Markos Tekle and Abdeta Beyene in Addis Ababa. Charles King, Tom Banchoff, Irfan Nooruddin, Sam Potolicchio, Kate Kimble and faculty chair Amira Sombol at Georgetown University lent support to our efforts in Doha and Washington. Hagar Rakha's leadership made our meetings possible in practical terms. Joshua Mitchell was a terrific soundboard early on in the project. Anatol in particular also acknowledges his new colleagues at the Quincy Institute for most interesting discussions of Indian Ocean geopolitics, and Michael Swaine in particular for his insights.

We want to thank various scholars who made part of the oceanic journey with us: Afyare Elmi, Marieme Lo, Amelia Fauzia, Zoha Waseem, Pranab Bardhan, Sharath Srinivasan, Amal Al-Malki, Sana Tariq, Jihane Benamar, Allen Isaacman, Abdullah Baaboud, Kjetil Tronvoll and Mohammed Hassan Ali. Not all of that travelling was smooth sailing; the wide-ranging substantive inputs, personal kindness and good humour of Eckart Woertz, Ricardo Soares de Oliveira, Phil Roessler and Christopher Clapham were even more appreciated than they usually are. Roger Haydon sent excellent comments on the first drafts of the introduction; Russell Martin's copy-editing was outstanding. Michael Dwyer's enthusiasm proved highly encouraging and gave us the confidence to complete the intellectual task at hand.

Christine Umutoni, Sofia Ahmad, Joan Bordon, Joe Piper, Jorge Codas Thompson Perez and Simukai Chigudu made, as usual, all the difference—physically in Indian Ocean locales or in spirit. So was Tom Matthijs who provided safe anchorage and subtle wit when it was most needed. Ms. Rose could always be counted on.

Finally, this book would not have materialized without the deep, deep love of our respective families. Home is home. To Katja and Mischa, Aliya and Mams, Sasha and Maimuna: thank you so much.

1

ORDERING THE GLOBAL INDIAN OCEAN

THE ENDURING CONDITION OF THIN HEGEMONY

Harry Verhoeven

Of all the macro-regions of the earth, the Indian Ocean world contains the greatest range of cultures and religions, political systems and commercial networks. Almost three billion humans live in the countries along the shores of the Indian Ocean and another half a billion reside in states adjacent to the oceanic rim. The populations here are, more than anywhere else, young, multilingual and likely to move in their lives from the countryside to the cities. It is in this region that many of the key challenges facing humanity in the next decades—adapting to climate change, responding to deadly pandemics and reducing poverty while creating meaningful employment—will demand a defining response.

Throughout the ages, land-based empires and the cosmopolitan port cities that supplied them dominated the shores of the globe's third biggest body of water and connected them with each other—forming, together with China, the beating heart of the world economy before the advent of capitalism. This mercantile tradition gave it a crucial role in the British Empire too, with India, positioned at the centre of most of its overseas possessions, as the jewel in the imperial crown. The region experienced lengthy economic decline in the 20th century, giving rise to nostalgia for a lost age: the quintessential image of the ocean-faring dhow sailing into the setting sun. Today, however, the Indian Ocean world is once again surging in global importance. Whatever metric one uses, its dynamic character is undeniable: the Indian Ocean has the densest flows of migration in the world; its trade routes, from the Straits of Malacca to the Cape and the Suez Canal, are crucial to global commerce; littoral states have been experiencing some of the fastest economic growth anywhere on the planet in the last thirty years; old and new superpowers alike are rapidly increasing their military presence onshore and offshore; and climate change is already disturbing weather patterns and altering coastlines in this macro-region, which is vulnerable like no other.

The Indian Ocean is also the fastest-changing and most unpredictable region on the planet in terms of its politics—local, regional and international. The countries of the region range from the bustling global cities of Singapore and Dubai and the enduring imperial states of Thailand and Iran to the violent fragmentation of authority in Somalia, with a great mixture of different experiences in between. The country that gives the Ocean its name, India, will soon be the world's populous polity. Rising global powers like China and regional heavyweights like Saudi Arabia and Ethiopia shape littoral societies, trans-continental trade networks and geopolitical calculations in a way that is leading security systems that hitherto were relatively contained (like the Gulf and the Horn of Africa) to enmesh. In this geographical space, the redrawing of borders and the violent emergence of new states are not a hypothetical scenario but a bitter reality—from the Partition of the Indian subcontinent in 1947 amidst genocidal killing to the hard-fought liberations of Eritrea and East Timor in the 1990s to the contemporary crumbling of Yemen's government. While the Indian Ocean is sometimes melancholically mourned as yesterday's world, it is, as the contributors to this volume will argue, also very much that of tomorrow.

Studying the Ocean is not just a fascinating endeavour in its own right, but sheds light on the nature of international order in the 21st century. After World War II, the United States assumed the responsibility of reforming the international system in ways that it thought would prevent cataclysmic conflict, spread economic prosperity and guarantee American security. The resultant order was clearly hierarchical in its underpinnings of unprecedented military strength but US hegemony prioritized liberal objectives and instruments to give it longevity. Procedurally, Washington invested in creating multilateral institutions and a web of rule-based arrangements that bound the hegemon and its allies together, ensuring authority would be legitimate, predictable and constrained. Substantively, the liberal order sought to protect the Western model of representative democracy and capitalism and to spread it all over the world in the face of the alternative promoted by the Soviet-led communist bloc. As the Cold War ended, the US-led system of alliances, institutions and norms did not disintegrate, but instead penetrated where previously its reach had been tenuous. The three pillars of the post-1945 global political economy that define this liberal order in our understanding—the Pax Americana, free markets and liberal democracy—appeared unchallengeable. The progress of states in the international system would be measured by their degree of convergence ("transition") towards these. For liberal theorists, the domestic foundations and international architecture of liberal order are mutually reinforcing and universally desirable (and desired). While few still explicitly use the "end of history" aphorism,[1] the notion of a global, teleological march towards a very specific modernity remains widespread and (until recently) taken for granted.

Yet what does liberal order amount to outside the core areas of the North Atlantic where it was most formally institutionalized? What do empirical realities in Africa, the Gulf and Asia reveal about the relationship between international order and its constituent parts? What happens when, following Chakrabarty,[2] we "provincialize" the US-led "global" liberal order and examine the ways in which liberal democracy, free markets and the US security umbrella have been understood, mediated, reappropriated, resisted and contributed to by actors in the Indian Ocean world?

There are several reasons why the Ocean is a particularly apt site for asking questions about the past and future of liberal order. As the home of more than a third of humanity, the Indian Ocean world is essential to any global aspirations of liberal order; it makes no sense to speak of "global" order if three billion people are analytically (and practically) ignored. Moreover, there are significant theoretical motivations for rethinking international order from an Indian Ocean standpoint. Contrary to the Atlantic or Pacific worlds, where regional order has for decades been dominated by a clear hegemon which spearheaded the development of an elaborate security architecture, encouraged parliamentary democracy and spurred the institutionalization of deep trade and investment ties, the post-1945 geopolitical landscape in the Indian Ocean has been relatively inchoate. There are no equivalents of NATO, the European Union or even the US–Japan defence relationship in the Indian Ocean world—and liberalism remains a deeply unpopular term associated with Western exceptionalism, whether in East Africa, the Arabian Peninsula, the Indian subcontinent or South East Asia.[3] The weak multilateral institutionalization of the Pax Americana, the dreadful reputation of laissez-faire economics, and the patchy record of elections and human rights in most regional states underline why it is unsurprising that Australia is the only Indian Ocean society that unambiguously identifies as liberal.

The structural condition of what we might call "thin hegemony"— a hierarchical international system with heterogeneous and relatively autonomous constituent parts that interact intensely and often consensually but whose normative preferences need not converge, nor do they mirror those of the dominant power which loosely structures (some of) the system and provides some public goods—offers an intriguing counterpoint to the international relations context shaping the Atlantic and Pacific. Thin hegemony allows us to explore the implications for international cooperation, ideological pluralism and market dynamism of an only irregularly present order-building superpower amidst remarkable political diversity. Moreover, historicizing such a tradition of order and the values and technologies of rule central to it also contributes to rethinking the political geographies of liberalism. Despite the Indian Ocean being on the margins of the priority list of the victorious American superpower post-World War II, historically the fabric of liberal thought and liberal order has been moulded by legacies of empire, with the Ocean serving as the canvas on which civilization, progress and the very meaning of "international" were defined. The "long 19th century" produced "a great transformation to global modernity" and shifted not only the distribution of power, but also the sources of power; an emergent two-tier international order would for the first time span the entire globe and result in the formation of International Relations as a discipline preoccupied with explaining and legitimizing that order.[4] The Indian Ocean world was in a material sense tremendously important to globalizing capitalism, technological revolutions and the forging of overseas empires. Moreover, it served in ideational terms as oppositional Other to an emerging, liberal "West" in the 18th and 19th century. It was here that, through genocidal violence, settler colonialism established Southern Hemisphere "White Dominions" under liberal-constitutional government such as Australia and South Africa. It was also in this region that piracy, *sati* (widow immolation) and slavery were fought, campaigns that proved foundational to liberal ideas of civilisation and international law. The very notion of a (liberal) Pax Britannica was meaningless without its ambivalent relationship with the Indian Ocean, which was simultaneously the core of empire and its Other.

That ambiguity, so closely related to thin hegemony, still defines the oceanic landscape today, as this book documents. On the one hand, the Indian Ocean is an important part of the international state system and global capitalism, which have been powerfully shaped and lorded over by successive European and American hegemonies; the societies that constitute the Ocean cannot be studied without considering extra-regional forces and actors. But it is also striking that no other part of the globe has witnessed such potent challenges to all three pillars of the US-led liberal order, even before self-doubt in the liberal West (re)surfaced with a vengeance. Liberal democracy, deregulated markets and the Pax Americana all coexist alongside, and indeed are all being confronted by, explicit alternatives in the Indian Ocean World. American politico-military dominance is challenged by China's deployment of geo-commercial power through the Belt and Road Initiative and the People's Liberation Army Navy, by the attempted jihadist caliphates of al-Qaeda and Daesh, and by the revisionist Islamic Republic of Iran, which undermines the American- and Saudi-dominated order in the Middle East. Domestically, most Indian Ocean societies are not converging on a liberal-democratic, laissez-faire horizon either. In view of the pluriformity in political economies that straddle the oceanic rim and its hinterland, an impending transition to an "end of history" settlement appears illusory. Neither the statist developmentalism of African (neo-)liberation regimes nor the patronage systems and economic sovereignty-focused policies dominant both in resource-rich states (Indonesia, Malaysia, Oman) and resource-poor ones (Bangladesh, Yemen) conform to the prescriptions of the "Washington Consensus". Across the Indian Ocean World, the state appears either too unable to protect Locke's "life, liberty and property"—in the case of governments struggling to uphold more than nominal control over swathes of their territory, including megacities like Karachi—or too strong, to the point of systemically circumscribing individual freedoms and property rights: the Indian Ocean and its edges host several experiments in state-building in which new Leviathans concentrate and project enormous political and economic power. From Singapore to the United Arab Emirates to Ethiopia, an important gamut of state-builders pursue illiberal recipes that differ resoundingly from the advice of the European Commission or Western-dominated international financial institutions.[5] The boldest such experiment has been pushed by Narendra Modi in Delhi since 2014. His BJP government implements tempered free-market reform, while trying to recast India as a Hindu-nationalist republic in ways that are significantly qualifying its democracy.

Exploring the idea of thin hegemony may enable us to more fruitfully analyse transoceanic processes that are hard to conceptualize, including the complex relationship between liberal globalization and the resurgent interest in how soaring flows of capital, goods and people between Malacca and Bab al-Mandab are producing a reworked "Afrasian Imagination".[6] Even without a strong push by a hegemon to tie regional states, markets and societies together, the Indian Ocean World is, increasingly albeit unevenly, again functioning as an integrated ideational, economic and military space. While this process cannot be seen separately from the impulses provided by the liberal international order, it cannot be reduced to it either. Travel—for education, health, leisure or work—between the different corners of the Indian Ocean has expanded exponentially, as has the consumption of one another's cultural products—from Bollywood's popularity in East Africa and the Gulf to the proliferation of Batik textiles in Arabian and African markets to the embrace of Saudi-promoted Salafism among worshippers in Aceh, Dhaka and Mombasa. Millions of accountants, doctors, drivers, construction workers, imams, IT specialists, nurses, teachers and hospitality providers, drawn from across the Ocean world, live and work in the Gulf and in South-East Asia and trade and investment volumes between different sub-regions have skyrocketed. Military exercises by land, sea and air between Ocean states are also being held with increasing frequency as are meetings to coordinate regional responses to piracy. Several forces drive this integrationist thrust: technological advances, most importantly transportation and communication revolutions; unprecedented capitalist accumulation, propelled by the hydrocarbon bonanza in the Gulf, the liberalization of India's economy and an ocean-wide commodity boom sparked by the economic miracle in post-1978 China; and successive waves of labour migration that have revitalized ancient and deep socio-cultural and economic links. These integrating vectors also include a growing militarization of seas and coastlines, initially spurred by the Global War on Terror. Such projection of military and geo-economic force is also catalysed by growing competition between China, India and the US, and by states caught in regional polarization dynamics such as Saudi Arabia, Iran, Ethiopia and the United Arab Emirates (in the Gulf and Horn of Africa). The Ocean is being reconceptualized as an integrated security space, though crucially without the governance architecture of the North Atlantic and North East Asia.[7]

The task of investigating the relationship between the macro-region and global hegemony is urgent considering the neglect of the politics of Africa, the Indian subcontinent and South East Asia in mainstream accounts of international order.[8] How material realities and guiding ideas of liberal order evolve across time and space and how actors in these regions welcome, resist or refract liberal norms, conditionalities and power structures form the subject of this book. Eight chapters and a conclusion draw on a range of approaches—some macro-comparative, others focused on inter-regional connections, still others dissecting continuity and change in specific communities. What unites the contributing anthropologists, historians, political scientists and sociologists is the prism of a Global Indian Ocean: such a "global" perspective does not entail studying the entire world, but rather analysing the structural conditions and structured transformations that affect disparate places and assessing what they, in turn, reveal about the global level.[9] This volume rejects a teleological account of the integration of states, markets and societies within the Ocean and of the Ocean world into the global system. Instead, it dissects how liberal order has been constructed, perceived, engaged with and/or subverted from the perspective of Indian Ocean states, societies and markets and what outcomes have resulted from processes of both integration and disconnection. This global outlook means at once recognizing the region's specificity as well as its embeddedness in global structures and processes.[10] On the one hand, the Indian Ocean is ecologically distinct from other parts of the planet and has a unique history of integration and disintegration, both as a region and vis-à-vis the global political economy.[11] Moreover, it has experienced—and continues to experience—a structurally different geopolitical context in the form of thin hegemony. At the same time, the Indian Ocean World is both heavily affected by global forces (climate change, organized crime, great power rivalries, etc.) and contributes significantly to them: what happens here is undeniably part of global convulsions and should not be analytically quarantined. Studying continuity and change in the Global Indian Ocean is thus an endeavour concerned both with rich local specificity and with global implications.[12]

Conceptualizing a "Global Indian Ocean" and concentrating on processes of (dis)integration through the mobility of capital, ideas, identities and people has important consequences for how this volume defines its scope of inquiry. Rather than wielding a narrow geographic definition (e.g. only current-day countries that have a coastline adjacent to the Ocean), we see the Global Indian Ocean as contracting and expanding through time. A state like Ethiopia, for instance, no longer lies along the oceanic littoral after the secession of Eritrea but has historically forged significant social, religious, political and military Ocean World connections and is developing many of these again today as an aspiring hegemon in the Horn of Africa, a source of cheap labour for Gulf states, a hub for travel between Africa and Asia, and a key partner of China's Belt and Road. Similar arguments for inclusion can be made for Afghanistan, which featured prominently in 19th-century Britain's Indian Ocean strategy to maintain the global balance of power and does so again today in the outlook of both the Pentagon and transnational jihadism. There are of course limits to this perspective—neither Argentina nor Côte d'Ivoire counts as a Global Indian Ocean society, today or historically—but we hope to convince the reader that a fluid and evolving approach (dovetailing with the growing tendency to approach regions as not merely or even mainly determined by geography)[13] through emphasizing the Ocean *in* the world offers more analytical purchase in appreciating how the interconnections between states, societies and markets shape core ideas and practices of order than conventional approaches do.

Rethinking global politics through oceans recognizes the central importance of key bodies of water as not just connectors of territories but as spaces at the heart of the formation of world-historic forces such as emergent capitalism and modern empires. Inspired by Fernand Braudel's seminal works on the Mediterranean,[14] historians began writing "oceanic histories" in the 1980s and 1990s. New nautical and financial technologies resulting from the growing proximity between the Old World and the New in the 16th and 17th century became the vehicle to expand European power into other realms, and the resultant colonial riches enabled the consolidation of the Westphalian state and a new unitary conception of territorial sovereignty in Europe.[15]

However, the ocean mattered not just in terms of the accumulation it facilitated; the "social construction of the ocean"[16]—its growing role in the imagination of order-builders as to what it meant to *think* transnationally—was also essential in nurturing incipient international legal norms and technologies of power. The development of sovereignty within the modern state system coproduced ideas of projecting authority over the non-state space of the seas and the legitimate use of armed force at sea as well as on land.[17] The imperial cartographies that accompanied these ideational developments and physical struggles over oceanic primacy gave colonial administrators greater self-confidence in controlling vast overseas spaces and sustained the fiction of European moral supremacy.[18] Such maps also helped to sell empire at home in the 19th century and in the process boosted nationalist sentiments.

This is but one of many examples of the ways in which thinking of oceans in the world facilitates an understanding of the inter-regional connections that underpin the making of political orders and a more fruitful assessment of how communities and systems around the globe respond differently (or similarly) to structured global transformations. This approach allows us to strongly foreground the *interactive* effects between global, regional and local ideas, norms and material flows—a point of neglect in the study of International Relations and some of the social sciences more broadly.[19] Thus, rather than assuming (liberal or any other) international order as a unidirectional, exogenous factor impacting on the international relations and politics of a specific region of the developing world, local and regional hierarchies and practices in the non-West are constitutive of what that order actually represents and how it works; the presumed periphery of liberal hegemony reveals as much as the core about the logics driving (and undermining) the ordering system. This book seeks to build on the excellent theorizing originating from the discipline of area studies, where new frames have been crafted by leveraging hitherto ignored or suppressed narratives, formative experiences and chronologies.[20] Our proposition is that an alternative historicization and spatial conceptualization of order allows us to see and reflect on fault lines, connections and dynamics that we otherwise would not: the "Global Indian Ocean" as method, to paraphrase one recent classic.[21]

The remainder of this chapter provides theoretical and historical background to our thinking about order, especially of the liberal kind. It discusses the key concepts deployed in the volume and narrates a history of the Global Indian Ocean through the lens of our concern with states, markets and societies in their relationship with liberal order: how the "Great Transformation"[22] of European political economies also redrew the oceanic world after 1750 through successive waves of imperialism and substituted one type of global-ization for another. This British-dominated order was replaced after 1945 (but especially from the 1970s–1980s onwards) with a more ambitious system of liberal governance which spurred renewed dynamics of both integration and exchange but also of violent resis-tance and heterodox imagination. In the course of this analysis I introduce the individual contributions that make up this volume and explain how they speak to its major themes. To do so, I think through one overarching question: what happens to our understand-ing of liberal international order—its history, material bases and ideological claims—if we read its development not solely as a social formation built by the West and exported around the earth, but rather as an intellectual, economic and political encounter with the world of the Global Indian Ocean?

The Global Indian Ocean and international order in historical perspective: From archaic globalization to the Pax Britannica

The literature on the Indian Ocean has mushroomed in the past twenty years and centres dedicated to its study are proliferating (at least twenty globally, and counting), as are chairs, curricular offerings and research programmes, especially in history, driven by South Asianists.[23] India, Mauritius, Oman and South Africa have tried to invoke a shared oceanic past as the basis for a regional cooperation body. Just like some of the Asian and African regionalisms of the past,[24] statist and academic initiatives today often project the Indian Ocean world as a space of both historical imagination and political utopianism. Such discourse frames the Ocean as a radical counter-point to Western hegemony and a site of heterodox cosmopolitanism and competing universalisms, often through "narratives of vindication … [anchored by] a (utopian) horizon toward which the emancipation-ist history is imagined to be moving".[25] The device deployed for this juxtaposition is usually to pitch Indian Ocean histories against the Atlantic omnipresence in historiography and in politics. Many Indian Ocean scholars refer to work on popular culture, literary traditions and subaltern resistance in the Atlantic world as inspiration[26] or aspi-ration[27]—but with a crucial difference. While the "Black Atlantic" literature locates resistance and alternative consciousness within the key institutions of colonial domination (ships, ports, prisons and plantations) and among those most subjugated,[28] its Indian Ocean peers seek alternative imaginings among communities who appear less colonized, maintaining remnants of earlier relationships that are assumed to be intrinsically more fluid and less violent.[29]

Much of this work both implicitly and explicitly rebukes the traditional international relations literature where the Indian Ocean remains largely absent and the concept of international order is often positively evaluated. Realists see the international system as anarchical and dangerous though at the same time powerful states ensure a modicum of stability by crafting a set of rules that render existential rivalries more predictable and that help govern the system. In such accounts, world politics is shaped by the order-building bids of successive hegemonic states which rearrange inter-state relations in the wake of large-scale conflict.[30] Hegemonic Stability Theory predicts that continued cooperation is dependent on a material distribution of power in which the hegemon—Rome in Mediterranean antiquity or the British Empire in the 19th century—who built the order remains dominant.[31] Power Transition theorists warn that when rising powers narrow the gap with the hegemon they seek to revisit the existing order, aligning it with the shifting distribution of material capabilities.[32] For proponents of both accounts, the decline of empire is coeval with the disintegration of order.

The scholarly riposte of the Indian Ocean as "globalization with a difference"[33]—a space stitched together by commerce embedded in reciprocal multicultural codes before the advent of coercive European colonialism—is not without empirical foundations.[34] Historically, international order and its constitutive institutions were (and are) far more diverse than traditional international relations accounts recognize.[35] The ecology of the Indian Ocean with its changing monsoon winds every six months led for over a millennium to a system of economic exchange embedded in the unceasing movement of people and the unifying force of Islam.[36] Contrary to Orientalist depictions of the Ocean as an unchanging space with extravagant despots ruling the hinterland, the region was in mercantile, intellectual and religious terms extraordinarily vibrant.[37] Islam, science and commerce stimulated each other, building a first Global Indian Ocean; in the footsteps of the monsoon-sailing traders followed *ulema*, administrators, craftsmen, literati, pilgrims and soldiers.[38] Although Muslims were a minority in many societies, they dominated the circles of learning, jurisprudence and political authority: Egyptian *qadis* served in Mogadishu, scholars from Comoros studied in Mecca and taught in Sri Lanka, Bahraini captains recruited crews in Kilwa, Hadrami generals commanded forces in Gujarat and Sumatra. As Dunn put it, "to be a Muslim in East Africa, southern India or Malaysia in the fourteenth century was to have a cosmopolitan frame of mind."[39]

Such "archaic globalization"[40] was remarkable because its sinews were woven together in the absence of an oceanic hegemon imposing a security regime and facilitating trade. No land-based power claimed sovereignty over the seas.[41] Diaspora communities in port cities around the Ocean were granted cultural and religious autonomy and their own jurisdiction. These were organized in self-regulating *natios* in which religious affiliations, ethnicity, commercial interests and professional codes overlapped, acting partly as embassy, partly as guild, partly as separate legal system, such as the Tamil nagara, the Persian milliya, and the Swahili taifa.[42] Like 21st-century offshore havens, contemporary rulers did not fiscally squeeze these expatriate networks, but instead wooed them by improving infrastructure, exempting them from duties, and lucratively rewarding their employment as civil servants, diplomats and military officers. Law—especially Islamic law—in the form of contracts, debt and an interoceanic web of rights and obligations, was as important a vector as trust in enabling transnational networks of expanding commerce and political authority.[43]

This multicultural world crafted without brute hegemonic force is almost inevitably upheld as the converse of European-dominated worlds like the post-1492 Atlantic or the Indian Ocean after Vasco da Gama's expeditions.[44] Yet while there can be little doubt as to the brutality of the lusophone conquerors (who burned alive Muslim prisoners and mutilated their corpses) and the shock felt in Indian Ocean communities faced with Portuguese claims to sovereignty over the high seas (demanding from them a *cartaz*, or licence tax, to be allowed to trade), the notion of a cosmopolitan paradise lost risks simplifying complex historical realities. First, the "globalization with a difference" of the Indian Ocean might have lacked a Pax Romana-style order dominating its different shores but it certainly was not wanting in violence. Indian Ocean slavery lasted much longer than its Atlantic equivalent, was properly multinational (every constituent region of the Global Indian Ocean imported and exported slaves), and involved proportionately more girls, young women and eunuchs.[45] A multitude of bonded labour systems existed from Mozambique to Aceh, with varying gradations of exploitation, state involvement and legal avenues for manumission.[46] Moreover, what detractors delegitimized as "piracy" conducted against (legitimate) commerce was widespread and deeply political: "pirate" attacks on centres of Indian Ocean trading such as Aden or the ports of Gujarat had everything to do with attempts by governments to force shifts in trade routes to rival centres.

Second, the narrative of a pre-Western melting pot underplays the extent of discrimination and the looming spectre of communal violence that periodically erupted. The position of Jews in many Islamic polities was to a considerable extent a function of the economic climate and the perceived vulnerability of the state vis-à-vis external challengers; this sometimes enabled them to be privileged intermediaries and sometimes rendered Jews as targets of popular anger.[47] Wealthy Arab, African and Asian Muslim merchants in South India benefited from legal protection from Hindu rulers and even served as their ambassadors but, along with poorer co-religionists, also faced widespread prejudice, reminding them of their hazardous minority status.

Third, the international order of the Global Indian Ocean was until two centuries ago more a set of distinct regional subsystems around the Arabian Sea, the Straits of Malacca and Karimata and the Malabar Coast, each with its own dynamic, than a closely integrated oceanic system. Seaborne commerce and intellectual syncretism tantalized the imagination, but empires in the various subsystems were primarily sustained by their control of the agricultural surplus, not transoceanic commercial exchanges. This also explains why they did not invest as much in conquering navies as they did in intrepid armies on land.[48]

The hegemonic unification of most of the Ocean—and thus the creation of the Global Indian Ocean in the modern sense, as part of a global system of political economy and imperial control—only succeeded after 1757, having been an elusive goal for the Portuguese, Dutch, Omanis and other aspirants in preceding centuries. The Pax Britannica became the first pan-oceanic order as the material capabilities of post-Industrial Revolution Britain and its use of innovations in communication, finance and transportation enabled it to shrink the vast distances of the ocean to an extent that finally allowed one power to be ascendant from the Cape to Melaka.

Much Anglo-Saxon-dominated international relations scholarship sees the advent of the Pax Britannica—not only in the Indian Ocean but globally—as a fundamental historical rupture with previous international orders. And, indeed, studying the material distribution of international power and the reproduction of (and changes in) hierarchy is insufficient.[49] What hegemons do with power depends on how they understand power, on their systemic preferences and on the character of the domestic polity, and on how its elites imagine their place in the world: order is an explicitly social concept, as attempts at building a durable pattern of rules to govern the system reflect and promote a set of values and norms.[50] Such an understanding of order underlines that legitimacy is what distinguishes (material) primacy from (more consensual) hegemony. The normative ideas produced by a hegemon are essential to attract support and to outflank rivals.[51]

The notion that not all orders are equal and that the Pax Britannica and (as we will see shortly) the post-1945 Pax Americana are qualitatively different from preceding episodes of primacy is essential for liberal order theorists.[52] Though a contested concept, which means very different things to different people, liberalism is premised on the secular faith that cooperation and peaceful competition between individuals and governments are natural as well as desirable and that economic openness, multilateralism and democratic debate are mutually reinforcing. Constitutional democracies are thus regarded as the appropriate leaders of an order they build in their self-image: one of reciprocal interests, learning institutions and peace through the spread of commerce and democracy.[53] As more and more states embrace the liberalizing road to modernity, the probability of violent conflicts recedes, as democracies do not fight with each other, because of their culture of dialogue and rules-based interaction. Convinced that a world of liberal states is more secure and prosperous than any other, defenders of the Pax Britannica and Pax Americana saw and see no contradiction in denouncing (illegitimate, illiberal) imperialism and defending (legitimate, liberal) empire.[54]

The narrative that British conquests began a (still ongoing) process of deepening liberal international order under the aegis of the "Anglo world" informed the cultural construction of "the West", but it is notably silent about how the violent past of empire, racial exclusion and the disciplines of History, International Relations and Political Science have intertwined.[55] The rise of liberal internationalism was premised on a bifurcated reading of world politics, pitting a nascent civilized and European international society (strengthened by white settler colonies under constitutional government), to which international law applied, against a literally lawless, barbarian periphery (including the non-white European colonies) which was beyond the normative pale and required policing, whether by the British Empire or, later, the League of Nations.[56] Nineteenth-century liberalism cast the societies that had spawned it as laying down universal standards of decency, performance and reason and propagated the spread of civilization, commerce and Christianity as the best guarantor of world peace.

Supporters of liberal order today abhor such racialized arguments, but the degree to which the non-Western world remains on the margins of their conceptualization is striking.[57] In the early 21st century, Ikenberry's classic works, for instance, place the North Atlantic at the heart of liberal order and frame politics in East Asia as a more bilateralized "hub-and-spoke" extension of that order but exclude, by his own admission, Latin America, Africa, the former Soviet Union and the rest of Asia from the discussion altogether.[58] The combination of ignoring most of the non-West or framing politics there in mainstream international relations studies through the lens of "failed states"—judging non-Western polities, just as under the Pax Britannica, mostly in terms of what they fail to do or to be, rather than what they are[59]—resurrects the 19th-century discursive distinction between (legitimate, liberal) empire and (illegitimate, illiberal) imperialism.[60] Such discourse underpinned the late-20th-century experiments in suspending local sovereignty[61] and imposing liberal

international governance in "the new protectorates"⁶² set up in the
Balkans, Afghanistan and East Timor. Associations with empire also
explain the continued resistance today to the very term "liberalism"
across the Global Indian Ocean, especially in former imperial anchors
like India, Singapore and South Africa. As Chua Beng Huat, one of
the contributors to this volume, observed: "Whereas liberal multicul-
turalism in the West is premised on the rejection of White supremacy, in postcolonial Asia and Africa liberalism is associated precisely
with Western White cultural supremacy. To reject one is to reject
both simultaneously."⁶³

Problematizing the genealogy of ideas and practices of liberal
internationalism should of course not lead to intellectually lazy cari-
caturing; replacing one impoverished reading of liberal order (as
universal and enlightening) with another (as inherently and irre-
deemably pro-empire and racist)⁶⁴ simplifies and underestimates a
complex, historically evolving concept. Its ambivalence was already
clear when the Victorian era reached high noon. While John Stuart
Mill and J.R. Seeley defended the civilizing mission of empire, other
icons of liberalism—like Richard Cobden and William Gladstone—
used the same vocabulary of freedom, emancipation and pluralism
to denounce imperial conquest and the denial of self-determination.
It is paradoxes like these that elucidate a key premise of this book:
liberal order has never been one thing to both its subjects and its
objects but, on the contrary, has changed greatly over time, substantively and procedurally and has functioned as a tool and foil in both
elite and vernacular discourses.

In the Global Indian Ocean it (re)made, the Pax Britannica embod-
ied these contradictions, changes and multiple meanings. For about a
hundred and fifty years, the crucial ingredient underpinning British
dominance was the Empire's ability to convert primacy into what was
earlier coined "thin hegemony": it did not just tolerate the continued
existence of other socio-political systems but embraced the pluriformity and heteronomy that have such long track records in the Indian
Ocean, as long as ultimate authority was, implicitly or explicitly,
recognized as lying with London. This dovetailed not only with the
fact that Asian polities were in the early-modern era often militarily
at least equals of European imperialists and sometimes clearly

17

superior,[65] but also with well-entrenched technologies of rule. For most of modern history, empire has been the default governing mode of the dominant polities, yet imperial rule seldom amounted to strong centralization and was often not only permissive of, but even symbiotic with, other forms of governance.[66] For both land- and (particularly) sea-based empires, the sustainability of their rule often required a softer, more indirect touch and an appreciation of the limitations of one's power.

The Pax Britannica relied for its prosperity and security on a dense, ever-changing web of overlapping treaties, arrangements, forms of (in)direct rule, buttressed by the Royal Navy and the Gold Standard. "It contained colonies of rule (India), settlement colonies (mostly self-governing by the late nineteenth century), protectorates, condominia (Sudan), mandates (after 1920), naval and military fortresses (Gibraltar, Malta), occupations (Egypt, Cyprus), treaty-ports and concessions (Shanghai), informal colonies of commercial pre-eminence (Argentina), spheres of influence (... like Iran, Afghanistan and the Persian Gulf) and a rebellious province at home."[67] This patchwork of sovereignties meant that the tangible reality of Empire to the peoples of the Ocean was represented as much by local intermediaries as it was by British proconsuls. This had the not unimportant advantage of being colonialism on the cheap; as tasks were outsourced, imperial administrators also did not have to bother with providing much in terms of services to subject populations.[68] The classic example are the Trucial States of the Gulf where overrule had minimal liberal substance. Lord Curzon, Viceroy of India (1899–1905) and in that capacity also responsible for the sheikhdoms, could not care less about Arabian political vicissitudes or internal policies as long as British security and commercial interests remained unthreatened: "These petty tribes exist for little else but internecine squabble, blood-feuds, puny forays and isolated acts of outrage or revenge. With their internal relations Great Britain, who claims no suzerainty over Arabia, would have been foolish to interfere. All that she took upon herself to do was to secure the maritime peace of the Gulf ..."[69]

The hegemonic order's systemic strength—its flexibility in tolerating different social orders and forms of political authority—was ironically also one of the reasons why the empire-builders themselves constantly felt anxious about "unfinished empire".[70] Myriad politico-legal arrangements without a singular imperial constitution fed fears of disintegration: could loyalty to the monarchy and the co-option of local auxiliaries ensure centrifugal forces remained in check? The proverbial cavalry was the Indian colonial army—by the late 19th century the most powerful force in the world outside Europe—charged with enforcing British power not just in the subcontinent but also in Iraq and East Africa.[71]

The liberal character of British hegemony in the Global Indian Ocean rested on two planks: constitutional government, property rights and elections in the White Dominions of South Africa and Australia and elsewhere the promotion of laissez-faire economics which, conveniently, absolved colonial mandarins from having to provide expensive public services and infrastructure, unless essential for enterprise (e.g., railways). The key nodes of imperial commerce were multiracial port cities that were either newly created by the British or owed their spectacular expansion to the business opportunities generated by the hegemon: Singapore, Penang, Bombay, Karachi, Aden, Durban. These sites of concentrated military, industrial and financial power fuelled regional integration that deepened, and frequently reworked, older patterns of inter-oceanic trade.[72] Gulf traders poured in unprecedented numbers into the entrepôts of the Swahili coast and South Asia.[73] Gujarati merchants dominated the markets of eastern and southern Africa. Their presence across the oceanic littoral was not new, but the lucrative possibilities offered by empire rendered their impact both quantitatively and qualitatively different.

The engine for economic integration was skyrocketing demand for the Global Indian Ocean's resources—cotton, jute, sugar cane, ivory, gum copal, gold, diamonds—as the West industrialized and transfigured its consumption patterns. But the transformative impact of the investment boom required to get commodities to Europe and North America also generated unprecedented demand for goods and services on the ocean's shores, from white settler populations and from migrants arriving from across Asia, Africa and Arabia to power the arteries of the emergent liberal order.[74] Thomas Blom Hansen in chapter 2 in this volume concentrates on the polyglot communities that constitute the latter group, recreating the tapestry of mercantile threads, legal pluralism, soaring migration and new ideas of belonging and citizenship under the Empire's regime of "distributed sovereignty". This regime turbocharged commerce and movement, allowing travelling ethno-linguistic and religious minorities to become some of liberal order's most proactive foot soldiers and main beneficiaries from Malaya to Natal. Through the partnership between British mandarins and networks of trading communities originating from northern and western India, Blom Hansen shows how novel modes of capital and labour dovetailed with the military and commercial umbrella provided by the Pax Britannica and flourished in the Ocean's multicultural ports, and thereafter also in their eastern and southern African hinterland. These communities were as important to liberal order as the brute force of gunboats and the soft power of imperial pomp. And although the nature of sovereignty in the Global Indian Ocean has evolved since those days and their cosmopolitanism is seen as suspect by many of today's nativist politicians and administrators, these networks are still among the main drivers of transoceanic interdependence in the early 21st century.

The intermediary role of South Asian and Arabian diasporas in weaving a transoceanic web was vital to capitalist accumulation and the ability of the British hegemon to leverage this wealth for its own, global purposes. The macro-region's main function was to sustain the Gold Standard: India's trade surplus vis-à-vis European countries and the US was so large that it helped offset the metropole's own declining ratio of exports to imports in relation to the continent and America.[75] London could only be the global creditor—investing as much in the non-Western world between 1865 and 1914 as it did domestically[76]—and stave off deflationary adjustments at home because of the Empire's Indian Ocean surplus.

Liberal order under Britain's aegis—essentially a combination of open sea lanes and a global investment regime that guaranteed creditors' rights and the soundness of their money—provided several ocean-wide public goods, but these were profoundly double-edged. Not only was India's trade surplus a consequence of the deliberate suppression of local incomes, but the Gold Standard meant that colonial possessions and societies importing capital were vulnerable to rapid inflows and destabilizing outflows and the associated brisk expansion or contraction of money supply.[77] The consequences of the forcible integration of the Indian Ocean World into the global economy were most horrifically experienced in the agrarian realm: food supplies flowed to those locations where they could command the highest price. Potentially this could have benefited rural producers in the Horn and Indian subcontinent, but when transoceanic market integration coincided with climatic turbulence tens of millions of people were rendered vulnerable to famine in the 19th century's final decades. These "Late Victorian Holocausts"[78] were not an unfortunate by-product of the building of a global liberal economy but a logical consequence of the demolition of local industrial capacity, the destruction of communal adaptation mechanisms to economic and ecological adversity, and the crushing of political and epistemological resistance to the British Empire. Smith, Bentham and Malthus provided colonial savants with the rationale to rely on the market and "natural checks"—rather than dreaded government intervention—when faced with mass starvation.[79] In India alone, the number of famine deaths between 1876 and 1902 is unlikely to be lower than 15 million.

In sum, from an Indian Ocean viewpoint, the Pax Britannica was liberal in the substantive economic sense, though procedurally liberalization was not pursued consensually or reciprocally but rather through the coercive discipline of the Gold Standard, the Royal Navy and deadly hunger. Politically, this order represented the liberalism of its time: democracy was limited to those belonging to the chosen race, class and gender. Empire's preference for "decentralized despotism"[80] and racial segregation in its cities and legal systems made clear that liberal internationalism was both practically and theoretically erected on profoundly illiberal foundations.

Embedded liberalism: Deconstructing and reconstructing the Global Indian Ocean

World War II marked the passing of British-led order to US hegemony. The conflict left Britain exhausted and the symbolic *coup de grâce* was delivered in the Indian Ocean with the surrender of eighty thousand troops in Singapore in 1942, described by Churchill as the worst defeat in the Empire's history. While British influence did not disappear overnight everywhere, and the extent to which London through the Royal Navy and key networks retained leverage in the 1950s and 1960s is still debated,[81] the shift to US dominance globally and later also specifically in the Global Indian Ocean was unmistakeable. Washington promised a reworked international order in the form of "embedded liberalism": multilateralism, regional integration and the spread of economic and political freedom would be mutually reinforcing so that market forces strengthened rather than threatened democracy, as during the interbellum.[82] But the soaring liberal language of the Atlantic Charter notwithstanding, the White House initially only reluctantly embraced the idea of hegemony, especially in the face of public opinion's isolationist sentiments. The Truman administration's operationalization of embedded liberalism—"a loose array of multilateral institutions in which the United States provided global public goods such as freer trade and freedom of the seas and weaker states were given institutional access to the exercise of U.S. power"[83]—came about more through ad hoc responses to the crises of the emergent Cold War than through any idealistic blueprint for a modern, liberal empire. Yet even if American actions were mostly about European allies fearing abandonment and warning the Soviet Union, the new hegemon did build on the liberal self-image of the Pax Britannica. For those who consider order-building in the last three centuries an "evolutionary process" driven by "liberal ascendancy",[84] the peaceful relay of the baton from London to Washington—so-called hegemonic succession[85]—has become a canonical image that helps make the case that liberal international order is qualitatively different from all its predecessors and potential alternatives. At the heart of an expanding international society is a like-minded core group of states, led by America and Britain, which share a sense of purposeful community steeped in norms such as self-determination, non-aggression and liberal tolerance. In this narration, the public goods benevolently provided by both the British Empire in the 19th century and the US after 1945—freedom of the seas, capital mobility, access to the hegemon's markets—allowed weaker states to achieve even faster growth than the hegemon itself.

The stylized narrative of hegemonic succession and the widening scope of order has the merit of underscoring the enduring allure of liberal universalist promises, but the differences between the Pax Britannica and the Pax Americana are as significant as, if not more so than, the similarities.[86] British hegemony was exercised in splendid isolation and without strong formal international institutions, contrary to post-1945 America, which built a liberal order that has been characterized by extensive multilateral coalitions and bilateral alliances. While both Anglo-Saxon powers dominated the monetary system and promoted global capitalism, they did so under radically different political-economic conditions. The British Gold Standard emphasized fiscal discipline and international capital mobility—at the expense of national monetary autonomy—whereas the Keynes-inspired mid-20th-century order encouraged domestic budgetary expansion and curtailed transborder financial movements. After World War II, Washington predominantly traded with its allies and institutionalized reciprocal liberalization, while London's 19th-century commerce was mostly with its rivals and UK dominance did not prevent the unilateral imposition of protectionist tariffs from 1880 onwards by Germany, France and other European powers.[87]

The differences between the Pax Britannica and 20th-century embedded liberalism are even clearer when studied in the context of the Global Indian Ocean, where different notions of sovereignty took hold, as they did before. Decolonization, starting in the late 1940s and peaking in the 1960s–1970s, drew strength from the inversion of liberal arguments against imperial overrule in the wake of the mobilization to combat Nazism and fascism: if colonial powers were unwilling to grant universal suffrage to their overseas subjects, then they should concede popular sovereignty through self-determination. For the states, societies and markets of the Indian Ocean this was, at least initially, a process of regional disintegration and distancing from liberalism.[88] Independent statehood implied introspective nation-building and institutional centralization. Tariff barriers went up, coups ended early democratic experiments, and transoceanic diasporas were often regarded as agents of neo-imperialism.

The setting of the sun on the Pax Britannica and its era of distributed sovereignty, in Blom Hansen's expression, augured trouble for those communities that had been the linchpins of British hegemony, or so it seemed. Chua Beng Huat, in chapter 3, examines how a city that owed its very existence to the British Empire reinvented itself in the age of nation-states and would subsequently become the Global Indian Ocean's most successful polity. Founded in 1819 as an East India Company trading post and subsequently the Pax Britannica's military and commercial fulcrum in South East Asia, Singapore under its post-independence elite took advantage of the Empire's mercantile and cosmopolitan legacy to both control domestic unrest and reinvent its international role. The early years were marked by fears of communist insurrection. Singapore drew close to the American superpower—its independence guaranteed by the US Navy—and opened its port facilities to foreign containers and warships; it was an early collaborator with multinational companies, which prized its multilingual, disciplined workforce and common law system. Simultaneously however, Prime Minister Lee Kuan Yew launched a social-democratic nation-building bid that prioritized state capitalism, social housing and public education, routinely violating liberal sacred cows such as private property and market competition. If in 2018 Singapore recorded the world's third-highest GDP per capita, it is because its policies have evolved in line with the demands imposed and opportunities created by international order: laissez-faire during the Pax Britannica; social democracy and nation-building as liberal hegemony changed in character after 1945 and independent statehood became a reality; strategically taking advantage of American-style globalization and China's growing dependence on Indian Ocean trade in the 1980s, 1990s and early 2000s. Liberal order always appeared as thin to Lee and his comrades, but, as Chua explains, it is precisely that which enabled and spurred pragmatic adaptation and selective borrowing.

The Singaporean example illustrates how the global context of the Cold War was ambiguous in its effects on the Global Indian Ocean. On the one hand, the US and Soviet Union were keen to replace European influence in the former colonies and each claimed to support self-determination and the sovereign equality of nations; potentially a radically new international order was in the making, bringing with it new opportunities for the peoples of the Ocean. But in practice, the Soviets were mostly focused on Europe and contributed only

ORDERING THE GLOBAL INDIAN OCEAN

in a limited way to decolonization and state-building in the Indian
Ocean, while US enthusiasm for self-rule was greater in the case of
British and Italian possessions than those of France and Portugal. Even
if individual US policymakers preferred dealing with (liberal-)demo-
cratic counterparts rather than authoritarian regimes, all other things
being equal, this was a largely hypothetical scenario and security
interests always trumped democracy promotion.[89] In reality,
Washington's key partners in Africa and Asia were one-party dictatorships and white minority regimes, staunchly anti-communist with
a formidable coercive apparatus and often not very economically
liberal either.[90] Moreover, American efforts to gradually reliberalize
international trade after the protectionist 1930s focused mostly on
industrialized economies and industrial goods—the developing world
was, from the perspective of embedded liberalism, a secondary front.

Lingering progressive currents, regularly the target of State
Department suspicion and CIA subversion, still linked societies across
the ocean and gave rise to new regionalisms and imaginaries of international order.[91] Like in the context of the Black Atlantic, contesting
global and regional racial hierarchies—many of which had underpinned the liberalism of the Pax Britannica, as already discussed—was
an integral part of establishing sovereignty and rethinking the foundations of international order, a project of "worldmaking" that has been
consistently underestimated, politically and intellectually.[92] Asian
leftists inspired liberation movements in Oman, Yemen and East
Africa, and the Non-Aligned Movement of Sukarno's Indonesia,
Nehru's India and Nyerere's Tanzania preached Third World unity
and imagined a different type of interdependence.[93] Drawing on the
physical struggles of comrades across the Indian Ocean and the polit-
ico-cultural imagination of Rabindranath Tagore, Frantz Fanon and
Mahatma Gandhi, transoceanic solidarity was meant to help post-
colonial nations carve out economic, intellectual and strategic autonomy to deliver on the promises to their people.[94] Diverse notions of
federation and confederation—beyond traditional cartographic logics
and old imperial zones of influences—were experimented with as
African and Asian political and cultural leaders were acutely aware of
the dangers facing the incipient nation-state, internally and externally.[95] Yet for all the well-intentioned thought experiments, the

25

sociocultural and transhistorical affinities and the political summiting, institutionally the idea of a new order to replace the Pax Britannica and compete with the Truman Doctrine was stillborn. Much was made of the "spirit" of the 1955 Bandung Conference, but because, owing to external sabotage, internal contradictions and formidable personal incentives, incumbents had first and foremost to consolidate power in their now independent states, Bandung remained just that— a spirit—never a threatening alternative to an American-led (or Soviet-led) order.

US objectives in the Global Indian Ocean, between 1945 and the 1970s, could afford to be limited. Its chief objective was denying direct Soviet access and countering communist subversion (including through alliances such as the Southeast Asia Treaty Organization (SEATO), the brainchild of US Secretary of State John Foster Dulles), while minimizing its own immediate involvement. Encouragement of democracy, human rights and free markets was rationed; support for dictatorships, their oligopolistic economies and vistas of authoritarian modernization was the rule rather than the exception in places like Iran, Pakistan and Kenya.[96] Yet the pragmatics resulting from bipolarity and the American preoccupation with Europe, East Asia and Latin America should not distract from the fact that US preponderance in the Ocean was real and significantly oriented states, societies and markets in ways that augured some meaningful continuity with, and not just difference from, the pre-1945 world of British Empire. The reliance on local auxiliaries and naval muscle to guarantee core security and commercial interests whilst backing regional clients to anchor thin hegemony echoed the earlier age. Cheap oil for Washington and its allies—essential for their balance of payments and thus for global liberal order's material underpinnings—was guaranteed by elite bargains with producing states in the Gulf and (to a lesser extent) South East Asia; even without a formal international regime, protection for Middle Eastern monarchies and US oil companies ensured plentiful energy to buttress the post-war economic boom.[97] The Pax Americana was legitimized through the Baghdad Pact and SEATO, which brought Australia, Iran, Iraq, Pakistan, the Philippines and Thailand together with the US, UK and France in collective defence structures. The base at Diego Garcia served as a nuclear-armed watch tower, monitoring threats to free navigation of the seas and Soviet naval activity. And through US overseas aid in Africa and Asia, the expansion of American multinationals and the post-1971 Generalized System of Preferences that encouraged trade-based integration of developing countries into the world economy, Washington increasingly shaped the material realities of the Ocean World.

A thicker hegemony? Liberal order in the age of neoliberalism and terror

American dominance of the Global Indian Ocean became more thickly hegemonic from the late 1970s and early 1980s onwards, even if that hegemony would remain considerably less institutionalized and rested on less liberal foundations than in the North Atlantic and Pacific. This trend started in the sphere where US supremacy was already greatest: military power. The 1979 twin shocks of the Soviet invasion of Afghanistan and the replacement of the Shah of Iran by Ayatollah Khomeini's Islamic Revolution led to the Carter Doctrine, which warned that America, if necessary, would intervene directly to protect its national security interests in the Persian Gulf. Washington greenlighted massive arms sales to Riyadh and large-scale military assistance to Islamabad to counter communism and revolutionary Shia Islam. This commitment to US allies also translated in support for the founding and consolidation of the Gulf Cooperation Council and for the increasing involvement of the Association of Southeast Asian Nations, led by Washington's associates in Indonesia, the Philippines, Singapore and Thailand, in containing Vietnamese and Soviet penetration. The Pentagon created the US Central Command in 1983 to act as its nerve centre for operations, which became increasingly plentiful, in the western Indian Ocean. Moreover, after the 1991 Gulf War and the 1993 Operation Restore Hope in Somalia, US forces established an enduring large-scale permanent presence in the region, most visibly through bases in Saudi Arabia and later Qatar and the 1995 formation of the US Fifth Fleet responsible for Persian Gulf, Red Sea and western Indian Ocean security from its headquarters in Bahrain. Following the demise of the Soviet Union, US military activities in the Global Indian Ocean were not scaled down but intensified through carrier strike groups, extraordinary renditions and drones, first as part of concerns about "failed states" and, after 11 September 2001, in the context of the Global War on Terror (GWOT), as Will Reno discusses in chapter 8. Both the US generals and intelligence operatives fighting the GWOT as well as their nemeses al-Qaeda and ISIS, have transnationalized the way the battlefield and security itself are understood, erasing borders in a never-ending conflict that creates a new imperial geography as it moves back and forth between core and periphery of the international system.[98] Yet the framing of myriad concerns around the Indian Ocean through the overarching prism of fighting "global" terror not only blinds Washington to the profoundly localized causes of violence but also leads US Central Command and its partners in targeting international jihadists and their resident fellow travellers to erect the Pax Americana on profoundly illiberal foundations. Afghanistan, Iraq, Kenya, Pakistan, Somalia and Yemen are front-line states where America's extraordinary coercive prowess and technological abilities have been showcased, but also where the contemporary liberal order has run into the same age-old dilemmas that previous hegemons faced. Reno argues that military intervention in these Badlands is time and again forced to scale back its ambitions; the instability that is claimed to threaten the regional or global liberal order can only be quelled by pragmatic means that prioritize security and local order-building over liberal mirages of societal transformation.

The Pax Americana in the Global Indian Ocean has sought to ensure open seas, energy security and regime security (the first a public good, the latter two club goods). Growing militarization of the macro-region has been accompanied by the gradual intrusion of the order in economic affairs too, especially from the 1980s onwards. The neoliberal wave unleashed by the Reagan and Thatcher administrations brought pressures for liberalization, privatization and deregulation, most visibly through the establishment of the World Trade Organization (WTO) in 1994 and the conditionalities imposed by the International Monetary Fund (IMF) and World Bank in exchange for further assistance to increasingly indebted states.[99] In South Africa, Nelson Mandela's post-Apartheid administration envisaged the transformation of one of the world's most unequal societies, but its ability to redistribute land, tax corporations and provide public services to the townships was gravely curtailed by the iron discipline imposed by financial markets.[100] Even without formal IMF and World Bank strictures, fears of a run on the Rand forced the ANC into a neoliberal straitjacket. Moreover, students returning from overseas study to Indian Ocean societies came back not only armed with the teachings of Hayek and Friedman but also with powerful connections in New York, Washington and California. The most (in)famous example was the so-called Berkeley Mafia in Suharto's Indonesia, US-educated economists in key government positions who sermonized monetary and fiscal conservatism and opened the economy to multinational corporations. Beloved by foreign investors for their resistance to land reform and their preoccupation with efficiency and capital mobility, they were instrumental in sustaining the close US–Indonesia relationship.[101]

The economic transformation of the Global Indian Ocean had been an objective of the US-led order, albeit a secondary one, since the Cold War's early days. The Truman Doctrine promised a "fair deal" in dealing with the newly identified problem of "underdevelopment", considered to be endangering world peace: "More than half the people of the world are living in conditions approaching misery … Their poverty is a handicap and a threat both to them and to more prosperous areas."[102] Overseas development assistance was meant to create "the right kind of revolution" in the form of modernization: newly independent Indian Ocean states were to build up physical infrastructure, boost agricultural productivity and check soaring birth rates, so reservoirs of potential socialist insurrection were transformed into industrializing, middle-class societies.[103] Such paternalistic policies were initially non-compulsory and merely encouraged by the World Bank or bilaterally by Western aid agencies. Neoliberalism, however, radicalized the reform agenda as its ideological one-size-fits-all was vehemently preached by the international financial institutions and imposed, on pain of non-dispersal of loans and a general financial crisis, through harsh "Structural Adjustment Programs". The disciplining effect was felt across the Global Indian Ocean, including in some of the strongest states such as India. Faced with a balance of payments catastrophe, the Indian government was bailed out in 1991 at the eleventh hour by a multibillion-dollar IMF loan in return for the dissolution of capital controls, tariffs, state monopolies and the fixed exchange rate.[104] The result of such drastic (if incomplete) economic liberalization, unchallenged by successive administrations since, has been breathtaking aggregate growth and the birth of a new millionaire and billionaire class, but also violent inequality and barely budging rates of malnutrition, illiteracy and social exclusion.[105]

In chapter 6, Lamia Karim traces the impact of liberal order's developmental fads—from the obsession with fertility rates in the 1970s to export-led economic expansion through apparel sweatshops in the 1980s and 1990s to the celebration of female entrepreneurship in the microloan business in the new millennium—in studying their impact on Bangladeshi women. Her chapter focuses on women and girls as the objects of liberal development, continuously recast as the potential saviours of an overpopulated, politically chaotic and desperately poor nation forever at the mercy of cyclones. While the strictures of donors have changed with great frequency, Karim highlights how external actors continue to ignore the lived experiences of these women under different developmental regimes and underlines the dissidence of ordinary Bangladeshis, especially when they challenge paternalistic prescriptions that unfailingly dovetail with the macroeconomic canon of the moment. Bangladesh's daughters have paid a high price for their country's perceived progress and prominence in the development landscape of the Global Indian Ocean, she argues.

The economic forces unleashed by the Washington Consensus not only cut new social cleavages in South Asia, but yielded disappointments elsewhere too; in Africa the neoliberal magic of price signals torpedoed industrial policy, led to the axing of social safety nets, and further contributed to the marginalization of rural areas.[106] Such "development in reverse" gravely weakened already feeble states and contributed to surging political violence and criminality in Kenya and Somalia. Yet the diagnosis among donors was not that laissez-faire economics failed to adequately capture the central policy dilemmas of markets in developing societies; it was that a supplementary transformation would be required to overcome resistance to structural adjustment. Political conditionality—multipartyism, free elections and the liberalization of the media—joined economic diktats in a bid to let African and Asian laggards join the irresistible long march to globalization.

The Soviet Union's collapse appeared to underline that there was no alternative to liberal democracy and free markets; Washington had tolerated authoritarian rule during the Cold War, but without Moscow's long arm there was no longer an excuse for leaders not to present themselves to voters. If before 1989 competitive elections in the Indian Ocean were few and far between (e.g., Bangladesh, Pakistan and Sri Lanka stopped holding them for much of the 1980s, while Burma, Mozambique and South Yemen did not hold any at all), in recent decades only Eritrea has refused to let its citizens cast a parliamentary or presidential ballot. In 1990, US democracy promotion funding stood at around US$100m; two decades later, the Obama administration spent twenty-five times that amount on democratization initiatives.

The question of liberal order's relation to domestic political institutions—constitutions, modes of citizenship, the monopoly on violence, and so on—across the Global Indian Ocean is approached by contributors to this volume from various empirical settings and conceptual perspectives. In chapter 4, Shandana Khan Mohmand propositions that elections are no mere epiphenomenon. Liberal order, through its promotion of accountability through the ballot box, has impacted on many polities more deeply than is acknowledged by cynical critics, but differently from the way naively optimistic "transitologists" expected. Through a longitudinal study of four villages in the Pakistani Punjab, she explains that electoral competition (no matter how violent, messy and procedurally dissimilar from voting in Denmark or Sweden) has opened up meaningful, hitherto nonexistent political spaces for marginalized communities. Feudal lords, private militia and wealthy incumbents continue to wield disproportionate influence and power, but local politics are becoming more inclusive and the quality of services delivered to historically excluded social groups is rising as patronage networks are compelled to shift in form, scope and intermediaries. Real democratic practice is emerging at the margins, even within severely dysfunctional political systems like Pakistan's, and though it may not fit Western liberal ideals of order,

31

this, Khan Mohmand argues, is what democracy looks like in practice in much of the Global Indian Ocean.

The (re)kindling of political communities under the umbrella of British and US hegemony in the Global Indian Ocean throws up complex questions about the relationship between ideas, institutions and practices. Yet if Khan Mohmand points to bottom-up empowerment of historically excluded groups who seize on the language and tools of liberalism to become political actors (rather than mere subjects),[107] others have catalogued a darker side to liberal order, intolerant of difference and nonconformist actors and vernaculars.[108] The Pax Britannica and numerous post-colonial nation-building projects were built upon—and, in turn, encouraged—strongly ethnically segmented societies, with divergent levels of political participation. Such stratifications and exclusions were legitimized by scholars and administrators who reshaped or even invented genealogies and traditions that identified imperial protégés and scapegoats.[109] Today's violent resurgence of ethno-linguistic differences in the context of elections and human rights discourses is therefore unsurprising to critics of the Washington Consensus and democracy promotion, as it re-energized historical narratives of liberal order's ethnically segmented winners and losers.[110] Such discourses, especially in their more culturalist incarnations, sometimes cast economic and political liberalism as un-Asian or un-African; in doing so, however, they ironically rhyme with 19th-century tropes that posited a fundamental incongruence between liberal civilization and the despotic (Asian) or anarchical (African) nature of its Other.[111]

From the vantage point of this book, liberal thought and practices should not be considered as one pole of a binary, but rather as a fungible and historically contingent set of instruments amidst a multiplicity of social and political registries in the Global Indian Ocean. This set has been important at some critical junctures in the last centuries and less consequential to others, and continues to merit careful and nuanced examination, because it has never served straightforwardly as the grammar of either oppression or liberation (however defined), but often of both: it has historically been found useful by ordinary people and elites alike in the construction of political identities, *pro* or *contra* hegemonies and alternative allegiances throughout the oceanic world.[112] Studying the resultant hybridity in political action and language and tracing how both similarity and difference, coercion and tolerance, have shaped conflict, dialogue and interconnectivity (between and within sub-regions, as well as vis-à-vis the wider international system) presents a more fruitful way forward to studying political modernity and order-building in the Global Indian Ocean.[113]

The search for hybrid socio-political dispensations in the context of the thin hegemony of liberal order has been the central theme of the post-independence history of polities in the Gulf, explains Steffen Hertog in chapter 5. The petrostates of the Arabian Peninsula are not only socially but also politically profoundly segmented. This predicament is at once at odds with liberal political theory yet also directly contributes to the integrative forces of capital and labour circulation that have knit the oceanic space much more closely together again: the migrant underclass, drawn from across the societies of the Indian Ocean, is both a product of historically embedded patterns of movement of people and of the peculiar ways in which Gulf economies have managed their resource rents under the Pax Americana. Hertog notes that royal dynasties have enthusiastically adopted liberal institutional and market recipes in some areas—finance, elite education, free trade zones, common (commercial) law enclave courts—but certainly not in many others including utilities, citizenship, housing, etc. Intriguingly, their laissez-faire attitude towards the massive blue-collar expatriate workforce is strikingly similar to that of the British Empire. The Pax Britannica was a deliberately thin hegemony that did not seek to remake its subject populations into proto-Englishmen, but instead emphasized social difference while facilitating transoceanic migration. Gulf sheikhdoms are the most global corner of the Indian Ocean, with their astonishing racial diversity, key role in channelling remittances to African and Asian backwaters, their massive military bases that anchor the Pax Americana, and their pivotal position in global air travel and maritime commerce. Yet at the same time, Hertog posits, extreme segmentation means that local citizens are governed by Sharia law and carefully protected from the disembedding market in these hyper-capitalist spaces; the social contract remains a distributive one, involving little political participation and no meaningful input from an independent civil society. The ideologically hybrid Arabian oil states are thus at once at the beating heart of the contemporary liberal order in the Global Indian Ocean and at its margins.

After hegemony, thin hegemony? The Global Indian Ocean and the future of liberal order

From its relatively reluctant beginnings, contemporary US hegemony has come to comprise three core pillars (the Pax Americana, free markets and liberal democracy), each seen as an irreplaceable complement to the other two.[114] The order-creating powers of this triad have been explained as emanating from the internal logic of liberalism itself and as being increasingly less reliant on military force—a project of progressively expanding freedom, institutionalization and rules-based governance that is attractive for states to join and almost impossible to leave. Such self-imagery presupposes that liberal internationalism requires liberal domestic foundations and, vice versa, that democracy and capitalism can only thrive under liberal hegemonic leadership. If one follows this line of argument, the rising number of democratic states accounts for why after 1989 American dominance has been consensual and why there has been no countervailing force against the unipolar hegemon as neo-realists expected.[115] Hence, for its (supportive) theoreticians, contemporary, US-led liberal hegemony is "in terms of the provision of security, wealth creation, and social advancement … the most successful order in world history".[116]

As this book proposes, the Global Indian Ocean reveals how ahistorical and parochial many of the assumptions of the narrative of liberal ascendancy really are. By rethinking liberal order not as an Anglo-Saxon export or bequest to the world but rather as an encounter between the North Atlantic and the world of Gujarati traders, Hadrami *ulema*, Swahili askari, Bengali construction workers and Gulf sheikhs, we conclude that neither the Pax Britannica nor US superpowerdom ever operated under such guiding logic. The liberal side of order has never functioned without the illiberal, materially and discursively. Contrary to those who see the Global Indian Ocean as somehow on the periphery of the liberal project—as unfinished empire or perennially in transition—this introduction has demonstrated how utterly constitutive of liberal order the encounter with the macro-region has been for decades: the freedom of navigation, the Gold Standard, the gospel of "development" and the GWOT's Freedom Agenda have all been articulated—and have run into their most fundamental contradictions—through their interactions with the states, societies and markets that form the transoceanic landscape.

It is by centring the encounter with the Global Indian Ocean that the changing scope of liberal order over time, and its practical limitations, becomes clearest. Initial American designs for the post-war system remained bifurcated, with, on one hand, a comprehensive military, political and economic alliance with Western Europe, and, on the other, self-determination for the non-Western world but no US commitment to multilateral institutions or societal transformation there. However, the Cold War convinced Truman to promise technical assistance to poor nations: their economic and political development became part, at least in theory, of the order framework.[117] The confrontation with the Soviet Union initially led US presidents in practice to downplay democratic values and free markets, yet pragmatic deviation became more difficult from the 1980s onwards. Unipolar military dominance, the spread of neoliberal economics and the apparent victory of liberal democracy exerted much stronger pressures for domestic reform across the Global Indian Ocean. The extent of this agenda would have puzzled Disraeli or Gladstone and made little sense to Roosevelt and Eisenhower.

The planetary ambitions for liberal order expressed since Reagan, Bush and Clinton run counter to the Global Indian Ocean's long tradition of thin hegemony—a very different kind of *e pluribus unum*. Historically, empire in the macro-region has benefited from, and adopted light-touch governance towards, a set of internationalisms produced by the movement of capital, goods, ideas and people, resting on politically and ethno-religiously segmented foundations. Mohmand's and Hertog's chapters, especially when read alongside the contentions put forward by Chua and Reno, speak to the underlying theoretical question: what is the relationship between current-day liberal international order and its constituent parts—states, societies and markets? This concern is all the more pressing, as

Michael Woldemariam highlights in chapter 7, because the domestic foundations of the US-led hegemony around the Ocean World seem to diverge completely from what liberal ascendancy predicts should be happening. Consider one of the salient features of the Global Indian Ocean's international relations: no region on earth has seen more successful state-creation—Pakistan (1947), Singapore (1965), Bangladesh (1971), Yemen (1990), Eritrea (1991/1993), East Timor (1999), South Sudan (2011)—a development crucially related to the liberal principle of self-determination and the encouragement and protection provided to secessionists by Western states, first and foremost the American hegemon. Liberal international order in the Global Indian Ocean has been a breaker-cum-midwife of states, but the emergent polities and rump states have seldom been very liberal in character; quite the contrary. Using the examples of Eritrea and Ethiopia, Woldemariam explicates how donors have aided the projects of illiberal state-builders and how liberal discourses and instruments—self-determination, referenda, decentralization—have been seized upon to consolidate highly authoritarian systems of rule.

Not only do such empirical findings run counter to liberal international order requiring (or dovetailing with) liberal foundations, but they also raise the question as to what difference an alternative hegemon—or at least the balancing of unipolarity by other powers—would make to the nature of both the international relations of the Global Indian Ocean and the domestic orders within it. After all, a common lament among liberal order's defenders is that it is suffering from a crisis of authority, especially as America confronts relative decline and self-doubt.[118] In chapter 9, Rana Mitter examines the extent to which the Chinese Communist Party is both in theory and in practice reworking the material sinews and the prevailing ideas that dominate the oceanic landscape. While there is no denying that the sums of money associated with Xi Jinping's Belt and Road Initiative are overwhelming, Mitter argues against the (new) cold warriors in Washington that Beijing is not seeking to transplant US hegemony, overthrow the existing liberal order and develop an autarkic bloc of economic influence. He maintains that the thin hegemony which sets the Global Indian Ocean apart from the Atlantic and Pacific worlds is much more suited to China's desire to advance its position in the world by averting direct confrontation with existing hegemons and by pragmatically cooperating on the basis of material interests (rather than shared norms). The Chinese Communist Party is half-heartedly selling an alternative imaginary in the form of the developmentalism of Belt and Road combined with illiberal government. However, it is likely to prefer benefiting from thin hegemony's historically anchored lowest-common denominator rules that facilitate coexistence and commerce rather than engaging in military adventurism or ideological proselytization.

As Anatol Lieven argues in his conclusion, dystopian narratives that paint the Indian Ocean as the next battlefield of violent hegemonic rivalry have more to do with the unsettled nature of politics in Washington, Delhi and Beijing than with a historically grounded study of how international order has evolved in the macro-region. Like Rana Mitter, Lieven is profoundly critical of the geopolitically weaponized term "the Indo-Pacific" which offers little analytical purchase but instead seeks to help identify a Chinese threat to US interests that needs to be countered by the so-called "Quad" that comprises the US, one Pacific power (Japan), one Indian Ocean player (India) and an actor linked to both oceans (Australia).[119] Constructs like the Indo-Pacific fail to capture the actual historical roots of international order in either oceanic world, their transcontinental connections or the heterogeneity of Indian Ocean societies. In spite of Sino-American competition, the *sui generis* character of the Ocean will ensure it is neither very liberal or Western nor especially illiberal or Chinese: rather than being coaxed into a tight external framework, political orders in the macro-region will combine elements of both, as well as of their own traditions, and continue to experiment with a startling pluriformity of ideas, institutions and practices. Criticizing policy tropes and accounts in social science that still echo modernization theory and "end of history" prophecies, Lieven believes that the political virulence of religion and nationalism will endure in the Global Indian Ocean and shape the varieties of statehood that characterize it.

As discussed above and explored in greater detail throughout this book, the varying liberal ambitions of the Pax Britannica, the Truman Doctrine and the last four decades of US hegemony were often strongly reappropriated and resisted in the Global Indian Ocean. In doing so, the macro-region has in more than one sense been prefiguring the recent contestation of liberal order in the core of the global political economy. At the very moment that the material distribution of capabilities is shifting and (re-)emerging powers are (re)forging systems of interconnectivity, the idea of mutually reinforcing liberalizations and multilateralisms that sought to give US hegemony and its "mythical world order"[120] legitimacy appears to be in ignominious retreat.[121] For various kinds of realists, the proposition that the nature of order will change as the distribution of power shifts is obvious, as were the self-defeating illusions of the liberal international order of the last thirty years.[122] Since the inception of our collective intellectual project during initial discussions in 2015, liberal order's core propositions have been assaulted by rising right-wing nationalism and a return of leftist class politics in America and the European Union— most prominently by the previous occupant of the White House for whom human rights treaties, Ricardian models of commerce and America's global network of alliances are inimical to US interests. The Doha Round of WTO negotiations has made marginal progress since 2001; the UN Security Council has been gridlocked for years over Syria and Ukraine; in the last decade, the IMF has lost global influence, loaning more money to European countries than to all other IMF members combined; and the optimism surrounding collapsing *anciens régimes* in the former Soviet Union, Middle East and South East Asia has dissipated in the wake of failed colour revolutions and an Arab Spring turned catastrophically violent. The 2003 invasion of Iraq gravely tarnished the agenda of global democracy promotion, just as the 2007 crash of the US subprime market followed by the Great Recession exposed the delusion that financial globalization was a tide that could lift all boats.

With both the attractiveness of liberal institutions and the raw power that underpinned them having eroded, how resilient and robust is what remains of the liberal order in the Global Indian Ocean of the 21st century? Can the legacies of "archaic globalization" and of the Pax Britannica shed light on the future of capitalism and state–society relations? What kind of alternative social contracts, modes of state-building and international security arrangements are being proposed, and by whom? And which geographies of political, economic and cultural inclusion and exclusion are emerging as new forms of regional awareness and circulation manifest themselves?

These questions guide the chapters that comprise this volume. The contemporary structural condition of the Global Indian Ocean is less what Robert Keohane famously termed "after hegemony"—the institutions created by liberal order endure when the material underpinnings of dominance have declined, because international regimes facilitate decentralized, interest-based cooperation among states to mitigate uncertainty[123]—and more yet another reinvention of thin hegemony. International order in the Global Indian Ocean has always been characterized by supple transactionalism and heteronomous concepts of political authority rather than rigid institutionalization and homogenization of relations between polities.[124] Dense interactions and interdependences in the Global Indian Ocean have consistently been rooted in, and have facilitated, various cosmopolitanisms and overlapping regionalisms rather than universalism and political or cultural unification. Even at the high point of "end of history", the states and societies of the macro-region reconfigured and contested liberal order, exploring its potential, marking out its limits, and laying bare its contradictions. The retreat of liberalism's most ambitious plans for transformation likely means that a historically recognizable pattern of myriad spatial networks combining geopolitical, linguistic, mercantile and religious affinities and contrasts will once again dominate transoceanic processes of interaction and (dis)integration. Such relations and flows continue to strike observers, sometimes even in the region, as disorderly. They also baffle conventional international relations analyses that struggle to offer a persuasive theoretical account of why the oceanic world is more than the sum of its parts and why the retreat of grand hegemonic ambitions will neither end deep interdependence, nor necessarily produce anarchy. Yet if the Global Indian Ocean teaches the study of political order anything, it is that the durable multiplicity of forms of statehood, society and markets and the variegated interactions between them under conditions of thin hegemony reveal not only important lessons about globalization's past, but perhaps also tell us something about the future of international order.

2

A HISTORY OF DISTRIBUTED SOVEREIGNTY

TRADE, MIGRATION AND RULE IN THE GLOBAL INDIAN OCEAN

Thomas Blom Hansen

In the longer history of European colonial expansion, and the creation of a global economy, the Global Indian Ocean holds a special place. Not only was the Indian Ocean world home to many, well-consolidated empires and kingdoms, but it also had a well-developed seaborne economy and large communities of sailors and navigators and naval power that often were more than a match for the European navies. As a result, Verhoeven points out in the introduction to this volume, the Indian Ocean emerged as Europe's Other, a space full of pirates, traders and armies that often opposed and thwarted direct European domination. In the Indian Ocean, the emerging Pax Britannica of the 19th century was based primarily on alliances and subsidiary arrangements with local rulers rather than on direct military presence. This "thin hegemony", in Verhoeven's formulation, also characterized the arrangements in the Global Indian Ocean after

1945, with the US now as a naval hegemon presiding over a complex, if unstable, set of alliances involving a large array of regimes from the Middle East to Indonesia.

In this chapter, I trace the origins and dynamics of patterns of sovereignty, economies and human movement across the Indian Ocean that seem to have been reproduced over centuries up to the present day. My argument has two parts. Firstly, that British hegemony could only be established in the Indian Ocean through an elaborate, if improvised and piecemeal, system of treaties and indirect rule which has left deep and enduring legacies such as widespread legal pluralism and layered systems of economic exchange, trust and credit. This is particularly visible in the way small, well-organized trading communities continue to dominate the economic life around, and across, the Indian Ocean. Secondly, consolidation of British power across the Indian subcontinent in the 19th century enabled diverse groups and communities on the subcontinent to establish trade networks, migration routes and cycles of labour migration across the Indian Ocean space. I illustrate this with three historical and ethnographic vignettes that demonstrate the path dependency of these migrations and networks: (a) the history of the Memon trading community's establishment in South Africa; (b) the history of the export of indentured Indian labour to South Africa and elsewhere, and the continued uncertainties of belonging and status that face their descendants six generations later; and (c) the economic and migratory ties between colonial Bombay and the Persian Gulf, and how these have been retained but reversed in the late 20th century with the rise of oil-based economies in the Gulf and neighbouring areas.

Patterns of sovereignty in the Global Indian Ocean

The Indian Ocean world has a long and deep history of competing trade routes and overlapping regimes of domination. Unlike the complete naval and commercial domination of the Atlantic world by European powers from 1500 onwards, these same powers did not enjoy any obvious military superiority in South Asia, South East Asia or other parts of the Indian Ocean until after the end of the Napoleonic Wars and its proxy wars on the Indian subcontinent. Beginning with

Portuguese and later Dutch trade and conquest, European expansion was almost exclusively based on domination of the sea, seeking security and bases on multiple islands while gradually establishing entrepôts and factories on the mainland. These entrepôts were precarious and entirely dependent on the maintenance of viable treaties with local rulers who could overwhelm them with great ease.

In the western parts of the Indian Ocean—the Arabian Peninsula, the Swahili coast and the Arabian Sea and western India—multiple trade routes expanded and thrived especially after the spread of Islam. From around 1500, the slave trade grew in importance, supplying a steady stream of labour and soldiers from various parts of Africa to the cities and kingdoms of the Arabian Peninsula, Persia and India. However, throughout the 18th and early 19th century there were also individuals from India arriving in the Middle East as domestic slaves and other forms of indentured labour.[1] The scale of this centuries-old trade in forced labour is contested but historians estimate that 1.5 to 2 million Africans were sold into slavery in various parts of Asia.[2] Persia and the Gulf were among the largest markets and the ports of Muscat, Jeddah and Aden became crucially dependent on slave labour by the 18th century.[3] However, unlike the system of chattel slavery and the hardening racial ideology that governed the Atlantic slave trade, there were multiple examples of relatively free labour, or freed slaves, becoming integral, if permanently subordinated and often marginal, to parts of societies across the western Indian Ocean.[4] Nowhere was this clearer than in the history of African slaves and soldiers in western India. By the 15th century, many kingdoms and sultanates in India began importing *habshis*, Abyssinian slave-soldiers, who were transported to the new ports of Bombay and Cambay by Arab as well as Portuguese traders. Habshis, mostly converted to Islam, became known as highly capable soldiers who soon set themselves up in 1489 as rulers of the fortified enclave of Janjira (south of Bombay), where they remained a military force to reckon with for centuries until Janjira was declared a princely state under British paramountcy in the 19th century. Around 1600, Malik Ambar, the most illustrious habshi of the era, became the vizier of the sultanate of Ahmednagar and later one of the most effective and legendary military commanders of the Deccan.[5] In the following centuries, there was a continuous trickle of African labour into Surat, Bombay and Goa as sailors, dock workers and manual labourers. Their descendants are today communities known as *sidis* (derived from *sayids*), spread across the coastal zones of western India. The largest group of Africans arrived on the Makran coast of what is today Baluchistan in Pakistan. This territory was part of the Omani state until the 1950s. The Omani rulers had for centuries relied on African slaves and free labour for soldiery, domestic service, and pearl diving. Today, the numerous descendants of these populations are known as *sheedis*, or Afro-Baluch.[6]

European colonial powers inserted themselves gradually into this already densely interwoven economy of trade and military power. The Portuguese, the Dutch and later the British experimented with a range of different arrangements and forms of layered, shared and partial sovereignty: Portuguese trading forts from Colombo and Cochin all the way to Bassein and Diu off the Gujarat coast,[7] penal colonies, the plantation economies on the islands of Mauritius and *Réunion*, the entrepôts in the Persian Gulf, and the old trading and slave ports on the Swahili coast forced into treaties with European powers, along with similar arrangements across South East Asia.

The primary instrument was not naked conquest but a range of treaties that established trading rights and dominion in smaller territories in order to secure free trade and curb piracy. As the British Empire emerged at the start of the 19th century as the world's preeminent naval and commercial power after the Napoleonic Wars, there was also an unprecedented push for legal regulation, treaties and contractual relations between the emerging Europeans powers and their multiple new subjects and subordinated "partners" and allies, from African kingdoms to East Asia and the Pacific.[8] Nowhere was this "rage for order", to use Benton and Ford's term, more complex and generative of many aspects of what in the late 19th century gradually consolidated as "international law" than the Global Indian Ocean. Hand in hand with the consolidation of territorial domination of India, a system of treaties began to proliferate across the Indian Ocean.

The most well-known system was the establishment of a plethora of princely states constituting 40 per cent of India's territory and population. Each of these states possessed what Beverley has called "minor sovereignty",[9] in that they retained their own government and taxation systems. The larger states had their own police forces, armies and foreign legations, all overseen and discreetly directed by the British resident.[10] In the hilly and peripheral regions of British India, other forms of government were conducted through tribal councils, headmen and small tribal kingdoms under the protection of the Crown.[11]

These forms of government and principles of indirect rule and limited autonomy were also applied to other parts of the Global Indian Ocean. Sultanates and towns in the Middle East and South East Asia had been forced by cannon-boat diplomacy to accept a status as "protectorates" with varying degrees of obligation to the Crown, such as the General Maritime Treaty of 1820 that established British "protection" in the Gulf region.[12]

The abolition of slavery across the British Empire in 1833 presented the British Navy and the empire's growing commercial interests in the Indian Ocean with new opportunities in their attempts at undercutting existing economic networks and establishing naval and commercial hegemony in the region. The sultans of Zanzibar and other rulers on the Swahili coast had for centuries played central roles in the trade involving slaves and a range of goods from the interior of Africa.[13] The area had a large number of powerful Arab and Indian traders, but by 1833 the Indian traders (now British subjects) were forced to free their slaves and give up their involvement in the lucrative slave trade. In the 1860s, and again in 1873, British warships arrived in Zanzibar to force the sultan to ban slave trading. However, the stand-off continued for decades and slavery was only formally abolished in Zanzibar as late as in 1897.[14]

By the 1880s, most of the British interests across the Indian Ocean, including the vast Indian Army, were no longer under the direct control of the Colonial Office in London but were run by a variety of offices and agencies out of Bombay, Calcutta and Madras, now effectively Her Majesty's government in the East. Across the Arabian Peninsula, Persian ports, and the Swahili coast it was prominent Gujarati traders, Muslims and Hindus who served as the formal representatives of the Crown. These agents reported directly to Delhi and called in armed assistance to discipline local rulers who had shown signs of insubordination or had failed to protect British commercial interest as stipulated in the multiple treaties that governed these often volatile relationships.[15] This complicated web of treaties, protectorates, local rulers and indirect control grew out of an adaptation to the realities of partial, overlapping and unresolved sovereignty arrangements already existing in the Global Indian Ocean.

One of these dynamics was Britain's long-standing, and ultimately effective, attempt to become a benign protector of the ailing Portuguese empire—a strategy initially forged in the competition with Spain in earlier centuries that eventually saw the rather advantageous transformation of Portugal into a de facto subsidiary empire under British protection.[16] During centuries of Portuguese colonial rule, many Goans had established themselves in Mozambique, where they came to play an important role in the national liberation movement in the 1950s and 1960s. In Goa, the Portuguese authorities had conventionally relied on Mozambican slaves and slave soldiers as police and armed forces. This practice, now employing enlisted troops, lasted until Goa's forcible incorporation into the Indian republic in 1961.[17]

From the point of view of the British Crown, the establishment of paramountcy (a term that gained popularity among imperial officials after 1857) through indirect control was always regarded as a cost-saving measure if also dependent on the fortunes and temperaments of local rulers. It seemed an effective strategy in promoting the long-term security interests of the empire though it was not always advantageous in the eyes of those interest groups that pushed for deeper imperial control. In the course of the 19th century, the expanding interests of planters, missionary societies and trading companies seeking deeper entry into the interior of India and other colonies became ever more vested in demanding political stability and permanent military protection by imperial forces. An important tipping point came during the great revolt in North India in 1857 when the much-publicized violence against white women and children swung popular opinion at home and in the British settler colonies in a more jingoistic and openly racist direction.[18] After this point, British policies became more invested in direct rule and systematic law enforcement, as well as more intense regulation of the economy and of public health across British India and other territories.[19]

Colonial rule as distributed sovereignty

How can one analytically understand the ways in which the British empire established itself as the force that reshaped the political order and economies around the Indian Ocean? Was it, as Sugata Bose has suggested, an attempt to extend a blunt form of modern unitary sovereignty into the Indian Ocean that merely resulted in domination but not hegemony?[20] Or was it, rather, a kind of hegemonic arrangement that worked through a multitude of complex and often fluid and provisional arrangements? From the trading post, settlement, enclave, factory and plantation to the trade corridor or treaty-bound indirect rule overseen by a duly appointed British resident—these were projections of British power in different ways, some commercial, others symbolic or military. These many arrangements constituted neither the "delegation" of British sovereignty from a fixed territorial centre nor "layers" in a hierarchy of British jurisdiction. Rather, they formed an emerging system of "distributed" sovereignty, by which I mean that each of the elements in this order drew on different, even incommensurable, legal and symbolic registers of legitimate rule. The claims over territory, resources or the symbols of power exercised by rulers, headmen, community elders and princes throughout this complex world were uneven and non-standardized, drawing on vernacular traditions, but were nonetheless incorporated into the imperial order in so far as they recognized the symbolic paramountcy of the British Crown. Without ever achieving effective dominance in many parts of the Indian Ocean world but relying on naval supremacy, territorial control, commercial power and a flexible system of treaties (many of which were revised or subverted by the British at their will), Britain succeeded in maintaining a hegemonic status in the Indian Ocean for almost a hundred and fifty years. This was the essence of what Verhoeven calls an enduring "thin hegemony".

This complex formation presents several challenges to the standard historical narrative of early, predatory colonialism as the mere disorganized precursor of a more full-blown and rational governmental control over territories and large populations, fixed by treaty systems and precise delineations of space and maps, which emerged by the early 20th century. As Benton has suggested, the resolute drive to map sovereignty onto space in an ever more detailed manner in the

20th century was in fact a concerted strategy pursued by imperial European nation-states in order to reduce the legal and political complexity of the systems of distributed sovereignty they had created in previous centuries. However, as we shall see below, the sovereignty arrangements in the Indian Ocean left deep traces with considerable path-dependent force.

The first challenge is the significance of the sea as a space of power and movement. Despite the current political and scholarly celebration of the Indian Ocean as a space of ancient cosmopolitanism and cultural fluidity,[21] it is worth reminding ourselves that control of seaborne power was the indispensable cornerstone of all European colonial expansions and it was what guaranteed their durability. It is impossible to understand the reach of British power in the 19th century without the dominance of naval power and trade, in that order. In the late 19th century, many strategists in Britain questioned the process of large-scale territorial domination and modern administration of millions of subjects of the Crown that was then under way in Africa and South Asia. The empire should instead rely on the time-tested conventional domination of the seas, islands and global trade, they argued.[22] The ocean was, in other words, never a counterpoint to empire; it was where empire began. Oceans were not a challenge to imperial control but actually its most important precondition. Similarly, the offshore economies and tax havens that today are portrayed as illegitimate outgrowths of global capitalism are not aberrations but rather pillars in the way modern sea-based capitalism grew—from Jersey and the Bahamas to Singapore and Dubai.[23] To this day, Mauritius, owing to its tax code and tax treaty with India, remains the most important node in capital flows into India. The contemporary grid of commerce and capital flows in the Global Indian Ocean—Singapore, Dubai, Hong Kong, Shanghai, Johannesburg—began as nodes in the elaborate system of treaties that was codified and elaborated by the British Empire. Even the ancient port city of Gwadar in Pakistan, today heralded as a new centre of trade and logistical access to the ocean from Central Asia, was for centuries part of Omani territory and protected by a treaty with the British until it was ceded to Pakistan as late as 1958. The complex system of international law, which took shape in the late 19th century, emerged in crucial ways from attempts to codify and regulate the plethora of legal "anomalies", special zones, and exceptions that encompassed much of the colonial world.[24]

The second challenge presented by the sovereignty arrangements of the Global Indian Ocean is that they run counter to the conventional distinction between pre-modern sovereignty based on public ritual and the public performance of loyalty and fealty to the ruler, and modern sovereignty based on effective daily administration of territories and populations. This distinction is the underlying theme of Michel Foucault's famous work *Discipline and Punish*,[25] which draws exclusively on European and especially French examples and sources. However, the global and colonial configuration of sovereign power in the late 19th century does not sit very well with Foucault's underlying teleological idea that sovereignty inexorably moves towards a more intensive bio-political regulation of populations.

In 1980, Clifford Geertz coined the term "theatre state" for the tradition of statecraft of pre-colonial Bali that centred on the performance of ideals of balance, perfection and stillness in public ceremonies.[26] Although it was framed as a comment on the poverty of the Western realist notion of power as "war, horses and guns", it is striking how inattentive Geertz was to very similar dynamics played out at the heart of the colonial state formations that evolved in the 18th and 19th century across the Indian Ocean world. The British colonial state, and the Dutch state in the Indies, relied very heavily on the theatrics of power, on pomp and circumstance, and on adapting local registers of authority to their own ends.[27] As the East India Company consolidated its rule in India, it experimented with Persian and Urdu as official languages, and its revenue collection was largely based on Mughal land records. In the early 19th century, the Company embarked on an ambitious experiment of micro-governance of temples and religious institutions in South India as a way of cutting straight to what was believed to be the religious source of political legitimacy in India.[28] Everywhere, in India, in Malaya and the Indies, treaties and alliances with local notables and rulers were the bedrock of territorial control and security. Colonial states were constantly worrying about their own legitimacy and the 1857 great rebellion only deepened this fear, impelling the colonial state to employ more systematic violence than previously. Yet, the system of treaties and indirect rule persisted and became more entrenched than before, creating a parallel aristocratic universe in the colony, where hunting and arcane rituals of rule were shared between British officers and local rulers.[29]

These alliances and theatrical imitations of local rituals of sovereignty were anathema to the progressives of the day—missionaries with abolitionist leanings repelled by the caste structure; administrators enthusiastic about the rationality of new techniques of governance; social reformers, nationalists and labour organizers who saw in the British Raj an unholy alliance between retrograde native cultural and political institutions and the interests of planters, settlers and commercial interests. These progressive groups pushed for more intensive, rational and indeed "moral" governance of the colonial subjects.[30]

The history of late colonial rule around the Indian Ocean was essentially structured by a protracted tug of war between these two faces of the colonial state: reformers pushing for deeper regulation and social reform versus conservatives pushing for a leaner operation that relied to the largest extent possible on methods of indirect rule through local aristocrats and "natural leaders" as well as the presence of an effective military force. This latter group argued that the colonial state should retain its hegemony by more distant performances of imperial paramountcy while leaving most details of governance to local authorities in a manner that was consonant with local customs and norms. The debate in a nutshell was about this: should the colonial state be an aspiring modern bio-political state or remain a colonial theatre state imitating local rituals of authority?

These two faces of the colonial state points to the third challenge presented by the patterns of distributed sovereignty in the Global Indian Ocean: the tension between territorial sovereignty and sovereignty over people. In the standard narrative of the evolution of the modern state, the technologies of bureaucratic permanence, borders, and cartographical and spatial control went hand in hand with deeper registration, regulation and control of populations through surveillance and policing of largely sedentary populations, as well as the collection of documentary and statistical evidence about them. However, with the rapid expansion of sea and rail transport and of the world economy at the beginning of the 20th century, the control of bodies, movement and people became ever more important and challenging than territorial control.[31] The vast colonial and "protected" territories under systems of distributed sovereignty were characterized by rather fluid and often contested geographical boundaries and even more unclear jurisdiction over populations and territories.[32]

As Verhoeven argues in the introduction to this volume, British hegemony was in the main based on control over territory and oceanic space, maintaining the right of the Royal Navy to control waterways, trading routes, ports and entrepôts, and enforce treaty obligations as interpreted by London. This hegemonic form allowed larger numbers of people than before to move across the Indian subcontinent and from there to other parts of the empire as indentured labourers, traders, pilgrims, sailors and soldiers. In the absence of systems of identification and verification, this soon presented a whole new problem of legibility and responsibility: who had jurisdiction over these brown bodies that, by virtue of originating from within a colonial territory, were generally defined as "imperial subjects"? The Government of India in Delhi, the Colonial Office in London, the sultans or princely rulers, or the (mostly) colonial authorities in their new permanent or temporary places of residence?[33] What kinds of care, amenities and entitlements could these newly mobile populations claim and expect as imperial subjects? As we shall see, this rapid expansion of the umbrella of paramountcy over vast populations without any concomitant intensification of bio-political governance generated durable social structures and informal community organizations of considerable path-dependent power across the oceanic space.

Let me illustrate some of these general observations by looking at three small moments in the larger story that made the Global Indian Ocean a space for the demographic and economic expansion of communities originating in colonial India.

Community and capital in the Indian Ocean

The overwhelming majority of capital assets in modern India are owned and controlled by a tiny concentration of trading communities

51

from northern and western India. The most successful were trading communities from the western coast of Gujarat and Sindh—the territories of Kutch, Kathiawar, Saurashtra—who successfully exploited the new possibilities opened by British naval hegemony in the Indian Ocean. Much of the capital accumulated in the oceanic trade in the 19th century was reinvested in property and enterprises on the Indian mainland in the 20th century.

Many were Hindu Bania communities like the Bhatia, Patel and Shah, and Sindhi traders who spread globally,[34] but Parsis and smaller Muslim sects were also highly successful. The Bohras, who are Shia, established a stronghold in colonial Aden and Yemen;[35] the Khoja Ismaili (Aga Khanis) established themselves from Persia to Zanzibar and Central Asia;[36] while the Memon communities from Kutch rose to prominence in South Africa, the Gulf and in Canada.

These communities arose from the complex network of puny self-governing princely states in this region—almost two hundred states in Gujarat alone, some of them as small as a few villages but with a carefully prescribed protocol regarding the number of gun salutes the rulers were entitled to when visiting areas under direct colonial rule or adjacent states.[37] In old trading cities like Surat and in the bigger princely states with thriving ports like Kutch, Bhavnagar and Porbandar, the trading communities had enjoyed substantial self-governance through local caste and community councils, under the protection of the ruling family.[38] This allowed these communities to develop intense and elaborate codes of trust and mutuality, which they deployed with great success in their oceanic trade and migration ventures. It also bound them back to their homeland in deep and enduring ways through property, credit, philanthropy, marriage and kin relations. As Edward Simpson has argued with respect to Kutchi traders and sailors, generations of transoceanic and global travel and investment did not make these communities "cosmopolitan". Rather the opposite, Simpson argues.[39] I concur, as my example will show.

Memons today number about 1.5 million people, equally divided between India, Pakistan and large numbers living in various parts of Africa, the UK, the US, Australia and Canada. They are a tightly knit community with most members registered on an online database (memon.com), which previously was printed every five years in a telephone directory. This was used by travelling Memons as a guide to where one could stay, and whom one could ask for favours, support and even credit when abroad. This community sees itself as a global mini-society, largely intermarried and interconnected, their loyalties to the Memon community far overshadowing any other priority—whether nationality or solidarity with other Muslims.

Memons constitute the single richest group of Asians in Africa, with concentrated wealth in Johannesburg and Durban and also in Mombasa and Nairobi. Memons make up the majority of a recent list of the 40 richest families in Pakistan,[40] while Indian Memons, like other Muslims in the country, have encountered major obstacles to scaling up their business operations across the country.[41] As a result, Bombay and Porbandar are today mainly places of philanthropy and property investment rather than business investment for Memons.

Memons were among the relatively marginal groups of coastal Gujarat that seized the opportunity for outmigration especially to eastern and southern Africa in the late 19th century. Memons also thrived in Burma and Sri Lanka and were successful in aligning themselves socially and commercially with other Kutchi communities, both Hindu and Muslim.[42] They also proved particularly adept at exploiting new commercial opportunities in coastal Kenya, Uganda, Muscat, Aden and indeed South Africa, which soon emerged as an important centre of Memon wealth and power. As the indentured labour system grew from 1860 across the Indian Ocean, local planters in South Africa requested that a small number of Indian traders be allowed to provision the "coolie" population. This was the beginning of a major migration of thousands of Memons and other Gujaratis who opened small shops and imported foodstuffs and commodities from their networks in India. They proudly described themselves in the colonial language of the day as "pioneers" and "settlers".

The abundance of cheap land and economic opportunities in the booming economy of South Africa after the discovery of gold and diamonds meant that Memons quickly prospered. Members of the community began to operate ships between India and South Africa and acquired very substantial holdings of land and commercial real estate. They graduated from being small dukawallah retailers to become major wholesale traders. By the 1920s, Memons dominated the market in building materials and agricultural implements and supplies across much of the country. Many small towns across the Afrikaner heartland of the old Transvaal still have Memon families and small mosques on their outskirts. Their integration into the Afrikaner farming economy spared the Memon community many of the indignities that Apartheid visited upon other communities of colour. Memons created a dense network of Muslim schools, orphanages and mosques as well as many Indians-only educational institutions. Some Gujarati Muslims became prominent lawyers and politicians supporting the African National Congress, but the Memons generally stayed out of politics and the public eye, working mainly on the inner lines of the emerging Muslim civil society in the country.

A small mosque was set up in the 1880 in central Durban by a Memon trader and it soon expanded to become the largest mosque in the Southern Hemisphere—open to all Muslims but entirely controlled by the Memons. Relatives of the same group of businessmen had established a charitable trust in Porbandar in 1884, and in 1891 it was decided to create an entity called Natal Porbandar Trust whose aim was to collect funds in Natal and channel them back to India to be spent on the education of the less fortunate members of the Memon community. In 1906, charges of irregularities in the transfer and collection of funds emerged in Natal and serious disturbances erupted. Local authorities feared that the members of two lineages on either side of the dispute would clash in the streets. The local ruler, Rana Saheb, decided to intervene and ordered a settlement of the dispute in Porbandar as well as in Natal. Although it was strictly speaking a legal dispute on South African territory, all parties involved in India and Natal decided to abide by the order of the Porbandar ruler.[43]

Although the state of Porbandar was dissolved into independent India in 1948, Porbandar is still the most important centre of Memon identification today. Many Memon men in South Africa prefer to this day the tradition of marrying brides from India. I met several Memon women who were born and raised in small towns in Sindh in present-day Pakistan. When I remarked that they were not technically from India, my informants would say, half-jokingly, "For us, India is where we Memons come from, that is what matters … whether they call it Pakistan or India today is not really important to us."

This sentiment is in no small measure informed by the growing influence of Islamic piety movements in South Africa. Today, many wealthy Memons and other Gujarati Muslims in South Africa and elsewhere on the continent are driving forces in the spread and power of Deobandi-inspired Islamic reform movements, such as Tablighi Jamaat, that promote a purified and "originalist" interpretation of Islam. In the early 20th century, some Memons tried to get officially classified as "Arabs" in order to distinguish themselves from the growing populations of lower-caste indentured labourers from India. Today, the same communities assert their deep connection to the Middle East as the cradle of Islam. In the early 2000s, a group of wealthy Memons related to me that they were being approached by both the Pakistani and Indian embassies in South Africa, who wanted them to invest back in their putative homelands. A senior member of the group remarked, "What these officials don't understand is that we are Muslims, first and foremost. We feel more at home in Jeddah or Mecca when we go for umrah,[44] or even in Dubai or Kuwait, than back in Karachi or Bombay."

From "coolie" labour to Indian immigrants

While the history of the Memons is an example of how the distributed sovereignty across the Global Indian Ocean afforded newly empowered commercial communities unprecedented levels of freedom and transnational autonomy, my second example concerns the opposite end of the social spectrum: the movement of millions of people as indentured labourers throughout the oceanic world. Here I explore how this phenomenon over time forced the colonial governments across the Empire to adopt incipient policies of protection and care of these populations. The abolition of slavery in 1833 had faced stiff resistance from planters and traders. Soon after, a system of "indentured labour" was initiated with a view to providing cheap labour from India on ten-year renewable contracts to plantations across the world. These were mostly British possessions such as Fiji, Natal (South Africa), Malaya and Trinidad but also French territories, such as Réunion, Guyana and Mauritius, and Dutch possessions in the Caribbean. From the 1840s until the 1920s, at least 3.5 million people of Indian descent were transported as indentured "coolies" across the world.[45] Mauritius was the first major importer of labour under the indenture system and, as the traffic increased quickly in the 1850s, the Government of India felt compelled to create some legal framework for its regulation.

In 1859, the office of the "Protector of Indian Emigrants" opened in Madras, and it was decreed that in every territory importing indentured labour on ten-year contracts, an "Office of the Protector of Immigrants" should ensure that employers were abiding by the terms of indenture and provided the minimum facilities for the workforce, such as food and shelter. Ten years later, Natal was by far the biggest importer of "coolie labour" and the influx created unruly situations in Durban harbour and on the rapidly expanding sugar estates where planters were unwilling to follow the most basic injunctions. The Natal authorities did not see the coolies as their responsibility and claimed that they were a kind of "free labour", but pressure from New Delhi and the Colonial Office forced an investigation in 1872. The recommendations of the "Coolie Commission" far exceeded anything that the government of Natal or India provided to its non-white subjects: labourers were to be given free medical care, free education for their children, supervision by a protector of Indian immigrants, and five to ten acres of land should they decide not to return to India.[46]

The episode created much resentment among the white authorities in Natal and was the beginning of one of the longest rifts within the Empire. Over the next five decades, high population growth and immigration made the Indian population in South Africa the largest outside India. The resentment against what was seen as "Asiatic penetration" of white residential areas and business fields—mostly by wealthy Gujarati traders and businessmen—led to persistent demands for segregation and also the repatriation of "Asiatics" whom white colonists saw as "alien" to Africa.

Many of these ideas went into the Class Areas Bill of 1922, which recommended separation of white from "non-European" residential areas and predated Apartheid's more infamous schemes by decades. This was, however, far from enough in the eyes of the National Party–Labour Party government, which came to power in 1924, and it began initiatives to prepare for large-scale repatriation of Indians.

The minister of the interior, Dr D.F. Malan (later the first Apartheid prime minister of South Africa), stated: "the Indian, as a race in this country, is an alien element in the population, and no solution will be acceptable to the country unless it results in a very considerable reduction of the Indian population in this country".[47]

The government's plans, which had widespread support among whites, caused a major stir in Durban and Johannesburg. A "National Day of Prayer" was held throughout the country on 23 February 1926. The South African Indian Congress sent a deputation to India to mobilize support for the cause of the Indians in South Africa. Mass meetings were held in various parts of India to protest and the Viceroy of India, Lord Reading, sent an official protest against the legislation. Interestingly, the Government of India clearly acted as an advocate of native Indian interests and pressed for a round table conference where the issue could be settled and negotiated between the two governments within the newly formed Commonwealth. A round table conference began in Cape Town. The Indian delegation consisted of six civil servants, three Indian and three British, and was led by Sir Mahomed Habibullah. The South African delegation was all-white. After protracted negotiations, the so-called Cape Town Agreement was signed in 1927. It laid out a new voluntary repatriation scheme that built certain financial incentives (such as free tickets, and a fixed sum per adult and child) into the repatriation procedure.[48] However, the more remarkable part of the agreement was that a review of Indian education was to be undertaken with the assistance of experts in education from India, that the South Africa government promised to provide better housing and living conditions for Indians, that Indians should receive "equal pay for equal work", and that no unreasonable obstacles should be put in the way of Indian business initiatives. It was also agreed that a permanent Agent General of the Government of India should be posted in South Africa to oversee the implementation of the agreement.

The issue continued to simmer. A series of laws limiting Indian purchase of land generated massive protests from Indian organizations in the 1940s, at this point powerfully represented by the Natal Indian Congress. This organization was founded by Gandhi to represent all Indians in the country, but it had from the outset been dominated by individuals from wealthy and educated business families who often felt directly targeted by the policies of residential segregation. Bending to massive pressure from white constituencies, the government of Jan Smuts passed the highly discriminatory Asiatic Land Tenure and Indian Representation Act in 1946. Indian organizations termed it the "Ghetto Act" and pointed out that it violated even the highly paternalist terms of indenture which had been administered by the Protector of Indian Immigrants, as well as the Cape Town Agreement. The Government of India, still under British administration, protested strongly and withdrew its High Commissioner in South Africa. The issue was one of the first put before the newly formed United Nations General Assembly. After a lengthy debate, where the Indian delegates defended a universalist agenda of human rights and accused South Africa of practising racial supremacy, while the South African delegation defended its right to treat the matter as one of "domestic jurisdiction", the vote went against the South African government—the first in a long series of international condemnations.

The question at the heart of this was whether the vast majority of Indians, descendants of indentured labourers, could be regarded as proper South Africans, or would simply remain what the South African government called "temporary sojourners". It was clear that the fate of the indentured labourers and their descendants once again had forced colonial governments, Indian and South African, to confront not just whose jurisdiction and sovereignty these people fell under but also what kind of care and responsibility, if any, the government was prepared to extend to these formerly imperial subjects.

It is noteworthy that independent India has maintained an office called "The Protector of Indian Emigrants", an authority under the Ministry of External Affairs, "responsible for protecting the interests of Indian workers going abroad".[49] It is to the story of contemporary labour migration that we now turn.

Bridging the Gulf

Until the early 1990s, the authorities in the booming economies in the Gulf region (see Hertog's chapter 5) preferred to issue *kafalas*— labour contracts—to fellow Muslims. Muslims in Bombay had been

the first to be squeezed out of the labour unions and the textile industry by Hindu nationalist militants since the 1970s, and Gulf employment opened a new income source for them. Many young Muslims
had technical skills, but recruitment was complicated. Most of the
kafalas were handled by well-established travel agents and businessmen—belonging to the long-established Muslim trading communities
such as Memon, Konkani and Bohra—who had direct kin-based contacts in the Gulf and in Saudi Arabia, and it was these traders who
handled the kafalas (for a fee) through a string of transactions largely
within their own networks. The same businessmen had lucrative business contracts with the Haj Committee, a government agency that
since the 1920s had issued short-term passports to haj pilgrims and
subsidies to poor Muslims in the form of discounted tickets. This
practice was part of a larger effort by the Colonial Office to frame the
Empire as the true friend and protector of Muslims worldwide. In
keeping with the incipient "bio-political" practices of the late Empire
which we saw above, the Haj Committee also guaranteed the return
of poor and destitute pilgrims to their point of origin anywhere in
British India.[50] In the post-colonial era, the haj subsidies became
something of a political perk, and also a source of considerable
patronage and power on the part of wealthy Muslims (again, many
Memons and Konkanis) who occupied key positions in the influential
Haj Committee bureaucracy.[51]

To obtain a kafala, applicants had to contact a recruitment agent
who would evaluate their skills and suitability. This process could
take weeks, at times months, and would often involve exorbitant
fees. Many of these agents operated a network of hostels and so-called
trade testing centres that would test the skills of applicants and issue
certificates of skills and qualifications as stipulated in the kafala and
visa rules issued by the UAE, Kuwait, Saudi Arabia and others. This
entire system was nominally supervised by the Bombay branch of the
Office of the Protector of Indian Emigrants. Inspectors did indeed
occasionally inspect offices and trade testing centres, but regular
donations to the inspectors ensured that the system basically functioned as a large, sprawling system of payments. Those who did not
pay up would be kept waiting or would return home, indebted, and
without a kafala. The system afforded the Muslim trading communi-

ties substantial sources of income and patronage and it reinforced their community ties across the ocean. At the same time, the massive flow of labour across the Arabian Sea in the last few decades has provided new groups of lower-status Muslims with new sources of income, new networks and contacts in the Gulf, and a welcome opportunity to compensate for the systematic social and economic marginalization experienced by most Muslims in India.[52] The decades of booming Gulf employment had three effects on the relationship between Indian Muslims and the Middle East, all of them profoundly shaped by historical ties.[53]

Firstly, the Gulf and the Middle East more broadly became powerful symbols of religious authenticity and piety in a way that had not been the case previously. While haj had been a durable aspiration but only within reach of those with education and some means, the intensified ties between India and the Gulf made haj more feasible for large populations. The presence of growing Indian and Pakistani communities of professionals and labourers across Saudi Arabia and other states in the region greatly strengthened the popularity of the Wahhabi- and Deobandi-inspired piety movements, which advocated a return to a purer and simpler form of Islamic life, and strict adherence to the conventions and ritual described in the Hadith literature. In the 1990s, I witnessed the growing presence of Tablighi Jamaat preachers in Muslim working-class neighbourhoods in central Mumbai, where they previously had enjoyed limited support. Most of the families in these neighbourhoods were devotees of particular Sufi shrines and tariqas across northern and western India, but now sons, brothers and fathers brought back new styles and ideals of proper Islamic conduct. Many working-class families began to practise stricter purdah at home, enrol their daughters in Muslim girls-only schools, and aspire to a purer pious lifestyle as a way of countering the powerful attractions of Bombay's popular culture, music, films, drugs and other temptations. While much was made in the press of rising "fundamentalism", most of the young Gulf returnees I met in Mumbai in the 1990s had a simpler story to tell. Riaz, a young, Bombay-born sales manager working in Riyadh, told me: "In the Gulf we saw Muslims living with respect, and self-respect. There you can walk with your head high and be a Muslim. You can live a good life there, you are safe but life cannot flow freely there … In Bombay we are so used to be careful and alert and not to attract any attention of the police. So, although I am a Muslim I still want to live here in Bombay—there is more humanity here."

What Riaz referred to obliquely was the harsh treatment, and often racist discrimination, that many South Asians faced in Saudi Arabia in particular. However, the pressure to retain the narrative of the Gulf as a clean and modern Muslim utopia was so strong that these stories mainly circulated among the young working-class men who experienced the worst abuses but could not relate any of their experiences to the wider community for fear of being stigmatized as a failure, as "a troublemaker and a bad Muslim", as one of Riaz's friends put it wryly.

Secondly, the historical relationship between the Maharashtra region around Bombay and the Gulf has been reversed in several ways. Colonial Bombay was for a more than a century the undisputed financial and commercial centre in the western Indian Ocean. The wealthy merchants and industrialists who dominated the oceanic routes demonstrated their new standing by building mansions, schools and public institutions across the emerging metropolis. Bombay was also a major centre for "religious entrepreneurs", powerful trading families that financed and sponsored the building of mosques, madrasas, printing presses and scholarly institutions throughout the western Indian Ocean.[54] Traders, workers and sailors from across the Middle East and East Africa, as well as a number of Central Europeans, flocked to Bombay to find employment and political shelter in its thriving and relatively liberal climate.[55] India's economic stagnation in the 1960s and 1970s and the decline of Bombay's industrial base reversed this trend. From the late 1970s, the burgeoning oil economies around the Gulf began the large-scale importation of labour from across the Global Indian Ocean, as Hertog highlights in chapter 5. Indian Muslims were some of the first to seize these new possibilities. By the 1990s, it was Dubai and other urban centres in the Gulf that, like Bombay a century earlier, had become symbols of modernity and magnets for labourers, professionals, fortune-seekers and businessmen from across the larger region. In Bombay, many of the labour migrants belonged to families that had experienced a considerable loss of social standing and income as the industrial economy declined. Asif, an elderly retired millworker, told me with some bitterness: "When we were young, getting a job in a mill gave you social respect. Millworkers always got good marriage proposals ... I educated my sons, but look at them now, living away from home, doing menial work just to support us all back home in Bombay."

Thirdly, the strong economic ties within community networks across the ocean had been a great strength during the age of empire, giving trading communities rich resources, extensive autonomy and diverse multinational ties. However, as India adopted a more protectionist model after independence, and as Muslims became ever more socially and economically isolated in India, this economic autonomy and reliance on community ties also became a major liability. Outside the relatively limited formal economy, a vast semi-informalized economy and labour market deepened segmentation along lines of community and religion. In this situation, the emerging Gulf migration economy made Muslims less dependent on employment at home in India but it also reinforced the ever-stronger stereotypes of Muslims as "anti-national", not loyal to India, and a "society unto itself", engaged in criminal and smuggling activity. The rise of criminal dons like Haji Mastan, and later Dawood Ibrahim (based in Dubai), who became hero figures among young Muslims, only strengthened the widespread idea of Muslim areas as dangerous, crime-ridden and lagging behind other communities in employment, health and education. Recent government reports have comprehensively documented the rapid and systematic marginalization of Muslims in all sectors of Indian society, and have detailed the systematic "over-policing" of Muslim areas, the systematic ill-treatment of Muslims at the hands of the police, random arrests after terror attacks, and a significant overrepresentation of Muslims in the penal system (Muslims account for almost 39 per cent of all undergoing trial, and 50 per cent of all prison inmates in the state).[56] The involvement of Muslim underworld figures in the retaliatory Bombay blasts in 1993, and later in the planning of terrorist attacks in the city in the early 2000s, lent credence to the Hindu nationalist charge that Muslims were aliens in India, belonging to a different world.

During the 1990s in Bombay, as militant supporters of Hindu nationalist organizations like Shiv Sena and BJP became known as *hindutva-vadis* (literally, devotees of Hindutva), many of my Muslim informants and former labour migrants to the Gulf began claiming that they, by contrast, were *duniya-vadis*, devotees of the world—a claim to adhere to an older register of Muslim cosmopolitanism as against what they saw as a provincial Hindu identity solely bound to the land, and to India alone.

Coda: National sovereignty and migratory flows across the Global Indian Ocean

The process of decolonization across the Indian Ocean space from the 1940s until the late 1960s irrevocably changed the older dynamic of distributed sovereignty. The biggest challenge for the new nation-states soon became that of mobile people and bodies—many of whom continued to move within the older pathways of empire—the trading communities, the hajis, the migrant labourers, the maids, and later flows of tourists, students and experts following new pathways. The new territorial maps interrupted the older pathways of movement of people, particularly the substantial migrations of populations from the Indian subcontinent to other parts of the Global Indian Ocean. The creation of national space also entails the projection of national populations, and the question soon arose whether populations from the subcontinent could be considered proper South Africans, Kenyans or Ugandans, or whether plantation Tamils really could become Sri Lankans or Malaysians.[57] Some of the historically most enterprising and creative communities of the Indian Ocean—the Muslim trading communities of India's west coast—have today become framed as security risks and are often portrayed as anti-national elements in their country of origin.

This effort at projecting national sovereignty by defining the nation's core majority is directly reflected in India's ever more active policies aiming at redesignating the descendants of indentured labourers and itinerant traders as "diasporic populations". From the 1970s, the Hindu nationalist affiliate organization Vishwa Hindu Parishad set out to create a presence in all countries with sizeable Hindu populations in Africa, the Caribbean, Europe and North America. Activists and business people affiliated with these early efforts formed an organization called People of Indian Origin (PIO) in 1989. Their campaign for recognition by India resulted in the PIO card, a quasi-passport that gave its holder most rights in India, except the franchise. Those who could prove Indian ancestry four generations back were eligible. A few years later, the Indian government began holding an annual meeting called Pravasi Bharatiya Divas (Days of Indians Abroad), where leading BJP politicians would appeal to the "Global Indian Family".[58] Soon after, the government announced the Overseas Citizens of India (OCI) card, which further expanded the rights of non-nationals of Indian origin. Immediately after Narendra Modi's electoral victory in 2014, his BJP announced that it aimed at granting voting rights to holders of OCI cards.

There were also more discreet efforts at mobilizing major business families and other notables of Indian origin, to act as unofficial ambassadors of India, lobbying for access to high-ranking officials, and spreading goodwill for Indian trade and investment. This strategy failed in East Africa and South Africa. Here, Indians historically have faced suspicions from many natives, and nativists, of not being loyal to their adopted country. In South Africa, the richest people of Indian origin are Gujarati Muslims, such as the Memons, many of whom are sceptical about how India treats its Muslim minority. Even more damning to this strategy has been the pernicious and deeply corrupting influence of the Guptas—a business family from Uttar Pradesh—on President Jacob Zuma (2009–18) and his family.[59] On the eastern side of the Indian Ocean, populations of Indian origin in Sri Lanka, Malaysia, Burma or Singapore had arrived as indentured plantation labourers, and the standing and nationality status of these communities remain controversial and unresolved to this day (see Chua Beng Huat's chapter 3).

As the paradigm of national sovereignty and nations of distinct peoples has redefined the way the Global Indian Ocean is governed and imagined, it is now a space of competing projections of sovereignty by major powers. The Indian government, and many elite Indians, view this larger space not just as a sphere of interest, but as naturally and historically connected to India by way of history, people, cultural practices and even religion. There are clear continuities between this view and the policies of the late colonial state, which also framed itself, successfully, as the protector of Indians everywhere in the world. However, within the model of distributed sovereignty during the colonial era, such dispersed populations were objects of governance but also of limited responsibility. Within a post-colonial model based on national sovereignty, such people of Indian origin from Myanmar and Malaysia to Kenya and Tanzania are considered minorities, or residues of an "alien" nation, though now they are being actively courted and addressed as diasporic citizens by their putative "mother country".

Herein lies one of the most complex legacies of the model of distributed sovereignty that evolved in the Global Indian Ocean over several centuries. To return to the matrix of sovereignty I outlined above, it seems that India is at least as focused on history and a projection of "soft" sovereignty over people (of Indian origin) as it is on territory, economy and space. In the post-colonial age, strong attachment to popular sovereignty and anxieties about minorities decisively shape societies around the Global Indian Ocean, and the presence of people of Indian origin has turned out to be less of an asset than the Indian government projects.

By contrast, as is evident from Rana Mitter's argument in chapter 9, the Chinese Communist Party steers clear in its pronouncements directed at foreign audiences of detailed and potentially controversial references to shared history or culture in the Indian Ocean. Instead, China is focused on pragmatic collaboration with regimes of all kinds—democratic (e.g. South Africa), Islamist (e.g. Sudan, Iran), monarchical (e.g. Gulf states), militarist (e.g. Myanmar), leftist (e.g. Eritrea, Ethiopia, Mozambique)—in a manner that is reminiscent of early British projections of naval and mercantile power. Could it be that China's project of flexible alliance-building across the Global Indian Ocean is the true successor to the model of distributed sovereignty of the previous century?

3

LIBERAL ORDER'S ILLIBERAL PRODIGY

SINGAPORE AS A NON-LIBERAL ELECTORAL
DEMOCRATIC STATE

Chua Beng Huat

After the collapse of the Berlin Wall, liberalism emerged as the pre-
sumptive normative standard of all modern democratic states,[1] and
liberal order—free elections, the Washington Consensus, the Pax
Americana and liberal multilateralism—became the teleological end
point of modern political development. All other modes of governance are decried as deviations that will eventually return to this
righteous path.[2] With the exception of a few communist states,
almost all constitutions in the Global Indian Ocean have instituted
multiparty elections at periodic intervals as a means for choosing the
government, along with the institutionalization, in varying degrees,
of some liberal rights and freedoms, such as freedom of assembly and
freedom of the press. Furthermore, capitalism has become an economic system without a competitor. Its long temporal and spatial
expansion globally, especially from the end of World War II till the

1990s, has certainly engendered growth, if not generalized prosperity in many post-colonial nations in Asia and Africa. These developments constitute the basis for the optimism of the "democratic transition" theorists,[3] who imagine the day when all authoritarian states will become full liberal democracies, like Taiwan and South Korea and, more recently (with ongoing challenges), Indonesia and Kenya. However, regardless of such triumphal universalistic projections, a quick survey of post-war political development shows that the initial experiments with liberal democracy seldom produced happy results in the South Asian and South East Asian states of the Indian Ocean. With the possible exception of India, liberalism, as a value system and a political order, has not sunk deep roots in the region even though electoral processes are in place. It appears that the liberal global order has ironically enabled successful political-economic developments that deviate significantly from its own ideological premises, as Verhoeven suggests in the introduction and as is evident from Khan Mohmand's chapter 4 on the nexus of democracy, patronage and local power competition in Pakistan.

This chapter argues that there is no linear link between the existence of a (thin) liberal hegemony at the global or even macro-regional level and the spread of democracy and capitalism in the states of the Global Indian Ocean. Drawing on East Asian examples, transitologists continue to predict that capitalist growth produces a broad middle class, which then will go on to overthrow authoritarian rule. Yet the evidence, even from Asia, is sketchy at best. Neither Taiwan nor Korea held competitive presidential elections until the early 1990s,[4] when military dictatorship and martial law were lifted, respectively. Even Japan, arguably the most democratic polity, has developed in effect into a single-party-dominant state under the Liberal Democratic Party since 1945.

In South East Asia too, despite decades of economic expansion and the strong encouragement by donors of liberal pluralism, democracy and liberalism remain difficult propositions, as has long been the case. In Indonesia, a large state within the Global Indian Ocean, President Sukarno instituted what he called "'Guided Democracy', with himself as president-for-life, within a year of the first nationwide elections in 1955. He was deposed in 1965 and succeeded by General Suharto, whose military-backed authoritarian regime produced plenty of growth. However, it took until the mass demonstrations caused by the Asian Financial Crisis in 1997 before he was overthrown and democratic elections were finally held. Under the dictatorship of Ferdinand Marcos (1965–86), the Philippines, a former American colony, was hailed for the spectacular growth he presided over, but his administration is now remembered as an emblem of political "cronyism" and "kleptocracy".[5] Even after "democratization", elections at all levels are still marred—and in some locations getting worse—by violence, corruption and ballot violations.[6]

The South Asian states have also largely failed to entrench liberal democracy. For about five decades, after independence in 1947, India successfully maintained a relatively stable Nehruvian liberal social democracy, under the Indian National Congress. However, the political decline of the Congress from the 1990s saw the rise of the Bharatiya Janata Party (BJP), an ethno-religious (Hindu) nationalist party (see also Anatol Lieven's conclusion in this volume). Under its charismatic leader, Narendra Modi, the BJP won an absolute majority in the 2019 general election. Since then, India appears to have regressed from its relatively liberal political order to a religiously intolerant, particularly anti-Muslim, state. On the other hand, Pakistan was explicitly created as an Islamic state, with two geographically non-contiguous parts, East and West Pakistan. Politics have always been unstable due to the presence of Islamic extremists. Martial law was first imposed after a coup in 1955. However, a general election was held in 1970, in which Zulfikar Ali Bhutto of the Pakistan People's Party (PPP) won the West and Sheikh Mujibur Rahman of the Awami League won the East; this split led eventually to the breakaway of what would become Bangladesh. Bhutto was blamed for the loss of the East, and arrested and executed by General Zia-ul-Haq, who imposed military rule from 1997 till 1988, when he died in a plane crash. Benazir Bhutto emerged to lead the PPP. She won two elections and was twice made the prime minister, until she was exiled to Britain by yet another general, Pervez Musharraf. When she returned to contest the 2008 general election, she was murdered. Although electoral parliamentary politics have been reinstated (see Khan Mohmand in this volume, chapter 4), political instability has prevailed.

From the outset, East Pakistan (see Karim's chapter 6) was a lesser partner of the West: finance flowed from the economically more developed East to the West; East Pakistanis (Bengalis) were discriminated against in civil service employment and Bengali cultural programmes banned from national broadcasts. The Awami League turned its win in the 1970 election into a call for independence. The Pakistan military reacted to the political agitation with repression. It was met with stiff resistance, particularly from the hastily established Bangladeshi National Liberation Army, and committed the strategic mistake of attacking the western border of India, allowing Delhi to assist the secessionists. The People's Republic of Bangladesh was established in March 1972, with Sheikh Mujibur Rahman as prime minister. He soon turned authoritarian and was murdered in 1975. What followed were alternating brief periods of martial law and electoral politics, in which politicians were essentially hostages to a military strongman. The last of the strongmen was General Hussain Muhammad Ershad, who was removed by a mass uprising in 1990. This ushered in the current parliamentary system, which is characterized by violent animosity between the leading factions, the Awami League and the Bangladesh Nationalist Party.

In Sri Lanka, persistent discrimination against the Tamil population was a key fault line undercutting democracy; Tamils were not given citizenship until 2003, more than fifty years after independence. In 1956, the prime minister, S.W.R.D. Bandaranaike of the (Buddhist) Sinhalese nationalist Sri Lanka Freedom Party, made Sinhalese the only national language, replacing English, and thereby further marginalizing the Tamils. As discriminatory policies piled up, revolutionary Tamil groups began to form, at home and in the diaspora. By the mid-1970s, the Liberation Tigers of Tamil Eelam (LTTE) was established, aiming to create an independent state. In 1983, a horrific civil war erupted that lasted until 2009, when the LTTE was defeated. Post-conflict politics remain unstable; in 2018, escalating disagreements between President Sirisena and Prime Minister Wickremesinghe created a constitutional crisis. The 2019 general election that followed saw the come-back of Mahinda Rajapaksa, the man who had violently crushed the LTTE. Returning as the prime minister, Rajapaksa immediately appointed his brothers and other family members to ministerial and other senior positions.

The key explanation for the failure of elections to produce actual democratic governance across these states and sub-regions of the Global Indian Ocean is situated in their histories of state formation. First, where there was a protracted violent decolonization struggle, military and political leaders who led the armed revolution often presumed that they, having shed blood for the birth of the nation, were automatically entitled to lead the state, rather than having to be elected, as in Indonesia. Second, where there was no violent decolonization struggle, indigenous political leaders could legitimately "reclaim" their homeland and insist on indigenous or ethnic primacy in the political, cultural and economic life of the new nations; non-indigenous groups could thus be denied citizenship or relegated to some form of "second-class" citizenship and subjected to highly undemocratic laws, in the name of pre-empting possible ethnic conflict, as in Sri Lanka. Third, where parliament was duly elected, prolonged negotiations among competing interests might cause delays in policy decisions, aggravating economic and social issues. Such normal parliamentary processes have often been intentionally reframed as political "instability" to create the excuse or opportunity for military leaders to intervene, such as by imposing emergency rule, as in Pakistan. Finally, even today insecurity and uncertainty undermine democracy. As newly minted nations in most cases, South and South East Asian states are still very much insecure countries in the making. Nationalism remains a vital social and political force that exercises strong affective hold on the citizenry. Given the multiple anxieties of nation-building, the emphasis on the rights of the individual and the demand for a minimalist state in classical liberalism and neoliberalism constitute threats to the "unity" of the emergent nation. All these reasons largely explain why so many Asian politicians explicitly reject liberal democracy. Meanwhile, rather than "transiting" anytime soon to liberal democracy, many have turned to "moral accountability" as grounds for political legitimacy to govern.[7]

Whereas liberal democratic accountability is based on the political authority of the citizenry, which may be modified by limiting majoritarian rule through guarantees of individual rights, moral accountability or authority is grounded, singularly or in combination, on metaphysics, charisma, or traditional sources such as religion, aristocracy and indigenous customary practices. Whereas liberal democracy evaluates the conduct of power holders in terms of their accountability to the electorate, moral accountability evaluates them in terms of "conformity to received codes of behavior", that is, in terms of "moral righteousness" and "personal integrity".[8] Governments are wont to claim their moral authority by invoking supposedly local or traditional ideas that valorize the "collective", "community" and "society", and these are reinscribed as "indigenous national values" that should serve as the basis of politics and governance; for example, *gotong royong* for Indonesia,[9] and 'Asian Values' or Confucianism for Singapore.[10] Often, the family is held up as the foundational, quintessential social institution. The unequal, hierarchical but supposedly harmonious relations within the family are ideologically mapped onto the nation at large. Discipline, subordination and acceptance of authority as fostered at home are expected to equally serve the nation. One can readily see how this can quickly open the door to authoritarianism and paternalism. Authoritarian regimes are often complicit in financial corruption. For example, Indonesia's Suharto "vigorously propagated a set of morals and ideological values under the rubric of *kekluargaan* (literally 'family-ness', from *keluarga*, family)",[11] even as his New Order regime progressively became emblematic of *Korupsi, Kolusi dan Nepotisme* ("*KKN*": corruption, collusion and nepotism) in government.[12] However, the apparent tendency of authoritarianism and corruption to be co-present is neither logically entailed nor inevitable. The People's Action Party (PAP) government of Singapore is the exception that proves the rule.

It is easy to criticize Singapore on account of the arrogant authoritarianism of the first and long-serving prime minister, Lee Kuan Yew; the detention without trial of political opponents in the years from 1963 to 1987; the financially ruinous libel suits against opposition party members; the extensive set of repressive laws on labour relations, race relations, media and civil society organizations, which are all constantly under threat of proscription and deregistration;[13] and finally, the aggressive gerrymandering of electoral boundaries and changes in electoral rules that have ensured the PAP's uninterrupted domination of parliament since 1959. Seen through liberal eyes, the aggregate effect of these measures amounts to a "suffocating atmosphere" of political and cultural repression. Ironically, it is just as easy to be seduced by the city-state's obvious success as a nation-state with its gleaming downtown banking district that signifies a global financial centre; the smoothly integrated transportation network of roads, highways and mass rapid transit trains; the endless expanse of high-rise public housing estates that house the entire nation; the intense sense of orderliness and public security without the ubiquitous police or armed soldiers that one has come to expect of an authoritarian state; and, finally, the high standard of material life of the citizens, all under an efficient, efficacious and non-corrupt government that makes and carries out long-term, future-oriented plans. From that standpoint, Singapore seems to epitomize the promise of successful adaptation to liberal globalization.

Economic success has elevated the small island nation in the esteem of the world and given Singapore a voice in the global economy and political arena that belies its small size; for example, its minister of finance and deputy prime minister, Tharman Shanmugaratnam, was appointed chairman of the International Monetary Fund's international monetary and finance committee (2011–15) and chairman of the G-30—the global group of financial experts—from January 2017 for five years. Singapore is now frequently regarded by many developing nations as a "model" for development.[14] A successfully capitalist authoritarian state with an expansive middle class that not only does not clamour for greater democratization but, repeatedly, elects by popular vote the same ruling party into parliament for six decades is a distressing idea in a world defined by liberal democracy. So how can we account not only for its success and failure but, more pertinently, for its peculiar character as a profoundly illiberal state and, at the same time, an exponent of the liberal international order?

Singapore as non-liberal electoral democracy: Governance as an instrumental transaction

Founded as a social-democratic political party, the People's Action Party was constituted by two leftist factions held together by shared anti-colonialism and "socialist" sentiments: a group of British university-trained professionals, who were influenced by the social democracy of the post-war Labour Party, and a group of radical unionists and student leaders, who were educated in local Mandarin-medium secondary schools and were heavily influenced by the cultural politics and civil war in China. The former had the education and skills to deal with the colonial government while the latter had the ability to deliver mass support. Such a partnership was not to last. In 1963, the radical faction was forced to split to form Barisan Sosialis, on account of disagreement with the terms of merger with Malaysia. This left the British-educated faction, under Lee Kuan Yew, to retain the PAP and control of the instruments of the state. Singapore's membership in Malaysia was short-lived, lasting only three years, and it became an independent island nation in 1965.

As a post-colonial settler nation in which the majority population was neither the colonial white race nor indigenous people, Singapore was established as a modern constitutional state with a Westminster parliamentary system enjoying all the conventional liberal rights and freedoms, albeit with a very significant difference. Singapore was constitutionally a "multiracial" nation, which stressed equality of race, among ethnic Chinese, Malays, Indians and others, owing to its demographic composition.[15] As a multiracial nation, maintenance of racial peace and harmony has been elevated as a social good above the freedoms and interests of individuals (cf. chapter 2 by Thomas Blom Hansen in this volume on sovereignty, migration and citizenship in the Global Indian Ocean). Secondly, the newly elected government argued that the survival of the island nation with its scant natural resources required the collective effort of all citizens in the nation-building process. Both the need to maintain racial harmony and the collective effort in nation-building continue to serve as the ideological justification for emphasizing social and political stability at the cost of liberal freedoms. Additionally, the emphasis on "collective well-being" enables the PAP government to recuperate its social-democratic values in some of its social and economic policies.

Throughout the 1960s and 1970s, protected from possible negative sanctions by the liberal democratic West with its Cold War anti-communism, the PAP government vigorously imposed political repression, particularly on its previous radical left partners, placing some under long periods of detention without trial.[16] In 1968, it first gained total control of parliament after Barisan decided to boycott the general election. Since then, the PAP has won every general election with an overwhelming majority of the votes cast. During elections, electoral rules and procedures are manipulated, by heavy-handed gerrymandering for instance, to the advantage of the incumbent PAP government, although there has been no tampering with the ballot box or violence.

By the mid-1970s, the PAP no longer had to be dependent on political repression to draw sustained electoral support, although repression of certain individuals continued, which was calibrated to cast shadows of fear among other citizens.[17] By then the PAP had come to depend on what is called "performance legitimacy": the delivery of security and material goods. Within two decades of independence and aggressive PAP economic policies, the party's astonishing success in guaranteeing what it promised meant that the high unemployment of the pre-independence years was already a distant memory. Moreover, PAP-directed public investment ensured that by the late 1980s more than 90 per cent of the resident population lived in highly subsidized high-rise public housing estates. Such social gains were paralleled by the rapid expansion of education opportunities, which have not only improved the productivity of the citizens but also promoted intergenerational upward mobility.

Singapore's investments in education, housing and infrastructure were consistently labelled "pragmatic" (supposedly rational, necessary and unencumbered by political ideology) policies aimed at sustained economic growth,[18] which in turn translates into the improvement of the material life of citizens across the board. While these economic policies were clearly not apolitical—on the contrary, they were essential to cementing the PAP's hold on power—they undeniably gave the party the performance legitimacy it so craved. Its spectacular economic performance was further buttressed by the state's relentless anti-corruption drive. During the early years of its uncomfortable partnership, Lee Kuan Yew's faction was in awe of the dedication and commitment of the radical unionists and student leaders to toiling for the working masses. They knew that to win the "hearts and minds" of Singaporeans, they would have to be as committed, clean and ascetic as, if not more so than, their radical partners.[19] A severe anti-corruption regime was imposed within the party and on the civil service. Self-discipline and incorruptibility became the operating principles and crucial symbolic political capital of the party, the government and the civil service. Anti-corruption now embodies the national ethos. "Good economic performance plus anti-corruption" equals "good government", of which the PAP sees itself as exemplary—a view shared by many states in the Global Indian Ocean that look to it for inspiration.

Governance is, above all, an instrumental transaction. The government delivers the "good" life in exchange for the trust, respect and votes of the citizens—reciprocity with different tokens. The periodic general election is an occasion when the party presents its "report card" (a favourite metaphor of the PAP leadership) of achievements since the last election to the electorate, as "evidence" that it has discharged the electorate's "trust" by governing in its best interests. To the PAP government, a general election is thus but a referendum on its performance rather than a multiparty political contest, although different political parties do enter the contest. Singaporeans are well aware that part of their comfortable material life has been built on abuses of their rights as citizens but they have largely quietly acquiesced in this trade-off.

The expediency of a parliament and government dominated by a single party—in making and executing long-term plans with few or no interruptions—has motivated the PAP to want to entrench its political system and practice in Singapore. Decades of uninterrupted rule have provided both the time and discursive space for the PAP leaders to rethink and rearticulate the ideological framework of their rule, as they continue to seek "social consensus", between themselves and the electorate. In the early 1990s, at a time in which socialism was in global retreat, the PAP began to rework its foundational social-democratic commitment to the "social" into a communitarian ideology.[20]

Redefining the terms of democracy

Significantly, unlike other authoritarian leaders who abolished general elections owing to weak legitimacy, the PAP government, perhaps as a consequence of their British university education, understood that elections are critical to their legitimacy to rule in the eyes not only of Singaporeans but also of the world of nation-states. As an observer succinctly put it: "Mr Lee may have been sceptical about the benefits of democracy, but he was not viscerally hostile to it; he understood its usefulness."[21] However, to stay within the discourse of democracy, it has had to reinterpret two fundamentally liberal ideas, namely, the "rule of law" and "political representation".

Rule of/by law

A central premise of a liberal state is the "rule of law", in terms of which a government and its citizens are both bound by the constitution and the laws that regulate their prerogatives and obligations and limit the state's authority. In spite of its disavowal of liberalism, the PAP government has continued to hang on to this idea and insist that it governs and is governed by this principle. However, Lee Kuan Yew argued that the British common law tradition had to be adjusted to local "contingencies"; specifically, laws must be instrumentally enacted to assist in securing the survival of the island nation.[22] To secure national survival meant no less than severely restricting conventional liberal freedoms and civil society activities. The law is thus used for the purpose of restricting rather than guaranteeing liberal freedoms. The 1966 Punishment for Vandalism law, for instance, has served to punish the painting of political slogans to avoid showing the state's hand in criminalizing political dissent. The Societies Act has been pressed into service to constrain civil society by restricting every civil society organization to activities within its declared purposes, preventing any coalition from fighting a common cause.[23] The Public Entertainment Licensing Unit (PELU) provides licences for the delivery of public speeches, which are considered "public entertainment".[24] The press laws constrain the mass media to support the developmental orientations of the government. The Legal Profession Act keeps lawyers out of commenting on law-making, and religious harmony regulations keep religion out of politics. This extensive use of laws as instruments to suppress overt dissent and the development of alternative bases of political power has been criticized, from a liberal point of view, as constituting more a regime of the "rule by law" rather than the "rule of law".[25]

The argument of public order above individual rights has always been endorsed by the Singapore judiciary. Former chief justice Chan Sek Keong argues that the PAP government's interpretation of the concept of "rule of law" is entirely defensible. He opines that the "rule of law simply meant the supremacy of the law, without reference to whether the law is just or unjust",[26] and has nothing to do with human rights or democracy. The parliament elected by the citizens is the only rightful and exclusive authority with respect to lawmaking because of its electoral mandate to govern. As long as laws are procedurally enacted properly in and by parliament, the judiciary's work is limited to the execution of the duly enacted laws, ensuring that they are applied equally to all, including the government. It is up to the people to change the government if they judge the ruling government to be mistaken in articulating the values of society. It is not the place of the judiciary to change the law. For the chief justice, the supremacy of the law has prevailed in Singapore, as the PAP government has always subjected itself to the laws it enacts. By way of illustration, when an opposition party leader sued two PAP ministers for libel, the latter apologized unreservedly in public to avoid going to court.

Singapore's "statist" interpretation of the function of the judiciary[27] is not without its merits, even within a democratic constitutional tradition, as "the idea of a judicial body modifying the will of the elected legislature, and therefore the sovereign will of the people whom the legislature represents, has traditionally been rejected as a distortion of the democratic process and the rule of law".[28] This statist conception is, according to Chief Justice Chan, precisely one that explicitly contests the liberal understanding of the rule of law which prevails in the West.

Representation/trusteeship

The PAP accepts elections as a necessary democratic process of selecting the ruling government but it rejects the liberal idea that an elected individual is obliged to represent the narrow interests of the constituency which has elected him or her. It sees competition among "representatives" of different narrow and particularistic "constituencies" as a recipe for gridlock in parliamentary proceedings and paralysis in governance. A prime example was provided by the US federal government during the Obama presidency (2009–16); it was frozen into inactivity because of the extreme ideological intransigence and partisanship of the two national political parties. On a larger scale, PAP ideologues posit, where a contest between several parties representing different particular interests results in a coalition government, that government is liable to be held hostage by the smaller coalition partners, giving them disproportionate bargaining power in exchange for their support for the continuance of the minority government, thus subverting the idea of democratic majority rule; a good example here is the small ultra-Orthodox religious parties in Israel or, before the rise to power of Narendra Modi, some of the regional parties in India and the constraints they have placed on bigger, national players and the centre of the federation as a whole.[29] Although the PAP government has never been burdened by either of the two conditions, it is nevertheless terrified of possible polarization of interests represented in parliament, which might lead to the fragmentation of Singaporean society. Consequently, while it has to "suffer" elections, it remains unconvinced that a two-party, let alone a multiparty, system of government is desirable for Singapore.

In a conventional liberal democracy—in the European heartland, Australasia and North America—the politics of representation is coupled with the politics of trust, that is, the elected government is entrusted by the electorate to act in the "national" interests. However, representing constituency interests takes precedence over evocation of trusteeship, limiting the latter to exceptional instances. Consequently, in practice, "trust" is invoked precisely when the actions of the elected government go against the wishes of the majority of citizens; for example, the exclusive right of the elected prime minister or president to declare a "national emergency" and suspend all normal processes of governance when the nation faces perceived or real security threats. This happened in 2003 when the British Prime Minister, Tony Blair decided to join US President George W. Bush in invading Iraq, against the express wishes of an overwhelming majority of the British public. He argued that he was morally compelled to act because the Iraqi president, Saddam Hussein, had to be stopped before he unleashed weapons of mass destruction on his people and potentially the world, including Britain. He might be said to have acted on the assumption that he was "entrusted" by the British people to act in the "national" interest, in spite of the nation's explicit objection.

The PAP government has inverted the priority of representation and trust. After taking over from Lee Kuan Yew, Prime Minister Goh Chok Tong would consistently invoke the idea of election as conferring "trusteeship". "My purpose is to ask you to ponder over this question: is a democratic system an end to be pursued in its own right, or is it a means to select a government to look after our lives like a good guardian or trustee? If it is the latter, how do we ensure that it returns a good government to serve the people? As we can see from examples around the world, simply observing the form of democracy does not necessarily deliver good governance and results."[30] This idea of elected government as trustee was repeated in the 2015 general elections by his successor as prime Minister, Lee Hsien Loong. "We are not the bosses of Singapore, we are not the commanders or the owners of Singapore, we are the trustees and the stewards of Singapore, we are like the *jaga* (Malay for one who is hired to watch over property, like a night-watch)."[31] The PAP government's claim of having fulfilled the electorate's trust to safeguard and improve their latter's collective interests is materially realized in many public policies. In what follows, I explore two critical examples: universal provision of public housing and state capitalism. Both illustrate once again the ways in which state-building in Singapore draws on the vocabulary of liberalism, but simultaneously reappropriates some of its key tenets to put them at the service of wider collective objectives. Singapore is of course not alone in doing so—see also Khan Mohmand's chapter 4 on local democracy in the Pakistani Punjab—but the degree to which it explicitly diverges is fairly unique.

The violability of private property: Singapore's National public housing programme

> "We have created a property-owning democracy, that's why we have stability in Singapore."

Lee Kuan Yew

Singaporeans, without doubt, are among the best-housed urban citizens in the world. One year after being elected to Singapore's first parliament, the PAP government established the Housing and Development Board (HDB), in 1960, with sweeping powers in the planning, allocation and management of comprehensive housing estates; only the actual construction of the housing blocks was outsourced to private constructions firms. For the freshly elected government, improving the living conditions of the newly enfranchised population, who were then mostly living in over-congested urban shophouses[32] or informal settlements of wood-panelled and thatch-roofed houses on the urban fringe,[33] was a pressing issue. Starting modestly with providing rental flats for the poor, the HDB moved quickly, selling 99-year leases on the flats to households eligible for state-subsidized housing. By the mid-1980s, 90 per cent of the population lived in public housing estates, of which more than 85 per cent owned a 99-year lease on the flat in which they resided. These initiatives transformed the population into a nation of homeowners.

The HDB's success was critically dependent on several essential factors, of which the availability of affordable land was primary.[34] Land cost is the most prohibitive factor in any government's attempt to provide social housing. Without low-cost land, no extensive public housing programme can be implemented. With its social-democratic commitments still fresh, the PAP government was aggressive in compulsorily acquiring privately held land for national development. The 1996 Land Acquisition Act empowered the state to procure any privately held land that it deemed necessary in the interests of national development, offering meagre rates of compensation to the landowners. The draconian land policy covered all private landholdings, effectively reducing speculation. Well aware that the Act violated property rights, which are sacrosanct to liberalism,[35] a former minister of national development argued it was "the most efficient and effective way of obtaining land" for the urgent need to resettle the poorly housed population; in any case, "the majority of the acquired private lands comprised dilapidated properties or neglected land where squatters had mushroomed. The government saw no reason why these owners should enjoy the greatly enhanced land values over the years without any effort put in by them."[36] The compensation rate was not adjusted upwards until 1986, when the government had sufficient land banked for development purposes, and it took another decade before it paid full prevailing market value for all acquisitions. With land transferred from the colonial regime, combined with radical land acquisition and an extensive land reclamation programme which transformed the entire coastline of the island, the state ended with owning approximately 90 per cent of the land in the entire country by 2010. Land was effectively nationalized, paving the way for public housing sold at affordable prices.

At the national budgetary level, sales of public housing flats have made possible the recovery of a substantial proportion of the cost of each cycle of construction, avoiding the drain on national wealth caused by the gap between the high cost of construction and the pittance collected in subsidized rent from socially disadvantaged families. Additional revenue is derived from rent collected from the provision of ancillary services such as parking charges and rent from commercial premises in the housing estates. Overall, the government was able to keep its annual subsidy to the national public housing programme at an estimated 3 per cent of its annual budget, from the mid-1970s till perhaps the late 1980s; the subsidy remained generally below S$2 billion annually during the first decade of the 21st century.[37] This was a small percentage of the annual national budget to "house the nation", compared with the high political capital and performance legitimacy return accrued in terms of popular electoral support and longevity in power.[38]

State capitalism and social distribution

For many outsiders (including the UK's Brexiteers and their neoliberal dreams of "Singapore-on-Thames"),[39] the PAP government appears as a champion of free market capitalism. It continues to invite foreign multinational enterprises with generous tax breaks and co-investments; the compliant labour unions under the state-controlled National Trades Union Congress are directed towards tripartite (state–enterprise–union) collaboration for peaceful labour relations that avoid disruption of production; the state provides the collective consumption amenities, including public housing, to reduce production costs for private enterprise. However, Singapore's first minister of finance, Goh Keng Swee, was categorical in stating that "one of the fundamental tenets of socialism [is] that the state should own a good part of the national wealth, particularly what is called the means of production" and "that the ultimate objective of this whole industrialization is not to provide fortunes for a fortunate few but to raise the standard of living of the entire working class".[40] Consequently, alongside the multinational corporation-driven industrialization is a state capitalist sector constituted by a constellation of state-owned enterprises (SOEs) and two large sovereign wealth funds.

There are broadly three paths to the building of Singapore's SOEs. The first is straightforward government partnering with local or foreign private investment. Where partners are not available, the government will invest and grow the enterprise on its own. The second is by transforming public services into commerce. Government service agencies are split into an SOE, which supplies the service on a profit basis, and a regulatory authority that monitors the profit margin of the service provider in the domestic market. This delinking avoids the common practice of providing essential public services, such as water and electricity, as state-subsidized "necessities". Families who are unable to meet the commercial prices of the essential services are assisted by the government through social transfers.[41] The third path involves spinning the services required by the new Singapore Armed Forces (SAF) into SOEs. The SAF is a complex institution that generates its own demands for industrial services. Each of these services can be made into an SOE which markets its service commercially, in addition to serving the SAF. The successful SOEs are corporatized and listed on the local stock exchange and are free to grow their businesses abroad without direct government supervision and to eventually transform themselves into multinational companies. A constellation of successful multinational corporations wholly owned or controlled through a majority share by the Singapore government has been engendered by these three processes: the Development Bank of Singapore (DBS Bank), now the largest bank in South East Asia;[42] Singapore Telecommunications Limited, or Singtel, which operates in twenty countries in Asia and Africa; and the SAF companies grouped into a single holding company, Singapore Technologies.

In 1974, to consolidate capital, improve the coordination of investments and pursue profit-making opportunities more efficiently, all the successful SOEs were placed under a single holding company, Temasek Holdings, with an initial capital input worth S$345 million. In 2002, Temasek established itself as an independent long-term investor in local companies with international growth potential and in multinational corporations. It operates effectively as Singapore's sovereign wealth fund, extending further the state's presence in global markets. Investments range across financial services; telecommunications and media; transportation and logistics; real estate; infrastructure, industrial and engineering; energy and resources; technology; life sciences; and consumer and lifestyle.

The dividends, interest and capital gains generated by the SOEs and the SWF constitute part of the national wealth. This wealth is divided into two equal halves. Fifty per cent is reinvested to grow the SOEs and augment the national reserves. The long-term expansion and deepening of the national reserve contributes to securing the stability and resilience of the economy[43] and protects Singapore's financial sovereignty.[44] The other 50 per cent is channelled as a revenue stream into the annual national budget as a subvention to the cost of governance; rough estimates place it at averaging between 12 and 20 per cent of the annual national budget. This constitutes a mode of non-targeted social redistribution: it reduces the tax burden on citizens yet enables the government to increase social expenditure, which is expected to increase annually as Singapore heads towards an ageing population and a mature, slow-growth national economy. Given the financial benefits it delivers, the majority of Singaporeans evidently have sound reasons to support state capitalism over free market capitalism.

Singapore's foreign policy: Be at the dining table or end up on the menu

Singapore's ability to sustain undisrupted economic development is due significantly to the fact that it is undisturbed by external political interventions, unlike some states in the Global Indian Ocean (Pakistan, Kenya, the UAE,...), which have been recurrently used as locations for interventions or proxy wars by external powers. This is also a result of years of meticulously cultivating friendships with nations, near and far, weak and strong. Self-determination for

Singapore's new leadership was also coterminous with redrawing old racial hierarchies.[45] This implied reactivating old Indian Ocean connections and creating new solidarities. The very first foray into diplomacy was Lee Kuan Yew's 1963 tour of seventeen newly independent African nations, including all those in the Horn, where questions of state formation and secession were most fraught (see Woldemariam's chapter 7). That year, Indonesian President Sukarno had violently objected to the formation of the Federation of Malaysia. Having hosted the Bandung Conference in 1955 for non-aligned nations, Sukarno's influence among post-colonial Asian and African nations peaked. Lee's tour was motivated by the need to solicit support for a threatened Malaysia at the United Nations.[46]

The need of support from other nations—and a concomitant embrace of international law and liberal multilateralism—has only intensified after becoming an independent, small island nation following secession in 1965. Lee Kuan Yew was acutely aware of the dangerous world Singapore had entered and would be forced to navigate in foreseeable decades: "the [balance of power] policy depends on the competing interests of several big powers in the region, rather than on linking the nation's fortunes to one overbearing partner. The big powers can keep one another in check, and will prevent any one of them from dominating the entire region, and so allow small states to survive in the interstices between them."[47]

In line with this vision, Singapore took the initiative to establish the Forum of Small States in 1992,[48] to improve their collective influence in the post-1989 global liberal order. The Forum, with an initial membership of 16, including for instance Global Indian Ocean locales such as Djibouti and Bahrain, has grown to the current 107 states, constituting half of all UN members. According to Prime Minister Lee Hsien Loong, the fundamental realities and vulnerabilities of small states in the international system have remained unchanged since the 1960s: "Our economies are smaller and more exposed to fluctuations in the global economy. More importantly, our margin of error is much narrower than for big states, which can absorb multiple hits." "If there is a war, we lack the strategic depth to defend ourselves. If we suffer an extreme weather event, we can take years to rebuild and recover;" for example, "rising sea levels threaten the very existence of island states". "[Small states like Singapore] must make a contribution to the work of the UN because it is in our interest to have a strong UN and a sound and stable multilateral system."[49]

As these statements illustrate, Singapore has a deep commitment to a rules-based global order, which it understands as essential to its survival and prosperity. This commitment to liberal order and especially multilateralism, international trade and collective security is a direct consequence not so much of an internalization of liberal values, as it is of an astute reading of its strategic predicament: the city-state has thrived in the liberal order of the Global Indian Ocean but is acutely aware of how vulnerable its success is.

Smallness has generated a host of aphoristic phrases that characterize its international relations: "The world does not need Singapore but Singapore needs the world", so it behoves Singapore to make itself relevant, especially economically, to the world and, as far as possible, be "friends of all nations and enemies to none". Occasionally, it will be subject to pressures from other states, neighbouring or distant. In such instances, it is not to be bullied and must stand firm to defend its interests, using its membership in international organizations and friendships to fend off threats; the aphorism favoured by the Ministry of Foreign Affairs is: "if you were not at the dining table, you will end up on the menu".[50] This stance was demonstrated very early in the PAP's rule.

During the Cold War, Singapore benefited hugely from the anti-communist security umbrella of the US in South East Asia and economically from increased trade and services derived from the American war in Vietnam.[51] At the same time, its leadership publicly emphasized its non-alignment. For instance, Lee Kuan Yew disclosed in September 1965 (barely a month after independence) that in 1960 an American CIA agent had tried to bribe him with three million dollars to cover up a covert operation in Malaya. When the State Department denied the charge, Lee promptly published a letter from Secretary of State Dean Rusk, forcing Washington to backtrack. He also took the opportunity to state categorically that Singapore would not allow the US to take over the naval base that would be soon vacated by the Royal Navy.[52] Such assertions of independence were (and are) crucial to Singapore's self-image, yet remain pragmatic.

When the US Navy withdrew from Subic Bay in the Philippines in 1992, Singapore readily agreed to let it use the services of Singapore's naval base, reaffirming its interest in having the US remain engaged in South East Asia to keep other powers in check. Singapore today is not only a "strategic partner" of Washington, but has had a bilateral free trade agreement with the US since 2004, which it sees as crucial to anchoring the economic component of regional order alongside the military Pax Americana.

This pragmatic view of hegemony—some of it is welcome, but a lot of it needs to be countered—also characterizes its relations with Beijing (and, indeed, as Verhoeven notes in his introduction, is quite typical of the international relations of the Indian Ocean). Reflecting the importance it placed in the Association of Southeast Asian Nations (ASEAN), Singapore was the last member to establish formal diplomatic relations with the People's Republic in 1990, after Indonesia, which had suspended its ties with China from 1967, after an alleged communist coup attempt in Jakarta. However, in spite of the absence of formal diplomatic relations, in 1976 Lee Kuan Yew visited China; in turn, Deng Xiaoping visited Singapore in 1978. Despite the PAP government's staunch anti-communism and its distrust of Communist China for its support of the Malayan Communist Party, trade expanded between the two states. The first foreign minister, S. Rajaratnam, announced in 1965, "Singapore, now it has become independent, is most interested in maintaining and consolidating trade links with China as with other friendly countries, which recognise our independence and political integrity."[53] Since the opening up of China to the world economy, relations between the two states have expanded dramatically, from collaborations in city developments,[54] to the transfer of Singapore's experience in "authoritarian modernisation",[55] and conferences between the PAP and the CCP, held in Beijing and Singapore each alternate year. If China is keen to experiment with the Indian Ocean as a space to project a new foreign policy identity, then Singapore sees it as its task to leverage its partnership with Beijing to bind it more closely to the thin liberal order that currently exists there.

Nevertheless, on occasions, Singapore's national interest-first policy has irritated otherwise friendly countries. A recent incident was the detention by the Hong Kong harbour authority of several amphibious military vehicles en route from Taiwan to Singapore. This was an expression of China's unhappiness at the continuing use of Taiwan as a military training ground for Singapore's armed forces.[56] Subsequently, a junior minister of national development was invited to the first Belt and Road Conference in Beijing, instead of Prime Minister Lee Hsien Loong. Singapore's response to such provocation is to stand its ground and let subsequent developments smooth over the hiccups.

Conclusion

This chapter has set out to explain a major puzzle in discussions on the liberal order and the Global Indian Ocean: how to account for the breathtaking success of one of the region's smallest polities, which is an exponent both of openness to globalization and of profoundly illiberal policies? On the one hand, Singapore is only able to scale these developmental heights by building on its historical role as a Pax Britannica trading centre. It has thrived under what Verhoeven termed "thin hegemony" in the introduction: the post-war global liberal political and economic order, secured by America as the benign hegemon, has allowed it to benefit from transnational flows in goods, services, people and capital more than any other Oceanic state. It has achieved this by a foreign policy of emphasizing, firstly, economic security and, secondly, neutrality with a strong commitment to a rules-based multilateral global order. At the same time, that liberal international context has made possible its domestic illiberalism. With its ideological origins in its quest to build a social-democratic state and manage the threat of communal violence, the PAP government in Singapore has consistently disavowed liberalism, ignoring persistent liberal critiques of its violation of conventional liberal individual rights and freedoms. Yet in spite of the undeniable political repression and the authoritarian leadership of Lee Kuan Yew and his successors, the ruling party has remained popular for decades and consistently continued to subject itself to the verdict of voters— and done so successfully. The material benefits delivered to Singaporeans are the primary reason why voters have rewarded the

PAP with successive parliamentary majorities. The economic and the political are thus mutually reinforcing in maintaining electoral support for the PAP; hence, its legitimacy and longevity in power.

With its spectacular economic success, Singapore has come to enjoy a space and a voice in global forums vastly disproportionate to its small size. Talk of a "Singapore model" surfaces regularly in policy discussions—or the utopian dreams of politicians—in the Global Indian Ocean.[57] This is a very valuable symbolic political resource which the PAP government is unlikely to squander with excessive and unnecessary crackdowns. Indeed, overt and blunt political repression, such as detention without trial and financially ruinous defamation suits against opposition party members, is increasingly rare, although the use of the law to constrain political and civil society activities continues. There has also been a progressive liberalization of the cultural sphere. However, this does not entail a path to liberal political pluralism. Instead, the PAP government has reconceptualized its ideological framework as a hegemonic single-party-dominant government. Especially after the collapse of "real existing socialism" in the late 1980s, the PAP has reformulated its social-democratic inclinations as a local articulation of "communitarianism", where the elected are trustees of the collective interests of the governed and where national and collective interests must take precedence over individual interests.

Significantly, that Singapore is "Asian" is a geographical fact, but this is incidental to what the government would call a "communitarian democracy". Distilled into a set of values and processes, the political practices of the PAP government—a social-democratic model for developing countries in the 21st century—appear to be replicable at least in part, if not in whole, in other nations. In politics, this would be to maintain an ethos of incorruptibility with a rigorous selection of ministers and members of parliament based on career achievements and commitment to serving, and the disposal of miscreants expeditiously; to conduct periodic general elections without tampering with the voting process (although gerrymandering is advised); and to emphasize general trust in the government to govern for the greater collective good over the representation of specific constituency interests. In economic matters, the model would be to focus relentlessly on the type of economic growth that translates into a better material life for the population; to invest in human capital development to improve workforce productivity and national competitiveness, including the universalization of homeownership; to promote individual and intergenerational upward social mobility through competitive, publicly funded education; and to establish a state capitalist sector that invests nationally accumulated wealth in profit-minded domestic and international enterprises to further grow the national reserves, and channel a significant portion of the profits from the state capitalist sector into the annual national budget to defray the cost of government, thus reducing the tax burden on the citizens and increasing redistributive social expenditure.

The most important evidence of possible replication can be seen in the way China observes Singapore for occasional "lessons" for its own developmental trajectory.[58] After his visit to Singapore in 1991, Deng Xiaoping, the paramount leader of the Chinese Communist Party responsible for the marketization of the economy, instructed Chinese bureaucrats to study Singapore: "Singapore's social order is rather good. Its leaders exercise strict management. We should learn from their experiences, and we should do a better job than they do."[59] This has resulted in the establishment of two urban management training programmes for potential Chinese mayors at the two national universities in Singapore. It has also led to joint government development projects between China and Singapore, such as the Suzhou Industrial Park,[60] the Sino-Singapore Guangzhou "Knowledge City" project, and the Sino-Singapore Tianjin Eco-City project. In addition, the head of China's State-Owned Assets Supervision and Administration Commission (SASAC), Xiao Yaqing, reportedly said: "Temasek (Holdings) has 'always been a role model'"[61] for the management reform of China's state-owned enterprises and its sovereign wealth funds.[62]

That the Chinese Communist Party studies Singapore for useful lessons is not entirely surprising, especially as Mitter reminds us in his chapter 9 that the Global Indian Ocean is where China keenly experiments and learns, much to the chagrin of India and the US. As a hegemonic single-party state, it would like to be able to replicate the PAP's success in economic development, with a strong state capitalist sector, a relatively reasonable income distribution, widespread upward social mobility for most citizens, and the growth of a very large middle class, without having to share political power;[63] in short, a Singapore writ large. If China succeeds, then free market capitalism may be said to have met its match. But how replicable Singapore's achievements are in actual fact remains debatable. The unique combination of domestic illiberalism, geography, a highly specific colonial legacy and liberal international order might be too hard to match, even for the Chinese Communist Party.

4

HYBRID CLIENTELISM AS DEMOCRACY IN THE GLOBAL INDIAN OCEAN

Shandana Khan Mohmand

Democracy and democratization have followed a very different trajectory in the Global Indian Ocean from that in much of Europe. Numerous scholars argue that democracy in Europe was an outcome of the reorganization of power and resources across social classes.[1] At the risk of oversimplifying, this general narrative suggests that as resources were distributed in favour of classes other than the aristocracy and landed elites, and as the middle class expanded, the demand grew for access to better and more equitable public services, leading to a reconfigured, modern and autonomous bureaucracy that could respond to this demand. In time, the demand for equal representation and political participation followed, and by this point one of the big challenges facing democratization in Europe was how to make a capable executive responsible and accountable to an elected legislature.

This is not the story of much of the Global Indian Ocean, where democracy came at the end of colonial rule and where it has a complex relationship with liberal international order, as discussed in Verhoeven's introduction to this volume. The countries of this region—from South Africa and Kenya in its west, through India in its centre, and all the way to Malaysia and Indonesia in its east—emerged from colonial rule with bureaucracies that were oriented, at varying levels, to extraction and revenue collection rather than to the equitable and rules-based delivery of essential services to the population. These bureaucracies maintained their colonial logic of extraction and control as the countries struggled through either nascent democracies or various forms of authoritarian regimes. In some states electoral democracy was introduced as European imperialists began leaving and preceded the establishment of effective public administration that could serve the needs of their new citizenry (such as in India, Kenya, Mauritius, Malaysia and Sri Lanka). In others the bureaucracy became entrenched in the politics of building authoritarian regimes (such as Burma, Indonesia, Pakistan and Tanzania). In both cases, bureaucracies became defined by the logic of particularistic delivery targeted at populations favoured by the rulers. (Singapore presents a real outlier in this case, as discussed in Chua Beng Huat's chapter 3.) Martin Shefter and Francis Fukuyama point out that sequencing matters.[2] Where bureaucratic capacity and autonomy developed before electoral politics was established, political parties connected with citizens in terms of larger programmes that could set the rules for how the public sector worked and delivered services. Where states democratized before they restructured their public sectors, the particularistic delivery of public services was more usual, as politicians used the state's resources and infrastructure to build and retain support bases. This system—clientelism—defines the norm in large parts of the Global Indian Ocean. Here, democratization did not work against clientelism but, rather, it created a political system whose very logic stemmed from clientelistic interactions between parties and citizens.[3]

Clientelism is the contingent exchange of public goods and services for votes.[4] The concept has, however, been stretched considerably and now connotes a few different modes of exchange, of which two broad types are clearly distinguishable and concern us most in studying the Global Indian Ocean. The first of these, the clientelism of mass parties, is the form in which the concept is most usually deployed in recent literature.[5] In this form, parties organize large machines or networks of brokers that amass votes, maintain and transmit information about voter needs and preferences, and ensure turnout. Such brokers are often entrepreneurial local actors who have political ambitions and who build their support through political means in which their power is based on their access to the party machine and bureaucratic offices.

The other form of clientelism was the subject of much of the initial work on the concept.[6] This type is based on personalistic, reciprocal relationships between actors of unequal socio-economic status. As political parties became the main organizers of politics after the "third wave of democracy", this form of politics, organized around the personalistic power of local patrons, was thought to have lost importance. Recent studies of political dynamics in Africa and Asia— including in South Africa, Tanzania, Uganda, Afghanistan, India and Pakistan—have now established that such patron–client relationships continue to condition political behaviour and outcomes.[7] Across these regions, local notables like chiefs, landlords, "big men" and religious leaders continue to draw on extra-political power based on economic and social influence to organize networks of clients within villages and neighbourhoods. These notables have strong support bases of their own which they can carry with them to the highest bidder, so they are less dependent on the patronage of any one political party. Lucas Novaes contrasts the party machine—networks of brokers tied to, and possibly coordinated by, a political party—with the phenomenon of "modular" parties produced under this notables-led model, in which parties are simply assembled modularly on the basis of a multitude of such local networks of clients.[8] This clientelism of notables reproduces the logic of colonialism to an extent, built as it is around political actors' use and encouragement of power asymmetries to extract support through the co-option and cooperation of elites.

A defining feature of politics in the Global Indian Ocean is that these two types of clientelism—that of mass parties and that of notables—are often found together within its political systems and are clearly identifiable even if they mix seamlessly. Party brokers may often overlap with local notables, and clients may value their local patrons not just for their traditional power but also for the inroads that they have made into party structures. Furthermore, parties that are modular in their interaction with rural intermediaries may actually have quite sophisticated machines that operate through networks of brokers in urban areas. Theoretical differences between various types of clientelism and political parties are muted by the empirical reality of politics in this part of the world. Why the clientelism of notables has not disappeared is based on another defining feature of the Global Indian Ocean—the existence of high levels of socio-economic inequality. Citizens here are segmented not just by access to economic resources, especially land, but also by ethnicity, race, tribe and caste, which trap populations in particularly immobile social categories—immobile not because they are immutable but because processes of state formation in the region have accommodated and built off these cleavages rather than challenged them (see Chua Beng Huat's chapter 3 and Steffen Hertog's chapter 5). The hierarchies created by such segmentation keep local notables in business.

This, clearly, seems an illiberal order that constrains the political choices of its citizens. And yet it would be a mistake to think that the politics of the Indian Ocean world sit entirely outside the democratic project, which represents such an important component, especially after 1989, of the liberal international order. Many political systems in the region are defined by genuinely competitive and regular elections that aim to elect representative parliaments and presidents. Every few years when these elections draw the national system down into localities, we know that poorer citizens not only come out to vote but actually seem to value democracy as much as richer citizens do, and feel significantly empowered by the vote.[9] The language of liberal democracy also shows up in exchanges between voters and politicians in terms of expectations around representation, responsiveness and accountability. Even under military regimes, political activists and civil society actors have drawn on this language, driven in some part by exposure to Western theory but in significant part by grounded demands for equal representation and accountability.

Nevertheless, the tone and texture of politics here are different from those in the North Atlantic, even though it would be a mistake to think they are the same across the entire macro-region. This chapter presents an attempt to look in some detail at how the poorer citizens of one country in this region, living in its villages and deeply embedded in these socio-cultural constructs, engage with ideas that are part of the liberal order's global repertoire. What type of micro-dynamic is created during elections that allows local notables to renew and reproduce their power, while simultaneously bringing to villages and neighbourhoods the often quite intense competition between mass parties at the national level? And in what ways does the unequal status of voters within their communities interact with the empowerment offered by the vote? This remains a gap within our understanding of current politics in the Global Indian Ocean. Most studies focus either on accounting for the historical roots of these types of state–society relations (e.g., the contributions of Blom Hansen and Hertog to this volume in chapters 2 and 5), or one type of clientelism (local or national), or on specific case studies that do not analyse variations across time and location. This chapter analyses the micro-interactions that create and sustain a hybrid clientelism by looking at how it functions across a group of differently structured villages as the political system moves from one election to the next, and voters within segmented communities are presented with different political parties and candidates as options in national elections.

I examine the political impact of hybrid clientelism in the context of current rural politics in Pakistan. There are two popular facts about Pakistan's politics that are widely accepted: that its military has been omnipresent in its politics, and so its political institutions, especially its parties, have remained weak without strong constituencies of their own; and that political parties have assembled in a modular fashion around the local power of large "feudal"[10] landlords and kinship-based political networks that organize the vote within communities. Nevertheless, as this chapter will demonstrate, electoral competition has opened up political space for marginalized voters. Electoral politics in rural Pakistan thus provide an evocative case through which to examine the political impact of the hybrid clientelism that defines much of the Global Indian Ocean. At a time when democracy around the world is experiencing indeterminate fortunes, it is interesting to look at how voters engage with this particular configuration of democratic practice from the ground up.

The analysis presented here helps advance a central concern of this volume—how democracy functions beyond Western-style liberal orders, and what happens to our understanding of democracy when we engage more deeply and without prior assumptions with the political reality of the Global Indian Ocean.

This chapter is organized as follows. In the next section I provide a brief history of Pakistan's tumultuous struggle with democratization and a description of its current political system. Subsequently, I define the dimensions of democracy as they are operationalized in this chapter, and describe the unequal contexts within which I explore them. I then examine the specific dynamics of clientelistic relationships that emerge around elections in four villages. I conclude by describing what these stories reveal about the ways in which clientelistic competition can alter the micro-dynamics of political inclusion within emerging democracies—places like India, Kenya, Indonesia and elsewhere around the macro-region.

Pakistan's struggle for democracy

The establishment of democracy has been particularly difficult in Pakistan. It has struggled between military and civilian rule for over seventy years since independence from British overrule and partition from India at the same time. After a tumultuous start in 1947 (see Woldemariam in chapter 7 on secession and the liberal order) and many years without an elected government during which it was run by the civil bureaucracy, Pakistan acquired its first military regime in 1958, largely at the instigation of the bureaucracy, which wanted to avert an election under which it stood to lose power to an elected legislature. The regime of General Ayub Khan lasted for 11 years till 1969, when it was brought down by a social movement. Pakistan's first election was then held in 1970, 23 years after it became an independent country, and this brought the Pakistan People's Party (PPP) into power under Zulfiqar Bhutto. In 1977 the country moved back to a military regime when General Zia-ul-Haq toppled Bhutto in a coup and took over power for another 11 years until 1988. A mysterious plane crash ended his reign, and for the next 11 years, four short-lived, unstable civilian governments of the PPP and the Pakistan

Muslim League-Nawaz (PML-N) came and went through four elections held in quick succession. The military regime of General Pervez Musharraf took over next in 1999, and was toppled in 2008 during widespread unrest by another social movement.

Pakistan has thus had numerous elections. Those of 1970 and 1977 were genuinely contested and suddenly opened up political space, especially for its poorer populations under the left-wing PPP. Party-based elections returned after a long hiatus in 1988, but the many that followed in the 1990s were held at unpredictable intervals and brought into power unstable governments, so that they did little to strengthen political parties or embed democratic practices. The 2002 election held under Musharraf's military regime suffered from the manipulation of political parties at the national level. The election of 2008 was largely openly contested and marked Pakistan's most recent transition to democratic rule. The transition was consolidated to some extent by the subsequent elections of 2013 and 2018, both of which were held at the stipulated intervals and marked the completion of full terms by governments led by the PPP and the PML-N respectively. The election of 2018 brought to power a new party, the Pakistan Tehreek-e-Insaf (PTI).

Politics in Pakistan are now organized predominantly around and by political parties, but a consequence of regular alternation between authoritarian and democratic rule is that the parties remain weakly organized and operate largely as conglomerations of clientelistic networks.[11] This is both because authoritarian regimes often encourage such politics by seeking legitimacy through established patrons and their networks of voters, and because political parties have been manipulated and engineered extensively to serve the needs of the military regime during Pakistan's history.[12] As elections became regular events in Pakistan, parties focused more on consolidating their positions through established clientelistic networks than on building strong internal structures and stable constituencies.[13] This resulted in fluid vote bases and voters who swung from party to party, organized as they were by local notables and not by party programme or ideology. The focus of this chapter is on how the imperatives of such a political system condition the political behaviour of Pakistan's rural and poor voting majority.

Democratization as contestation and inclusion

In order to understand how rural citizens experience democracy and electoral competition within unequal and clientelistic contexts, we must first define how democratization manifests itself within the politics of Pakistan's villages. There are two stylized facts about rural politics in Pakistan that will help us greatly in sighting democratic practices at the local level when they occur.

The first is that rural voters vote collectively within local vote blocs that form at the village level. I have established elsewhere that about 80 per cent of rural voters may vote through these local political institutions.[14] This means that rural voters often do not make individual decisions about who to vote for but, rather, gather within their families, caste or kinship groups or even at the level of the entire village to pick their preferred candidate or political party. This is not unlike the village factions that John Powell described in Italy and Venezuela, or those that John Gaventa documented in the southern United States.[15] These vote blocs are led by local men (almost always men) of influence, whose ability to organize politics is often based on their ownership of land. It is the contestation between these local leaders and the vote blocs which they organize that defines electoral competition at the local level, rather than that between political parties. Therefore, to sight increasing contestation within villages, we would expect to see new challengers to the power of the traditional landed elite in the form of emerging political leaders who organize vote blocs of their own. I call this dimension "contestation".

The second stylized fact is that Pakistan's villages represent sites of great socio-economic inequality. Part of Pakistan's instability has been attributed to the disproportionate political power that "feudal" landlords exercise over the countryside. These elites use their landed wealth to exclude the landless, the poor, women and minorities from power, and they manipulate these groups to support the political preferences of the rural landed elite, largely through the organization of local vote blocs. This inequality directly conditions village politics, but it does not affect or constrain all village citizens in the same way. Local leaders of vote blocs have different types of relationships with village residents. To some they may be an employer while with others they may share a common tie of kinship. To yet others they may be patrons through whom state services and jobs may be accessed, or a neighbour, a religious leader, and so on. Given unequal socio-economic conditions and the existence of collective voting, it is conceivable that these different relationships between vote bloc leaders and voters create political spaces of different sizes and shapes for different village residents. Those that are dependent on the landlord for employment, or those that belong to lower-caste groups,[16] will face greater political constraints and more limited space than those from higher-status groups or those with more independent income sources within the same village. Therefore, we would expect electoral politics to expand options for marginalized voters in two possible ways: either local vote blocs become more inclusive of the preferences of poorer voters (largely so that they can increase their numbers and their chances of attracting higher-tier patrons) or voters start to organize beyond village borders by connecting up to supra-local collectivities, such as kinship networks, class-based mobilization, or political parties, that may increasingly organize the rural poor according to their specific collective interests. I call this dimension "inclusion".

How have these two dimensions of democratization—increased contestation and inclusion[17]—played out in rural Punjab over the course of a democratic transition? This involves a story of four villages in the same district of central Punjab, Sargodha: they are Tiwanabad, Sahiwal, Chak 1 and Chak 2.[18] I tell this story through observations made over multiple elections that marked Pakistan's transition to democracy in 2008. I observed local political organization in these villages in the years 2006–7, when the country was ruled by a military regime, and then returned to them six years later as they prepared for the election of 2013, which is widely believed to have provided some initial signs of democratic consolidation.

Elections, inequality and the rural poor

Despite their proximity to one another, there are important differences between these four villages: some lie in more remote parts of the district while others are close to urban centres and jobs; and in some there is a more unequal distribution of land. Most importantly, some have hierarchically organized social structures, while others are relatively more egalitarian. This particular variation traces its history to colonial land settlement patterns; when the British Raj incorporated Punjab in 1849, it sought to "settle" its largely pastoral population. Political logic and the imperatives of revenue collection led to different types of land tenure systems even within the same district, and resulted in important differences in their social structure based on the extent to which landed elites were given state-sanctioned social privileges that allowed them to dominate other village groups. In some villages such social authority was dispersed across different groups and actors, while elsewhere it was concentrated in a single landowner. Importantly, though, regardless of the extent to which authority was dispersed across different members of the village population, it almost always remained within the kinship groups of the *zamindar*, or landowning, caste.[19] Variations arose from the fact that in some villages all of the land, and, with it, social authority over village residents, was granted as private property to a single man (again, always men) or family. In others, multiple kinship groups of the agricultural caste were given ownership rights. Both of these are called "proprietary villages". In yet other villages, landowners never received proprietary rights. Instead, they remained lessees of the state until 1941, with serious constraints placed on the extent to which the agricultural caste could exercise any social authority over residents from other caste groups. These were "Crown villages".

The four villages in this chapter capture these differences, and together they provide sufficient variation to allow us to observe the impact of changing electoral politics on different social and economic structures. All of these villages are deeply unequal: their Gini coefficients for land distribution range only between 0.85 and 0.94, which is extremely close to perfect inequality. But the fact that two of these are proprietary villages while two are Crown villages (typically called "chaks") means that they differ greatly in terms of the dispersion of social authority across the village population. They also vary in terms of their proximity to urban centres. Using indicators of different types of inequality, I position the four villages along a spectrum from the "most likely to be competitive and inclusive", where landed elites here may be least able to constrain the political space available to other village groups, to the "least likely to be competitive and inclusive", where the landed elite has a repressive hold on the political behaviour of other village groups.

Figure 4.1: Likelihood of villages being politically competitive and inclusive

| Most likely | Chak 2 | Chak 1 | Sahiwal | Tiwanabad | Least likely |

Close to the left-hand end of this spectrum in Figure 4.1 lies Chak 2. Chak 2 is only about ten kilometres from Sargodha city, and was settled as a Crown village. Land here was given in small parcels to different people, none of whom were private owners. The ten families that received land grants in this village remained tenants of the colonial state until 1941. This means that those with access to land here had circumscribed social authority over other village residents. This fact, together with the distribution of land across multiple *chaudhry*[20] families and its proximity to non-land-based jobs in the urban market of Sargodha, makes Chak 2 the most likely to respond to democratic changes. The largest landholding here is just 55 acres, and there are four households that own around this much land. People from about fifty different *biradari* (kinship groups) live here.

Chak 2 had two main vote blocs that divided almost all the village votes between them in 2006–7. Both were led by men from the higher-ranked kinship groups who were bitterly opposed to one another, even though they usually collaborated with the same electoral candidate. The animosity was so pronounced that the two local leaders refused to sit on a joint village council (*panchayat*). Both also worked to regularly undercut each other vis-à-vis their common electoral candidate. Yet neither leader had a very strong hold over the members of their vote blocs, so that they were both unsure of their actual membership numbers. This was unusual compared with vote bloc leaders in other villages, and was a result of several factors. First, the landlords' limited landholdings meant that most people were not economically dependent on either leader. Second, the proximity to Sargodha city had opened up the possibility of alternative forms of employment to residents. Finally, it seemed that villagers actively used the extreme animosity between the two leaders to their own advantage on a regular basis, playing one against the other to extract greater benefit and more political space for themselves. Both leaders confirmed that a large portion of the village's voters swing between the two vote blocs. About 300 to 400 voters (out of about 1,200) change their support for a vote bloc from one election to the next, and both factions had become increasingly unsure of voters' alignments over the recent years.

It was clear, however, that the main alignment between voters and either leader was defined by expectations of service delivery and access to the state, especially the police. To maintain voters' support on this basis, both leaders spent lots of energy negotiating with politicians. Lacking other traditional ways of ensuring support for his own vote bloc, one of the local leaders had even managed to convince villagers that they needed his official stamp as the *lambardar*[21] to get anything done in a state office, and to get this, they needed to remain on his side. Voters did not generally connect directly or individually with either leaders. Instead, they first came together either as *biradaris* or as a neighbourhood—which in this village could be considered a class-based organization, given that the upper, middle and lower classes live in different parts of the village—and then decided collectively which of the two leaders to align with. Their decision depended on how much each leader could promise them in benefits and support, which in turn depended on how much each leader had been able to negotiate with the electoral candidate. Politics in Chak 2 seemed to be defined almost entirely by bargains, and the village provides evidence of both high levels of contestation and greater negotiation space for village residents vis-à-vis their landlords.

Next to Chak 2 on the spectrum lies Chak 1. This too is a Crown village where the social authority of its landlords was historically circumscribed. It was originally leased in 1902 to three families of agricultural castes from three different villages. Even though several other families received some land as well, land packets here are larger than in Chak 2—the two largest landowners own just over 100 acres each. Like other Crown villages, Chak 1 became home to a number of unrelated landowners, or *chaudhries*, from different *biradaris*, of which there were in total about thirty in the village. Unlike Chak 2, however, this is a more remote village and offers far fewer employment opportunities to its residents. People remained dependent on the land-based jobs offered by landowners for much longer than in Chak 2, though the recent development of quarries and a stone-crushing industry near the village now provided its landless population with an alternative source of daily wage employment. More upwardly mobile village residents had also diversified into public employment and many families had at least one person in the army or other state employment.

The interaction of diffused social authority with a history of relatively greater economic dependence of village residents on landowners had given rise to a very different kind of politics here. Instead of the factionalized clientelistic relationships we saw in Chak 2, Chak 1 had a high level of class-based conflict that politically divided its landlords and poorer citizens. There were two main vote blocs in 2006–7, but these were dramatically different in nature. The first, with about 56 per cent of the votes, was led by the *lambardar* and included all the *zamindar biradaris* along with their dependent populations. The second, with about 37 per cent of the votes, was made up almost entirely of lower-caste groups—the *kammi* and *muslim sheikh* population that lived in the village's physically segregated "colony". This colony was the result of a 1970s reform that turned state land in villages into residential schemes of small plots which were distributed amongst *kammi* and *muslim sheikh* groups in order to reduce their homestead-based dependence on landlords. Families that moved to the colony were no longer dependent on the *chaudhries* for residence (unlike those that remained in the main village settlement) or for employment because of the nearby quarries. With these two sources of dependence reduced, colony residents no longer saw a reason to come together politically under the *chaudhries*—whose repressive behaviour over the decades had led to feelings of great resentment among lower-caste groups—and so "colony politics" was born.

Colony residents organized their own vote bloc to link up independently with provincial and national politicians. This bloc was led by a smallholder farmer (who owned a single acre) and a member of the lowest-ranked *muslim sheikh* caste group who worked as an agricultural labourer. Through these men, colony residents provided stiff competition to the political authority of the landowning *chaudhries* of their village by linking up with political parties that represented the polar opposite of the landlord's party. In all of Sargodha district, landlords prefer to align with the landlord-friendly, right-wing PML-N, while more marginalized voters generally align with the labour-friendly, left-of-centre PPP. These were indeed the political alignments found in Chak 1, though the *chaudhry* bloc supported the PML-Q in this case, a breakaway group of the PML-N that was created by General Musharraf to support his regime. The open rebellion of the colony caused great dismay and embarrassment to the *chaudhries* but delighted colony residents in equal measure. Members of the *chaudhry* families spoke often about how their counterparts in other villages now looked down on them for allowing such resistance to develop in their village, while colony residents relished relating accounts of their resistance, including how even the servants of the *chaudhries* were voting with them without the knowledge of their landlords. Like Chak 2, Chak 1 displayed high levels of contestation and a larger political space for poorer voters, though this was defined more by class-based organization rather than by the strategic negotiations between leaders and voters that were aimed at mutual benefit in Chak 2. In some ways, given the lower status of their leaders and the weak organization of direct voter–party linkages in Pakistan, such organization constrained poorer voters more in Chak 1 than in Chak 2.

Further along on the spectrum in Figure 4.1 are two proprietary villages, Sahiwal and Tiwanabad. Landowners in these villages had not only received much larger grants from the colonial state, but, more importantly, these grants vested full ownership rights in the individual landowners, who, over time, developed historically grounded, officially sanctioned and entrenched social authority over the rest of the village population. Politics here looked significantly different from those in the Chaks, but with variations. The original settlers of both Sahiwal and Tiwanabad had been granted thousands of acres each, but while the former village lay close to a growing and important urban centre, the latter was remote. Voters in Sahiwal are thus more likely to have greater political space than those in Tiwanabad, a village that combines extreme land inequality with the historically entrenched social authority of a single landlord, and a lack of nearby employment opportunities that can aid social mobility.

The village of Sahiwal was awarded as a *zamindari* grant of 4,572 acres to one man in 1860 with full ownership rights, as a reward for services rendered to the colonial government.[22] Sahiwal was managed by the family as one unit until 1920, when a feud between two grandsons of the original grantee allegedly led one to instigate the murder of the other. This split the village into two separate shares (*pattis*), with each *patti* headed by a single *zamindar maalik*,[23] who played an important role in the economic, social and political life of the village. The two heads of the families owned only about 250 and 140 acres individually in 2006–7, but their social authority was far more pronounced than that seen in Crown villages. The *maalik* families of these large proprietary villages have a different kind of influence: their political alignments connect them directly to national leaders, presidents and prime ministers. Within their villages, they have historically controlled employment opportunities, access to fodder, dispute resolution mechanisms, and all links with the state. The proximity to an urban centre means, however, that many village residents have been able to break their dependence on land-based jobs and have invested in upward mobility through the education and employment opportunities afforded by a town that is only six kilometres away.

The two *pattis* maintain a somewhat united front politically, and so they control most of the village votes as part of one large vote bloc which is led by the family together. Greater physical and social mobility has prompted some *biradaris* to venture out and build kinship-based links of their own with groups in other villages. Nevertheless, they remain politically aligned with the *maaliks* because the influence of their own connections cannot compete with those of the *maaliks*. There is thus far more limited challenge to the power of the landlords in Sahiwal than in the Crown villages. What little there is comes entirely from a small landholder who rose against the power of the *maaliks* at the time of the two elections held in the 1970s, which brought the PPP to power between the Ayub and Zia dictatorships. Contemporary class-based politics gave this ex-tenant of the *maaliks* the political space in which to support opposing candidates. He continued this opposition over the years by providing some limited contestation in the form of a small class-based vote bloc of about 400 votes (out of 2,000 in total) that brings together Sahiwal's middle strata of smallholders and traders. By drawing on links with influential members of his own *biradari*, the Mekans, in the district, he has managed to make this faction an alternative channel of access to state services for some village residents. Despite this, the smallholder farmer had not managed to establish any stable links as a local organizer for a political party. Overall, Sahiwal provides evidence of the pervasive power of large landlords, with some fissures in parts where limited contestation is visible. The political space for its marginalized populations remains very limited, and is entirely defined by the preferences of the traditional landed elite.

To the absolute right on the spectrum lies Tiwanabad. It too is dominated by a large landlord whose ancestors received a large land grant from the colonial state in return for services rendered during the Sikh Wars in the mid-1800s.[24] Colonial inspection reports record this as a *zamindari* grant of 2,281 acres owned by only one landholder in 1917. Land fragmentation, land reforms and land sales have reduced the holding to about 300 acres now, but the landlord remains the undisputed *maalik* of the village, regularly referred to by residents as their "*maee baap*".[25] The power and authority of the *maalik* appeared to be more oppressive and obvious in Tiwanabad than in Sahiwal. Some of this control is based on the continuing economic dependence of the village residents on the landlord for work, given that the village is 25 kilometres from the nearest town. The family's historical social authority over all the residents of the village is constantly emphasized by various means. For example, village residents considered themselves to be living on the landlord's land, and therefore beholden to him, even though they had all been given ownership certificates for their homesteads by different governments in the 1970s and 1980s.

The power of the single landlord had been challenged by a local family of ex-tenants in local government politics, but this did not extend to national and provincial elections. In these, the landlord's political power was secure and largely uncontested. This was because even in the months leading up to the 2008 election, which marked Pakistan's transition to democracy, there was no opposing vote bloc leader in the area who could compete with his political influence and connections. The landlord led the village's single large vote bloc with about 88 per cent of the village vote and made all its decisions.

Typically, he would decide hundreds of kilometres away in his home in the provincial capital, Lahore, whom he wanted to support in the upcoming election, and then pass the decision on to his farm managers in the village, usually on the phone. The managers would announce the decision to the village on the loudspeakers of the main mosque, and would then monitor the voters in the lead-up to election day to ensure that votes were cast accordingly. The remaining 10 per cent of voters were the few independent landowners who had moved out of the main village settlement after they purchased agricultural land that the landlord was selling off. The fact that they now lived on their own land meant that they could vote "independently" outside the landlord's vote bloc, and many chose to do so as a mark of their social mobility. Tiwanabad provided little evidence of either contestation or any real political space within which voters could exercise agency.

This was the state of affairs in the four villages in the year before the landmark February 2008 election. The next election was in May 2013, and marked the completion of a full term by a democratically elected government. Only the Bhutto government of the early 1970s had managed to complete a full term in power before this. A democratic consolidation seemed to be under way at the national level, and it seemed things had changed significantly in three out of the four villages as well. Politics in Chak 2 had remained as they were. It still had two competing vote blocs with shifting membership, and voters still had both bloc leaders guessing about the numbers they might be able to secure. One bloc leader had put a list of very public demands from the village to his preferred candidate from the PML-N, the party that was slated to win, while the other was running as a candidate himself on a PTI ticket, a party whose fortunes were still uncertain at the time. The clientelistic organization of voters had only intensified under the impression that regular elections were here to stay, and would determine the political landscape and the imperatives of the actors who operated within it. What had changed quite visibly was the fact that landlords were now out and about canvassing from door to door for votes; this was now considered an absolute necessity based on changed voter expectations. The traditional way of gathering people at the landlord's compound was no longer effective. "We now need to personally visit people at different locations,"[26] explained the main leader's brother. He went on to say that the old traditional landed elites (referring to those in proprietary villages) would now start losing their influence because they had not yet grasped the import of this changing situation.

Chak 1 had experienced much greater change, though it was not unambiguously positive. The class consciousness and "colony versus *chaudhries*" politics that had defined this village had transmutated into one large vote bloc that had almost entirely co-opted the colony's vote. Some colony residents had remained steadfastly with the PPP—interestingly, these were mostly women, led by a female vote bloc leader—but the colony bloc had largely unravelled when its leaders joined the *chaudhries*. Changing politics had made the colony's large numbers of marginalized voters indispensable to the landlords. Under a new, younger leader, the *chaudhries* had courted the colony vote with greater humility, and had offered to place their specific demands before their electoral candidates.

From the colony leaders' points of view, they were willing to shift their politics because the *chaudhries'* attitude towards the colony had changed—"they now speak our language,"[27] said the smallholder farmer who had led the colony bloc and was now a leading organizer of the main bloc. Another reason was that colony leaders had had little success in accessing national politicians on their own. Parties relied on local notables, the *chaudhries*, to pull in the votes, and within such a system of modularly assembled parties, lower-caste voters striking out on their own evoked little confidence. But now with the landlords by their side, they sat down in meetings with national and provincial politicians and were finally able to place their demands before them. The new *chaudhry* leader explained, however, that all this applied only to the contest for seats in the national assembly. "For the MPA[28] seat there are too many candidates and too many direct connections between the village and politicians. We have no real control there," he said.[29] The landlords in Chak 2 observed similar dynamics: "the elections this time are more confusing than they have ever been before. There are so many candidates for every seat, especially for the MPA seats. This has made the constituency-level picture look uncertain. In the past, when there were only one or two main parties, things were more clear-cut. Results were often known before votes were cast. Now we have no idea what is going to happen."[30]

Sahiwal had seen a nigh-identical change. A member of the Mekan *biradari* had quickly risen to political prominence in the area, and was slated to win a ticket from the PML-N for the provincial seat in the constituency, for which he was competing against a member of the traditional landed elite of the district. This had taken the *maaliks* to the doorstep of the smallholder Mekan farmer who had traditionally opposed them with his small vote bloc. Basic pragmatism had made the leader realize that the village vote now stood to be divided more evenly between the two blocs than it ever had been. To avoid this scenario, she courted the small bloc to join her and form one large village-wide vote bank. The leader of the small bloc was happy to do this for a number of reasons: because it was he who was choosing the candidate they would all support;[31] because it promised to bring in the whole village's votes for his kin brother; and because "she requested me personally, and she is a better politician than the men of her family".[32] Both Chak 1's and Sahiwal's class-based second vote blocs had disappeared under the growing logic of clientelistic and kinship-based politics. However, the leaders of the co-opted vote blocs were now indispensable organizers of the new village politics, and were expected to open up greater political space for their own supporters within vote blocs organized by the village elite.

The changes in Tiwanabad had also been dramatic. For the first time in the village's history there was now a second vote bloc that was bitterly and openly opposed to the landlord. This vote bloc was based on an expansion of the political activities of the independent peasant proprietors who lived just outside the village, and it now included other more disgruntled and more independent middle-tier village residents. They now controlled about 30 per cent of the village vote, and were aligned with the PPP, a party that the landlord abhorred for having organized the peasants of his village against him under the left-leaning Bhutto government of the 1970s. This suited the new bloc's members well, for it underscored their open rebellion against him and his social authority. A prominent member of this new bloc explained: "Our helplessness has decreased as choice has increased. People are now more willing to oppose the landlord visibly and openly."[33] It was clear that politics were far more competitive than they had been earlier, but Tiwanabad had only now arrived at the class-based organization that Sahiwal and Chak 1 had already reached on their way to a more clientelistic form of politics.

The implications of hybrid clientelism

These cases provide us with a detailed and nuanced perspective on how the clientelism of notables engages with the clientelism of mass parties in Punjab's villages to condition local politics. The two dimensions of democracy—contestation and inclusion—highlight where spaces emerge for marginalized voters as the logic of electoral politics becomes embedded in unequal contexts. With the exception of Chak 2, politics shifted in each of the villages, but it is along the dimension of inclusion, rather than contestation, that electoral politics seem to have created the most space for more marginalized voters. This is somewhat surprising. We expect elections typically to lead to greater competition, and that more substantive structural reforms may be required to make local politics more inclusive. Instead, the accounts provided in the previous section show that while the villages behave differently in terms of contestation, it is in respect of inclusion that they all perform better than before. Vote blocs are now more consultative and reflective of the preferences of non-elite members, and their mobilization methods include more individual contact and negotiation. Non-elite emerging intermediaries who had attempted to strike out on their own were unable to consolidate their own vote blocs in two villages. Instead, they now play an indispensable and central role in the politics of their landlords. There were no such emerging intermediaries in one village, while in another the fortunes of the newly emergent leader were as yet unclear.

An explanation for this is that the imperatives of elections and clientelistic competition at higher tiers ensure that every vote matters, and so they drive local notables towards greater inclusion of even the poorest voters. This allows villagers to create or renew reciprocal relationships with local notables to gain access to basic public services such as electricity, health centres, schools, paved streets and sanitation drains. So, inclusion increases but clientelistic relationships become entrenched. This matters little to poor rural voters living in severely under-provided localities, for whom this represents a significant step up from when their own preferences and demands did not figure at all in the politics of the landed elite. However, the fusion of the clientelism of mass parties and notables means that despite intense competition in national politics, contestation at the local level does not increase. Local notables, empowered under colonial rule and unchallenged under post-colonial instability, continue organizing local politics despite the fact that they are no longer able to draw on their economic wealth and social power. Instead, they cultivate and maintain links with state officials and with politicians within modular parties, and voters learn that access to a distant state is possible only through these links. This political system places severe constraints on the ability of emerging political entrepreneurs to provide comparable access to the state, thus curtailing contestation. If the clientelism of mass parties had existed here without that of notables, new political entrepreneurs might well have become party brokers that challenged the political power of local notables and provided them with some competition.

Findings from four Punjabi villages in Pakistan may not obviously extend to explain wider political trends in the world's most populous macro-region, but it is not altogether unimaginable that the impact of hybrid clientelism produced here may be observable elsewhere in the Global Indian Ocean. The situation on the ground in Pakistan reflects neither a classical strong state nor what is generally seen in the West as a weak state. Yet, it is a state which is present and shaping politics and interactions between citizens in the same way that it does in Kenya, Indonesia, Tanzania and South Africa. Above all, it is a source from which local forces extract patronage. This does not qualify it as an "objective" provider of impartial services but it does often help sections of the population. Competition for access to state resources has over the decades heavily restructured local politics, not only in Pakistan but wherever states are present and have anything to distribute. This helps explain why we see vibrant democratic debate and practices coexisting with expanding, not shrinking, clientelistic practices.[34]

Rather than continuing to grapple with how countries will (or will not) become liberal democracies, these facts help us ask the much more fascinating question whether clientelistic dynamics, fuelled as much from above by politicians as from below by voters or citizens, undercut the notion of democracy or strengthen it. Voters are now genuinely holding politicians to account for public service delivery, and politicians are under pressure to be responsive to ensure re-election. This is producing real democratic practice at the margins even while national systems may not exhibit signs of deepening democracy. It may not fit our ideals of liberal democracy, but this is what democracy looks like in practice in Nairobi, Johannesburg, Calcutta and rural Punjab. The corollary is of course the debate on whether this is a stepping stone on the way to (Western-style) liberal democracy—which also emerged from decades of machine politics in places like America, where democracy also preceded public sector reform—or a different variety altogether, with a different end point (if any at all).

Recent literature suggests it may be the latter, but defining how exactly this may look is complicated by the impossibility of generalizing with any value across the incredibly varied macro-region of the Global Indian Ocean. We may be able to reach broad agreement on the fact that politics here function under competing and simultaneous pressures from (at least) the rhetoric of a global liberal international order and the specificity of local cultural contexts. Beyond this, answers must be grounded in the empirical reality of each system, both because clientelism does not present a steady state and because it is conditioned by the local socio-economic context as it changes.

The answer is also complicated by the fact that much of what we understand about how clientelism died out around the (North) Atlantic is observable around the Indian Ocean too. A combination of industrialization, urbanization, increasing incomes and rising inequality makes vote-buying practices less attractive to voters; increases the appeal of ideological and programmatic policy positions; and increases the number and anonymity of voters so that brokers and party machines have a hard time monitoring behaviour.[35] As clientelistic linkages weaken at varying rates based on these factors—all of them visible across this macro-region—voters connect with politicians and parties for a variety of other reasons, including ideological identification, populist appeal or valence competition. This is visible in recent scholarship that argues that voters are increasingly building linkages with parties based on these motivations.[36] Within these linkages we may continue to see glimpses of ethno-religious mobilization in some places while not in others. But given that the politics of race and migrant status continue to define politics even around the Atlantic, it is not this that sets apart the Global Indian Ocean.

What may distinguish it more is its processes of state formation. Clientelism works because politicians can divert public expenditure to fulfil promises through particularistic, discretionary delivery of services. It also works because the under-provision of basic services creates a space for such relationships in the first place. But it is not necessarily popular with politicians—clientelistic exchange is expensive, with high transaction costs, and makes party elites dependent on the personalities, whims and agendas of brokers. Even in Pakistan's cities recent evidence suggests that non-contingent, party-based linkages between politicians and citizens are increasing.[37] The politics of this region may therefore be conditioned more by the weakness of its bureaucracies and the lack of transparency in its public expenditure functions, than by the primacy of primordial socio-cultural constructs. And the nature of these bureaucracies is linked to the very recent experience and nature of colonialism and order-building, as discussed earlier here, in Verhoeven's introduction and in Blom Hansen's chapter.

The challenge here is now the opposite of that faced by Europe when it sought to strengthen democracy at the start of the 20th century. Europe's challenge was to make a capable executive more responsible and accountable to newly emerging elected legislatures. The challenge in the early 21st century around the Indian Ocean is to incentivize elected legislatures to reform their extractive executives into capable, transparent and impartial institutions. The variety of democracy in this region in the future thus depends in good part on whether the global order or its more indigenous regional manifestations can create such incentives for political elites. This is a more difficult question to answer, and one that will be affected by two other concurrent forces visible in the Global Indian Ocean at the moment. The first is the mixing of the liberal order with the increasing influence of the more illiberal Chinese order, which remains uninterested in the promotion or deepening of democratic practice (see Mitter's chapter 9). The second is the growing political polarization around populist ideas and personalities (similar to that in other regions) that may dull the push for impartial governance reforms in favour of greater ideological partiality.

5

THE ARABIAN OIL STATE

INFRASTRUCTURAL POWER AND SOCIAL SEGMENTATION

Steffen Hertog

Oil rents allow institutional experiments—forms of statehood that would be difficult to imagine without the availability of large, state-controlled and externally derived surpluses. Muammar Gaddafi's experiments of abolishing the modern state, for instance, would have been impossible to sustain without Libya's large and stable oil income.[1] I have proposed more recently that oil rents have enabled the building of an unusually heterogeneous state in Saudi Arabia, whose technocratic, religious and royal components operate in parallel and according to very different rules.[2]

This chapter argues that the building of deeply segmented states characterizes not only Saudi Arabia, but Arabian oil monarchies more broadly (Bahrain, Kuwait, Oman, Qatar and the United Arab Emirates), which have gone through state formation processes under similar historical and structural conditions. I furthermore demonstrate a point that I paid scant attention to in my previous state-centric work: segmentation characterizes not only the state, but also local society itself, in which different social groups live in spatially, culturally and administratively separate enclaves.

This separation is reminiscent of pre-modern empires, notably the millet system in the Ottoman Empire[3] and the self-governing, transnational ethnic communities in port cities of earlier orders in the Indian Ocean (see Verhoeven's introduction). Yet, in ways different from old empires, segmentation exists here under a state with strong infrastructural power that can directly reach into and regulate the lives of local residents. This unique blend of institutional and social segmentation with omnipresent state power is what makes Arabian oil states unique. Perhaps the only similar case, at the edge of the Global Indian Ocean, would be the small, absolutist petro-monarchy of Brunei.[4]

The segmentation of Arabian oil states makes for an intriguing form of ideological hybridity in the context of this volume's focus on liberal order. Some outward-oriented, elite parts of the state apparatus espouse liberal if outwardly apolitical discourses of social modernization, civil society development, entrepreneurship and global cultural openness, often in close cooperation with white-collar expatriates and advisors. But in other segments of the state, including the education and religious sectors, discourses are much more conservative, inward-looking and oriented towards non-elite citizens who often have little contact with the state's elite-level liberal spheres. Finally, in the large social enclaves inhabited by blue-collar expatriate workers, the Arabian oil state has no ideological ambitions at all, allowing foreigners to build separate ethno-cultural spheres as long as the regime does not perceive direct security risks—not unlike the British Empire's traditional approach to subaltern peoples in the Indian Ocean, as outlined in the volume's introduction and Blom Hansen's chapter on the genealogies of distributed sovereignty.

The position of the Arabian oil states vis-à-vis the "liberal state" hence is uneasy. Elites have enthusiastically adopted liberal institutional, market and social recipes in some areas, deeply imbricating them with capitalist globalization. At the same time, with the exception of Kuwait, the Gulf monarchies remain deeply illiberal in political terms and reproduce a segmentation of social and ideological spheres, of local populations' identities and legal rights, that is at odds not only with the liberal state, but with the very concept of the modern nation-state (cf. Lieven's argument in chapter 10 about modern ethnopolitics and bifurcated societies across the Global Indian Ocean). Especially in the richer Arabian monarchies, citizens are served by the capitalist market yet also protected from it.[5] And in a different way from ideal-typical liberal states, Arabian oil states have been built in a top-down fashion, rather than resulting from the interplay of capitalist development and emerging civil society. The social contract with the citizen constituency is distributive and involves little political participation. Democratization is not on the cards—not to speak of liberal democracy.

It is an unusual set-up that has been enabled by unusually high per capita oil rents and has persisted thanks to historical security guarantees from Britain and, since the 1970s, the Pax Americana guaranteed by the United States.[6] Under this arrangement, the US has eschewed imposing liberal political and social values which it has promoted within its Western alliance, confirming Verhoeven's observations in chapter 1 about the illiberal foundations of the global liberal order outside its Western core. It has instead provided security guarantees in return for stable oil supplies and Gulf petrodollar recycling in the US financial system after the 1973 oil shock, a time when the US lost its control over the international oil market.[7] The result is an example of the "thin hegemony" analysed throughout this volume, with a strong US security presence and significant integration into global capitalist circuits, but only very partial ideological integration into the US-led liberal order—all of which is highly compatible with the transactional nature of regional order that Verhoeven describes in chapter 1. The prominent role of the US has in turn met rather limited local social challenges compared to the wider Middle East and North African regions, as Gulf societies for the most part have been less politically mobilized.

This chapter first investigates the historical roots of the Arabian oil state, documenting how oil has allowed the building of heterogeneous but by and large high-capacity states, while also engendering large-scale transnational migration that has increased social heterogeneity. The next section investigates dimensions of social, spatial and ideological segmentation. The final section summarizes the argument and discusses the comparative significance of the particular forms of sovereignty that the Arabian oil state has developed, and places it on a wider Global Indian Ocean canvas.

Historical roots of the Arabian oil state

Rentier state theory posits that oil rents increase regime autonomy.[8] While this is not true at all times, Gulf ruling elites have indeed enjoyed large autonomy in shaping the state apparatus in the early phase of rent-finance state-building after the onset of large-scale rents. This mostly happened with the start of oil exports after World War II (with the partial exception of Kuwait and Bahrain, which had access to some pre-WWII rents), and accelerated drastically across the whole region after the 1973 oil crisis and the associated hike in hydrocarbon prices.

Elite autonomy was considerable because of the scale of resources suddenly available, and because pre-oil state apparatuses were so embryonic as to impose little constraint on specific institution-building decisions. Moreover, there were few modern interest groups in society that would have made specific demands on institutional design beyond, if at all, expecting a share of the material spoils.[9] In this setting, ruling elites were able to use oil rents to create very different institutions for different purposes, including self-enrichment, the building of administrative capacity in priority areas, and mass co-optation of different strata of local society. The Arabian oil monarchies stand out for the resulting heterogeneity of their state apparatus.

Fiefdoms and pockets of efficiency

I have previously documented the emergence of personal princely "fiefdoms" in Saudi Arabia,[10] where individual state agencies over time became indelibly fused with particular Al Saud members or family branches. Such fiefdoms have acquired parallel infrastructures, built their own health and education services, and operated with high decisional autonomy. This has made them "states within the state" until at least the rise to power since 2015 of Crown Prince Mohammad bin Salman, who has kept the parallel institutional structures largely intact but has recentralized decision-making power at the top level.

Similar personalized fiefdoms exist in other Gulf monarchies: in Bahrain, the Crown Prince controls economic policy-making through the Economic Development Board, a kind of parallel cabinet, while the "Khawalid" sheikhs rule supreme over the Bahraini security apparatus.[11] In Qatar, the Emir's mother, Sheikha Moza, controls the Qatar Foundation with its Western universities, Qatar Science and Technology Park, cultural programmes, mobile phone franchise and real estate operations—all of which exist in parallel to and with a high level of autonomy from the rest of the education and state apparatus.[12] In Abu Dhabi, the state-owned holding company Mubadala has built its own economic and residential zones, hospitals and higher education projects, and has functioned as a personal vehicle for Crown Prince Mohammad bin Zayed.[13] While personal fiefdoms also exist in other state apparatuses, oil rents have allowed them to acquire particular scale, depth and resilience in the Gulf while—in the short run—reducing the opportunity costs of building parallel and redundant institutions.

The level of elite fragmentation at the top level varies strongly across Gulf monarchies. Saudi Arabia used to have the most fragmented, oligarchic ruling elite with the deepest personal "fiefdoms", yet it has become much more cohesive under Mohammad bin Salman. The modern Omani state was built around one person, Sultan Qaboos bin Said,[14] while personal empire-building in Kuwait has been constrained by an active and powerful parliament.[15] As a result, not all countries have built royal fiefdoms to the same extent. Oil rents have allowed the rapid building of parallel institutions across the region, but family politics and balance of power have inflected the specifics.[16]

In all cases, however, ruling elites used at least some of their unprecedented surpluses to also build high-functioning, elite technocratic bodies in priority areas, so-called pockets of efficiency.[17] Different from the ruling family fiefdoms, they are almost invariably controlled by commoners. These are often, but not always, state-owned enterprises. In Saudi Arabia they include the central bank SAMA,[18] the Royal Commission for the industrial cities of Jubail and Yanbu, and the heavy industry giant SABIC.[19]

In other Gulf countries, they include sovereign wealth ADIA (Abu Dhabi), Qatar Petroleum and Qatar Telecoms, the Jebel Ali Free Zone, port operator DP World, and Emirates airline (Dubai), aluminium smelter Alba (Bahrain) and Oman Airways.[20] In Kuwait, where the public sector is more politicized due to conflicts between parliament and government,[21] historical pockets of efficiency like the central bank and the auditing bureau have been under more political pressure and there are no conspicuous success stories among the country's state-owned enterprises.

Pockets of efficiency typically also enjoy high autonomy from the rest of the state apparatus, as they have separate budgets and staffing regimes and are run by close (commoner) confidants of the rulers. Elite agencies flourish, of course, in many countries outside the Arabian Peninsula,[22] and have even come to be the norm in places like Singapore (see Chua Beng Huat's chapter 3) where "efficiency" has been the mantra of illiberal state-building. What is striking in the context of the Gulf is the unprecedented pace and scale at which these agencies have developed, considering that as late as the 1950s there was pretty much no modern administration in the region. Such a transformation would be hard to imagine without large oil surpluses that autonomous rulers could quickly deploy in priority areas. As a result, Gulf monarchies have built segments in their state apparatuses that are highly modern and "Weberian", even if they serve a system that remains patrimonial at its core.

An important auxiliary factor that arguably allows elite agencies to flourish in the Gulf is situated in these states' unusually close reliance on select Western advisors (especially British ones in the smaller sheikhdoms—a legacy of the particular type of colonialism that the Pax Britannica brought to the region, as highlighted in Verhoeven's introduction). These helped with building new bodies in line with Western templates. The absence of a strong nationalist ideology—reflected, for example, in the avoidance of nationalizations—made it easier to selectively adopt foreign models, including the pro-market liberal discourse that came with them. Socially liberal discourse has become especially visible in outward-oriented enclave institutions like new universities, cultural foundations, and museums that have flourished since the early 2000s.[23]

Mass co-optation of citizens

The dominant and arguably most unusual aspect of Gulf state apparatuses is, however, the extent to which they have been used for the material co-optation of the local citizen population. The level at which Gulf monarchies provide direct employment, free public services, housing, cheap credit and subsidies is unparalleled—with the earlier-mentioned exception of Brunei, a small oil monarchy on the other side of the Indian Ocean World, which is structurally very similar to the states of the Gulf Cooperation Council (GCC). The British and, then, US security umbrella (discussed in the introduction to this volume— allowed rulers to avoid the deep militarization of society that occurred in many other Arab states after independence. Owing to the external-ization of security provision, they have instead been able to focus on concentrating power domestically through expanding civilian public services and patronage structures.[24] And under the system of "thin hegemony", the American patron has made few demands on how to organize the Gulf monarchies' internal order, allowing regimes to reject political liberalism despite much public rhetoric (and some action) about civil society and social modernization.

Oil riches do not automatically translate into generosity. There are high-rent authoritarian hydrocarbon producers like Equatorial Guinea or Angola in which poverty is rife and corruption so rampant that the state fails to deliver even basic goods to its population.[25] Primary sources show that the "generosity" of Gulf rulers towards their populations was to an important extent triggered by the sub-versive challenges that the region faced during the heyday of Arab nationalism from the 1950s to the 1970s. Rulers like Qaboos of Oman, Faisal of Saudi Arabia, and Zayed of Abu Dhabi explicitly justified their development efforts as necessary counter-revolution-ary measures to placate local populations and fend off clandestine nationalist and leftist movements.[26] As was the case with both fief-doms for ruling family members and technocratic pockets of effi-ciency, oil provided rulers with an unusually wide range of institu-tional choices, but which ones were taken was a result of historical context, elite incentives and agency.[27]

The extent of material welfare in the GCC is quickly illustrated by some figures on public employment, energy subsidies, and human development outcomes. Figure 5.1 shows that the share of govern-ment workers among employed citizens is uniquely high in the Gulf, ranging from about half to around 90 per cent, which contrasts with government employment shares in the rest of the world, which cluster around 20 per cent. Since the 1970s, GCC governments have de facto provided an open job guarantee for male and sometimes also female citizens—an arrangement that has come under pressure in Bahrain, Oman and Saudi Arabia with the decline in oil prices since 2014, but whose legacy will shape labour markets for decades to come.

Figure 5.1: Distribution of employment by sector and nationality in the GCC (2009)

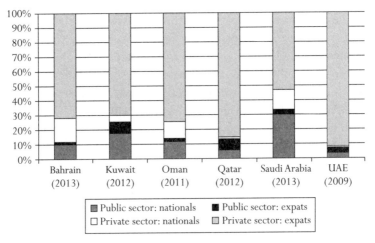

Source: National agencies, author's estimates.

Gulf monarchies also provide generous energy subsidies, at least if these are calculated as the difference between local energy prices and global benchmark prices. While these have been cut back in recent years, the absolute costs and per capita benefits remain substantial. In several cases, citizens are subject to separate higher water and electricity tariffs than expatriate residents.[28]

Finally, the Gulf monarchies all provide free universal health care and education to their citizens. While the quality of neither is on a par with that in the wealthiest OECD countries, the GCC countries stand out in terms of the rate of improvement in education and health outcomes which they have been able to achieve since the 1950s. Four of the world's ten countries with the fastest post-WWII reduction rates in child mortality are in the GCC, and few have managed to reach universal primary and secondary school enrolment as quickly as the Gulf monarchies.[29] This is reflected in human development index results—incorporating GDP per capita, years of schooling and life expectancy—that nowadays are close to those of rich OECD countries and much above those of many other oil-rich states, as shown in figure 5.2.

Figure 5.2: Human Development Index vs GDP per capita

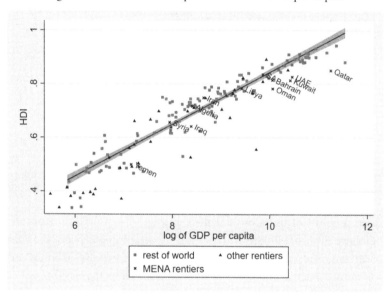

Source: World Bank Development Indicators, UN HDI.

Using the state as employment machine for citizens has to some extent compromised administrative efficiency.[30] Yet, all things considered, the Arabian oil states have built impressive state capacity in a short time span. They deliver a wide range of public goods, provide expansive modern infrastructure, and have built several impressive, high-capability agencies that are insulated from the pressures of patronage employment. In the World Bank's measure of government effectiveness, the Arabian oil states score worse than rich non-oil countries, but all lie above the global median and outperform most other oil-rich developing countries (see figure 5.3).

Figure 5.3: Government effectiveness vs (logged) GDP per capita (2010)

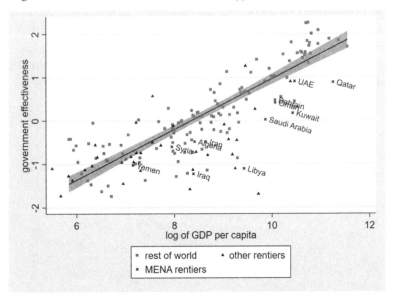

Source: World Bank Development Indicators, World Bank Governance Indicators.

As a result of decades of well-resourced distributive institution-building, Arabian oil states are now able to penetrate deep into the lives of citizens and foreign residents. This has led to the weakening and sometimes disappearance of old intermediary elites that used to act as go-between between local communities and the state, in particular tribal leaders and urban notables. The central state used to be weak and remote, while society was locally organized and self-reliant. Today's situation is the opposite: the state is omnipresent and has deeply pen-etrated a society that—in the case of citizens in particular—is highly reliant on resources directly provided by government.[31] This flattening of non-state social hierarchies is not unlike the modernization processes that happened in liberal states[32]—yet, in contrast to the liberal image, the relationship to state and ruling elites remains hierarchical, and pri-mordial identity markers within society remain powerful.

Arabian oil states have developed typical mechanisms of infrastruc-tural power like taxation and conscription, only several decades after independence or still not at all.[33] Yet they are able exert tight political

THE ARABIAN OIL STATE

control through well-resourced security services and are deeply involved in citizens' lives through the provision of public services and the employment of the majority of national workers in the state. The balance of power and resources between state and society has shifted fundamentally. At the same time, Arabian oil states are less coherent than other modern national states with comparable levels of bureaucratic capacity, like Malaysia or Turkey. Owing to the sprawling and often disjointed process of institution-building in the Gulf, state apparatuses remain fragmented and heterogeneous, with different organizations serving very different social and political purposes.

Social fragmentation: Locals

State-building through oil rents has also fragmented local society. To be sure, in some regards the citizenry has become more integrated owing to the power of modern media, education and labour markets, and as a result of deliberate policies of national identity-building, including patriotic education, national festivals and a plethora of state-financed cultural programmes.[34]

But in key aspects of society, state-building and co-optation strategies have also reproduced and deepened separate social identities. In Saudi Arabia, the *ulema* elites were co-opted into the new judicial and educational bureaucracy, which they were allowed to run with a high level of autonomy for many decades, all the while creating world-scale organizations for Wahhabi proselytization.[35] Their activities could not be more opposed to the liberal international order on the ideological level; yet they operated under a regime that had entered a close and durable geo-strategic alliance with the US, a fact that highlights the deep heterogeneity of the Saudi system. Select tribes were co-opted into the National Guard, with its own hospitals, schools, residential cities and other infrastructure—in the process both expanding modern state infrastructure and reproducing segmentary politics.[36] As the state provided parallel space for separate social forces, it reinforced its own internal segmentation.

Similar if less extreme "granting" of state organizations to specific segments of society also happened in other GCC countries. Men of tribal background with lower levels of education are typically

127

recruited into the police and other security forces; every Gulf state has a share of nationals without clear tribal descent who are treated as socially inferior. This bifurcation thus leads to state institutions structured along tribal or sectarian lines. In Bahrain, specific government agencies like the Ministry of Labour are generally known to be "Shiite" agencies—a phenomenon that has survived the sectarian polarization and repression that Bahrain has seen since 2011. In Kuwait, specific government agencies have been dominated by (modern) political groups like the Muslim Brotherhood. This means that the state provides space for different identities and ideologies to be reproduced within the administrative apparatus, which in turn contributes to the segmentation of the state. While "capture" of state agencies by specific social groups has also happened in other countries in the Global Indian Ocean (e.g. the Malay dominance of the Malaysian bureaucracy or the Punjabi dominance of the Pakistani army), the resources and scale of the process relative to the national population are much larger on the Arabian Peninsula.

The segmentation of the state is reflected in spatial separation. Government agencies often have their own residential cities and infrastructures, and institutions like ministries of defence, National Guards, the Qatar Foundation, Mubadala, Saudi Aramco or Dubai's free zones operate their own mini-cities with separate public service and utility systems. Abu Dhabi Global Market, the Qatar Financial Centre and the Dubai International Financial Centre are spatial enclaves that even operate their own legal system.[37] Saudi Aramco in turn applies radically different social rules in its cloistered corporate compounds, where women have been allowed to drive, go unveiled and mix with men for decades.

As their institutional heterogeneity underscores, Arabian oil states are ideological hybrids. Parts of the ruling elites and technocracy are Western-inspired, adopting foreign managerial models as well as liberal, globalist language about social modernization, civil society development, entrepreneurship and global cultural openness. Elite enclave institutions like MiSK in Saudi Arabia or the Qatar Foundation—whose motto for a while was "Encouraging the people of the world to start thinking"—speak the language of the international NGO world and pursue a liberal social agenda (politics is, of course, eschewed). High-profile, outward-oriented humanitarian, cultural and environmental summits in the Gulf signal modernity, tolerance and openness and seek to build Gulf states' international "soft power", as do elite university projects like KAUST in Saudi Arabia, NYU Abu Dhabi or the transplant universities in Qatar's Education City.

Yet these segments of the system operate in parallel to much more conservative and inward-looking parts of the state apparatus and official education system. Citizens' lives are often distant from the official liberal ideologies, including in lower rungs of the state apparatus where most male national employees have their jobs. In some cases, like the cultural and education projects of the Qatar Foundation, attempts by enclave institutions to project liberal social values beyond their own confines have triggered open conflict with conservative local society.[38]

Local citizens' buy-in for many environmental sustainability, civic education and education reform projects has been limited. Despite official denouncements of tribalism and a rhetoric of (sometimes global) citizenship, employees in national security and police apparatuses often cherish their tribal identities—and are often recruited along those very lines (albeit with notable exceptions like the Saudi armed forces, which avoid tribal recruitment). While states have managed to strengthen national identities quite significantly (see Chua Beng Huat's chapter 3), there remains much space for parallel infranational and transnational tribal identities, even if these nowadays are rarely the source of autonomous collective action. Similarly, the religious and educational spheres in Saudi Arabia, and also in other Gulf monarchies, have provided space for conservative and even reactionary social attitudes. Attempts to make the mainline education systems less xenophobic and socially conservative are under way across the region, but are progressing slowly. By and large, the Arabian oil states still provide parallel institutional spheres and physical spaces in which different social ideologies can be reproduced.

In sum, oil rents and political autonomy have allowed Gulf rulers to build states that are both highly heterogeneous and have significant infrastructural power, reaching deep into the lives of local residents. But oil rents have not only permitted the construction of fragmented states. As important, state-building has allowed the reproduction of local social cleavages. As the next section will show, it has also brought with it deeper cleavages between citizens and foreign residents as well as among foreign residents. Social fragmentation is the second distinct feature of the Arabian oil state.

Social fragmentation: Expatriates

The Gulf oil booms led not only to rapid state growth, but also to the extremely fast growth of the local population, partially through rapidly dropping child mortality but, more importantly, through large-scale labour migration, much of it across continents and seas—indeed, it is constitutive of the Global Indian Ocean, as underlined by Verhoeven's introduction. While such migration predates the discovery of oil by many centuries and shaped the Red Sea and Gulf of Aden littoral,[39] it was turbo-charged by oil rents, and the social status of labour migrants relative to the local population has dropped precipitously since the introduction of modern citizenship in the Arabian oil states, deepening social segmentation. Migration patterns have mostly been driven by local employers, who through the "sponsorship" system could import and control workers with few official restrictions, exerting tight control over their workforce. In practice, much of the migration is managed through the types of transnational ethnic networks described by Blom Hansen in chapter 2 (especially the section "Bridging the Gulf"), but with local employers in the Gulf as the most powerful players.

It would have been impossible to build the GCC states' infrastructure and public service provision so fast without large-scale labour imports. The widespread use of foreign workers shielded national populations from the vagaries of menial work and precarious private employment, while public employment was used as the key tool to spread wealth broadly among the citizen population. This is a key difference from the Singaporean model described in chapter 3 by Chua Beng Huat: like the Gulf monarchies, Singapore is an authoritarian state that draws legitimacy from the welfare it provides to its citizens and relies on a large, transitory expatriate population. Yet nationals in Singapore are expected to work hard, including in the

Figure 5.4: Share of nationals vs non-nationals in GCC populations (%, most recent year available)

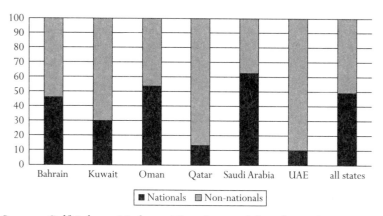

Source: Gulf Labour Markets, Migration, and Population Programme (EUI), based on national sources.

private sector alongside, and indeed competing with, foreigners. Their role in the (real) economy is much more central, and welfare provision much less generous than in the Arabian oil state.

Large-scale migration in the Gulf has increased the heterogeneity of local society, dividing it rigidly into citizens who (at least in principle) enjoyed expansive material privileges and "expatriate" workers whose official status is temporary, and whose material privileges are limited, often strictly so. Gulf populations before the onset of oil production were also culturally and socially heterogeneous and exposed to migration to and from Asia, Africa and the Middle East.[40] But the creation of modern citizenship systems and sponsorship laws drastically deepened the legal and social boundaries between locals and "foreigners", while migration increased the ratio of foreign to local residents as well as the cultural heterogeneity of foreigners. Oil-driven migration has propelled the share of foreigners in the total population to globally unparalleled heights (see figure 5.4).

As a result of rapid migration combined with deep social and legal boundaries, Arabian oil states host many, very different expatriate societies that often have only minimal contact with each other and live in separate residential enclaves, often under the control of their

131

employers. While white-collar expatriates—many of whom are Western citizens—live relatively privileged lives, expatriates with Arab, African and Asian passports predominantly do low-wage work in construction, domestic services, security and transportation with limited labour rights, competing in what is essentially a global market for low-skilled labour. While the parallel presence of different social systems could be read as typical for the Global Indian Ocean's cosmopolitanism, the deep segmentation between social groups has little to do with modern cosmopolitanism.

Very different social rules and practices apply in different residential areas depending on which nationalities live there. A rather extreme case is expatriate compounds in Saudi Arabia, where genders mix and officially prohibited alcohol is safely consumed as the religious police are informally prohibited from entering. But social practices also differ strongly in the UAE between areas dominated by Western expatriates and tourists—where women are often scantily clad and national dress is explicitly prohibited in some bars and clubs—and more conservative locales populated by nationals, like Al Ain in Abu Dhabi.

Many expatriates are long-term residents, and an increasing share of them are born into and bred in the expatriate societies of Arabian oil states, even if there is no formal provision for permanent residence. Some of them constitute a business elite which, while socially entirely separate from local business elites, enjoys good access to decision-makers—as is the case notably with Indian billionaires in Dubai, who retain close links to their country of origin.[41]

The vast majority of expatriates, however, are much less privileged. Many second- and third-generation residents rely on formal sponsorship from employers to be able to stay in the country.[42] The status of a significant share of the multi-generational non-citizen residents is unrecognized. All Gulf monarchies have informal Eritrean, Filipino, Indian, Nepalese, Pakistani, Sri Lankan or Sudanese communities, in some cases numbering in the hundreds of thousands, which call whole city quarters their own and which are, yet again, socially separate from shorter-term and official expatriate residents.

While segregation and discrimination run deep, the modern Arabian oil state retains a monopoly of violence. There are no communal clashes as in the old Indian Ocean sphere (see chapter 1). Yet while Arabian oil states enjoy strong infrastructural power, in some cases they deliberately neglect communities and city areas, de facto allowing them to self-organize. In the case of Kuwait, according to local sources, criminal networks of Bangladeshis in informal quarters are policed by Syrians intermediaries, who in turn act on behalf of the Kuwaiti police force, which does not want to get directly involved in policing these communities.

Several Gulf monarchies also have significant populations of stateless individuals who claim local origin.[43] In the case of the UAE, the government has arranged for thousands of them to be given passports by the government of the Comoros, a poor Indian Ocean archipelago state with which they have no link whatsoever. In practice, the arrangement does not entitle them to any consular support or residence in the Comoros, thereby creating yet another legally separate social group with no parallel anywhere else in the world. The arrangement gives the government the level of control over individuals that nation-states typically exert over their citizens, yet without granting them citizenship as nation-states usually would. The stateless are leftovers from the pre-nation-state era in the Global Indian Ocean when the migration regime was, ironically, far more liberal than that of today's liberal order.[44] Today these stateless individuals have become regulatory subjects of powerful modern states yet are not admitted into modern citizenship.

Probably nowhere else in the world is the social separation between different national groups so deep, and nowhere else are there so many long-term residents with formal temporary status. Expatriates of all stripes are exposed to the forces of private capitalism, be it formal or informal, and almost invariably have no path to citizenship or permanent residence (Qatari plans to create a permanent residence status have yet to be implemented). That many of them are de facto permanent residents[45] makes their status all the more unusual.

The presence of expatriate workers and their exposure to the vagaries of capitalist markets do in fact help to shield nationals from exactly the same forces. Expatriates provide much of the labour force for the local construction and service sector on which publicly employed nationals rely. Their low wages—which often lie below their marginal product[46]—are critical for keeping prices affordable and in practice they often allow the cross-subsidization of the better-paid minority of nationals employed in the private sector.[47] While modern capitalism has penetrated GCC economies in the course of state formation, citizens by and large remain protected from it. Ironically, this is the case especially in the more "Westernized" and ostensibly capitalist environments that have a larger expatriate-to-local ratio, in particular the Emirates. The UAE model, while at first glance a beachhead of freewheeling capitalism, is at its core a patronage-based system that defies the liberal order in which citizens are supposed to be subject to (and thrive because of) private markets. This distinguishes the Arabian oil state from the neoliberal marketization that poorer Indian Ocean countries have witnessed (see Verhoeven's introduction and Karim's chapter 6 on gender and Bangladesh's integration into global supply chains).

In the early oil age, transnational labour migration sometimes had a direct impact on local politics and ideologies. Arab nationalist and leftist thought percolated into the region through regional labour migration from the 1950s on.[48] Arab expatriates with affiliations to the Muslim Brotherhood in turn played a critical role in spreading modern Islamist thought and shaping the region's education and charity sectors[49]—in that sense, colonizing new sectors of the state just as different segments of local society were doing.

But regimes have fought these influences actively, and they have waned, even if Islamist influences had longer staying power.[50] As boundaries between citizens and expatriates have deepened and political monitoring of expatriate communities has increased, nowadays very few foreigners come to the region with a political agenda, and even fewer have a direct impact on local ideological networks. Foreign workers do engage in occasional collective action over their labour rights, yet the protests are almost invariably issue-specific and expatriates who are perceived as a security threat are easily expelled. If anything, ideological flows have reversed since the 1970s, as some foreign workers have brought local notions of Salafi Islam back to their home countries (see Karim's chapter on Bangladesh or Reno's chapter on Somalia), supported by global networks of Gulf-funded charities.

Conclusion: The comparative significance of hybridity in the Gulf

Few countries in the world combine authoritarianism, wealth and state capacity as effectively as the Arabian oil states do. But what really makes their form of statehood stand out—globally and historically—is how deeply the state apparatus and local societies are segmented, despite the considerable infrastructural powers of the state.

The top-down state-building process in the Gulf oil monarchies since the 1950s has created multiple statehoods within the Gulf rentier systems. Oil rents have allowed the parallel creation and maintenance of very different institutions and social sub-systems, some very insular and inward-oriented, others very outward-oriented and often separate from local society. Some are patrimonial and informal, others bureaucratic and bloated, while yet others are efficient and meritocratic. The deep heterogeneity of the Gulf's oil states is perhaps their most original contribution to the varieties of modern statehood.

The Gulf monarchies have built the most expansive systems of mass patronage anywhere in the world—yet the Gulf states are used for many other purposes: the building of personal fiefdoms, large-scale industrialization and attempts to create global hubs of logistics and finance, as well as world-scale "soft power" projects in education, culture and religion. States are deeply segmented and at the same time multi-purpose, following sometimes parallel, sometimes conflicting and sometimes mutually reinforcing logics.

The building of Arabian oil states was accompanied by citizenship, migration and labour regimes that fragmented local societies, creating separate social and spatial spheres for different nationalities with different informal rules and formal legal rights. In the economic sphere, the exposure of expatriates to capitalist labour markets makes the protection of nationals from exactly these markets possible. The internal fragmentation of Gulf oil states and societies explains the paradox that they are deeply integrated in world capitalist, cultural and migratory flows yet are able to shield their own citizens more than any other state from a globalized economy. They are "liberal" to the hilt in some parts of the administration and private economy, yet are based on patronage, patrimonial rule and parochial identity in others.

The Arabian oil states represent a curious hybrid of nation-state and empire, unique to the Global Indian Ocean and, indeed, the wider world. On the one hand, their penetration of most of local society is deep; state capacity to supervise, regulate and provide services directly to residents is high. While they do not extract taxes on any significant scale, their infrastructural power is that of a Tilly-style modern nation-state. On the other hand, these states contain parallel social communities that communicate little, share no common identity and operate under different rules. This is not unlike the multi-layered structure of British suzerainty in the 19th-century Indian Ocean, described as "patchwork of sovereignties" by Blom Hansen in chapter 2. Gulf rulers have no "bio-political" ambition to create political or ethnic uniformity among the large non-national communities in the Gulf—if anything, the interest is to reproduce existing divisions to prevent the formation of unified class and ideological interests.

This is not what a nation-state looks like—it is the social composition of an empire, in which different primordial communities and identities exist in parallel. On occasion, community leaders also speak on behalf of specific ethnic groups, as is the case with Indian billionaires in the UAE, who are informal representatives of their community vis-à-vis the state and finance local community societies and schools. Such intermediation through communities' separate social elites is characteristic of empire and is deeply embedded in the historical patterns of labour, migration and power of the Global Indian Ocean.

And yet, not all communities have leaders, and, where they exist, they have much less regulatory power and autonomy than, say, the leaders of millets in the Ottoman Empire. The state can reach out to individuals and regulate their lives directly when it needs to. The migration regime is permissive, yet states have the power to easily exclude individuals or communities if it wants to. The sovereignty that the Arab oil states have developed is unusual. They exert tight and direct state control over society yet have no ambition to integrate or reshape large parts of it. While most nation-states, especially liberal ones, eventually convert permanent residents into citizens, GCC states instead deliberately reinforce boundaries, using infrastructural power that is built on modern administrative tools imported from the West.

How does Arabian state-building compare to state formation processes in other world regions? It is commonplace to contrast genealogies of statehood in the Global South with Charles Tilly's account of European nation-states in which inter-state wars created modern states through the building of fiscal systems and powerful bureaucracies.[51] The Arabian oil states are obviously very different—but how? Existing theories of statehood outside the West sometimes describe weak states with limited infrastructure or geographic reach,[52] or infrastructure that was mostly built for lopsided purposes of colonial extraction,[53] or even "quasi-states" that only exist because international norms of sovereignty prop them up.[54]

The Arabian oil state is obviously much stronger than this, yet it is also quite different from the quintessential non-Western strong state, namely the East Asian "developmental state". In such states, powerful bureaucracies were built on the back of rapid capital accumulation, tight controls over and surplus extraction from the local working class, and—in at least some accounts—a strong sense of national cohesion.[55] The Arabian oil state is not extractive, private capital is relatively weak, and societies are not cohesive but deeply fragmented. It is the combination of social fragmentation with strong statehood that makes the GCC states stand out. State and society interpenetrate in some areas, notably in the patronage-oriented parts of national bureaucracies which provide employment for citizens.[56] At the same time, state elites retain strong autonomy and high capacity in other parts of the state.

The Gulf oil monarchies do not constitute an outright challenge to liberal order. They have adopted liberal social and economic rhetoric outside the political sphere, selectively appropriating liberal institutions and ideas, and do not actively seek to counter the (thin) dominance of global liberalism. At the same time, these are by no means liberal states and they pursue different objectives with different instruments from those of liberal states: the social and economic liberalism of Arabian oil states is reserved for elite state institutions and the private market. The states are patronage-based and conservative in areas controlled by and run for nationals. With the exception of Kuwait, the oil monarchies also espouse a political illiberalism that is more pronounced and unapologetic than even in Singapore, as serious elections and parties are absent. Conflicts between separate constituencies are not settled through an open political process, but through Gulf rulers' paternalistic adjudication, an essentially imperial strategy of rule. As the Kuwaiti example has shown, open political competition in a socially and economically segmented rentier society can indeed bring out deep cleavages and distributional conflict—which in the Kuwaiti case have undermined economic modernization.[57]

The Gulf states remain deeply integrated into the Global Indian Ocean and indeed are situated at its very core. As in the pre-oil imperial era, the GCC states have maintained strong linkages of transnational migration across the Indian Ocean, more so than other nation-states. Yet with growing state capacity, their control over these flows has become much tighter than used to be the case—while GCC citizens themselves have by and large ceased to be part of the migratory flows. Gulf oil states have imposed their sovereignty, albeit a sovereignty that is divided over different social and ethnic spheres in a way that is unusual for nation-states.

What then, in conclusion, is the outlook for the hybrid Gulf state model, at home and abroad? The system discussed in this chapter is predicated on oil rents and, with the potential exception of the free port of Dubai, not sustainable in its current form if and when rents drop further. As a result, while the UAE might seem to offer an attractive model to rulers in the rest of the Arab world, the paradigm is not replicable and does not pose a global threat to the liberal model.

Massive fiscal deficits in the lower-rent countries Bahrain, Oman and Saudi Arabia have already put considerable strain on public employment and forced citizens to gradually enter private labour markets. As citizen privileges erode, it is likely there will be growing social and economic friction between national and migrant communities of the type known from other countries with sizeable immigrant populations. A reduction in the number of expatriates is on the cards, which could in turn make it easier to allow some of them permanent residence. The state apparatus is likely to be trimmed and streamlined. Under Mohammad bin Salman, Saudi Arabia has recently undergone a process of elite consolidation in which he has reduced the autonomy of religious and princely fiefdoms. And while shrinking from dismantling the Saudi system of mass rent distribution, the prince also wants to make Saudi citizens part of the private market.

Jill Crystal has pointed out that a new Gulf social contract is emerging which is more focused on the provision of security and less on patronage.[58] If this is indeed the case, we are in the very early days of the transition, as reflected in the continuing scale of mass patronage for GCC citizens. Smaller, high-rent countries like the UAE, Kuwait and Qatar will be able to maintain the segmented Gulf state model for decades to come, based on mass expatriate employment in the private sector and ring-fenced patronage for citizens. Altogether, however, the coming decades will see growing pressure to integrate citizens into the private economy, reduce dependence on expatriate labour, and consolidate bureaucracies across the region. This all means, in essence, the erosion of the Arabian oil state model, despite its considerable achievements. After a long detour of institutional experimentation, the GCC countries might in the end evolve into more recognizable nation-states in the Global Indian Ocean, for better or for worse. They will in all likelihood remain politically illiberal, but be less unusual in their structures of authority, distribution and social identity.

6

WOMEN AS OBJECTS OF DEVELOPMENT

NEOLIBERALISM IN BANGLADESH

Lamia Karim

Since the 1980s, the Washington Consensus has dominated the international political economy as a template for economic growth and social modernization. Liberalization and deregulation have been sold not just through predictions of rapid economic expansion but as important to the emancipation of the female half of the population held back by tradition, state planning and other anachronisms in the Global Indian Ocean. Sri Lanka, Cambodia, Ethiopia and Mauritius can all be cited as prominent examples of women supposedly leading their country's integration into global markets.[1] While as, described in Harry Verhoeven's introduction to this book, the degree of adoption and imposition across Africa, the Middle East and Asia has varied considerably under liberal order's "thin hegemony" (see chapter 1), this chapter focuses on arguably the most prominent laboratory of blueprints for market-driven development: Bangladesh and its women. How did Bangladeshi women become the face of (neo)liberalism in the Global Indian Ocean?

141

Soon after its birth as an independent state on 16 December 1971, Western donor agencies identified Bangladesh as a laboratory for development and made its fledging non-government organizations (NGOs) a key ally in delivering market-friendly policies to the rural poor. In the context of weak states and impoverished economies, Bangladesh has long had an advantage over peer countries because it possesses an effective and vast NGO movement and prominent leaders (including Nobel laureate Muhammad Yunus of Grameen Bank and Sir Fazle Abed of BRAC, the world's largest NGO) who wanted to bring economic growth to rural areas by capitalizing on Western interest in rural Muslim women's economic and social emancipation.[2] From experimentations with population control in the 1970s to microfinance and the garment industry in the 1980s, global capital, development organizations and international trade agreements joined forces with the Bangladeshi state, local businesses and NGOs to invent women as disciplined market subjects. In the absence of a robust political left in the country to counter this offensive, Bangladeshi women were rendered voiceless by donors and their local allies. Development institutions and their researchers repackaged rural women as ideal market agents though they were not asked for their opinion. Their virtues were extolled in development literature, which showed them as controlling their reproductive bodies, managing financial resources to become small entrepreneurs, and working as docile factory workers for long hours to help the global economy grow. The market was the new god.

This chapter examines the role of women in the unfolding of the liberal order in the Global Indian Ocean from the vantage of Bangladesh, a peripheral state on the Indian subcontinent that has successfully instrumentalized women as agents of change. Much scholarship and policy literature continues to depict Bangladeshi women as the entrepreneurial vanguard of neoliberalism with a human face. Organized by NGOs as model citizens, they have come to symbolize the struggle to break the chains of rural patriarchy. Brochure after brochure shows Bangladeshi women sitting in groups learning about fiscal responsibility, raising ducks and chickens as small-scale entrepreneurs in their homes, walking to markets to sell products, and sitting in assembly lines stitching T-shirts and jeans for

Walmart and H&M. In 2018, more than twenty million rural women were microfinance beneficiaries and another four million worked in the global garment industry in Bangladesh. Even more significant, this phenomenon was occurring in a predominantly Muslim society where women were often assumed to be "oppressed" and without much economic agency, let alone entrepreneurial instincts, a point that has been strongly countered by feminist anthropologists.[3]

The chapter builds on the idea of liberal order as "the Pax Americana and the promotion of free market and liberal democracy", as defined in Verhoeven's introduction to the volume. The study is located within a tradition of critical scholarship seeking to understand the multiple logics of neoliberalism, which was pioneered by David Harvey. For Harvey, neoliberalism is a political project. He argues that when organized labour in the US gained influence through the Environmental Protection Agency and the Occupational Safety and Health Administration, the capitalist class reorganized to fight back, first at home in America and later through the export of the Washington Consensus to the Indian Ocean and other developing regions (for details, see Verhoeven's introduction). Capitalists sought to break the power of labour by making "domestic labor competitive with global labor".[4] Manufacturing jobs were offshored to countries like Bangladesh, Indonesia and Lesotho where wages were very low and workers' rights practically nonexistent. On the political-ideological front, by 1982 the World Bank and the International Monetary Fund had replaced virtually all their Keynesian economists with supply-side theorists who argued for austerity programmes, that is, less government interference, withdrawal of subsidies, and deregulated labour and product markets.[5] The Bank designed austerity policies (also known as structural adjustment programmes) for developing countries through their loan schemes. Almost from independence onwards, Bangladesh was financially dependent on such external programmes and on Western aid organizations. These agencies played a pivotal role not only in shaping the economy but in inventing rural women as market agents: the Washington Consensus merged social and macroeconomic policies as it sought to broaden and deepen capitalist growth.

Several global trends converged in the 1970s–1980s that would ensure Bangladesh became a centre of neoliberalism for the poor.

Market deregulation and the offshoring of manufacturing jobs in the West coincided with the demand for the inclusion of women in development projects by feminists working in international aid agencies. Bangladeshi figures partnered eagerly with these social activists and global financiers. The founder of Grameen Bank, Nobel laureate Professor Muhammad Yunus, became a purveyor of these neoliberal ideas to the global community. Seen as an iconic figure of capitalism for the poor who was admired by both the neoliberal right and the feminist left, Professor Yunus famously declared, "Human beings are not born to work for anybody else. For millions of years that we were on the planet, we never worked for anybody. We are go-getters. We are farmers. We are hunters. We lived in caves and found our own food, we didn't send job applications. So, [entrepreneurship] is our tradition." The fact that Yunus glossed over the central role of slavery and servitude in human history is remarkable. What is perhaps even more astounding is how the global media and the international agencies adopted his ideas and created him as an ally of the poor, a "Gandhi-like" figure who gave capitalism a human face. The newly independent state of Bangladesh was fertile ground for such an experiment in neoliberal ideas.

This chapter offers a case study of women's evolving economic roles under market reforms. Harvey has elaborated on the dismantling of the Ford–Keynesian welfare state as well as of security of employment under Thatcher in England and Reagan in the US and its replacement by "a regime of flexible accumulation".[6] He notes that flexible accumulation rests on remaking labour processes, markets, financial services, products and consumption into forms that have intensified "uneven development" between geographical areas.[7] The concepts of flexible accumulation and "accumulation through dispossession" have entered the Bangladeshi economy by inventing women as willing market subjects, free agents who enter into financial transactions as informed actors. These women are trapped in a condition of postmodernity where unrestrained capital dramatically reorganizes their lives while simultaneously they remain within the patriarchy of the home.

The growing emphasis on laissez-faire capitalism in Verhoeven's the historically "thin liberal order" of the Global Indian Ocean—what some would call "market fundamentalism"[8]—has led to a shift away from states as the pivotal players to an alliance with international donor agencies, NGOs and multinational corporations. These actors often have contradictory objectives that create conflict with the objectives of states. For example, Scandinavian donor agencies encourage more women in local government through their aid programmes whereas a state may want to consolidate its power by absorbing local male elites into its governance structure.

But has the state withered away under the growing impact of global liberalism? I believe we need to be cautious about accepting this argument, especially when we witness the power of the state in maintaining borders and regulating particular ethnic groups, for example in the Rohingya crisis in Bangladesh and Myanmar (see also Chua Beng Huat's chapter 3). Leela Fernandes reminds us that "an effect of these very real processes of restructuring is a danger of presuming that the state has in effect retreated or vanished in the post-liberalization period or that the neoliberal state is marked by a clear historical break from earlier forms of modern state power".[9] Instead, she urges us to consider how the state is being reinvented rather than disappearing into the dustbin of history.

Women and the liberal order

Ester Boserup's *Woman's Role in Economic Development* (1970) was path-breaking in drawing attention to women's exclusion in national planning. Boserup analysed how the Green Revolution and large-scale projects in Africa failed to consider *actual* women's economic activities and instead ended up further impoverishing women. In fact, rapid mechanization of agriculture adversely affected women across the globe. Large-scale development projects closed off the commons, and dams flooded adjacent lands, areas where women had traditionally gathered firewood, vegetables and fish. Boserup, along with the rise of second-wave feminism in the West, positioned women as a central part of development schemes.[10] Simultaneously, feminists in the Global South also critiqued the Western paradigm of female emancipation that saw women as autonomous subjects.[11]

Despite the growing intellectual and practical discontent with mainstream discourse, Bangladeshi NGOs and feminists did not look to Indian Ocean societies for alternative models, such as the Self-Employed Women's Association (SEWA) in India, a trade union of small-scale women producers and vendors that offered low-interest loans, savings and pension plans. The liberal development blueprint, accompanied as it was by lucrative financial assistance, became the chosen model. Feminists working inside organizations such as the World Bank, USAID and the UK Department for International Development advocated the inclusion of women in development projects. As early as 1973, the US Congress passed the Percy Amendment, which required all US bilateral aid programmes to "enhance the integration of women into the national economics of developing countries".[12]

In 1975, a global consensus was reached at the International Year of the Woman Conference held in Mexico City. Participants agreed on the "critical importance of increasing women's economic and decision-making roles not just to help women but to accelerate the achievement of national development".[13] Following the conference, a programme officer at the Ford Foundation, Adrienne Germain, wrote in the *New York Times* that "Hundreds of thousands of women in Bangladesh and Indonesia have lost their only source of income (rice husking) because machines can do the job faster".[14] In her ground-breaking piece, Germain went on to debunk three views against the inclusion of women in work:

(i) "Policymakers, primarily male, believe that the issue is 'women's lib' and therefore culturally imperialistic. It is neither. The issue is how to enable all people to be productive in order to reduce poverty."

(ii) "Policymakers have their own ideals of what women should and should not do, which often contradict the reality of poor women's lives."

(iii) "It is argued that national economic development problems have to solved before women's lives can be improved. The argument ignores the fact that women's work is part of the solution."

These discussions among feminists working in the United Nations, USAID and other international organizations led to the United Nations Decade for Women (1975–85), mandating development agencies to come up with new models that included women as participants. From the 1970s through the 1990s, policymakers and feminists working on women's issues advocated the end of gender discrimination,[15] resulting in the Convention for the Elimination of All Forms of Discrimination against Women (CEDAW) in 1979. At the Cairo Conference on Population (1994), representatives from 179 countries came together to address impediments to women's full realization of their potential. The 1995 Women's Conference in Beijing further advanced issues regarding women's economic, legal and political rights and participation, and signatory countries were required to give women access to legal and political spheres. One such provision aimed for one-third representation of women at the lowest rung of government (e.g., the union council in Bangladesh, the panchayat in India). By the 1980s, the idea that women's economic participation amounted to progress had firmly entered global discourse and practice. Aid officials working in various agencies identified women in poor countries as "resources" for donors and nations. The focus was on mainstreaming women into the economy, instead of understanding the social restraints imposed on women's activities in society.

According to liberal feminism (here I refer to feminists working in multilateral agencies such as the World Bank), women's work led to better fertility control, improved family welfare, and an intensified individual ethos of succeeding despite the absence of social safety nets.[16] As Carla Freeman has noted, "this neoliberal logic fits nicely with the microfinance agenda, which promotes women's empowerment through market-disciplined employment and entrepreneurship".[17] As the liberal order seemed victorious and without opposition after 1989, women were reimagined as motivated, self-driven, entrepreneurial market subjects who did not need the assistance of the state for credit, education and training. Instead, with microloans, they would operate successful petty trades. Some did succeed, but many fell through the cracks.[18] When small enterprises operated by women failed, the women were seen as being incapable of fiscal discipline, as having failed—not the policies themselves that targeted women without adequately vetting the profitability of operating small enterprises in the rural economy.

The question of how many egg-sellers a rural village in Bangladesh or Nepal could sustain was not one that policymakers posed while making funds available for loan schemes. Instead, what was taken for success was how many women were enrolled in these programmes, how many loans were extended, and how many loans were recovered. These statistical measurements were hardly the best method of evaluating how well the programmes worked on the ground. It should also be noted that success stories are rare within development circles, and hence the story of poor, Muslim women in Bangladesh making it on their own took on a life force of its own, with policymakers, researchers and the media all becoming enraptured with its endless possibilities. It is no surprise then that ideas of self-help for women remained unexamined within the liberal doctrine, and success stories of women's empowerment proliferated through NGOs and multilateral aid organizations.

Nonetheless, many feminists critiqued this model as the "add and stir" approach. Harding termed this trend "dedevelopment". According to Sandra Harding, "development has often meant only incorporating women into work that benefits others but not themselves; that destroys the environment upon which their daily subsistence often depends; that leaves them with no time or resources to provide for their children and others who are dependent upon them".[19] To bring capitalism into pre-modern societies, NGOs wrote scripts that showcased the "third world" woman as resourceful whereas her male counterpart was the key obstacle. While the "third world" woman was hailed as an unsung entrepreneur, the "third world" man was depicted as a drunkard and a gambler who would squander resources. Thus, agencies targeted women as central to economic transformation for their industry, morality and thriftiness.

This bias in market-driven liberalization had multiple effects. The focus on the woman individuated her as an autonomous market subject who was now positioned against the interests of the patriarchal family. If the family wanted money for a new roof on the house, she was supposed to defy them and instead invest in her chicken business in the expectation that a few years later she would earn more money to invest in her family. This development logic was incompatible with the way women's social roles were circumscribed by family and society. In farming communities, men and women work together, although their spheres of work are different.

In this neoliberal reimagination of women as hamstrung by rural patriarchy, the role of the state was ignored. Under the privatization policies of the World Bank, which required the removal of subsidies, the state was forced to abolish agricultural subsidies on seeds, fertilizers and pesticides, thus making prices skyrocket. Unable to purchase necessary inputs in the unregulated market, millions of farmers fell deep into debt. In India, these policies led to widespread suicide among farmers. In Bangladesh, suicides did not occur at the same rate because since the 1980s NGOs had stepped in with massive amounts of loans for rural women, who then passed them on to their husbands. What occurred instead was that women became the hidden face of rural indebtedness since they were the borrowers, a point that was ignored by NGOs, which needed to show success in order to receive funds from their Western donors.

Localizing the global

Bangladesh is unique for a number of reasons. Except for Bangladesh, no other independence movement in South Asia has resulted in an independent state (see Woldemariam's chapter 7). The very nature of its secession from Pakistan in 1971, after a relatively brief, nine-month freedom struggle, pushed Bangladesh with its 75 million people onto the global stage. The first prime minister experimented with some socialist policies in 1972 by nationalizing banks, and jute, paper and sugar mills. By 1975, the country was under a military dictatorship, which introduced privatization and deregulation to attract foreign direct investments, long before the neoliberal revolution fully hit the Atlantic world or demanded structural adjustments in Africa. This early-onset market liberalization in Bangladesh offers a unique perspective on free market ideology and the positioning of rural women as market agents. Interestingly, designating women as the drivers of economic change was not a well-articulated plan of the Bangladeshi state. Instead, it was an ad hoc process in which global discourses of Women-in-Development (WID) of the 1970s coincided with the military state's eagerness to court overseas dollars.

149

At its birth, Bangladesh posed a massive challenge to both its leaders and development economists and aid organizations. The war of independence had wrecked the country's infrastructure, leaving its national exchequer empty. Ten million refugees who had fled to neighbouring India had to be resettled. The rapidly growing population was among the world's poorest. In a famous study of the 1974 famine that killed 1.5 million people, Faaland and Parkinson noted the requirement of a "continuing massive injection of aid" to jumpstart economic development. For them, the importance of Bangladesh did not lie in its geopolitical significance but in its "availability as testbench for two opposing systems of development, collective and compulsory on the one hand, and a less fettered working of the private enterprise on the other".[20] These economists argued that if the poverty problem could be solved in Bangladesh—a land facing Malthusian catastrophe with a very high population density, poverty and illiteracy—then lesser problems could be alleviated in other contexts. But the first democratically elected government was rife with corruption and inefficiency, leading Henry Kissinger to call Bangladesh "a bottomless basket", even if US aid money kept flowing to Dhaka, the capital. These circumstances made Bangladesh uniquely positioned to become a laboratory for development ideas.

At a national level, the ruling generals (1975–90) followed the roadmap of market reforms favoured by neoliberals as a pillar of domestic prosperity and international order in the Global Indian Ocean as elsewhere. They implemented structural adjustment policies, to "reduce the budget deficit, reform the public sector, withdraw subsidies on such items as food, fertilizer and petroleum, and liberalize the trade regime".[21] The first military dictator, Ziaur Rahman, proposed the 1975 Revised National Industrial Policy; he went on to say that "the state would never nationalize private enterprise".[22] The military's focus was on consolidating its urban base by building alliances with an emergent business elite class in Bangladesh. In the 1979 national elections, 28 per cent of the newly elected members of parliament were industrialists and traders; a third of the executive committee of Rahman's Bangladesh National Party was composed of business elites who helped to shape government policy.[23] Many of these political cronies borrowed heavily from public banks and then defaulted, and the clannish relationship between the government and the business elites prevented any formal prosecution of the defaulters. The second military ruler, General Muhammad Ershad (1982–90), accelerated the pace of liberalization and privatization to court more capital from the international financial institutions.

The military's aims were twofold: to attract development dollars from the West and to support efforts in women's economic development. The military allowed Western aid agencies unfettered access to rural areas. These international organizations depended on local NGOs to carry out their development mandates. The development agencies needed a streamlined and efficient aid delivery system; whereas the state was weak in rural areas, the NGOs were locally present and willing to implement externally designed programmes. This led to an alliance between Western development organizations and the local NGO sector which over time flourished into a mutually beneficial relationship. The development agencies needed the NGOs to take their messages of women and development to villages, and the NGOs needed these agencies for funding. Western development assistance went to the NGO sector, and not to the state, which was regarded as corrupt and inefficient.

Another feature that set Bangladesh apart from India was the evisceration of its left. In the 1970s, the Naxalite movement was strong in West Bengal (later to be brutally eliminated by Indira Gandhi), while across the border in Bangladesh the left political parties had already splintered over the liberation struggle. For the hardcore communists, the 1971 struggle for independence did not include the question of class struggle; it was a bourgeois movement rooted in Bengali language and culture. The less orthodox leftists saw the liberation of the country as an opportunity to rebuild society through the NGO sector. Their goal was to educate, organize and agitate for land distribution and control of the rural power structure through the NGO sector. Thus, the NGO sector bifurcated the left. Later, under military rule, the left political parties were pushed to the brink of extinction. By 1989, with the fall of the Berlin Wall, the left also lost its ideological moorings, and some within the group began to consider how to think about politics outside a political party affiliation, and formed the National Committee to Protect Oil, Gas, Mineral

Resources, Power and Ports.[24] As for the rural people, they made calculated choices. While the NGOs could offer them resources and jobs, the left political parties only offered them ideology. As villagers have said to me, "I cannot feed my children with ideology". They went to the NGOs for money, resources and training. And through their involvement with NGO activities and training sessions, rural subscribers were inducted into an ideology of entrepreneurship.

The state and its women

Alongside these economic changes, each decade after independence introduced a new role for women in Bangladesh. At the country's birth, thousands of women were marked as war heroines —*biran-ganas*—having been raped by the Pakistani military during 1971. These women bore the brunt of social ostracism as the patriarchal nationalist state used their violated bodies as a symbol of the suffering of East Pakistanis (now Bangladeshis) under West Pakistani (now Pakistan) military rule, without rehabilitating these women socially and economically.[25]

Simultaneously, Malthusian fears of overpopulation in the 1970s configured Bangladesh as a population at risk from diseases, famines, and floods and in need of a "Green Revolution".[26] This made it the ideal testing ground for bold—some would say morally, politically or ecologically unacceptable—developmental initiatives. International organizations stepped in and introduced birth control devices, including Depo Provera for poor women.[27] Today, Bangladesh has a lower birth rate, at 2.14 per woman, than Pakistan at 3.55 and India at 2.40 (2015 figures). Large-scale population planning intervention programmes were introduced by the government with the support of international organizations. Yet while population control was considered a success in Bangladesh, thousands of unmarried young women and men were sterilized without their consent. However, this population control programme was not investigated by the media or by Western governments that funded these programmes, unlike in India where activist groups raised these issues after the end of emergency rule in the 1970s. The government has never been held to account for its brutal Malthusian policies, nor were its international partners.

Military dictatorship turned the country towards a pan-Islamic nationalism and to the Arab states of the Middle East. Thus, from the late 1970s, a national discourse inflected by Islamic ideals began to develop. Scores of Bangladeshis went to work in the oilfields and boom towns of the Gulf and they brought back with them a newfound Islamic identity rooted in Saudi cultural practices around Islam. While Blom Hansen's chapter 2 illustrates the inter-oceanic diffusion of values, customs and political ideas through migration across the Global Indian Ocean from the perspective of the *longue durée*, this new connection between a historically syncretic Bengali Islam[28] and more recent Salafi practices from the Gulf bifurcated an earlier Bengali identity rooted in Bengali language and culture. This new idea of being a proper Muslim was also influenced by the regional politics of the Indian Ocean. Bangladesh's closest neighbour is India, a country that is hegemonic and uses its power to shape the economic policies of the Bangladeshi government. Indian geopolitics also influenced many Muslims in Bangladesh to seek an identity that separated them from Hindus in India (for many Bangladeshis, these two terms are conflated) and turn towards Saudi Arabia as a source of selfhood.

While a segment of Bangladeshi society sought its identity in the Islam of Saudi Arabia, another part championed a Bengali national identity grounded in the liberation war. The incursion of these competing ideas was reproduced in the bodies of Bangladeshi women as many women began to adhere to more conservative (sometimes fully Salafi) attire and decorum, some by choice, others because of security reasons while working in public places. Along with it, changes in forms of address (*Allah hafez* as opposed to *khuda hafez*) and the increased use of Arabic words in Bangla have become the new norm. The implications of these transformations were projected onto the bodies of poor women who came out to work neither for modernity nor for democracy, but simply to feed their hungry children. These vulnerable women were deemed "un-Islamic" by the clergy and rural powerbrokers, who felt that NGOs and women's new economic and political roles disenfranchised them, and women faced a series of backlashes in the 1990s.[29]

By the early 2000s, women in Bangladesh had secured two achievements: in 2006, the Grameen Bank won the Nobel Peace Prize, a first for the country; and by 2010, Bangladesh had the second-largest garment industry in the world. In both sectors, Bangladeshi women dominated as entrepreneurs and factory workers. It was a development miracle whereby women took control of their lives without any assistance from the state. Scores of researchers arrived to study the hidden potential of Bangladeshi women as disciplined subjects of the liberal order. They wrote books, reports and surveys, illustrating the promise of liberalism for poor women. This iconic woman of development was entrepreneurial, hardworking, thrifty, invested in her children's well-being, and an asset to her family.[30] More fundamentally, she was breaking the chains of Islamic patriarchy, transforming gender relations and becoming a market subject. But this story of Bangladeshi women's remarkable progress under economic liberalism is also full of traps that these studies have largely failed to address.

Women's roles in two sectors

In the final section, I examine women's economic roles in two sectors that have been celebrated as beneficial to their financial and social empowerment. The first narrative is about the creation of Grameen phone ladies or cell phone operators in the rural economy. The second story concerns the life cycle of garment workers who sew clothes for retail giants like Walmart and H&M. Both case studies show how women's work and agency are nested inside the competitiveness of the market about which they lack knowledge or navigational skills.

Cell phone operators

In 1999, the Grameen phone lady was a highly celebrated entrepreneurial idea promoted in the West, especially in the *New York Times*, which published images of women posing as cell phone operators. Bangladeshi women, called "phone ladies", were sold cell phones through the Grameen Polli Phone programme. They received a loan to purchase the phone and all its accessories (such as battery and charger), and they would charge a nominal price to rural people to make phone calls. The idea was to create greater connectivity in rural areas while generating an income for these women. For example, a rural farmer could call the markets in several towns and find out the price of rice before he decided what, where and how much to sell. The availability of market information would also help to cut down the middleman who procured rice from farmers at below-market prices. The idea appealed to Western publics and development agencies because of their lack of knowledge of how local markets operated and of women's restricted social mobility in rural society.

When Grameen Bank launched the rural cell phone programme in the late 1990s, there was almost no market penetration by other cell phone companies. Grameen Polli Phone was a joint venture of Grameen Phone and Grameen Bank, which cost-shared different aspects of the rural phone operations. Grameen Phone had the responsibility of making the network available, they activated the phones and sent the bills directly to Grameen Bank. Grameen Bank remained responsible for identifying the cell phone operators, issuing the phone loans, and recovering the payments. The "phone ladies" were carefully selected by Grameen Bank personnel. Women who had a successful loan payment history, and whose husbands had a retail shop in the market, were chosen. At least one family member had to possess some fluency with English so they could recognize the letters and numbers on the phone.

With the loans, the women purchased the cell phone, battery charger, SIM card, antenna and so on. These phones either stayed with the women in their homes, or, if the family owned a retail shop in the market, the husband or an adult son handled the phone business. Those women with cell phones in their homes operated as rural phone kiosks. They had a husband who was either overseas as a migrant worker or was too ill to work: these "phone ladies" thus operated as de facto heads of households. Customers visited them and rented the phone by the minute. In the early days of the programme, women often hosted customers in their homes late at night when making calls to their relatives living overseas. Between 2005 and 2007, most of the women I met had successful businesses, sharing several features. They had autonomy within the household, their husbands supported them, and they possessed a certain market *savoir faire*. An important social dynamic that ensued from their business was that women met non-kin males in their homes to conduct these phone transactions.

155

Grameen Polli Phone started as a rural monopoly, but within a few years other cell phone operators (Banglalink, Telecom, City Cell, Warid, Teletalk) began to compete for rural subscribers by underselling Grameen Phone. Within a short time, a majority of rural people had access to cell phones and they no longer came to the Grameen phone ladies to make calls. Among the 300,000 phone ladies in 2007, the few women who had paid off their loans and invested in some alternative operation, such as opening a tailor's shop or a small grocery shop, fared well. The rest, however, found themselves heavily indebted. In 2002, phones were sold at $696, which included the phone purchase loan, mandatory security deposit, mandatory Grameen pension scheme, and one-time connection fee. These rates have since then come down substantially. By 2005, many of these women were stuck with huge loan payments but with no income from their phone investment. Part of the reason was the incursion of new telephone companies. But the more important point is that these women had no knowledge of how the phone market could change through competition. The NGOs used the women's lack of knowledge as well as their poverty and vulnerability to build their own institutions.[31]

Cell phone technology has revolutionized communications in Bangladesh, and it has had a positive effect on small businesses where owners (mostly male) could monitor their sales through communication. What is less clear is to what extent these phone sales have helped to move women out of poverty. Sterne and Stabile ask whether "Bangladeshi women, who certainly know their needs better than USAID, non-governmental organizations (NGOs), and multinational corporations that stand to benefit from expansion of markets for various new technologies, [were] consulted about their everyday life and needs".[32]

Loans and entrepreneurship are precarious activities. Women borrowers did not control the environment in which these loans circulated. For example, if the phone was stolen or broken, the woman, as the primary borrower, still had to repay the loan to the NGO. Unlike the rural moneylender, who had resources such as "muscle men" to coerce payment, women had no recourse. They depended on the goodwill of people to pay them back. Accordingly, when loan defaults occurred, women came under tremendous pressure from the NGOs to pay up. The borrowers were constantly on the verge of precarity since their ability to pay was dependent on a range of factors over which they had no control.

Women in the garment industry

On 12 December 2012, 112 workers burned to death in the Tazreen factory fire in Bangladesh. Four months later, on 24 April 2013, the eight-storey Rana Plaza factory collapsed, killing over 1,100 workers and injuring 2,500 more. The factory collapse, the worst industrial accident since the 1911 Triangle Shirtwaist Factory fire in New York City, brought to global attention the horrific conditions under which workers were forced to stitch clothes for Western labels like Joe Fresh, Gap, Mango, H&M, Zara, Old Navy and Walmart.

Industrial work has led to a radical transformation of expected gender norms, social roles and identities that shape family, marriage and human relations in contemporary Bangladeshi society. There are four million women in this industry. They are recent rural-to-urban migrants, entering around the average age of 15 and exiting by 40. Poverty, environmental degradation and domestic abuse have forced these women to come to the city in search of a better life. This is precariat labour—workers with very low wages, in unsafe work conditions, without union representation, and often without any hiring documents. These women tend to have low levels of literacy. They are often divorced or abandoned by their husbands, and have thus become single heads of households, a new social formation in a conservative Muslim society. The migration of workers has also led to a weakening of the extended family system, as these women weave nuclear families in the city that are not connected to traditional forms of familial support.

Within the span of thirty years, from 1978 to the 2000s, the ready-made garment manufacturing industry (RMG) in Bangladesh became second to China in apparel production, and, according to experts, it may soon replace China as Chinese garment labour migrates to higher-paying jobs.[33] This rapid and unregulated growth has resulted in over four million young women working in 4,328 factories scattered around the capital city, Dhaka.[34] By the end of 2017, garment exports totalled $30 billion—four-fifths of total Bangladeshi exports, and 15 per cent of its gross domestic product (GDP).[35] The phenomenal rise of this industry can be attributed primarily to low wage competitiveness in Bangladesh. The fledging garment industry of the 1970s was a beneficiary of the Multi-Fiber Agreement (1974–94), which restricted the import of manufactured clothes from middle-income countries of the 1970s—China, South Korea and Taiwan—to US and EU markets, but allowed unrestricted access to garments produced in the least-developing countries like Bangladesh, Sri Lanka and Vietnam. The EU was particularly influential by giving apparel exports preferential access to its markets.

On a global scale, market liberalization and the tariff-free status for least-developed countries encouraged South Korean garment manufacturers to seek out joint partnerships with Bangladeshi business elites, and the first company was set up in 1978. When the garment industry began to take off in the 1980s, the Bangladeshi state encouraged the industry to grow in an unregulated way in order for capital formation to develop. The 1990s saw greater flexibility in trade liberalization policies worldwide. The WTO's Agreement on Clothing and Textiles (1995–2005) allowed Bangladesh to continue its exports to Western markers without quota restrictions. By the end of WTO's tariff-free status in 2005, the ready-made garment sector had ballooned from $3.5 billion to almost $10 billion in exports.[36]

In the aftermath of the Rana Plaza fire in 2013, EU governments initiated an Accord on Fire and Building Safety with 150 global retailers and factory management to ensure factory safety standards. Factories were upgraded to international safety standards, an eight-hour workday was scheduled, overtime was limited to two hours per day, wages were increased from $30 to $67, and unionization was made easier. However, workers' victories were short-lived. High inflation and housing costs eroded their earnings. At the same time, companies pressured workers to produce twice as many pieces per day, without any overtime pay during regular work hours. If workers failed to meet their new daily quota, the company docked their wages and managers called them lazy and stupid. Inability to meet one's daily quota for several days meant losing one's job altogether.

Despite these changes, factory management routinely failed to pay workers the wages and bonuses they had earned, ignored weekly holidays, and kept wages flat between 1994 and 2006. Prior to 2013, the sector typically had factories with faulty electrical outlets; no fire escapes, fire doors or sprinklers; crowded stairwells; and padlocked doors and windows with iron grilles. Factory owners illegally locked workers inside factories and often forced them to work 12- to 14-hour shifts to meet quotas. As a result, factory accidents and workers' injuries and deaths have been an ongoing feature of the apparel industry.

Failure to guarantee factory workers the protection of a social clause in the WTO trade agreements was a major setback for women's labour rights. While the WTO introduced patent rights protections for pharmaceutical companies and agro-businesses, it failed to include a social clause to protect workers. Adding the social clause would have ensured minimum labour standards, including "prohibition on child labour, forced labour and discrimination, and with union rights as the key measure for addressing all working conditions".[37] Within the WTO debates, EU countries advocated higher labour standards for workers, whereas developing countries argued that these labour codes would handicap their manufacturing advantage.

Among feminists, the issue of the social clause was hotly debated, with one group supporting improved protection of workers' rights,[38] while another group looked upon garment jobs as "good jobs in context", which referred to the absence of alternative employment opportunities for women: in this view, garment factory jobs were the best available option for poverty-stricken women.[39] It was the latter group that successfully defeated the inclusion of the social clause in WTO trade agreements in the 1990s.

These women are workers but they are also lovers, mothers, daughters, sisters, wives and political subjects. Yet, most of the voluminous research produced about female labour in Bangladesh refers to them in statistical terms—as the lowest-paid workers in the world ($30 in 2013), the poorest workers working in extremely hazardous situations, and so on. While these statements are true, they do not reveal what these women aspire to through work. A sense of pity engulfs these narratives, obscuring the aspirations of these women, diminishing their humanity, and centring them as abject and immobile subjects. While their lives are often harrowingly sad, these women can still create moments of pleasure in their lives, which many fail to recognize.

At work, their bodies are injured beyond repair from repetitious assembly-line work under strong lights. Poor wages have prevented workers from getting adequate nutrition or medical attention, worsening their health within a few years of factory work. At home, they are often at risk from gender-based violence from their husbands and partners when they refuse to turn over their wages. In fact, this nuclearized private life in the city is far more precarious than their former village life. These women are disconnected from the traditional forms of familial support (a father or an uncle who could intervene on their behalf) that they could depend on in the village. So, in the event of a misfortune, whether at work or in their private lives, they are on their own as isolated young women in the anonymity of the city.

Conclusion

As this chapter has shown, Bangladesh has long been a laboratory for various experiments of "development" as defined by the powerful in the contemporary liberal order. From birth control in the 1970s to the idea of finance as holding the key to helping the poor escape poverty, Bangladeshi women have been the guinea pigs for change and its supposed cheerleaders. Despite evidence to the contrary, they continue to be held up as a model to promote liberal economic and social policies, most recently under the theme of "financial inclusion of the world's poor". Bangladeshi NGOs now play a pivotal role in offering their services to the international banking sector. For example, Mastercard Foundation and BRAC have partnered to bring financial services to poor people in Uganda. The head of BRAC, Fazle Abed, has said that what they have learned in Uganda would help them scale up their programmes all through Africa.[40] Similarly, garment factory owners from Bangladesh went to advise the Ethiopian government on how to set up garment factories, and garment workers from Bangladesh have been taken to Jordan and Mauritius to work in factories owned by Chinese and Indians. This global circulation of neoliberal ideas and practices occurs through circuits in which vulnerable Bangladeshi women are represented as capitalist agents but in reality have little say or influence over these processes.

Market liberalization in the Global Indian Ocean has created some avenues for income generation for women, but it has also positioned them in precarity as a result of market uncertainties. Two of Bangladesh's most prominent sectors, microfinance and the garment industry, which are vital to the global image of itself that the Bangladeshi government projects into the world, are connected through women's work. Rural women can borrow loans from microfinance institutions when they have daughters working in garment factories in the city. These factory women's paychecks help the family to pay off its loans. Small loans give poor people money with which to settle old debts, invest in petty trade, pay dowries, and purchase consumer goods that they did not previously have access to. Similarly, the garment factory worker brings home a steady paycheck that allows her to invest in herself and her family, while gaining self-confidence through industrial work and an urban lifestyle. These are some of the positive aspects of work in the shadows of the capital.

The Bangladeshi economy has benefited enormously from the garment industry. In 2017, the industry earned $30 billion, making it the backbone of the country's exports. What remains unexamined is to the extent to which women's lives might have fared better had they access to social safety nets. If the state had regulated the microfinance and garment industries from their inception and implemented laws to protect rural borrowers and workers, there might have been a different scenario. While some regulations have been implemented since the mid-2000s (a Microcredit Regulatory Authority in 2006 for greater accountability and transparency, the passage of a labour law in 2006, and the post-Rana Plaza upgrades to factories), they have failed to address some core issues. In the microfinance sector, Professor Yunus has spoken out against the commercialization of microfinance loans which led to the suicide of hundreds of farmers in 2010 from the SKS Microfinance scam in Andhra Pradesh, India.[41] In the garment sectors, unions are still dysfunctional. In the US, the 1911 Triangle Shirtwaist Factory fire, which killed 146 workers, mostly young women and girls, gave rise to stronger workplace safety protection, a workday and better wages, as well as the emergence of unions—a true turning point. In contrast, four years after the Rana Plaza accident, 97.5 per cent of garment factories still remain non-unionized, despite the government's acceptance of an EU demand to ease unionization rules. The factory owners, the Bangladeshi state, EU governments and global retailers are all aware of this situation, yet change is slow in coming.

Neoliberal ideas have entered into the lives of NGO loan recipients and factory women with far-reaching effects on individuals. Recipients call themselves "entrepreneurs", a euphemism they have adopted from NGO discourse. When it is pointed out to them that they do not own their materials (the phone for example), and that the phones are confiscated if they cannot pay their loan obligations, they admit that they are actually contract workers for NGOs. In contrast, the factory workers are slightly more educated than their rural counterparts and have exposure to living in the city. Unlike the rural entrepreneur, the factory worker thinks of her wages as her right, and routinely takes to the streets to demonstrate if she remains unpaid. Factory workers are more political, but they are not organized because the trade union movement was crushed at the inception of the industry. For these women, living in the city, walking the urban streets, seeking new jobs, meeting potential spouses at work, these novel situations have contributed to some modest notions around autonomy in their lives. Some of the workers want to go overseas to Mauritius or Jordan to work for higher wages. A window has been opened to a new life of opportunity. This is a tragic chimera because the worker still has little control over her life circumstances. This chapter offers a cautionary tale. If we look behind the masks of these stories of success, we find extremely vulnerable and highly indebted women.

7

DIVIDE AND RULE

PARTITION AND ILLIBERAL STATE-BUILDING
IN THE HORN OF AFRICA

Mike Woldemariam

Partition—defined as "the division of sovereign states into new, functionally sovereign political units"—has been a major political feature of the post-World War II Indian Ocean world, perhaps more so than any other region of the globe.[1] The collapse of imperial orders in the Global Indian Ocean after World War II made the issue of partition relevant through various historical processes. In the Indian subcontinent, late colonial administrators decided in 1947–8 that the only way to preserve the stability of their previously unified colonial possession was to "divide and quit".[2] This produced astonishing levels of violence and forced migration and, subsequently, decades of rivalry between the independent states of India and Pakistan. In Yemen, the colonial subdivision of the territory in the 19th century became the basis for two independent states that struggled to find a route to reunification for much of the Cold War. In 1990, North and South Yemen were reunited by force of arms, but that union remains tenuous. Britain's colonial partition of the Malay Peninsula reasserted itself in 1965 when the early post-independence merger of Malaysia and Singapore fell apart and Singapore became independent (see Chua Beng Huat's chapter 3). In Ethiopia–Eritrea, Somalia–Somaliland, the Sudans, and Indonesia–East Timor, the incorporation of smaller territories with distinct colonial identities into larger neighbours triggered long wars of secession that eventually resulted in formal or de facto partition at the end of the Cold War.

This chapter examines the relationship between partition and the domestic political arrangements of resulting successor states in the context of the "thin liberal order" that characterizes the Global Indian Ocean (as discussed extensively in Verhoeven's introduction to this book). Here one notices interesting variation. The partition of the Indian subcontinent, for instance, yielded two successor states whose domestic political trajectories diverged in important ways: India emerged as the world's largest experiment in democracy, while Pakistan suffered decades of weak civilian government, repeated military intervention in politics, and periodic bouts of authoritarianism. In yet another case, the Sudans, partition produced two fragile authoritarian states that were beset by mass violence, economic collapse, and existential challenges to the integrity of the central government.

What then determines the kinds of domestic political systems that have emerged after partition in the Global Indian Ocean? Why, in some contexts, are democratic institutions built and sustained? Why do illiberal models of political development emerge in other contexts? And what explains differences in state capacity, both at the centre and the peripheral margins of the state? Under what circumstances are successor states strong and robust, or fragile and weak, with contested ability to exert their authority across geographic space and various policy domains?

The intellectual stakes of such questions are two-fold. First, partition has been a hotly debated issue among international security scholars. This is particularly true in the context of the contemporary Global Indian Ocean, where policymakers have considered alternatives to protracted (and expensive) state-rehabilitation efforts in Somalia, Yemen and Iraq. Many argue that partition can be a viable solution to protracted civil wars; others believe that it is counterproductive, and leaves old conflicts unresolved while creating new lines of dispute.[3] The debate largely turns on the empirical question of conflict reduction: Does partition reduce levels of violence across newly partitioned entities? And under what conditions might this be the case? The resulting successor states, and the domestic political arrangements that undergird them, are obviously critical to this entire equation.

Second, post-partition state-building projects—and their marked variation—highlight an important paradox of the liberal order in the Global Indian Ocean. While the thin liberal hegemony of Pax *Americana* (see Verhoeven's introduction) officially discouraged partition on the grounds that it would undermine the stability of the international system of states, partition's key corollary—self-determination—is a decidedly liberal precept. The noted political theorist Daniel Philpot goes so far as to say of self-determination that "liberal democracy requires it" and that "self-determination ... was invented by liberal democrats, and its intellectual history is a discussion among them". As a result of this linkage, the thin liberal order of Pax Americana inadvertently inspired a generation of secessionist projects in the Global Indian Ocean. And the underlying paradox of these projects was this: although they espoused a discourse of self-determination that was embedded in the liberal intellectual framework, they often yielded decidedly illiberal state-building experiments. This disjuncture is no mere intellectual curiosity, of course, as it cuts to the heart of the issues engaged in this volume: the multiple permutations of the liberal order in the Global Indian Ocean, and the ways in which this order was translated, reconfigured and contested in zones beyond its Western core.

This chapter explores these issues by examining the partition of Ethiopia–Eritrea in 1993. It attempts to explain what was perhaps the most significant outcome of the 1993 split: that it produced two highly resilient experiments in illiberal state-building dominated by the ideology and interests of rebels-turned-ruling parties.[4] While this outcome was highly contingent—indeed, most macro-political transitions are—I argue that the 1993 partition is best seen as an elite-level "political settlement" designed not only to partition Eritrea and Ethiopia, but to enhance the political monopoly of rebel elites in the emergent successor states. While this settlement—what I dub a "pact of domination"—would fall apart during the Eritrea–Ethiopia border war of 1998, the initial bargain had lasting effects, enabling the early consolidation of political authority by rebel elites and paving the way for the emergence of resilient illiberal building projects. Robust autocracy was thus the path-dependent outcome of a deal between newly ascendant rebel elites on both sides of the Mereb River to "divide and rule".[5]

In making this argument, this chapter shows that partitions can be meaningfully distinguished by the degree and nature of political settlement they involve; that these distinctions have long-run consequences for subsequent state-building and conflict dynamics; and that the domestic political trajectories of both rump and secessionist states are deeply interdependent. The chapter proceeds by mapping out key theoretical concepts, uses them to explore the Ethiopia–Eritrea case—focusing specifically on the period immediately prior and subsequent to the partition—and closes by highlighting the broader conceptual and comparative significance of the argument.

Partition and state-building

When partition occurs, it by definition puts in motion processes of state-building. In successor states that are newly sovereign—Eritrea, Croatia, South Sudan, etc.—the task of state construction is necessary and fundamental: laws must be promulgated and state institutions built from the ground up so that public goods can be delivered. Even in partitions that yield rump states—a remnant of the once larger state that retains its sovereign identity—the old state must often be reconfigured on a new basis, since the boundaries of the state, and who does and does not count as a citizen, have been altered. Additionally, partition is often associated with political transition in rump states, as it frequently serves as a capstone to a period of protracted conflict. In some instances, partition also involves the collapse of the previous regime at the old political centre—as occurred in West Pakistan following the 1971 departure of Bangladesh (see Karim's chapter 6 in this volume) or in Serbia just a year after its 1999 withdrawal from Kosovo.

Thus far, the research programme on partition has not directly addressed the question of succeeding efforts in state-building. Given that the normative case for partition has often hinged on the liberal discourse of self-determination—which in the tradition of Woodrow Wilson insists that it is only through democratic forms of government that a "nation" can truly determine its political destiny—one would expect succeeding state-building projects to possess all the virtues of liberalism: regular elections, institutional checks and balances, a free press, an autonomous civil society, guarantees of individual liberty, and so on. The reality, however, is that many (but not all) post-partition state-building experiments fall well short of these lofty liberal ideals.

Why is this the case? Central to the scholarly discussion of this topic has been the contrast between Pakistan's descent into military autocracy and India's consolidation of democratic governance in the years after Britain's partition of the Indian subcontinent in 1948.[6] Two categories of explanation seek to explain this divergence. The first largely focuses on the character of the movements that took over leadership of the Indian and Pakistani states. In this version of events, India's Congress Party was organizationally and ideologically more able to craft a functioning democratic system than Pakistan's Muslim League. The roots of Congress's relative strength, in turn, had a number of sources, including the skill and survival of its leadership (Jinnah would die just months after Pakistan's independence), the development of robust party structures decades prior to partition (the Muslim League lacked real institutional capacity until as late as the 1930s), and the underlying class interests that drove it (the Muslim League was driven by the interests of Punjab's feudal, landed elite).[7]

Others point to the national-level constraints that Congress and the Muslim League did, or did not, face in the aftermath of partition. Pakistan was founded as a Muslim homeland, and the appeal to a religious ideology was constantly invoked by elites that sought to ward off the pressures for democratic governance. Colonial legacies also left Pakistan's new leaders with much less state infrastructure to build upon—in part because the administrative resources of the old colonial state were not divided equitably—and pushed Pakistani elites to prioritize political centralization over and above the demands of democratic institution-building. And, finally, there was the external factor: Pakistan was in many ways defined by the military asymmetries between itself and its Indian neighbour, creating insecurities that empowered the Pakistani military domestically.[8]

Political settlements, pacts of domination, and resilient illiberal state-building

It is the last of these explanations—focusing on external dynamics—that is most relevant to this chapter, in so far as it suggests state-building efforts in successor states are deeply interdependent. Consider the logic of the following argument. When partition is the result of formal agreement between elites designed, in the first instance, to end a period of protracted conflict, we can think of this bargain as representing a "political settlement". The "political settlements" literature has been critiqued for its lack of precision, in part because it has been applied to intellectually disparate projects ranging from post-conflict stabilization to historical political economy. In its broadest and most conventional sense, political settlements can be defined as the "forging of a common understanding usually between political elites that their best interests or beliefs are served through the acquiescence to a framework for administering political power".[9] These elite agreements, in turn, reflect the balance of power between contending parties—often political organizations—rather than liberal normative considerations about who gets what and how.[10] Political settlements are also closely linked to the literature on regime transition, "elite pacts" and critical junctures.[11] Accordingly, when partition represents a real underlying bargain rather than political posturing or tactical considerations, its design can "lock in" long-term consequences, both intended and unintended, for the successor states it creates.

At the heart of the political settlement involving partition is an agreement to end a civil war and divide an existing state. By its very nature, agreements of this type are elite and exclusive: while partition may have a greater or lesser degree of mass support—as expressed through referenda, opinion polls or other metrics—the very principle of separation, and the details surrounding it, will be contentious, generating public discontent and opposition. Years of violence also tend to have eroded civil society, and empowered militarized actors and the political interests they represent. In such contexts, then, partition—as a formal, negotiated outcome—is something that is orchestrated from above rather than below. Indeed, it probably could not occur otherwise.

The elite nature of partition means that the political settlement tends to reflect elite interests, as well as the prevailing balance of power between them. The privileging of elite interests can often be seen in the formal details of the arrangement—on economic relations, citizenship rights, borders, restitution and reparations, security arrangements, and so on. However ambiguous the underlying deal, formal partition cannot occur without some understanding on these issues, as they define the terms of the split and relations between the emergent successor states.

But depending on elite preferences, there can also be an additional, more informal bargain intended to define the state-building projects in emergent successor states. At its root, this informal political settlement is designed, through collaboration and coordination, to protect and guarantee the political monopoly of partitioning elites in the new states they seek to govern. This modus vivendi varies depending on the context, but, in general, it means that partition, to borrow from Adam Przeworski, can sometimes be considered a "pact of domination" through which elites attempt to divide, and then rule.

When they work as intended, informal settlements can be foundational to the construction of illiberal but nonetheless resilient political orders—even in the most inhospitable of post-partition state-building contexts. This is because the relations between successor states and the elites that forged them do not constitute normal bilateral relations: once part of the same state, the political, economic and social interdependencies between these entities are profound and far-reaching. For better or worse, the bilateral relationship between successor states becomes the most significant form of diplomatic liaison for both of them, particularly in the fragile months and years after the split, when nascent state-building projects hang in the balance. Consequently, leveraging these specific cross-border linkages—which are potent precisely because they were once domestic—is central to the viability of the illiberal state-building project in post-war, post-partition contexts.

Of course, not all partitions are "pacts of domination". In fact, many probably are not: either aspiring political elites in soon-to-be successor states lack the will or capacity to strike such a bargain, or the bargain falls apart too quickly to realize its intended effects. This failure to strike a political settlement is also consequential, because it means the state-building experiment will necessarily be more contested, opening up the possibility for alternative trajectories of state development that include democratization and the implantation of a liberal political framework (a best-case scenario), or state-weakness and collapse (see Reno's chapter 8 in this volume on Somalia).[12] In the next section, I show how the aforementioned concepts explain the emergence of robust and resilient illiberal state-building projects in Eritrea and Ethiopia.

Illiberal state-building in Eritrea and Ethiopia

The formal partition of Ethiopia in 1993 was the result of a sustained struggle waged by a coalition of armed movements originating in northern Ethiopia—the Eritrean People's Liberation Front (EPLF) and the Tigray People's Liberation Front (TPLF). The EPLF was based in Ethiopia's coastal province of Eritrea while the TPLF was based in Tigray, the adjoining province to the south. Together, the two ousted the Marxist junta of Mengistu Hailemariam (referred to as the "Derg") in May 1991, partitioned Ethiopia, and entrenched themselves as ruling parties in the newly created successor states. The TPLF's transformation into the ruling regime of an Ethiopian rump state, organized along the lines of ethnic federalism, occurred under the cover of a TPLF-dominated alliance of ethnic parties: the Ethiopian People's Revolutionary Democratic Front (EPRDF). The EPLF, for its part, chose a more straightforward approach to asserting its hegemony over the new order, transforming itself into Eritrea's sole political party, the People's Front for Democracy and Justice (PFDJ), in 1994.

The political orders forged by the guerrilla elites in Addis and Asmara after 1993 differed in notable respects. Some of the challenges they faced were distinct. Eritrea is a small country that would fall out of international favour, while TPLF-led Ethiopia was a large state that was able to forge strong ties with critical players in the international system. This had little to do with the nature of their political systems—as both were decidedly illiberal—but much to do with the exigencies of the Global War on Terror, which rendered Ethiopia a key counter-terrorism partner of the West.[13] By contrast, in building a new Ethiopian polity, the TPLF had the disadvantage of a relatively small political base, while the EPLF had much more broad-based support within Eritrea. Perhaps as a result, TPLF and EPLF strategies of state-building would differ as well, as TPLF elites employed a system of ethnic federalism in which the veneer of democracy and decentralization along ethno-regional lines was maintained, but the substance of politics remained autocratic and centralizing. Eritrea, over time, converged on a Maoist model of state-building in which even the pretence of alternative power centres and dissent was obliterated, and the exercise of state control over the lives and labour of individual citizens was near complete.[14]

Despite these differences, the two state-building projects shared key similarities: they faced common challenges in the form of internal political crises, external conflicts and serious economic headwinds. And, more importantly for this chapter's purposes, despite these challenges these illiberal state-building projects were consolidated. Understanding the early political settlement that was the basis of Ethiopia's partition is central to understanding their survival.

Prelude to partition

The long secessionist rebellion in Eritrea was the result of a controversial 1952 UN decision to federate the former Italian colony with Ethiopia, its large southern neighbour. This federation, and the Eritrean autonomy enshrined in it, would not last long, even though it was guaranteed by a UN resolution. In 1962 Emperor Haile Selassie, a centralizing autocrat, abrogated the federation and transformed the coastal territory into an Ethiopian province lacking any special autonomous rights. The destruction of the federation had been a creeping effort, involving a campaign of Ethiopian subterfuge that unfolded over much of the preceding decade. As a result, Eritrean nationalists began to organize resistance even before the federation's formal dissolution. In September 1961, the Eritrean Liberation Front (ELF) launched military operations in the territory. The organization largely drew its membership from Eritrea's predominantly Muslim, western lowlands.

The ELF was the dominant resistance organization until 1967, when a schism within the movement culminated in the creation of a rival in 1972. This group, the EPLF, had a different social base, drawing its early membership from Eritrea's highland Christian towns and the port area of Massawa. Following a period of strife between the ELF and EPLF between 1972 and 1975, the two organizations struck a truce that lasted until the early 1980s. When the rivalry again exploded in 1981, it resulted in the EPLF's conclusive victory over the ELF by 1982. Once ensconced as the pre-eminent rebel faction in Eritrea, the EPLF defended its northwestern mountain bases for much of the 1980s, facing down repeated military offensives from the Ethiopian government. In 1991 the EPLF–TPLF secured a joint victory over Haile Selassie's successor, Mengistu Hailemariam. Following a two-year transitional period, Eritrea became an independent state.

As the war in Eritrea unfolded in the 1970s, the spirit of rebellion spread to the Ethiopian province of Tigray. Tigray sits directly south of Eritrea, and is demographically dominated by the Tigrinya-speaking Orthodox Christians who cross-populate the Eritrean highlands. The province had long chafed under the centralizing policies of the Shoan Amhara monarchs who had controlled the Ethiopian state since the 1880s.[15] The TPLF, founded in 1975, was an expression of these long-running grievances, but the immediate precipitant of the group's emergence was the Ethiopian revolution of 1974. While the revolution culminated in the ouster of Emperor Haile Selassie and his replacement by a military junta, its immediate effect was to throw the Ethiopian state into disarray. This led to a collapse of state authority in the periphery and created ample opportunity for armed rebellion.

The TPLF's early history was, like that of the EPLF, marred by competitive struggles with other rebel factions in Tigray. The TPLF would prevail over these competitors by 1979, in part through some early EPLF support, and by the late 1980s the TPLF had emerged as a significant military actor. Between 1988 and 1991, the TPLF combined with the EPLF to oust Mengistu Hailemariam in a decisive fashion.

The 1993 split and the "official" bargain

The EPLF and TPLF shared important commonalities that served as a platform for cooperation in the war against the Ethiopian government. Much of the leadership of both organizations hailed from the Tigrinya-speaking highlands of Eritrea and Tigray. These ethno-linguistic linkages were reinforced by the shared life experiences that bound elites across the two organizations, as many had left student life in Ethiopian universities to join the rebellion. The leaders of both movements were also closely aligned ideologically, extolling the leftist student radicalism of the 1960s and 1970s and nursing a deep resentment of the Amhara-centric nature of the Ethiopian state.

The EPLF and TPLF began close cooperation almost immediately, including joint military operations. In the 1970s, the EPLF was the more mature organization, and provided critical support to the TPLF in its earliest and most vulnerable days. Over time, the two organizations developed an interdependence that was central to their survival.

Yet despite the affinities and pragmatic interests that tied the EPLF and TPLF together, there were moments of tension. Differences over military tactics and political programmes created a serious break in relations in 1985. The TPLF disagreed with the EPLF's insistence that it engage Ethiopian forces in fixed positional warfare—most notably by defending its mountain redoubt of Nakfa, in the northwestern Eritrean district of Sahel. The TPLF and EPLF also differed on the rights of Ethiopia's various "nations and nationalities", with the TPLF taking the radical view that all ethno-linguistic groups—including those in Eritrea—should have the right of self-determination up to and including secession. Separate talks between the EPLF and Ethiopian government in the mid-1980s, brokered by the communist bloc, also created profound distrust between the two rebel fronts.

The rupture between the two organizations was significant. Military coordination and diplomatic engagement ceased. The EPLF prevented the TPLF from using supply routes that ran through western Eritrea connecting Tigray to Sudan, at precisely the moment that northern Ethiopia was hit by a massive famine. The TPLF, in turn, conducted a propaganda campaign against the EPLF among Eritrean refugee populations in Sudan in attempt to discredit its former ally.[16]

It was the changing face of the war in northern Ethiopia in the late 1980s that precipitated the rehabilitation of the EPLF–TPLF alliance. A critical EPLF battlefront victory at Afabet in March 1988 encouraged the parties to merge their efforts and defeat a regime that appeared to be on its last legs. By May 1991, the TPLF and EPLF had together marched on Addis Ababa, toppling what remained of the Derg regime. This effectively led to the partition of Ethiopia and Eritrea's formal entrance into the international system of states in 1993.[17]

Thus, the "official" political settlement that was partition evolved as the war took its decisive turn in the late 1980s. The TPLF recommitted itself to Eritrean self-determination and dropped any sympathies it might have had with notion of extending those same rights to Eritrea's various minorities. This position was affirmed at several crucial junctures between 1988 and 1993: in the TPLF's public memoranda and statements; in the EPRDF's own 1990 transition plan; at the London Conference of May 1991, where the TPLF, EPLF and others crafted post-Derg transitional arrangements; at the Addis Ababa transitional conference of July 1991 where a transitional charter was agreed upon; and in April–May 1993, when the TPLF-led Ethiopian government endorsed the resounding results of Eritrea's independence referendum, and the TPLF's chairman, Meles Zenawi, spoke as a distinguished guest at Eritrea's first independence day celebrations.

Just a month later, the EPLF and TPLF signed the Asmara Pact, which formally consummated the relationship between the two sovereign states after Eritrea's de jure independence in May 1993. The pact involved 25 protocol agreements, and established three joint technical committees and a ministerial committee to oversee full implementation of these arrangements. The pact dealt with cooperation on a range of issues including borders, trade, investment, education and security. Most critically, it provided Ethiopia—now the world's most populous landlocked country—unfettered access to its former ports in Eritrea. These arrangements were designed to set post-partition relations on a stable and mutually beneficial course, and envisioned amicable ties between the two countries.[18]

The 1993 partition as a "pact of domination": The TPLF view

Yet partition also constituted an additional political settlement between the EPLF and TPLF. In effect, it was a "pact of domination", in which the EPLF committed itself to the support of TPLF hegemony within Ethiopia, while the TPLF committed itself to a smooth transition to independent statehood for an Eritrea dominated by the EPLF. This pact was of necessity informal, since both parties paid lip service to liberal precepts of democracy and human rights in order to placate various domestic and external audiences, the latter viewing the supremacy of liberal governance frameworks as an article of faith following the collapse of the Soviet Union (see Verhoeven's introduction).

For the TPLF, this bargain was central to its consolidation of authority across Ethiopia in the months and years after the Derg's ouster. Three critical points illustrate why. First, the very act of partition served as an EPLF guarantee to Meles Zenawi and his comrades that it would not attempt to compete politically with the TPLF. This mattered because the EPLF was the older and militarily stronger front, and was perfectly capable of challenging the TPLF for supremacy within Ethiopia. In addition, several stakeholders were pushing the concept of EPLF rule of a united Ethiopia. This included the US assistant secretary of state for Africa, Herman Cohen, who was the American point person for the Ethiopian transition, and a number of unionist Ethiopian factions. Although Eritrean public opinion was firmly on the side of independence, as was most of the EPLF politburo, EPLF chairman Isaias Afwerki was reportedly taken by the idea of unity with an Eritrean accent.[19] Such a possibility was one the TPLF was wary of, for obvious reasons, and the EPLF's eventual rejection of unity meant a de facto recognition of TPLF supremacy within Ethiopia.[20]

But it was also the manner in which this "non-compete" clause was formulated during the transition period that was particularly advantageous to the TPLF. After the Derg's collapse, the EPLF set up its own administration called the Provisional Government of Eritrea (PGE), which governed the territory pending a referendum. Simultaneously, it effectively forfeited any political stake in the transition process that was occurring in Ethiopia proper during this period, even though the PGE lacked the full legal personality of an internationally recognized government and thus had some interest in the decisions of the emerging government in Ethiopia. At the critical Addis Ababa Transition Conference of July 1991, where Ethiopian actors met to forge a transitional charter and government, the EPLF maintained only observer status. Moreover, the EPLF did not have any representation within the transitional government that emerged out of the July meetings. These facts gave the TPLF free rein at a critical juncture in its state-building project, as it attempted to impose a framework for governance that would ensure its hegemony for years to come. As a result, the TPLF officials would come to occupy the most critical portfolios within the new government—including the post of president—and in July 1992 EPRDF forces transitioned into Ethiopia's national military. That same month, Ethiopia's first regional elections were held, and the TPLF and its EPRDF coalition, using their dominant status within the transitional arrangements, won over 90 per cent of votes cast. By 1995, the EPRDF had redrawn the administrative map of the Ethiopian state and imposed a new constitution. In the end, the transition was by and large consistent with the EPRDF's original May 1990 plan, and the ethnic federalism that was its chief outcome reflected the TPLF's ideological commitments as articulated in the bush.[21]

It is important to note that the EPLF's strategic withdrawal from the process of state reconstruction occurring in Addis was paired with more overt support for the TPLF. The TPLF's major strategic challenge was that its political base was small—only about six per cent of the Ethiopian population can be categorized as Tigrayan. Perhaps the biggest threat was the Oromo Liberation Front (OLF), which claimed to represent the Oromo, Ethiopia's largest ethnic community and inhabitants of a vast, resource-rich territory that includes Addis Ababa. As the TPLF won critical victories against the Derg in 1988 and 1989, it sought to boost its power relative to the OLF in two main ways. First, it established the Oromo

People's Democratic Organization (OPDO), which would become an important component of the EPRDF coalition, to undercut the OLF's Oromo support base and extend the TPLF's influence into Oromo lands. Here, EPLF support was vital. The OPDO was made up of government soldiers of Oromo descent, captured by the TPLF and its EPLF ally. The EPLF transferred charismatic officers like Abadula Gemeda—who was probably the single most important OPDO politician in the organization's pre-2018 history—to the TPLF for the express purpose of setting up the new party.[22] Backed by the TPLF, these soldiers were to be the TPLF's political vanguard in administering strategic Oromo territories.

The OPDO's creation enabled the TPLF to push into Oromo territories in the late days of the war, a fact that made possible its final, unilateral seizure of Addis Ababa in May 1991. While the TPLF's quick advance on the capital can be explained by the military necessity of ousting the Derg, the TPLF also crossed into the Oromo territory of Wellega, in the far west of the country, effectively blocking OLF access to one of its traditional operational zones.[23] Here again, EPLF military support was essential, as EPLF armour and combined arms paved the way for rapid TPLF advances into western and southern Ethiopia, allowing the TPLF to capitalize on the Derg losses as the OLF were outmanoeuvred.

The TPLF's strategy was designed to create a fait accompli, establishing itself as the dominant force in the anti-Derg camp just as the central government began to crumble. And it worked. The OLF was well aware of a decisive shift in the balance of power occurring in the late days of the war, and protested vociferously, raising the spectre of armed clashes in 1991. Yet again, the EPLF interceded, applying critical pressure on the OLF to accept the new realities. Two important meetings where this pressure was applied were the London Conference of May 1991 and the Senafe meetings of June 1991, the latter of which was hosted by the EPLF in Eritrea. In the end, EPLF pressure and guarantees—something OLF figures have openly acknowledged—pushed OLF leaders to participate in a transition process heavily slanted in the TPLF's favour.[24] Throughout this process, in what appeared to be a well-calculated ruse, the EPLF attempted to feign neutrality in the context of the TPLF–OLF rivalry.

The TPLF–OLF relationship again began to unravel in the run-up to the 1992 regional elections, as the TPLF sought to use its administrative power to reduce the OLF's electoral potential. It was here that the EPLF's support for the TPLF was to prove most decisive. The EPLF stepped into the fray, mediating meetings in Mekele designed to cool tensions. Amid clashes and provocation, an encampment accord was signed in February 1992, which would be overseen by the Council of Ministers (of which the EPRDF and OLF were a part) with the EPLF playing a vital monitoring role. What happened next remains a matter of some dispute, as the degree of bad faith on the part of the TPLF and EPLF is hard to ascertain. What is clear, however, is that the initial agreement didn't hold. The TPLF, with EPLF military support and political complicity (EPLF troops and monitors were in the Oromo territories at the time), discarded the encampment accord and struck at territorially concentrated and vulnerable OLF troops. It was a disaster for the OLF: 18,000 troops were captured and hundreds killed. The OLF was forced to boycott the elections, and withdraw its representation from the Council of Ministers, and its leaders fled abroad. The EPLF laid the blame on the OLF, providing the TPLF with political cover for its hegemonic bid. The result was that the OLF would never again pose a significant threat to TPLF hegemony within Ethiopia.[25]

The final way that the "pact of domination" helped propel TPLF hegemony within Ethiopia was the manner in which the EPLF handled the political blowback associated with Eritrea's secession. The departure of Eritrea, combined with the TPLF's proposed model of ethnic federalism—which the transitional charter of July 1992 indicated would guarantee the right of Ethiopia's nationalities to self-determination "up to and including secession"—sparked the ire of Ethiopian nationalists. Just one day after the TPLF-led EPRDF captured Addis, angry mobs of thousands marched through the city's streets to reject TPLF rule. They reserved special venom for the US Embassy in Addis—which they attempted to storm—because of the widely held belief that the Americans were aiding and abetting a TPLF plot to fragment the country. The furore seems to have been triggered by a comment from Herman Cohen earlier that same month, in which he appeared to endorse the TPLF–EPLF plan to partition the country.[26]

The protests were a harbinger of a central problem for the TPLF: many Ethiopians considered them "narrow nationalists" committed to undermining the unity of the Ethiopian people. This compounded the dilemmas of the TPLF's already limited political base. Political factions inside and outside the country appeared to tap into this sentiment, threatening the TPLF's prospects as a truly national hegemonic force.

The EPLF could not fully eliminate this burden for the TPLF, as the only way to accomplish that task would have been to drop the notion of partition altogether—but they could reduce it. Thus, the EPLF avoided a unilateral declaration of independence when they occupied Asmara in May 1991 as part of a tacit understanding with the TPLF that such a move would render TPLF rule in Addis untenable.[27] This threw the TPLF a lifeline at its most vulnerable moment. Second, the EPLF guaranteed continuing and uninterrupted Ethiopian access to the sea with no duties or tax. This assurance was publicly given by the EPLF on numerous occasions, and was formalized with the signing of the Asmara Pact in 1993. Since the port question was a central pillar of Ethiopian nationalist resistance to partition and TPLF rule more generally, the EPLF knowingly helped take the sting out of the argument that the TPLF was a Trojan horse bent on dismembering Ethiopia.

The 1993 partition as a "pact of domination": The EPLF view

While the EPLF did not face the same obstacles to the consolidation of its authority in Eritrea as the TPLF faced in Ethiopia, the informal "pact of domination" was of important value. First, the EPLF did face some notable challengers to the establishment of its hegemony. In 1992, the EPLF-dominated PGE passed a proclamation that outlawed alternative political organizations during the transition phase, but a number of opposition groups remained active. The EPLF thus embarked on a protracted campaign to neutralize this collection of opponents in neighbouring Sudan and Ethiopia. The TPLF was to be of crucial support. Just days after the signing of the Asmara Pact, the TPLF arrested 26 top officials of the ELF-RC (a remnant of the ELF), signalling that Eritrean dissidents would have no quarter in Ethiopia proper.[28] There were high-profile killings and kidnappings of Eritrean dissidents in Ethiopia as well, including the murder of ELF-RC member Tesfamichael Giorgio in April 1992 outside his Addis Ababa home in broad daylight, and the 1996 assassination of Eritrean Democratic Liberation Movement chairman Zecharias Neguse in Dessie. These operations and others were not executed by the TPLF but were likely carried out with its complicity. Indeed, the widespread belief at the time was that the TPLF had given EPLF assassination squads a free hand to roam Ethiopia and liquidate their Eritrean opponents.[29] The TPLF-enabled campaign eviscerated important networks of resistance to EPLF rule.[30]

The TPLF would also facilitate the EPLF's neutralization of another potential threat to its hegemony: a large contingent of Ethiopians residing in Eritrea that were said to have been Derg collaborators. While a large portion of the Derg army in Eritrea had disintegrated, and its remnants had either surrendered or fled to Sudan, the EPLF regarded its collaborators and sympathizers as a destabilizing force. In June 1991, over 100,000 of these Ethiopians were deported from Eritrea, and their economic assets seized. The move was a contentious one within Ethiopia, as the deportation process was regarded as lacking any semblance of due process and as a power grab by the EPLF driven by its desire to accumulate economic assets and assert its dominance over Eritrea's political economy. The deportations created a humanitarian crisis in Ethiopia that was only averted by emergency assistance from the US.[31]

The TPLF was not enthusiastic about the deportations because of the humanitarian and political costs. At the same time, it understood that it was of great importance to the EPLF's bid to consolidate its hegemony within Eritrea, and thus a key part of the TPLF's "pact of domination" with the EPLF. Meles Zenawi thus publicly confirmed that many of those who had been deported were indeed Derg collaborators.[32] Ethiopia's defence minister at the time, Siye Abraha, went a step further, dismissing the deportees as the "running dogs of the Derg".[33] The effect of the TPLF's rhetoric was to give the EPLF cover for an otherwise contentious assertion of authority within the Eritrean political sphere.[34]

By 1994, the EPLF also faced additional challenges from armed Islamist opposition groups like the Eritrean Islamic Jihad Movement, who were backed by Sudan's military-Islamist regime. Indeed, by the summer of that year, western Eritrea was becoming increasingly unsafe, as militants infiltrated Gash-Barka and Sahel to launch attacks. Events reached fever pitch in December 1994 when the EPLF-dominated government broke relations with Khartoum and transferred the Sudanese embassy in Asmara into the hands of the Sudanese opposition.[35]

The TPLF-led government had its own issues with Sudan. However, the acrimony between it and the Islamists in Khartoum was nothing like the fissures between the Khartoum and the EPLF (at least until the attempted assassination of Mubarak in Addis in June 1995).[36] In fact, the TPLF attempted to position itself as a neutral mediator at several junctures. Nonetheless, the TPLF provided political support for the Eritrean position as early as January 1994, when the Ethiopian foreign minister, Seyoum Mesfin, openly accused Khartoum of destabilizing Eritrea and "helping religious groups to undermine the security and stability of neighbouring states, including our own".[37] This was the first of many expressions of solidarity with the EPLF throughout 1994 and 1995 at a time when Sudanese–Ethiopian bilateral relations were generally sound. In the end, such support was important in bolstering the EPLF's diplomatic position in the wake of the embassy closure of December 1994: as the host nation of the Organization of African Unity (OAU), and the holder of the OAU chairmanship throughout 1995, the TPLF administration in Addis retained significant diplomatic clout. When the EPLF government got in another diplomatic row with Yemen over the Hanish Islands in 1995, the TPLF again repeated this pattern of support for the EPLF.

The final element of the "pact of domination" that bolstered EPLF hegemony within Eritrea was that the TPLF cleared any and every obstacle to Eritrea's acquisition of sovereign statehood. For the EPLF chairman, Isaias Afwerki, in particular, sovereign statehood was an essential political requirement, since its achievement would bolster his position within the EPLF while solidifying the legitimacy of the EPLF among the Eritrean masses. It would also allow the EPLF government to seize the practical benefits of international recognition.

Consequently, the TPLF attached no formal conditions to Eritrean independence; it delegated the conduct of the 1993 referendum to the EPLF and allowed the EPLF to design a referendum ballot that some argued was slanted in favour of a "yes" vote (although, to be clear, the overwhelming majority of Eritreans would have supported independence anyway); the Asmara Pact, signed after formal partition but an essential part of the partition arrangement, deliberately left many important and difficult separation-related issues ambiguous and unsettled in order to rapidly push forward Eritrea's secession; and, finally, the broader Ethiopian public had no input on the question of Eritrean independence, and, where resistance emerged, it was quashed.

As the TPLF facilitated Eritrea's transition to independence, it also sought to help the EPLF manage the economic burdens of de facto statehood between 1991 and 1993. Eritrea had been devastated during the thirty years' war, much more so than any other part of Ethiopia, but when the EPLF captured Asmara in May 1993 it did not yet have the legal standing to sign international aid agreements—even as the spectre of drought appeared in 1991–2. In response, the TPLF-led government in Addis shared aid with the EPLF, and even signed a few international arrangements on their behalf, thus filling resource gaps until the EPLF was able to acquire the full legal personality of a recognized state.[38]

It is notable that in facilitating Eritrea's transition to sovereign statehood, the TPLF studiously sought to avoid any expectation that Eritrean independence and democratic elections would go hand in hand. According to Medhanie, "the refusal of the EPRDF to try to ensure democracy in the referendum was in line with the understandings and the deals involving Washington and the EPLF that Eritrea can secede but with the EPLF in state power". In explaining the TPLF–EPRDF posture on this issue, Medhanie concludes that "strictly speaking the EPRDF could not have insisted on a really democratic referendum without transgressing the agreements and understandings which were important in its coming to power".[39]

Conclusions

As this chapter makes clear, the partition of Ethiopia—formally consummated in 1993—involved an informal "pact of domination" designed to guarantee the political monopoly of insurgent movement elites in both Eritrea and Ethiopia. At a critical juncture in the TPLF's and EPLF's drives to construct new political orders—between 1988 and the mid-1990s—the reciprocal support that each movement provided to the other was crucial to the emergence of durable illiberal state-building projects. In the final analysis, the elite collaboration embedded in the partition deal—which was essentially a plan to "divide and rule"—was to have long-lasting effects.

Of course, there were other factors that helped forge resilient illiberal political models in Eritrea and Ethiopia. Once these systems were initially established, they had to be consolidated and reconsolidated on a recurring basis. The elite bargain struck by the EPLF and TPLF was shattered in 1998 amid a fierce border conflict, and thus their initial collaboration tells us little about how their autocratic projects were consolidated over time. For the TPLF-led EPRDF, the pronounced tension that emerged after the September 11 attacks between the normative aspirations of the US-led liberal order and US policymakers' practical need for counter-terrorism cooperation from autocrats (see Verhoeven's introduction) allowed it to carve out significant political and economic support from Western donors. This external support, along with the seemingly impressive economic achievements of the EPRDF's "developmental state", was central to the maintenance of the TPLF's internal political monopoly. For those who sat at the helm of the EPLF/PFDJ, particularly President Isaias, the break with the TPLF provided a pretext to engage in a systematic and far-reaching internal crackdown that deepened Eritrea's illiberal project.

Nevertheless, in focusing our attention on the nexus of partition and its subsequent state-building projects in Eritrea and Ethiopia, this chapter teaches us much about how liberal projects of self-determination can morph into decidedly illiberal experiments in the Global Indian Ocean. Here, there are three key points that need to be understood. First, partitions can be meaningfully distinguished by the degree and nature of the political settlement they involve. Indeed, political settlements that produced partitions in the Sudans (2011), East Timor (1999) and Somali territories (1991) looked fundamentally different from what we saw in Eritrea and Ethiopia: in Somalia—

Somaliland and East Timor–Indonesia there was no pact of domination, and in the Sudans it quickly fell apart.

Second, such distinctions have long-term consequences for the state-building and conflict dynamics that follow partition. In Somalia and Somaliland, the collapse of the former and the democratization of the latter were intimately tied to the absence of a pact of domination (see Reno's chapter 8). Meanwhile, state weakness in Sudan and state collapse in South Sudan were linked to the collapse of the pact of domination between the ruling factions in each territory just after the formal split in 2011. And, of course, as this chapter has shown, the strong pact of domination between the EPLF and TPLF was crucial to the contrasting trajectories of the state-building experiments in Eritrea and Ethiopia.

Finally, the chapter demonstrates that the domestic political trajectories of both rump and secessionist states are deeply interdependent.

What, then, for the future of partition in the Global Indian Ocean, particularly in terms of its state-building outcomes? Whatever elite compacts might exist across successor states, post-partition state-building will be mediated by a number of macro-level forces. One possible result is that the disjuncture between the liberal impetus for projects of self-determination in the region and their subsequent illiberal trajectories will become more stark. Much of this has to do with the changing nature of the liberal international order and the thin hegemony of the Pax Americana in the Indian Ocean world. As the War on Terror-era partnership between the TPLF–EPRDF and the US illustrated, since 1945 Washington has at times been willing to discard liberal precepts and underwrite illiberal projects when its core strategic interests required it.[40] The ideology of "America First" and associated transactional foreign policy approaches are likely to reinforce this particular tendency.

As Mitter's chapter 9 shows, the Global Indian Ocean is also being increasingly shaped by the geo-strategic ambitions of China. Here, again, it seems that macro-forces may further harden the liberal paradox associated with post-partition state-building projects. Beijing's model of authoritarian development, and its emphasis on stability and non-interference in its external relations, will likely enhance the viability of authoritarian modes of rule, both in post-partition contexts and beyond.[41]

Of course, beyond their independent effects, the interplay between these competing orders in the Indian Ocean world—the first American, and the second Chinese—will reinforce illiberal effects, if for no other reason than that it will further securitize regional and local politics. These dynamics, and others, will be important considerations in the evolution of new and old post-partition successor states in the Global Indian Ocean, from the Horn of Africa to South East Asia.

8

INTERVENTION AND ORDER IN FAILED STATES

William Reno

Somalia has lacked an effective central government since the collapse of the Siad Barre regime in January 1991. This country occupies a perennial position at or near the bottom of various prominent failed or fragile state indexes for its recurrent factional violence, the absence of effective state security forces, and dismal economic conditions. Somalia was also a focus of US President Donald Trump's policy "to eradicate terrorist safe havens, to cut off their finances, and to discredit their depraved ideology".[1] To this end, the US military command for Africa (AFRICOM) deployed "dozens" of troops from the 101st Airborne Division to Mogadishu to train and equip Somali and African Union Mission in Somalia (AMISOM) forces.[2] This was the first presence of US military forces in Somalia, other than small units of counter-terrorism advisors, since March 1994 when Washington pulled out of a UN operation after 18 US soldiers were killed in a battle with Somali militias. This response of the US and its allies in Somalia reflects a general set of policies for dealing with other so-called collapsed or failing states in in the Global Indian Ocean, such

187

as Afghanistan, Myanmar, Yemen and Iraq. While this chapter focuses mainly on Somalia, the lessons of this intervention also apply to these other states and should be seen as symptomatic of some of the key contradictions inherent in the liberal order that this volume is centrally concerned with. In particular, intervention in Somalia as part of a Global War on Terror highlights the disjuncture between the deeply rooted historical realities of layered, shared and partial sovereignties that Blom Hansen in chapter 2 identifies as integral to the Indian Ocean, and the desperate efforts of intervening forces to impose a standardized form of statehood commensurate with the liberal international order.

Both the categorization of Somalia—or any other country—as a "failed state" and the effort to "fix failed states" to better fit a Pax Americana[3] impact considerably on the evolving character of order that exists on the ground. This intervention in the first instance is premised on integrating the failed state into a liberal international order that is organized around participation in open markets, membership in multilateral institutions, acceptance of the institutions and practice of liberal democracy in its domestic politics, and acceptance of the leadership of the US and its allies.[4] But this interventionist vision is not the only possible order. Some scholars of Somalia view locally constructed orders as viable indigenous alternatives to a centralized state.[5] Islamist groups like Somalia's al-Shabaab and the Union of Islamic Courts before it, identified in the US official view as the beneficiaries and exporters of disorder and therefore needing to be confronted militarily, have been the most proficient architects of coherent and effective alternatives to liberal order.[6] Likewise, some Western government agencies tacitly acknowledge that Afghanistan's Taliban are able to provide a stable—and decidedly illiberal—order for the tens of millions of Afghans who live under their rule.[7]

In the age of the Global War on Terror, external intervention targeting those spaces and groups deemed hostile to the inter-state system generally, and the Pax Americana specifically, plays a critical role in shaping local orders that exist in those territories branded as "failed states". A closer look, however, reveals that intervention, in Somalia and elsewhere in the Global Indian Ocean, has two dimensions. The first dimension is embedded in the pursuit of a democratic domestic order compatible with a liberal international order. This aim is reflected in the official policies of interveners to build professional police and military forces in the recipient state. These domestic security forces are supposed to defeat insurgents—often proficient providers of illiberal order—and disrupt the international networks that (supposedly) provide resources and recruits to insurgents. Strong security forces are also supposed to maintain the rule of law and to protect a new, pro-Western government that will provide a growing array of public services to citizens while it consolidates democratic reforms.[8] The intention, at least in theory, is to rebuild state institutions and enable that state to take its proper role in the liberal international order, an idea that privileges the extension of a standardized hegemonic conception of liberal hegemony.[9] But, as the Somali reality shows, this is, in Verhoeven's words in the introduction to this volume, a "thin hegemony" indeed.

The second dimension reflects how intervention *actually* unfolds on the ground in failed states, even though most Western officials are reluctant to acknowledge it. This dimension of intervention seeks order but dispenses with the project of liberal democratic transformation. It instead deals directly with the reality that the recipient government lacks the capacity or political will to support professional security forces or to transform their political systems into liberal democracies. It accepts that officials responsible for security often share important networks with insurgents and that some even collude with the insurgent activities that their security forces are supposed to counter. Western intelligence and military operatives thus often turn to ad hoc measures to leverage local social networks in the failed state to address external security concerns that host state "partners" do not necessarily share. In doing so, these agents of a hegemonic Pax Americana play an important role in undermining the liberal democratic dimension of this hegemony, a "thinning" of this hegemony, as they engage with the realities of asserting military dominance in this diverse and overlapping networked environment.

While still opposed to the specific illiberal order of Islamist statebuilders, this second dimension of intervention presents an alternative illiberal model of order in failed states. This dimension of intervention overrides inconvenient elements of global norms of state sovereignty, as domestically it ignores or just plays lip service to the project of democratic reform and simply bypasses important officials of the incumbent government. Ironically, it is the promoters of liberal internationalism that come to depend upon highly authoritarian and often violent solutions to the problem of establishing a hegemonic political order in Indian Ocean societies like Somalia and are thus, in practice, not all that different from other interveners.[10]

This process is even more striking when viewed against the internally driven authoritarian hegemonic projects in Ethiopia and Eritrea that Michael Woldemariam examines in chapter 7. This development is at odds with other aspects of Western policy, such as the adversarial American approach to Iran's government. The US State Department, for example, takes issue with "the Iranian regime's destructive behavior at home and abroad" in a report titled *Outlaw Regime*.[11] This pragmatic actualization of intervention addresses the defining feature of many contemporary failed states: namely, the transformation of politicians into leaders of competing networks of armed groups that hedge their bets between the insurgents that intervention is meant to fight and the governments that intervention is supposed to support. These politicians often have kinship and other personal ties which they use to generate local support for their armed group, and transnational networks by virtue of their service in government and the illicit commercial and political networks that their positions of power enabled them to exploit. Foreign interveners identify these networks as elements of the instability that their intervention is supposed to remedy. In Afghanistan, for example, American officials were well aware of allegations that the half-brother of President Hamid Karzai (2001–14) was involved in illicit drug trafficking in collusion with Taliban insurgents. Yet despite American pressure, the president refused to remove his relative from his position as a kingpin of Kandahar politics and illicit commerce.[12]

This collusion causes interveners to question the agendas of their host country "partners" who use foreign security assistance to promote their personal interests while simultaneously undermining interveners' goals. The common intervener response is optimistic official declarations of redoubled efforts, alongside private expressions of disdain and repugnance for those with whom they are supposed to work.

This political reality of cross-cutting networks grows out of pre-conflict authoritarian government strategies across societies in the Global Indian Ocean—Afghanistan, Eritrea, Somalia, Yemen—that targeted social bonds right down to personal levels, which rulers feared might otherwise support popular rebellions. The rulers' more reliable political and business partners are allowed to build personal militias for personal gain, often involving illicit commercial activities, and to menace regime opponents. This regime survival strategy drew upon, and in other states in the Global Indian Ocean continues to draw upon, different transnational personal and commercial networks that are incommensurate (hence "illicit") with the contemporary hegemonic order of which these states are supposed to be subordinate parts. This strategy also created intense domestic social fragmentation, as competition between militias prevented any one from becoming strong enough to challenge the ruler. But once the central authority collapses, social fragmentation continues to impede cooperation and confound conventional security assistance efforts to build institutions while strongmen stake out their own territories and assume brokerage positions to represent their personal interests and networks over those of the state.[13] Armed Islamist movements represent an attractive alternative to many people in this context because these groups are able to build orders drawing upon a different set of social networks in business and religious organizations which cut across these harsh divisions that the collapse of the state has generated.[14] This is the real social context in which intervention occurs, rather than a chaos in which people readily accept the idealized and ahistorical project of liberal state-building that conventional assistance programmes articulate. The irony is that the intervention in this and other "failed states" is meant to preserve a Pax Americana partnership with local actors whose everyday survival strategies push the "thinness" of this hegemony. Meanwhile the armed Islamists who are identified as threats to this state-centric hegemony are in fact the more proficient state-builders, albeit in an illiberal and decidedly non-American mould.

The rest of this chapter focuses on these two dimensions of intervention in Somalia. The next section explores the liberal theory underpinning the logic of foreign intervention and its supposed results and is followed by a survey of the reality facing this dimension of intervention, deconstructing the flawed assumptions associated with conventional wisdom about fixing so-called failed states. The argument then turns to the actual record of intervention in Somalia and its real role in creating order; to its ad hoc adjustments and compromises that international actors make when they recognize that conventional intervention will not create liberal order. As Harry Verhoeven's introduction notes, contemporary illiberal orders like Somalia's reflect the historical experience in the Global Indian Ocean in which great powers have sought empires on the cheap through the use of mercenaries, military advisors and bargaining with local intermediaries. The latter, as Blom Hansen notes in his chapter 2, are rooted in non-standard vernacular traditions of "distributed sovereignty" reliant on regional networks and layered arrangements that fit uneasily at best with the modern "bio-political state", which asserts a uniform hegemonic rule over people and territory within its borders.

The conventional wisdom versus reality

Foreign assistance to Somalia's government regularly encounters "partner" officials who have a stake in the networks and activities that assistance programmes identify as threats to security. Many officials exhibit a distinct lack of political will to seriously undertake basic reforms. This situation resembles problems that Karl Eikenberry identified when he was the US ambassador to Afghanistan: that President Karzai and his allies "consistently oppose foreign efforts to create transparent, rule-bound Afghan institutions because such projects threaten to undermine their political domination and economic banditry".[15] By the mid-2010s, more than a decade after the initial US-led invasion of Afghanistan, that country's domestic revenues funded only 10 per cent of all public expenditures.[16] Likewise, in Somalia foreign assistance (which did not include security force assistance) overshadowed domestic revenue by more than ten times.[17]

In spite of this reality, Somalia's security sector assistance programme followed a textbook design that combined assistance to the host state's military to fight insurgents and extensive political reform to build a liberal state. First, soldiers of the African Union's AMISON mission chased al-Shabaab from Mogadishu in August 2011. This enabled the Transitional Federal Government (TFG), until then a largely virtual executive based mostly outside the state's borders, to move into Somalia's capital. A conference in London in 2012 included dozens of governments and most major Somali political groups to produce a plan to reconstruct state institutions and revive social services.[18] Foreign officials promised logistical and financial support for AMISOM and pressed Somali leaders to select a new legislature and write a constitution.[19] A legislature convened in 2012 and chose a professor with technocratic credentials as president to head what was now the Federal Government of Somalia (FGS). The 2016 legislative elections reserved 30 per cent of the seats for women to signal the government's "commitment to inclusion",[20] the 2017 presidential election included the country's first female candidate for this office, and so forth.

Security assistance followed in step with this political progression. The European Union Training Mission for Somalia moved from Uganda to Mogadishu in 2013. In 2014, the US announced substantial training assistance to the Somali National Army (SNA). Somalia's defence minister later announced a strategy to build a capable, self-sustaining force, including female officers, which should take primary responsibility for security by 2017.[21] Considerable Western resources have been spent on building this security apparatus to buttress a supposedly nascent responsible stakeholder in the liberal international order. Somalia absorbed 38 per cent of US Defense Department and State Department Africa programme expenditures, about $742 million for 2016.[22] The European Commission provided €1.2 billion (about $1.5 billion) from 2007 through 2016, primarily to train and pay AMISOM troops and Somali police.[23] The US also trains and equips armies of the countries that contribute soldiers to AMISOM. In 2016, for example, the US spent about $170 million for military assistance to Uganda's army.[24]

In spite of this considerable security force assistance, Somalia's government is a frequent target of al-Shabaab attacks. Attacks in Mogadishu in 2016–18 killed legislators, a government minister, an SNA general and other security officials, alongside scores of low-level state employees. Attacks struck the Criminal Investigation Department headquarters, the airport, the port, police stations, the Ministry of the Interior's headquarters and the presidential compound. Hotels are prime targets because international organizations pay the bills for legislators who are housed in these fortified hotels run by warlord-businessmen. Some of these entrepreneurs in the mid-2000s received financial help and advice from the Central Intelligence Agency (CIA) in a failed effort to get them to use their militias to capture or kill people suspected of links to al-Qaeda.[25]

Al-Shabaab regularly overruns AMISOM forward bases. Al-Shabaab fighters killed more than 50 Ugandan AMISOM soldiers at their base in September 2015 shortly after killing at least 50 Burundian AMISOM soldiers at their base. Al-Shabaab fighters attacked an Ethiopian base in June 2017.[26] Throughout 2017, al-Shabaab set off car bombs in the capital, ambushed dozens of AMISOM and SNA troops, looted an SNA base, assassinated police officers in Kenya, stormed a Kenyan army base on the Somalia–Kenya border, and killed an American soldier during a raid. A huge truck bomb attack in the capital in October 2017 slaughtered at least 512 people, though informal estimates suggest an even more deadly toll. Two months later, a suicide bomber murdered 18 police officers inside the main police academy. Car bombs near the Presidential Palace in February 2018 killed at least 38 people. The attackers' access to intelligence service ID cards and uniforms facilitated entry to the palace, which raised suspicions of collusion with intelligence service members.[27]

Infiltration of Somalia's security services reflects the nature of local politics in failed states. A good example is the January 2013 French attempt to rescue an intelligence operative held captive since 2009 after he and a compatriot were kidnapped from the Sahafi Hotel.[28] The French team sought information to find the hostage from Somalia's National Intelligence and Security Agency (NISA), a beneficiary of CIA assistance.[29] But this information led the French force into a trap and two French soldiers and the hostage were killed.[30] UN experts affirmed that al-Shabaab infiltration "includes sensitive Government agencies, such as NISA and various levels within the Presidential Palace."[31] Regular amnesty programmes since 2014 add to this problem.[32] Insider attacks against NATO soldiers and Afghan security forces played a similar role in continued insecurity in Afghanistan.[33]

Al-Shabaab infiltration of the police force is a factor in frequent hotel bombings, and when suspects are arrested, often they are released later without charge.[34] Possible motives behind attacks include political goals of extremists and personal and family retribution for security force killings of pardoned al-Shabaab members. Infiltration was suspected in the 2017 attack on Daallo Airlines flight, in which the attacker prematurely detonated a bomb hidden in his laptop computer and was sucked out of the blast hole in the airplane fuselage. Some passengers were on board because their Turkish Airlines flight was cancelled shortly before the departure of the Daallo flight 159 allegedly on account of bad weather—a decision that later raised suspicions since the cancellation occurred during normal weather conditions. It also emerged that the bomber had stayed at the home of a government minister with whom he shared kinship ties and that several airport workers facilitated the operation.[35]

On the whole, attacks and infiltration do not push Somali officials to greater efforts to build the state institutions that foreign providers of aid and advice envision as part of a liberal state order. Frustrated UN observers reported that "the systematic misappropriation, embezzlement and outright theft of public resources have essentially become a system of governance", as individuals make demands on state resources that officials cannot resist due to obligations of kinship.[36] In 2014, payouts constituted 70–80 per cent of Somalia's Central Bank payments.[37] A World Bank report observed that "although a Central Bank was in existence … it apparently was (and continues to be) largely circumvented by the Transitional Federal Government executive branch and their key staff, while civil service and security force salaries go unpaid".[38] The head of the UN Assistance Mission in Somalia declared that "corruption is a blight … The effects can be seen in all areas of public life, from business to politics, justice to security, while playing into the hands of extremists."[39] Some diplomats labelled the 2017 election as "a milestone of corruption, one of the most fraudulent political events in Somalia's history", while an anti-corruption activist noted that "this election has been awesome for the Shabab", because the corruption free-for-all makes al-Shabaab look upstanding by comparison.[40]

The SNA's real size remains a mystery. Official statements refer to 22,000 soldiers, but a realistic figure is closer to 10,000, while officials divert salaries of real and non-existent soldiers.[41] The United Arab Emirates recruit real SNA soldiers to fight Houthi rebels in Yemen, for which the UAE government allegedly pays $2,500 per soldier each month.[42] These problems reflect the realities of SNA commanders who serve clan interests and who have minimal allegiance to the Somali government.[43] Unpaid soldiers seek out officers of their clan and support those who take their patron's side in intra-clan disputes, some of which have involved clashes between elements of the SNA.[44] Some SNA units act as clan militias, allying with local strongmen and even with elements of al-Shabaab when they stand on the same side of local clan disputes.[45] SNA troops without patrons "set up illegal checkpoints to shake down civilians" so they can feed themselves and their families.[46]

This failure of liberal intervention highlights the two essential problems noted above that confront the liberal state-building paradigm in failed states. Somalia's government is unlikely to seriously engage in liberal reforms or support a real security force to protect its citizens in the foreseeable future. Creating a liberal order requires the participation of local politicians and other influential people who view the state's construction along these lines as feasible and desirable. These core assumptions fit poorly where political boundaries are hard to identify while armed groups, including state security forces, infiltrate one another and selectively collaborate with people that they fight. Moreover, it is difficult to distinguish licit from illicit behaviour when the real networks of authority are so deeply rooted in the social structures of failed states and stray so far from the formal state institutions and procedures that liberal interveners require.

Under Baathist (officially socialist) rule, Iraq in the 1980s saw a similar proliferation of "tribes", which were really the personal networks of neighbourhood strongmen that could be mobilized to fight regime critics, collect intelligence, and build their own patronage networks through exploiting illicit commercial opportunities with Saddam Hussein's personal consent. At the time of the 2003 US-led invasion of Iraq, these political-economic networks were invisible to those who were in charge of the American agenda to modernize, democratize and liberalize Iraqi government and society (though visible to planners in the State Department whose pre-invasion reports were rejected and discounted by the Bush Administration).[47] As in Somalia, interveners in Iraq eventually accommodated themselves to these interests in their hasty, pragmatic efforts to create an illiberal order that they could use as a bulwark against the armed Islamist orders, first of Al-Qaeda and then Daesh, the so-called Islamic State.

The failed 2013 French hostage rescue mission in Somalia shows how these networks shape armed group interactions to frustrate interveners who seek to reverse the collapse of state authority. Simultaneously, these very same networks are leveraged highly effectively by Islamist groups to create their own illiberal order. It is no coincidence that the abduction of the French agents appears to have been masterminded by a relative of the interior minister and a deputy leader of the Islamic Courts Union (ICU).[48] The ICU's former leader, Sharif Sheikh Ahmed, became the president of the TFG in 2009 in an externally brokered attempt to divide the Islamist opposition against AMISOM and neighbouring Ethiopia. However, this manoeuvre had profoundly ambiguous results as, among other things, it enabled the ICU to position its members in the security services.[49] One faction within the ICU, Hizbul Islamiyya, rejected the power-sharing deal that Sharif Sheikh Ahmed benefited from and declared that it would continue to wage jihad against the TFG. Confusingly to outsiders looking at Somalia with liberally tinted lenses, this did not entail all-out opposition, all of the time. Thus, when the kidnap of the French agents occurred, ICU and Hizbul Islamiyya members fought together against the TFG in Mogadishu while opposing each other in Kismayo.[50]

Hizbul Islamiyya's capture of the French hostages asserted a sub-clan's place astride both insurgent and government camps. At that juncture, the kidnapping looked like an inside job. But when al-Shabaab operatives arrived and demanded one of the hostages, they left Hizbul Islamiyya with only one hostage to sell to the French.[51] Thereafter the situation became a power play by a hard-line faction, while also settling scores between kinship groups following the ongoing struggle to control territory and clan positions in southern Somalia. After ransom was finally paid, the receipt activated cleavages when the original kidnappers and the recipients of the ransom quarrelled over how this resource would affect the power of factions within the larger collection of Islamist groups, inside and outside formal government. This convoluted situation reflected the complex nature of the Islamists' selective participation in the TFG and anxieties to smooth over kinship relations while still personally benefiting from the ransom. After that, the situation only got more complex.[52]

In any event, these situations in which insurgents, criminal groups, neighbourhood militias and government forces share information and shift sides so easily devour liberal intervention's security assistance programmes and political reforms from within. The local actors upon whom intervention relies to create a domestic liberal order pursue their interests and organize their own security in the networks that are integral to the social structure of state failure and that interveners regard as obstacles to this transformation. This frustrating situation has led on occasion to more extreme suggestions among supporters of liberal intervention, such as the proposal of Anne-Marie Slaughter, former president of the American Society of International Law. Referring to countries that were targets for liberal intervention, she argued that if all else fails, the UN Security Council should consider targeted killings of state leaders who are threats to "human security" in order to promote a liberal international order of fundamental human rights and "the equal rights of men and women and nations large and small".[53] The recent history of Western intervention in Afghanistan, Iraq and Libya casts a shadow over such ambitious proposals. The focus of external intervention instead has hence shifted to the more modest goal of creating a new local order, authoritarian or otherwise, that at least does not openly challenge the liberal international order while possessing the capacity to frustrate the construction of alternative Islamist orders.

The illiberal dimension of intervention

Conventional liberal intervention and those who view this order as weathering its crises ignore the durable realities associated with state failure[54] and, as the situation in Somalia shows, proves to be unable to promote democracy and effective security sector reform. Meanwhile, armed Islamists also work to build their vision of illiberal orders. Into this situation step security experts who are charged with dealing with the consequences of the real politics of failed states.

Task-oriented security experts working on the ground, including indigenous and foreign Special Forces units, private security contractors and intelligence operatives, are less inclined to think in terms of the norms of liberal international society or the democracy promotion of conventional intervention programmes. These security experts are concerned with disrupting plots and targeting specific individuals, not the elaborate liberal reforms that their governments prescribe for Somalia and other failed states. These awkward activities force foreign and local security experts to try to understand and work within the political realities of the collapsed state. They thus pay a great deal of attention to how and why people fight in this environment of a failed state as they develop their own tactics to promote order.

This alternative approach to intervention values experience, often in ways that are in tension with the conventional liberal state-building strategy. These security practitioners have to adapt to new concepts of public and private spaces and devise new local–global relationships to achieve their goals in this environment in what Rita Abrahamsen and Michael Williams term "global security assemblages".[55] In everyday terms, practitioners often prioritize collaborations with ostensibly non-state armed groups, even if this means acting directly against the interests of host state officials and against the grain of democracy promotion. This alternative mode of intervention creates a new network of security professionals, who are found inside and outside Somalia. In some ways this network resembles the jihadist networks they oppose. Both draw upon experts in violence who are insulated from the social obligations of their own society and are connected instead to a global network of professionals. They seek to understand the cultural and political contexts in which they work to create a new order that bridges existing societal divisions at the same time as it mobilizes and redirects existing conflicts in the interests of a new order. That is, both global networks operate as classic insurgents in that their visions of a new order do not so much displace older forms of political contention or the values they embody as add their own layer of leadership and doctrine and recruit local leaders to their cause.[56] This pursuit of illiberal order is far less disruptive than the social revolution that liberal intervention requires of societies in failed states. Those focused on fighting armed Islamists (like their enemies) are effective at extracting information from myriad social networks to accurately identify and target perceived security threats—in the case of Somalia, ranging from al-Shabaab members to state officials and soldiers who collude with them.[57] The result is that intervention on the ground plays out more like the Pax Britannica that Verhoeven and Blom Hansen describe in chapters 1 and 2, in which the hegemon is forced to experiment with and accommodate itself to the diverse arrangements and layered and shared networks of authority through which these places are actually ruled.

The simultaneous bombings of US embassies in Kenya and Tanzania on 7 August 1998, which killed 224 people, generated mounting anxiety in Washington about the nature of failed states. This and particularly the 2001 al-Qaeda attacks on New York and Washington, DC, caused US officials to step up order creation in failed states like Somalia, even if this meant intentional violations of basic precepts of the liberal international order, including turning a blind eye to grave human rights violations. These officials were willing to deploy the kinds of tactics used to counter Soviet influence during the Cold War, such as support for proxy militias, targeted killings and subversion of unfriendly governments. While promoting democracy remains a desirable goal, it takes a back seat to protecting Western security through promoting order in deeply illiberal ways in failed states like Somalia.

US officials noted that the 1998 bombers were connected to members of the Egyptian Islamic Jihad group and ultimately to al-Qaeda, and the architect of the attacks, Fazul Abdullah Mohammed, took refuge in Somalia. This concern led to US recruitment of Somali businessmen in Kenya, referred to earlier, who in 2004 returned to Somalia to use their heavily armed security details drawn from their kinship network to collect information and target individuals in coordination with US advisors.[58] In February 2006, these businessmen formed the Alliance for the Restoration of Peace and Counter-Terrorism (ARPCT) to fight the emergent ICU in Mogadishu and capture or kill suspected al-Qaeda members. CIA support for these proxies caused State Department officials to describe this as a "parallel Somalia policy", though one that ultimately failed to prevent the ICU from controlling much of the city.[59] Some members of the ARPCT opted to serve the interests of the kinship networks they shared with Islamists whom they were supposed to fight. Meanwhile, back in Washington this "parallel Somalia policy" and its shortcomings exacerbated tension between government agencies over how to deal with political instability in Somalia. In any event, the ICU-imposed Islamist order attracted popular support, while the ICU's puritanical and expansionist rhetoric raised foreigners' suspicions that it harboured domestic and foreign terrorists.

This alternative approach to intervention unfolded with the creation of Somali agencies that largely operated autonomously from the state and outside the conventional liberal intervention paradigm. From 2008 NISA received assistance from US advisors, and has operated with varying effectiveness while a variety of Somali governments and Islamist armed groups fought to control Mogadishu.[60] Foreign advisors and private firms sustain budgeting, staff and command structures that they try to insulate from the rest of Somalia's government and from the social pressures to share information with those they are supposed to pursue. In an illustration of Abrahamsen's and Williams' "global assemblage", foreign advisors aim to build a cadre of Somalis who integrate into global networks of security professionals to target coercive capacity against insurgents.

These externally sustained armed forces develop the capacity to act, even when the host government plays a minimal role in the force's activities. During AMISOM's 2011 offensive to drive al-Shabaab from Mogadishu, residents reported that well-trained fighters appeared on the scene with foreign support. "We initially thought that Alphas were foreign soldiers," said a businessman who did not believe that Somali authorities could sustain such a force. "Even when we discovered that definitely they were Somalis, we can't tell where they came from. They are completely covered so you can't see their faces and they don't interact with army or AMISOM."[61]

A US official acknowledged support for special units to fight al-Shabaab: "The aid we provide includes training support for the Somali advanced infantry company, also known as *Danab*—the Lightning Force. This is a 150-person unit we believe can become a source of future leadership for the entire army."[62] These fighters train separately from other Somali forces and some Somali officials are kept at arm's length.[63] For example, an aide to a former deputy minister reported that his boss was prevented from entering a compound housing private security forces near the Alpha compound, and speculated that "Americans there hesitate because they aren't confident about the Somali government's reliability" because of the tendency of officials to share information that reaches al-Shabaab.[64] An observer of the July 2014 al-Shabaab attack on government offices attributed the efficient response of Somali special units to US training and especially to their segregation from the influence of Somali government officials.[65] This operational effectiveness is a concern to Somali politicians, since an autonomous security institution that US personnel supervise can easily run foul of politicians' networks, especially if the networks are implicated in activities that Americans see as threats to security. A US Army logistics officer who was deployed to Mogadishu observed, for example, that Danab fighters and armed components of NISA fight other elements of Somalia's armed forces in clashes that "can often be as violent as their clashes with Al-Shabaab".[66]

Foreign security assistance focuses on similar elite units in other countries. The Crisis Response Unit 222, under Afghanistan's Ministry of the Interior, and Golden Division, directed by the Iraqi Counter Terrorism Service, are relatively small forces of elite troops that are militarily and politically reliable providers of security as their foreign benefactors define this concept. Iraq's Golden Brigade (36th Commando Battalion) was the only major component of the Iraqi military that survived the collapse of the Iraqi Army in the face of Daesh's advance in 2014. As in Somalia, these Iraqi and Afghani forces enjoy far better pay, equipment and living conditions than the typical soldiers in their armies. They are equipped almost identically to US Special Forces and are far more cohesive and resistant to infiltration from political militias and Islamist groups than their regular military counterparts. Their officers and NCOs are far more likely to speak English, and to have travelled internationally in the course of training.[67] Foreign trainers, whether Special Forces or contractors, remain embedded with these forces to ensure high fighting capacities, management of information, and insulation from the political agendas of political militias and factions of the governments which these forces are supposed to serve. This insulation facilitates these forces' connections to a global network of security experts that chase and kill armed Islamists but are comfortable doing so in ways that do not require promoting democracy or even major reforms of the host government.

This form of intervention requires logistical support independent of the (institutionally weak) state of which they are supposedly a part. In Somalia, private firms provide an alternative to the forlorn hope that the current government will take on more responsibility for domestic order, let alone building a democratic society. Bancroft Global Development, registered in the United States as a charity, is considered a private security firm by UN rapporteurs. They note that the firm was active in Mogadishu from 2007, engaged in a variety of projects involving AMISOM and Somali armed forces.[68] By 2007 US security agencies and local Somali partners collected enough information to enable US Special Forces to target insurgent leaders.[69]

The arrangements between special Somali forces and foreign security experts insulate these forces from the influence of social embeddedness and free them to direct violence against the groups that foreign backers define as threats. This insulation leaves units with the capacity to provide the deterrence that individual fighters need when they must deal with the family members of insurgents they have killed or captured. The family members often want to avenge these acts, but free-standing Special Forces that are insulated from this particular aspect of the social environment of the failed state can protect their members from attacks. Private security firms and special units are effective in training recruits but especially in insulating special units from the influence of state officials. This quality frees them to be "good fighters" in the eyes of counter-terrorism experts. Indeed, foreign personnel would be even more insulated, but they would lack experience and personal connections that would be critical for receiving and evaluating important targeting information. Importantly, insulation from both social pressures and government control enables these special units to escalate counter-insurgent violence through targeted killings, detentions, black sites and so forth.

This realistic understanding of the politics of security in Somalia informs commanders in AMISOM contingents too. The Ugandan People's Defence Force used the militia of Omar "Finnish", a former member of the ARPCT and, later, a member of parliament and

Mogadishu real estate developer, to hold a buffer zone between AMISOM forces and al-Shabaab-controlled areas of Mogadishu before the 2011 offensive to drive al-Shabaab out of the city. This strategy required careful attention in selecting a militia that was better than others at preventing reprisals from family members against recruits for acts committed in the course of fighting while accepting the reality of personal networks of influence in armed groups.[70] In these situations, the national army cannot provide such guarantees for soldiers, which helps to explain why armies in this context usually are as ineffective in battling insurgents as they are in benefiting from security assistance more generally.

Arrangements of this sort provide foreign interveners with soldiers who, removed from their domestic politics, redirect their personal connections and loyalties to a commander to become more consistently effective fighters. Their personal loyalties to individual commanders become an asset in this new context, as commanders are more inclined to focus on a single goal (i.e. fighting insurgents) rather than hedging bets and simultaneously playing multiple sides in their efforts to assert influence across different networks. Special militias in Somalia and in other places operate as an exclusive source of patronage and avenue for upward mobility for their members—a social strategy that recognizes the reality of the failed state environment. This strategy also separates counter-terrorism from dependence on liberal state-building in the conventional broad-spectrum counter-insurgency model to promote order. In doing so, hegemony becomes "thin" as liberal democracy drops out of the picture and its agents learn how to accommodate "free markets" that rest more on violent and often illicit networks of control than on the beneficent, democracy-sustaining liberal economic order.[71] Pax Americana in this version is not liberal, and is hegemonic only in so far as US military might disrupts competing orders.

"Security" and order in failed states

The basic assumptions guiding intervention for liberal state-building in the Global Indian Ocean clash with the realities of fighting insurgents and creating stable political order in places where most officials lack the capacity or political will to carry out these tasks in ways that conform to a liberal global order. Pragmatic intervention in Somalia and elsewhere is part of a process of learning and adaptation to this distinctive political environment, much as Pax Britannica entailed experimentation with a range of different arrangements of governance across a 19th-century landscape of varying degrees of often overlapping sovereignty. Some scholars recognize the durability of this condition and historicize the diverse elements of this order and juxtapose it with the rigid legal and institutional framework of the contemporary state system.[72] Two officials in neighbouring Ethiopia who deal directly with security challenges from Somalia have examined these practical aspects of power asymmetries between successful and failed states within the constraints of current norms and practices of sovereignty.[73]

Adaptation can produce arrangements that violate even basic liberal norms. For example, the use of children may be a rational adaptation in Somalia on the part of NISA to identify insurgents, but it raises predictable concerns about ethics.[74] Individuals under the NISA's control, including some captured from areas under al-Shabaab control, were separated from families and encouraged or coerced to identify insurgents. This practice insulated these individuals from the constraints of the wider social system, an effective but highly problematic way to collect valid information about insurgent presence in these communities. This practice also undermines the performative aspects of progressive ideals like human rights and the status of the child that are integral to the legitimation of the ambitious project of remaking societies so that they conform to liberal hegemony's ideal of progress. In colonial India, British accommodations to realities on the ground involved systems of treaties and indirect rule and even a selective reciprocal assimilation of elites, which created political space for practices that progressives condemned as "odious native customs".[75] The contemporary disjuncture between hegemony's promise and the realities of its enforcement leads instead to a more naked reliance on military might in which the synergy between that military might, free trade and liberal democracy that is supposed to ensure stability is notably absent, and the prestige of the hegemon suffers as a result.[76]

This ad hoc approach to intervention works around conventional norms of sovereignty, diplomacy and international supervision of failed states aimed at building democracy. It does not require a great deal of political discussion in Washington or other capitals, as this "light footprint" approach incurs few casualties among intervening forces. When casualties occur, such as the death of an American SEAL in Somalia and four SEALs in Niger in 2017, politicians profess to be surprised that US soldiers are even deployed in these countries. Casualties and unwanted political attention reinforce the bureaucratic tendency to rely even more heavily on elite Western trainers and contractors to sustain these anti-terrorism forces. This is unsurprising, given that the US has been involved in much bigger campaigns in two out of every three years since the end of the Cold War (i.e., Iraq, Afghanistan, fighting Daesh) with dismal results. Since these wars invariably fail to achieve their objective of creating liberal orders in the invaded countries, the public becomes sceptical of more interventions and begins to doubt the competence of their political leaders—an undermining of hegemony from within.

Is pragmatic intervention able to create a sustainable illiberal order in states around the Global Indian Ocean given that a liberal political dispensation appears to be entirely illusory? The consolidation of reliable coercion in the hands of a small group inevitably raises concerns about fairness and legitimacy and increases the probability that foreign security assistance will be used to consolidate the power of authoritarian leaders. Yet organizing armed forces in this manner provides a basis for building the hegemony of a narrow elite coalition and for more clearly defining the boundaries between state order and myriad parochial and personal contentions. This autonomy removes these key actors from the societal relationships that pre-conflict leaders of Somalia and elsewhere incited and exploited in their divide and rule strategies and that prolonged insecurity and made Islamist-provided orders appealing to people fed up with the strains of uncertainty and predatory violence. Pragmatic intervention picks sides in local conflicts and thus moves in the direction of creating a hegemonic force that is able to use coercion to build and maintain an authoritarian order. Woldemariam notes in chapter 7 that the authoritarian order in Ethiopia and Eritrea initially depended upon what eventually became international relationships between two former rebel groups once Eritrea seceded from Ethiopia. The difference in failed states like Somalia, however, is that the push for this authoritarian order comes from those abroad who are supposed to be promoters of liberal order.

The case of Somalia illuminates some of the dangers that pursuit of a Global War on Terror that bring interventions in "failed states" pose to liberal hegemony, even when objectives are trimmed back from earlier ambitions to remake these societies and their politics. This pragmatic approach to intervention reflects the political strategies of the recipients, which are almost certain to be authoritarian, rather than the ostensible liberal goals of the interveners. While the interveners in this revised approach take account of the specific social conditions of failed states, their focus is tactical: to find more effective ways to conduct counter-terrorism. But tactical effectiveness lacks the broader vision that links pragmatic assistance to overall political development. In lieu of a strategy, it empowers cadres of security professionals who are sure to play important roles in shaping what kind of political order emerges in Somalia and in other failed states. In doing so, it shows to the rest of the world that the foreign interveners have given up on their own hegemonic goal of liberal state-building.

9

CHINA IN THE INDIAN OCEAN

THE SEARCH FOR A NEW HEGEMON?

Rana Mitter

Today, Chinese and Indian naval vessels patrol uneasily in the waters of the Indian Ocean. Piracy is a shared concern, but also an opportunity to test out new naval strategies and deploy force outside traditional areas of influence. General elections in states such as the Maldives and Sri Lanka have become proxies for that same, understated confrontation between Asia's two great powers. Meanwhile, new Chinese investment, trade flows and aid transform states on or near the coast of Africa—Ethiopia, Kenya and Tanzania prominently among them.

As the chapters in this volume argue, there is now a growing sense of an emerging political—but not predominantly liberal—order in the Indian Ocean space. Regional or even global links bring together political and economic interests ranging from East Africa to South East Asia. The question of the Global Indian Ocean has re-emerged at the same time as Chinese power. A range of analyses, some reassuring, some alarmist, make the case that China is seeking to become a global power and even replace the United States.[1] In practice, it is in its own backyard, the Asia–Pacific, that China has sought most actively to dominate. In the Americas and Europe, while Chinese economic and political influence is growing stronger, China is still a relatively minor actor. However, in the Indian Ocean, there is little doubt that in economic, military and political terms, China is expanding its "backyard" considerably.

Since the start of the 21st century, China has changed the geopolitical balance not just in the Asia–Pacific (where it was always important), but far more drastically in the Global Indian Ocean. The sub-regions within the rim of the Indian Ocean have all been profoundly affected by the growing Chinese economic and security presence in the region. The littoral states of South Asia have been recipients of the capital reallocation that underpins the Belt and Road Initiative (BRI); Pakistan is due to receive some $62 billion of funding well into the 2030s as part of the BRI. The Indian Ocean is also vital for China's energy security: roughly half of China's crude oil imports come from the Middle East; according to a Chatham House report, China imports 49 per cent of its crude from the Middle East and 37 per cent of Middle Eastern oil exports are destined for China.[2]

Yet the Chinese role in the Indian Ocean remains much more in flux than the equivalent disputes over the growing Chinese presence in the Pacific. In the latter area, a variety of existing geopolitical structures, such as America's alliances with Japan and South Korea, and the well-documented disputes over the South China Sea, have set the tone for a growing confrontation between Washington and Beijing. However, in the Indian Ocean, such Cold War-era alliances are less clearly delineated. While the US, China and India all play a significant role in the macro-region, it is far less clear who dominates, and what the political stakes are overall on both sides. In the introduction, Harry Verhoeven refers to this condition as "thin hegemony", a circumstance very different from that of the Atlantic or Pacific spaces, and one that is particularly suited to China's desire to create a new type of order which matches its ambitions.

The Indian Ocean provides a clear arena for two questions that are increasingly urgent in the geopolitics of the 21st century: how global will the Indian Ocean be, and how global will China be? The questions can be answered in at least two ways: in terms of the realism of power politics, and in terms of the creation of a new narrative of regional order.

Overall, this chapter concludes that the Indian Ocean will indeed be the site of a whole range of new global connections as well as potential confrontations. China is taking clear steps to create a commercially driven network in the region, a probable corollary of which is an increasingly militarized presence. This is highly likely to lead to reactions and hedging by India and the US among others. However, Beijing will also find itself vulnerable as it becomes increasingly global. It will not be possible for China to develop an autarkic economic system in the Indian Ocean, even if it wished to do so.

The Global Indian Ocean is also the inheritor of its own traditions of a very thin order in the region. Both in realist and constructivist terms, the Indian Ocean has rarely had much history of either a powerful hegemon or of shared norms and values—certainly not in the conventional liberal sense that much of the IR literature proposes. This has produced a new opportunity for China. A significant part of China's attempts to advance its position in the world in recent years have been less concerned with direct confrontation with existing hegemons (certainly outside the Asia–Pacific), and more with finding ways to create new realities in places where order is still less clearly defined. Its operations in the Global Indian Ocean certainly fit into that definition, attempting to create new opportunities from the "thin hegemony" that it finds there.

These developments provide an important new angle to one of the most important timely discussions in contemporary international relations: the likelihood of China becoming a fully integrated, or at least not actively revisionist, member of the contemporary liberal international order. For much of the past few decades, there has been a body of scholarship on this question that was broadly reassured, or at least not fundamentally concerned, about such a prospect. In the early 2010s, David Shambaugh could write of the China of the Hu Jintao era that it was "*in* the community of nations but is in many ways not really *part* of the community"; his concept of China as a "partial power" reflected the analysis that China was not, in a fundamental sense, a challenger to the existing liberal order.[3] Alastair Iain Johnston argued strongly in 2013 that the development of a "new assertiveness meme" to explain China's international behaviour was not supported by evidence; he has argued more recently, after General Secretary Xi Jinping's foreign policy had had several years in which to bed, that China has to be understood as engaging with different elements of global order in different ways: to refer to one "order" is too simple.[4] The prominent Chinese international relations scholar Yan Xuetong has also recently declared, albeit cautiously, that China's current international behaviour is not intended as a fundamental challenge to the existing order. Yan suggests that while China and the US will be the two major powers of the 2020s, "there is no ideology able to replace liberalism through establishing a set of new mainstream values to guide the international community over the coming decade".[5]

These scholars' analyses of the endurance of the liberal order over-all remain entirely valid. The idea that China desires a new type of order, in the sense of (say) an international order of the sort envisaged by Lenin and Trotsky, is misleading: the current balance of state sovereignty and international institutions suits China well in various ways. However, China's leaders have raised their global ambitions in the mid-2010s, with a range of indicators, including the establishment of the Belt and Road Initiative, increased military spending, and increased presence in and spending on international organizations such as the UN. The argument, then, is not just about whether China is revising the liberal order, but rather about how it is inhabiting it and adapting it to its own preferences.[6] The development of China's presence in the Indian Ocean is a good example; little that happens there is a sign of China's desire for a fundamental shift in order, but rather it provides an example of how China can retool existing norms (and the lack of them) to its own needs. Below, I will discuss the historical origins of China's presence in the Indian Ocean arena and then reflect on the way that the country's role is shifting there in the present day. Overall, I will suggest, the Chinese presence in the Indian Ocean is likely to grow as China's global presence increases. This does not, however, mean that it can act exactly as it pleases; the region's own actors have their own motivations and agency, as do the liberal powers—should they choose to exercise them.

CHINA IN THE INDIAN OCEAN

The historical imaginary

China's engagement with the Indian Ocean is not new. During the first half of the second millennium CE, Chinese communities settled extensively in South East Asia. As Tansen Sen and other scholars have shown, the Mongol Yuan dynasty (1279–1368) undertook an assertive series of maritime expeditions to South Asian ports as well as numerous diplomatic missions.[7] These then set the stage for the Ming dynasty, when the Yongle emperor sent out a series of expeditions under Admiral Zheng He to demonstrate the power of the Chinese empire, to trade and even engage in conflict. The performativity of the Ming court was both external and internal. The Ming intended that the states that they visited in Asia and Africa should recognize the high status of Chinese civilization. However, there was also, at least for court elites, a sense of prestige that came from being associated with the extensive reach of the voyages and the exotic commodities and creatures brought back from them.[8] These voyages, which have been well documented, extended as far as the coast of East Africa, as well as many parts of South and South East Asia. However, they did not at that point lead China to extend its reach to the wider Indian Ocean on a continuing basis. There was no meaningful Chinese order in the Indian Ocean to match the spread of Confucian-imperial values within the Eurasian landmass during the Qing dynasty, or in South East Asia during much of the imperial era.

Nor did the modern era give China much scope to engage with the Indian Ocean. From the Opium Wars until World War II, China was under siege much of the time by the Western world and Japan, with little time to consider issues other than preventing the disintegration of the fragile Chinese state. During the 19th century, the Pax Britannica consisted of "a patchwork of sovereignty" (in Thomas Blom Hansen's words in chapter 2) during that period, which ended up integrating—and subduing—China within a fast-changing new order. Up to the mid-19th century, China ran a massive trade surplus with Britain and its empire, which presented a major problem for the London-centred order, as Verhoeven shows in his introduction. However, the arrival of an Indian Ocean crop, opium from Bengal, allowed a new dynamic to emerge, as a British network emerged that sent raw opium to South East Asia and on for shipping into China, famously reversing the trade surplus into a deficit and leading to the Opium Wars of the mid-19th century.[9]

The post-war era of the 20th century, however, provided the first stage on which China could attempt to recreate regional order beyond its own boundaries. Chiang Kai-shek's Nationalist government came out of World War II with a strong sense that it wished to become the hegemonic state in East Asia.[10] It saw itself as an American ally, yet with a strong role in the United Nations with its own permanent seat. It also saw itself as a model state for new post-colonial states, as well as an ally in the emerging anti-colonial wars. The Indian Ocean states of South East Asia were very much part of this vision. First, these countries had significant overseas Chinese diasporas, which had connections either to nationalist or communist movements. In addition, Chiang had begun to develop a stronger role as a voice of anti-colonialism even during World War II, for instance during his visit to see the Indian nationalist leaders Nehru and Gandhi in 1942.[11] Therefore, the recolonization by European powers of Indonesia, Malaya and Vietnam provided an arena in which a putative non-communist anti-colonial movement could be stimulated by Nationalist China. This movement had little time to develop, of course, because of the communist victory on the Chinese mainland. Yet the years from 1945 to 1949 did mark an incipient step by a newly sovereign China to project its power beyond its immediate littoral, as well as drawing on networks that had existed before its reassumption of full sovereignty after the treaties of 1943 that ended extraterritoriality.

The Cold War saw the emergence of a new order in which liberal values were more evident in name than in reality, as chapters 3 and 6 especially underline. The US claimed that it was sustaining "free" states, but "freedom" frequently meant little more than the absence of communism. Japan was the only full democracy that lasted through the period; in South Asia, as Lieven in chapter 10 rightly notes, only India—which was explicitly not a US ally, keeping up a strong relationship with the USSR and advocating non-alignment—stuck to democratic norms throughout the period (barring the 1975–7 Emergency). Nonetheless, there was a detectable division into Cold War blocs in much of Asia, and US and Soviet allies (or client states) were fairly easily defined in the region, with Taiwan and South Korea on the one side, and a unified Vietnam on the other.

In contrast, the Global Indian Ocean was witness—as throughout its history (see Blom Hansen's chapter 2)—to a variety of experiments in government, few of which had much pretension to liberalism. A major turning point for China, but also for a sense of unity for the states of the Indian Ocean zone, was the Bandung Conference of 1955. This continuing presence allowed a space for a discourse shaped in part by the Chinese presence in the post-colonial world after Bandung.[12] This conference marked a significant turning point for an Afro-Asian world in the post-war world. It was especially significant for Beijing, not just because of the positive impression made by the suave foreign minister, Zhou Enlai, but also because it marked a definitive point at which China was seen as a powerbroker outside the Sino-Soviet alliance. Yet China was not the only dominant presence there. India's prime minister, Jawaharlal Nehru, also made a powerful case for his nation's role as a regional leader. Furthermore, the Indian Ocean itself took a more prominent role, albeit not expressed in those terms. The meeting itself was held in Indonesia, one of the most prominent of the newly independent South East Asian states. Furthermore, the idea of a shared Asian–African–Arab solidarity at various points around the Indian Ocean rim came from a range of other points within that geography: Nasser in Egypt, Sukarno in Indonesia, and Nehru in India itself. They would later be joined by Julius Nyerere in Tanzania, the left's standard bearer in East Africa, who dreamed of a new regional order.[13]

Most formal anti-colonial struggles were over by the 1950s in East and South East Asia (the Vietnamese–American war of 1965–75 falls into a different category as the US-backed South Vietnamese regime was not a colony). The states around the Indian Ocean outside South East Asia were a space in which colonialism was still a dominant factor well into the 1960s, and (neo-)imperialism was a powerful, enduring factor in a way that was less true than in the Asia–Pacific. Kenya (which gained its independence in 1963) and Tanzania (1961) were British colonies into the 1960s, as were South Yemen (1967), the Maldives (1968) and Oman (1970).

This provided new opportunities for China to project its revolutionary influence. In Rhodesia, for instance, China was able to play a role by providing support for Robert Mugabe's ZANU liberation movement (as opposed to the Soviet assistance to Joshua Nkomo's ZAPU), a partnership that has endured to the present day.[14] It also sponsored the Tan-Zam railway, working with Tanzania and Zambia to provide a way for those states to avoid white settler-controlled Rhodesia (shades of the high-speed trains which have become an iconic part of the BRI);[15] the US became alarmed enough about the project to sponsor a rival Tan-Zam highway. China was certainly able to define a distinctive role for itself on the African side of the Indian Ocean world: revolutionary, developmentalist, and clearly not liberal.

However, such initiatives were held back by the reality of China's poverty. Mao's China had some success in projecting itself as the face of a new global order centred on the developing world. But it was in no economic position to make more than relatively limited gestures in pursuit of its vision. It was further hampered in those goals by the ending of the Cultural Revolution in 1976 and the adoption of Deng Xiaoping's more pragmatic policies toward the wider world. Deng's famous sixteen-character maxim ("Bide your time, hide your greatness ...") indicated that China would not seek an active role in challenging the US-led global order as it sought to build its economy.[16]

By the 2010s, that economy had not just been built, but had grown into the world's second largest. This meant that for the first time in perhaps two centuries, China had not only an active vision of how it conceptualized the regions around it, but enough economic power to shape that vision. This was also the time at which Beijing turned more actively towards influence in the Global Indian Ocean.

The politics of naval power in the Indian Ocean

Two crucial determinants of international relations, namely geography and the question of norms in the international system, have come to acquire a new significance in the Global Indian Ocean since the end of the Cold War. The North Atlantic has remained, overall, a region that defends liberal values (despite the questions about these norms triggered by the Trump presidency) which sit at the heart of its self-image, external relations and domestic political order. The Asia–Pacific region, a definition used here to exclude South Asia (contrary to the much in vogue discourse in Washington and London of an

"Indo-Pacific"), has been in flux; a growing sense of economic and political liberalization (in Indonesia, Thailand, South Korea, etc.) has been thrown into question by a combination of indigenous illiberal movements (such as the 2016 election of Rodrigo Duterte in the Philippines), along with the growing sense that China offers a major challenge to the existing liberal post-war order (a sense promulgated not least by Chinese scholars).[17]

As Verhoeven argues in his introduction to this book, the Indian Ocean, in contrast, has not been subject to any one tightly united order for much of the period since 1989 (or, indeed, before it). India had a relatively limited interest in naval projection during much of that period, and other major powers, in particular the United States, cleaved in large part to formations that had emerged during the Cold War. South East Asia, in contrast, became something of an "American lake", with US alliances, defence and trade agreements, and political understandings with countries including the Philippines, Thailand, Singapore and even Vietnam.

An important factor that has changed the dynamics of the region is the rapid growth of a Chinese blue-water navy along with a two-ocean strategy (Pacific and Indian). China has noted that there is no hegemonic power in the Indian Ocean, unlike the Atlantic and Pacific, and has sought to place itself in that position. For the last two decades, China has made significant investment in its naval prowess. By 2018, the PLA Navy had some 300 vessels, compared to 287 for the US Navy. The ChinaPower analysis notes: "New ships are being put to sea at an impressive rate. Between 2014 and 2018, China launched more submarines, warships, amphibious vessels, and auxiliaries than the number of ships currently serving in the individual navies of Germany, India, Spain, and the United Kingdom."[18] This rise must be kept in perspective: US military spending is still some four times that of China. Nonetheless, the significant upgrading of China's ability to project its naval power into new spaces has already changed the strategic outlook in the Global Indian Ocean, and will continue to do so in decades to come.

The early 2000s created new circumstances for all actors in the region, not just China. Jonathan Ward has insightfully analysed the three key factors which shape current geopolitical issues in the Indian

Ocean world. First, China's economic model depends on the reliability of high volumes of shipping coming through the Indian Ocean, especially at its key chokepoints: the Suez Canal and Bab al-Mandab, and the Straits of Malacca. Second, there is a new enthusiasm for India developing a more extensive naval presence in the region, as it seeks to preserve its own room for manoeuvre. Third, many other Asian powers aside from India and China—Pakistan, Indonesia and Iran most prominently—have a stake in the region and are likely to resist or, at least, mediate Chinese preponderance while balancing Indian and US interests.[19]

China has used both its naval power and its economic weight to shift relationships in the region since the new millennium. The first manifestation of this presence was defined by an alarmed India as the "string of pearls" strategy—that is, the idea that the medium-power nations of South Asia were being "picked off" by China as potential allies (or at least as a bulwark against India).[20] However, the past decade has seen a more ambitious strategy in which military and economic elements are brought together across the Ocean itself to create a new geography of power projection. The string of pearls, if such it is, now stretches across the Ocean, with Chinese concentrations of power in East Africa (especially in Ethiopia, Kenya and Sudan)[21] now looking out across to the Maldives, Pakistan and Bangladesh.[22]

From the early 2000s onward, China has placed ever-greater emphasis on the growth of its navy, giving it more prominence and importance than the development of ground forces. In the Indian Ocean, the Chinese naval presence has been largely posited around the promotion of anti-piracy activities off the coast of Somalia (cf. Reno's chapter 8 on interventionism). This has been helpful to the creation of a Chinese narrative of greater global citizenship, but has also enabled China to develop its ambitious programme of naval renewal, along with providing opportunities for warfighting experience.[23]

An important moment occurred in 2017, when China opened its first overseas naval base in Djibouti, providing it with projection capacity across the Indian Ocean. While China is by no means the first state to have developed a base in that state, there is little doubt that this move indicates a significant upgrading of China's intention to make itself a permanent state of influence in the region.[24] The

renewed interest of the US in strengthening its AFRICOM commitment to a military presence in Africa owes at least part of its origins
to growing concern about other actors, including China as well as
non-state perpetrators of terror.[25]

Challenging the norms governing the Global Indian Ocean?

The majority of analyses of China's international relations, particularly in the post-Mao era, have been realist in tone both in China
and the West, as is seen in the discussion above of China's changing
naval strategy.[26] Realism was the most appropriate lens through
which to argue (quite reasonably) that China tacked towards the US
to balance the USSR in the 1970s and 1980s, with China's growing
regional influence in Asia a function of its growing economy.
China's foreign policy was defined, in large part, by what China did
not want (interference in its domestic policy; international and
transnational institutions with coercive power over China) rather
than by what it did.

Yet realism is not, in itself, enough to explain what is happening in
China's foreign policy more broadly, and in the Indian Ocean in particular. While there have been significant changes in the values driving
Chinese foreign policy throughout the 1990s and 2000s, the rise to
power of Xi Jinping in 2012 marked a major change in the formulation of domestic and foreign policy, giving it an ideational element
that had not been seen since the Maoist era.

First, Xi's speech to the Party Congress on 18 October 2017 made
it clear that China was choosing a system which was, self-declaredly,
different from any to be found in the liberal world. The dominance
of the Chinese Communist Party and the determination that the party
would be the dominant force within Chinese society seemed to move
away from the trend, in the 2000s, of establishing governmental
rather than party structures (such as the State Council) as drivers of
policy. His speech made the point that

> the Chinese Dream can be realized only in a peaceful international
> environment and under a stable international order … We will
> uphold justice while pursuing shared interests, and will foster new
> thinking on common, comprehensive, cooperative, and sustainable

security... China will continue its efforts to safeguard world peace, contribute to global development, and uphold international order.

Such sentiments were hardly new, but Xi went on to relate the idea to the Belt and Road Initiative, declaring:

> We should pursue the Belt and Road Initiative as a priority, give equal emphasis to "bringing in" and "going global", follow the principle of achieving shared growth through discussion and collaboration, and increase openness and cooperation in building innovation capacity. With these efforts, we hope to make new ground in opening China further through links running eastward and westward, across land and over sea.

A further declaration, that "We should ... resolutely reject the Cold War mentality and power politics, and take a new approach to developing state-to-state relations with communication, not confrontation, and with partnership, not alliance", was a clear statement against the foreign policy of the United States.

By rejecting "alliances", Xi was protesting against the extensive presence of US defence agreements and bases in the Asia–Pacific. However, the statement could also be read as a marker for policies being developed in the Indian Ocean, where alliances in general remain weak to nonexistent. The statement that "We will strengthen exchanges and cooperation with the political parties and organizations of other countries, and encourage people's congresses, CPPCC committees, the military, local governments, and people's organizations to engage in exchanges with other countries" also implies a willingness to influence the civil societies of other countries in a way that China had not previously explicitly stated.[27]

The 2010s have seen an increasing explicitness with which China chooses to define its own political system as a "model" which might have applicability beyond China itself.[28] Previously, Chinese leaders used language, most notably the expression "with Chinese characteristics [Zhongguo tese]", that indicated that China was a self-declared anomaly. In his 2017 speech to the Party Congress, Xi made it clear that China should try to engage its political model more strongly with the wider world.

This shift provides the context in which the move towards a more constructivist, discourse-driven model of shared values and norms emerged as part of the new BRI-oriented strategy. So far, in the late 2010s, this is a work still in progress. Its most obvious manifestations are in the Asia–Pacific region, where a discourse of "community of common destiny" is used to create language that suggests a shared moral as well as geopolitical purpose. However, the nature of the "common destiny" has yet to be clearly defined.[29]

As this volume has shown through many different perspectives, the post-1945 (and especially post-1989) liberal international order did, despite its many flaws and contradictions, put forward normatively liberal goals, including cooperative regional order, liberalization of trade, and (putatively) democratization, under the Pax Americana. The Chinese alternative is still inchoate. However, there are clear attempts to create a new discourse that defines the emergent order in terms beyond the purely realist. Ideas of development are at the heart of this discourse: the assurance by China that it will provide huge sums in infrastructure is used as a sign that it can combine economics and morality. Linked to this is a nod to an older idea, drawn from the Cold War, of non-interference: unlike the Western-dominated institutions which demand certain norms in governance and supervision when providing support, China does not seek to question the bona fides of the regimes accepting its funds.[30]

This still leaves many ideational holes to be filled; essentially, this is a negative rather than positive definition of order. In particular, it gives no sense of any internal normative values *within* the polities that make up the order. China does not yet have the courage of its convictions; despite Xi's declaration that its model is capable of export, the specific Chinese combination of authoritarian government and market-driven exports and consumption has yet to be reproduced widely (not least because that model was indeed rather specific to China's unusual developmental circumstances).

Of course, it is also entirely plausible that a very thin order, with a lean set of norms, is more suited to China's still protean project in the region. As Verhoeven points out in his introduction, the absence of any deep normative order is the rule rather than the exception in this region, certainly from a historical perspective. The lack of liberal states in the region, and the concern that such liberal states that there are (such as India) have to maintain non-intervention as part of the post-colonial legacy in the region, may mean that China's ideas of how a thin order should be run might fit better with at least some non-liberal or even illiberal actors in the region.

The Global Indian Ocean and BRI

A great deal of work has concentrated on the changing Chinese role in the Asia–Pacific.[31] Such scholarship recognizes that the power relationships in the region are changing but disagrees on the likelihood of confrontation in the region; there are existing hegemons whose relationship with each other is now in question.

The situation is different in the Indian Ocean. As this book argues, no single hegemon has managed to impose a thick order in the area, and the types of norms and expectations that operate in the Pacific and, indeed, Atlantic have not emerged.

The fluid nature of China's aims in international society has become particularly important in the late 2010s, when one particular factor came to change the way in which China engaged with the Global Indian Ocean: the Belt and Road Initiative. This ambitious plan has been labelled, albeit not by the Chinese Communist Party officially, as a new "Marshall Plan".[32] It is the proposal that under Chinese leadership, some US$8 trillion (or more) of infrastructure funding should be brought into a region that stretches across the Eurasian continent and beyond. It has become the subject of immense interest as well as controversy both inside China and beyond. Although its antecedents can be seen from the early 2000s, it is associated in particular with General Secretary Xi Jinping, and as his rule becomes more authoritarian and China's vision more wide-ranging, there have been many accusations that the BRI is in fact a method by which China will seek to create a new economic hegemony across much of the world.[33]

However, although the majority of attention on the BRI project has been on its Asian aspects, maps indicate that in, its widest form, it very explicitly brings East Africa into the network. This, of course, intersects neatly with the growing Chinese presence in countries such as Ethiopia and Kenya. It also maps out the framework for a nexus of influence around the Ocean.

The role of infrastructural aid in creating power structures is not new in the Global Indian Ocean, including key regions like the

Arabian Peninsula.[34] The history of empire is, of course, one example of this, as studies show with the development of India's railways along paths that suited the British colonizers rather than indigenous market patterns. Odd Arne Westad has demonstrated that colonial thinking was still highly relevant in the mindsets of the Cold War hegemons as they reshaped the Third World, including Africa.[35] The term "neo-colonial" has been thrown at China in hostile interpretations of the BRI (and rejected by China with equal fierceness).[36]

However, there is a range of issues that have emerged even during the short period of China's new interest in the Indian Ocean. India and Japan see the BRI as an attempt to create a Beijing-centred economic and social model, and have expressed their lack of enthusiasm for it. Even among states initially enthusiastic for BRI investment, there have been developments whose appearance has been harmful to the Chinese aim of creating a positive normative discourse around their presence in the region. In 2018, Sri Lanka announced that it had agreed a 99-year lease (with unfortunate overtones of the British lease on the New Territories and Kowloon in 1898) on its port facility at Hambantota. This was the result of what has been termed "debt diplomacy", by which China paid for only part of the new installation, imposed repayment terms that proved impossible for Sri Lanka to repay, and reacted by seizing the port. The September 2018 presidential election held in the Maldives was widely interpreted as part of a struggle for power between Chinese and Indian interests. Incumbent pro-Chinese president Abdulla Yameen, whose actions suggested a preference for authoritarianism over liberalism, was unexpectedly defeated by Mohamed Solih. India, which (perhaps along with the voters) had become alarmed at the growing number of BRI projects in the strategically important Maldives, welcomed Solih's victory.[37]

The issue that haunts the Chinese presence in the region is the lack of ability, so far, to provide a convincing narrative of what it might mean. Of course, realpolitik remains a core interest. However, the Chinese presence in the Global Indian Ocean has not yet brought about a sense of "common destiny", despite the rhetoric. The phrase had a certain extra poignancy in the mid-2010s, at a time when ideas of "common destiny" were less in favour in the West, with the UK leaving the EU's project of a common European identity, and the US under Donald Trump seeking a much more transactional relationship with partners who were formerly joined with it at least by bonds of rhetoric. While China uses the term "common destiny", it is still highly transactional in terms of its economic and security-linked behaviour in Asia and beyond.

However, China's initiatives have standing in part because the alternative models posited for the region have also failed to find much traction. Since the early 2000s, the idea of "the Quad" has provided much of the framework for the security pushback against China's aspirations in the Indian Ocean. The United States, India, Japan and Australia have been engaged informally since around 2007 in the Quadrilateral Security Dialogue, which has sought to engage with the creation of a new security community within the Indian Ocean. During the brief tenure of US Secretary of State Rex Tillerson (2017–18), he declared that India and the United States were "bookends" that would act to keep "the Indo-Pacific region" safe.[38]

However, the ostensible idea of bringing together major democracies in the region to provide an unstated but clear buffer against China has proved implausible. Part of the problem has been the different set of calculations that each of the actors has to make. Australia cares about Indian Ocean security—as understood and defined by its key Western allies—and is simultaneously highly dependent on trade with Beijing; Japan is keen to contain China but is ultimately more concerned with keeping the East China Sea safe for its shipping; India is, conversely, more worried about the Indian Ocean yet cannot risk open confrontation with Beijing. Under President Trump the United States also had less traction because it was unclear how committed Washington was to maintaining traditional networks of security and economic cooperation, and targeted China specifically in a way that actors such as Australia found uncomfortable.

The South China Sea disputes are also closely linked to the new control of the Indian Ocean. Myanmar, Indonesia, Malaysia and Singapore are Indian Ocean states, and their attitudes greatly affect what China has come to think of as a major problem: the pinch point of the Straits of Malacca, which runs the danger of cutting off Chinese shipping between the Indian and Pacific Oceans, if regimes unfriendly to China are in control of it.

CHINA IN THE INDIAN OCEAN

The BRI opens up new possibilities that may change the dynamics of the Indian Ocean. The development of the China–Pakistan Economic Corridor will involve some $62 billion of Chinese investment in a 15-year period from 2018.[39] Much of the investment is to build up the port of Gwadar, which will become a shipping hub that links the overland route through Pakistani Kashmir to Xinjiang, and onward further into China. The port itself will become a major factor in easing the Straits of Malacca problem but will also increase the liabilities for China. This has led to growing reports, such as a Pentagon report of 2017, that China will move to install military and naval bases in Pakistan.[40] If this were to be the case, then a joint commercial and military nexus would protect Chinese interests from Djibouti to the Pakistan coast, with rail and road freight connections through problematic land areas (Pakistani Kashmir, which is claimed by India, and Xinjiang, where the state has been undertaking highly coercive measures to control the population). The Global Indian Ocean would become much more oriented toward Chinese interests than those of any other power, and would become much more integrated with a Chinese-oriented Halford Mackinder-like aim to exercise powerful influence on the "world-island".[41]

Although China continues to profess that it has no military interests and no domestic political agenda in Pakistan, or indeed in the BRI as a whole (for Pakistan's experimentation with democracy, see Mohmand's chapter 4), it is clear that at least some groups in Pakistan regard China as now being a political actor in the country, as shown by the murder by terrorists of four diplomats from the Karachi consulate of the People's Republic of China on 23 November 2018. The transnational and asymmetric threat of terrorism also exposes another area in which new dynamics in the Indian Ocean run the potential risk of causing wider confrontation. There have been repeated confrontations and all-out wars between India and Pakistan since Partition in 1947 (cf. Woldemariam's contribution in this volume). Aside from the two wars in 1965 and 1971, there was a major confrontation in the Kargil region in 1999, and in March 2019, the two countries had a brief confrontation over a terror raid in Indian Kashmir. Although there was significant international involvement, particularly in the 1971 war, India–Pakistan conflicts were ultimately resolved within the subcontinent, not least because South Asia was less of an arena of direct Cold War confrontation than East or South East Asia.[42] However, there are signs of a possible growing US–China confrontation in the region that might change the situation. If a future Indian attack on Pakistan were to compromise Chinese commercial or military interests, that might run the risk of bringing China into a South Asian conflict. Similarly, any attempt by a future US administration to raise the status of the Quad could create the possibility of a confrontation with American interests in the region, particularly if the Indian naval presence in the Ocean is increased in response to the growing Chinese naval presence. This is not to argue that confrontation is likely. Rather, it is to show that there is the potential for an emergent order in the Indian Ocean which could create new international alliances and tensions in a space that had previously had few such entities, in a bid to manage new uncertainties and insecurities.

What next for China's role in the Global Indian Ocean?

In the first respect, there has already been significant change within the last decade. The PLA Navy is now a major actor in the Ocean, and India's Navy has responded in kind. States from East Africa to Australia are now drawn, willingly or not, into the tensions caused by the two rising powers in the region, India and China. Unlike in the Pacific, in which rising Chinese power is undeniable, there is still no real sense that any one actor has genuine dominance in the Indian Ocean, and this situation may persist for quite a while longer. Liberalism's historical thinness may in that respect be useful.

In the second respect, the answer is less clear and very much in flux. For much of the post-Cold War period, countries were divided, rather crudely, into democratic or democratizing states and authoritarian ones. However, the assumption was that there would be convergence towards a liberal international order. This assumption is now under threat from various directions, as multiple contributions to this volume underline: democracies have in many cases become less liberal than they once seemed (India among them, as Lieven explains in his conclusion), some of them never were very liberal (see Chua Beng Huat's discussion of Singapore in chapter 3) and China's

226

politics have moved toward an unembarrassed embrace of illiberal politics. At the moment, however, these ideological changes do not map onto a neat new set of political contours within the Indian Ocean world. Individual cases such as the Maldives show the importance of Chinese (and Indian) influence but do not in themselves necessarily show a major pattern of change.

The case study of China's presence in the Global Indian Ocean space gives us the chance to throw new light on a question that has become increasingly urgent at the start of the 2020s: speculation on the prospects of a "new Cold War" between China and the US, or even a hot one. This debate has moved on fast in a short time. The position of much of the 2010s is lucidly argued by John G. Ikenberry, who has made a strong case that dominance of the liberal order is such that China will, broadly, have to be absorbed into it.[43] However, the darkening tone of US–China relations from the mid-2010s has brought to the fore analyses that are more cautious about that liberal future. Graham Allison has explored the "Thucydides trap" which might lead to confrontation between the US, as the established power, and China, as the rising power in the region, noting that while conflict is not inevitable, the risk of it is real.[44] It is odd that Arne Westad, reflecting on the possibility that China may become a new hegemon in Asia, thinks it unlikely that China will take up the role of the US, "not just because great power needs time to be socialized into a community of states" but "also because today's emphasis on bellicosity, self-interest, and narrow nationalism is a by-product of the way that China is governed under its current regime".[45]

These sobering observations are a timely warning that the western Pacific, where the US and China face off directly, is a fragile and potentially dangerous arena. For that reason, however, the Indian Ocean space provides a significant contrast. The Chinese presence in the region has been built up slowly, and with the economic rather than military element to the fore, precisely because there are no plausible claims of geographical proximity or historical contact (Zheng He apart) that could argue for a Chinese presence there as of right. This also provides a more objective testing ground for the success, or otherwise, of the BRI. China competes to a large extent with Western and other actors in the region on a much more equal basis than in the

Asia–Pacific, where a combination of economic and military power has enabled it to dominate. In contrast, in East Africa, South Asia outside India, and the Gulf, China has had to provide an offer which it can sell to leaders, and in the case of democracies (Kenya and perhaps post-2018 Ethiopia) there is a coherent if still fluid message: the developmentalism of the BRI combined with an embrace of an illiberal political model (recent geopolitical events have shown that illiberal democracies are more than a passing phenomenon).

How does that help us think about the role of the Global Indian Ocean in understanding the changing international order? Inevitably, it forces us to rethink the liberal internationalist model, but not to the point of dismissing it. It is still the case that many of the public goods provided by the liberal order are valued by China, including the operation of international law relating to commerce and against piracy, not least in the Indian Ocean itself. Nor is it yet evident that China's influence is actively creating new authoritarian states as opposed to being indifferent to regime type as long as it is sympathetic to China's interests (stable democracies are preferable in economic terms to weak authoritarian states, as can be seen in China's refusal to help Robert Mugabe in his hour of need when a coup removed him as president of Zimbabwe in 2017). Verhoeven's introduction to this collection writes of "thin hegemony" in the Indian Ocean as a powerful framework for thinking of the changing power dynamics in the region. China is not yet a hegemon in the region. However, "thinness" certainly appears to be the defining characteristic of the framework within which it wishes to operate there. The Global Indian Ocean may yet be the place where China finds an arena to develop that model in a way less confrontational but perhaps more lasting than what we see in the western Pacific. Watch this (thinly governed) space.

10

CONCLUSION

THE INDIAN OCEAN AND GLOBAL PATTERNS
OF ORDER AND DISORDER

Anatol Lieven

In the Global Indian Ocean, both the post-colonial era and the era when the West could dream with conviction of unilaterally setting models for local progress are now definitively over. As illustrated by the collection of chapters in this volume, rather than either common patterns of Western-influenced post-independence state formation or the emergence of an alternative overarching ideological hegemony, what we see is an extraordinary pluriformity of political orders. These stretch from Singapore, which is both the liberal order's most successful economy and an exemplar of efficient authoritarianism, to Pakistan's incompetent democracy dominated by patronage and "big men", and heavily influenced by the armed forces (Australia, as a British settler colonial democracy, is *sui generis* in the region). The economic results of the Covid-19 pandemic may cause unrest that will severely weaken polities around the Indian Ocean; this is extremely unlikely to lead to those states developing in a common liberal-democratic direction.

The conclusion to this book will review these emergent patterns of global order and disorder and offer its own critical reflections on the main themes and arguments that have emerged from the various chapters. I start off by tackling the fading importance of imperialist legacies. The political orders of the macro-region often retain certain colonial institutions but are equally shaped by pre-colonial pasts and present economic realities. Outside academia, memories of European empire are vanishing and have long since ceased to serve as political organizing principles.

US hegemony in the region has not vanished, but from a (relatively brief and unsuccessful) attempt at "thick hegemony", it reverted to a thin one, in line with the historical pattern discussed in Harry Verhoeven's introduction. US ambitions for a grander project now look positively emaciated. They also depend heavily on US partnership with India, as part of the US strategy of imagining and constructing a new "Indo-Pacific" geopolitical region—a term this book deliberately does not use as an analytical frame, given its obvious geopolitical purposes in emphasizing a Chinese threat to be countered by a Washington-led group of states in both the Indian and Pacific Ocean.

This is in line with US history in the region: during the Cold War, the US never attempted to create a thick hegemony based on formal institutions, as was the case in Europe. The second section takes this as its subject: the growing irrelevance of Western shibboleths and the need to re-theorize political systems and developments in the region. The macro-region exemplifies a contemporary pattern described by Stephen Hopgood:

> The global system is now religious and secular, Christian and Islamic (and Hindu and Jewish etc.), about human rights and traditional social hierarchies, about sexual orientation and gender identity and sexism and homophobia. Both liberal and authoritarian democracy will be permanent features of our world, as will women's rights and patriarchy. We have entered an era of multipolar authority where what is "normal" or "appropriate" no longer has one answer. Traditional values and conservative religious doctrine will not be outposts, like

the Barbary Pirates, waiting for the "universal modern" to arrive. They will be global-level alternative discourses to Human Rights.[1]

This book has argued strongly in favour of accepting the pluriformity of polities and nations in the Global Indian Ocean as a permanent, historical fact that continues to matter hugely to the region and to broader international relations today.[2] Within each state there is also a permanent search for enduring political order. Questions of how order-building and diversity intersect are the core of the fourth and fifth section of this conclusion and are logically followed by a discussion of the enduring salience of nationalism and religion along the oceanic rim. I conclude with critical reflections on what US thin hegemony still amounts to in the region.

As in the rest of the world, the countries of the Global Indian Ocean are developing individually but within a wider context of capitalist globalization, which profoundly constrains their behaviour and opportunities—a process elites and citizens are conscious of now that the dreams of the post-independence world have dissolved.[3] Several of them are also closely connected to and influenced by their diasporas, around the Indian Ocean and in Europe and North America. These diasporas help to make the region truly "global" and, in turn, bring the region to the rest of the world: they are the particle accelerators of the Global Indian Ocean.

In particular, the economies of Pakistan, Nepal, Bangladesh and the Indian state of Kerala are all heavily dependent on remittances from migrant workers in the Gulf monarchies, as Hertog underlines in chapter 5. As Blom Hansen detailed in chapter 2, smaller numbers of South Asian merchants and professionals have been established in these countries for generations and sometimes even centuries (though without citizenship and without intermarriage with the indigenous Arab populations), helping to weave together the far-flung regions under the Pax Britannica. Dubai in particular is also a highly important entrepot for South Asian trade and finance—but also increasingly for African population groups, including Sudanese, Somali, Kenyan and Ethiopian diaspora communities who are tightening commercial, social and political links between the Horn of Africa and the Gulf, but also between the Arabian Peninsula and locations in Europe and North America where compatriots and co-ethnics reside and work.

BEYOND LIBERAL ORDER

Pakistani and Bangladeshi diasporas in the West (especially Britain and Norway) retain close links to their countries and districts of origin, and due to their growing size, their future role in relations between these countries and the West is likely to be a significant one, even if its nature is still unclear. The much more economically successful Indian middle class diasporas in the US and Britain are beginning to have a visible effect on the politics of these countries, with a row of politicians of Indian origin rising to high positions—including UK Chancellor of the Exchequer Rishi Sunak. Contributions from sections of these Indian communities have played an important part in financing Narendra Modi's political movement; and Indian lobbies, sometimes working closely with Israel lobbies, are helping to shape US and British policies towards India and the Indian Ocean. The virulent hostility between India and Pakistan means that these diaspora politics raise the future possibility of South Asian political and geopolitical battles being also fought on the streets of Europe and North America.

The post-colonial era was to a great extent the era of the Cold War, and state-building processes and liberal order itself were deeply intertwined with the geopolitical and ideological stances of that era.[4] Today, assiduous efforts are being made in the US to foster a new bipolar confrontation, this time pitting the US and India against China. Beijing for its part sees the Indian Ocean as part of the canvas on which it is drawing up a new and more expansive foreign policy identity, as Rana Mitter argues in his chapter 9. This risks not only drawing neighbouring countries into opposing camps, but also desta- bilizing them internally, as the great powers back rival political forces.

These alignments are, however, in fact largely independent of ideology: subscribing to the Pax Americana is clearly more important than embracing what this book has defined as the other two defining pillars of liberal order, the Washington Consensus and liberal democ- racy. The US is aligned with communist Vietnam against China; Beijing is aligned with semi-democratic and Islamist Pakistan against the US and India.

The fading colonial legacy

In line with the ancient and deep syncretism of the political history of the Global Indian Ocean highlighted in Harry Verhoeven's introduc-

CONCLUSION

tion, the colonial legacy continued after the end of empire in the
institutions and elites inherited by the post-colonial states. This was
as true of the victorious opponents of colonial rule as it was where the
empires had handed over power to their own imperial clients, as in
Malaya or Ceylon. Discussions of the colonial and neo-colonial impact
continue to dominate a good deal of academic writing on the region.[5]
With time, however, this impact has become much less relevant to
contemporary realities.

Jawaharlal Nehru, though from an Indian Brahmin elite background, was a product of the British education system and a famous
writer in English. He and the Congress Party struggled against imperial rule, but largely through institutions created by the British. After
independence, Nehru governed through parliamentary, administrative, military, judicial and police institutions bequeathed by the
British Empire (which in turn had derived some of its basic approaches
to administration, taxation and land distribution from the preceding
Mughal Empire).

Where the rejection of colonialism required violent struggle and
was therefore more violent and absolute, as in Vietnam, the
Portuguese African colonies and (to a degree) Indonesia, the post-
colonial states were naturally products of that struggle and therefore
in their own way also deeply marked by the colonial period. Even the
communist states of the region were ruled by parties deriving their
formal ideology and institutions from a European political and economic philosophy. And in most post-colonial polities, the first generations of rulers owed their charisma to the fact that they had
struggled, more or less heroically, against foreign overrule.

In some cases, like Nehru's, they were able to hand this charisma on
to their children, though with diminishing effect. In other cases, they
were eventually overthrown, whether by American-backed or Soviet-
backed coups. This was also true in countries which had never (or only
for brief periods) been under direct colonial rule, but where British
imperial hegemony was succeeded by that of the US, as in Ethiopia.

The 1970s and early 1980s saw not only the height of Cold War
rivalry, but also the appearance of forces that cut across superpower-
led alignments and continue to do so, rapidly eroding the centrality
of colonial legacies. Thus Ethiopia (see Michael Woldemariam's

chapter 7), the lusophone colonies and Afghanistan all experienced initially successful communist rebellions. In Africa, these new regimes defeated their rivals with Soviet and Cuban backing, and after the end of the Cold War they went on to morph under US influence into highly corrupt forms of state-led capitalism.[6] In Afghanistan, however, the anti-communist revolt was spearheaded by Islamist forces which, though armed by the US, were much more responsive to Saudi Arabia. Parts of these eventually became America's arch-foes, the Taliban and al-Qaeda.

And in 1979 in Iran, America's client ruler, the Shah, was overthrown not by communists but by religious-nationalist revolutionaries who were equally hostile to the US and the USSR, and who continue, in a modified form, to rule Tehran to this day. America is still embroiled in bitter rivalry with Iran, but this is now largely due to the US being dragged into the regional fears and ambitions of its Israeli and Saudi "allies"—the latter pursuing a conflict going back to the Ottoman–Safavid wars of the 16th and 17th centuries rather than anything resembling the Cold War.[7]

Nor of course do the Saudis make anything but the very flimsiest of pretences to be aligned with the US in ideological and cultural terms. They are strategically part of the Pax Americana but are normatively hostile to both liberal democracy and the Washington Consensus—both so important to the post-1989 liberal order—as Hertog details in his chapter 5. As displayed in the Saudi–Russian oil price war of early 2020, the Saudis also pursue their energy interests regardless of US interests and, increasingly, of US pressure.

Outside the Middle East, geopolitical and ideological alignments today are variegated and shifting. They are beholden neither to past empires, nor to the struggle against those empires, nor to outside superpower backing. It is, after all, now two or three generations since the end of colonial rule. The Portuguese empire came to an end 45 years ago, the French empire 55 years ago, the British empire in South Asia 71 year ago. In Ethiopia, the emperor was overthrown and killed by the Marxist-Leninist Derg 44 years ago. The generation of political leaders who shaped and were shaped by these events is long departed from the scene. As with China's "century of humiliation", resentments of past colonial rule still exist, but, though they can be occasionally mobilized as a political resource, they cannot form the bases for political movements.

The end of the post-colonial era is perhaps most clearly seen in India. There, the aristocratic, British-educated Nehru–Gandhi dynasty was able to hang on for three generations after independence because of its founder's prestige as the leader of the independence struggle, because the Congress Party remained by far the most widespread political machine, and also because its Western cultural alignment was belied by its quasi-socialist domestic policies and its independent and often anti-American foreign policies; nobody could accuse it of being a puppet dynasty like that of the Shah.

The triumph of Narendra Modi and his Hindu-nationalist movement has been a crushing defeat for the Nehru dynasty and the post-colonial elites, marking the rise of what may prove to be the Global Indian Ocean's most formidable illiberal state-builder—unless of course all his plans, and Indian economic growth, turn out to have been wrecked by the coronavirus.[8] The fact that Modi—the son of a tea-stall owner from the lower (though not lowest) castes, speaking poor English—is so manifestly not from an elite background has been an immense asset for him.

The Nehruites were colonial products and in their more honest moments admitted the fact. Congress prime minister Manmohan Singh paid tribute to the British Indian Civil Service—so many of whom, like him, were Oxford graduates—and its role in creating modern Indian statehood.[9] That is not a thought that would ever occur to Narendra Modi. As an enemy of the Nehru dynasty and the English-speaking post-colonial elites, Modi could possibly be seen as an inheritor of the left-wing anti-colonial mantle. Far from it, of course. He is an ally of big business, a proponent of a particular mode of capitalism (with clear limits imposed by his middle-class base) and of alliance with the US, though only on Indian terms—more evidence that the old anti-colonial alignments have ceased to apply outside academia.[10]

Modi's regime is not really that of the Bharatiya Janata Party (BJP), whose traditional leadership he also displaced. Rather it is that of the Hindu chauvinist paramilitary volunteer movement, the Rashtriya Swayamsevak Sangh (RSS), and its affiliated organizations, through which he rose and from which he draws his top supporters. The formation and structure of the RSS did owe a great deal to Western influences—but not those of British colonialism.

Rather, as described by Blom Hansen in his leading work on the subject, the RSS (like the Baath Party in the Arab world) was formed on the model of the European fascist parties of the 1920s and 1930s.[11] Unlike the Baath, but like France's Front Nationale and other extreme rightist parties of Europe today, Modi today does not aim at explicit dictatorship based on a local version of the *Führerprinzip* (as did Modi's spiritual ancestor Vinayak Damodar Savarkar). Instead, he is willing to work through the institutions of parliamentary democracy, which so far he has been able to dominate through a first-past-the-post electoral system, mass organization, personal charisma and intense propaganda, including the assiduous employment of social media. Part Mussolini, part Donald Trump, part Veer Savarkar, but hardly anything of Nehru or his British imperial predecessors.

The concentration of much of Western and Western-led academia on anti-colonial and post-colonial themes therefore represents in many ways a distraction from the main issues and the main patterns affecting the Ocean world. A more useful approach, as several contributors to this book (Hertog's chapter 5 on the Arabian Peninsula, Chua Beng Huat's study of on Singapore in chapter 3 and Woldemariam in chapter 7 analysing secession and regime change in the Horn of Africa and beyond) have advanced, is to view the Global Indian Ocean as wrestling with the challenge of modern state- and nation-building under conditions of capitalist globalization.

What most of these figures and movements have, above all, in common is nationalism; and faith in the inevitable disappearance of nationalism is perhaps the greatest intellectual flaw in the liberal global vision.[12] As in the decades before World War I, the economic, social, cultural and demographic dislocations caused by liberal globalization have themselves been responsible for a tremendous surge in nationalism, which underpins equally authoritarian regimes such as Eritrea, and Iran, and the elected ones of India under Modi, Sri Lanka under the Rajapaksas and, beyond the Indian Ocean, the US under Trump, Hungary under Orban and Brazil under Bolsonaro. Nor do any of these countries show any signs of impending collapse. Nationalism therefore increasingly rules the world; but, at the same time, it takes very different forms in different nations, states and cultures.

Moreover, as Blom Hansen underlines in his chapter 2 on the genealogies of distributed sovereignty, also of capital importance are much older cultural, economic, ethno-religious and political legacies, albeit often incorporated by the colonial powers into their system of governance. In fact, the most important determinants of state success seem to be a combination of ancient traditions of statehood with a sufficient degree of national homogeneity, as in Iran and Thailand. This homogeneity, however, certainly does *not* resemble the "classic" ethno-linguistic nationalisms of Europe. Instead, after traditions of statehood, the most important determinant of national cohesion in the Global Indian Ocean appears to be a common religion (though, like almost every statement on this macro-region, this one immediately needs to be qualified by exceptions).

Thus the relative success of contemporary statehood in Ethiopia and its complete failure in neighbouring Somalia, or the relative success of electoral (but not liberal) democracy in India and relative failure in Pakistan, cannot be fitted neatly into any general theoretical framework, but can only be understood through a deep knowledge of the specific regions concerned. After all, by many standard analyses of ethnic nationalism, Somalia, as a homogeneous nation in ethno-religious terms, ought to have a solid basis for state-building.[13]

As the chapters in this volume have emphasized, the states of the Indian Ocean are immensely varied in terms both of political and economic forms and of political and economic success. None of them, however, conforms to Western, liberal models of what states and economies should look like; and, as Verhoeven and Hansen argue in chapters 1 and 2, American strategic agendas continue to have a profound shaping effect on the geopolitics of the region; though when it comes to shaping the internal structures of states, the US impact is becoming less and less important. A thin hegemony indeed.

The widespread irrelevance of Western models

The differences of the post-colonial world highlighted above were supposed to be erased on the ideological lathe set out by Thomas

Friedman in *The Earth is Flat* and so many other Western works of the 1990s trumpeting the inevitable victory of liberal order, internationally and domestically.[14] Following the end of the Cold War, and rising to a brief hysterical apogee after 9/11, the bipolar ideological competition was supposed to be replaced by a unipolar world dominated by the West, or just the US.

The era's catchphrases make this clear: The "Washington Consensus" sketched a universal path to free-market democracy, also summed up in the slogan "getting to Denmark". *The Earth is Flat* laid down as a supposed fact of nature the necessity for complete openness of all societies to free-market capitalism, as a result of which all would have equal chances of success and all would come basically to resemble each other. Above all, Fukuyama's notorious "end of history" identified one liberal capitalist democratic model for humanity for all foreseeable time.[15]

Even those Westerners who professed to reject some of the economic aspects of this generally bought its political ones, like the US liberals who after 9/11 expressed their support for Bush's "freedom agenda" in the Middle East, and declared that all the ideological "isms" had become "wasms"—except their own of course.[16] Where necessary, US military intervention was supposed to ensure successful democratic state-building, but in Afghanistan, Iraq, Libya and Somalia (as Will Reno in his chapter 8 describes) this has proved a complete failure.

The liberal-internationalist teleology has turned out to be as empty as the faith-based Marxist prediction that in the wake of socialist revolutions the state would wither away and be replaced by a peaceful global anarchist society without borders. The liberal equivalent of this Marxist vision was "democratic peace theory"—the idea, going back in its origins to Immanuel Kant, that democratic states would not go to war with each other.[17]

This has been accompanied by two other beliefs, often conjoined in US establishment thought, and endlessly promoted by journals like *The Economist*:[18] that history was pointing inevitably towards the spread of liberal democracy, and that these new democracies would inevitably look to the US for leadership, thereby shoring up US global hegemony for all foreseeable time.[19] Any states that resisted these processes, or engaged in "backsliding" from democracy, would inevitably end up on what the communists used to call the "scrapheap of history", doomed at best to stagnation and isolation, at worst to collapse and revolution.[20]

These beliefs had important consequences. In some cases, by encouraging indifference to considerations of real national strengths and great power interests, they encouraged Western overconfidence, as in the attempted expansion of NATO and the European Union into the former Soviet Union against the opposition of Russia. The result has been disastrous for Ukraine and Georgia.

In the case of China, these beliefs led to a different kind of Western overconfidence: that steep economic growth would inevitably lead both to the democratization of China,[21] and to Chinese acquiescence in what has been called a "rules-based global order".[22] The first has not happened, and the second is seen by most Chinese as no more than a hypocritical cover for US domination.[23]

As a result of this overconfidence (and the distractions created by the Afghan and Iraq wars), the US delayed for a considerable number of years both responding to China's trade surplus and taking account of what the return of China to superpower status would mean for America's global position. In consequence, the eventual response has taken the form not of well-considered measures but a precipitate rush to trade war, geopolitical rivalry and ideological hostility, on the part both of the last Republican administration and of Joe Biden's Democratic Party.

This Western strategy gained its supposed basis in evidence from the (apparently) successful expansion of a mixture of free-market capitalism and liberal democracy to Eastern Europe, enforced as the price of joining the EU and NATO and therefore securing these states against any renewed Russian hegemony. However, nations are reverting to previous forms of elected populist nationalism, while in the rest of the world it never worked at all, including the US's own backyard of Mexico.

The failure of the North American Free Trade Agreement to develop the Mexican economy, build successful democracy and thereby reduce the flow of migrants to the US contributed greatly to the triumph of Donald Trump, which—together with the successes of nationalist parties in Europe and an ambiguous EU approach to important aspects of liberal order[24]—undermined the liberal project at its core. Even one of the liberal international order's arch-defenders had to concede in astonishment:

> Is the world witnessing the demise of the US-led liberal order? If so, this is not how it was supposed to happen. The great threats were supposed to come from hostile revisionist powers seeking to overturn the postwar order ... Instead, the world's most powerful state has begun to sabotage the order it created. A hostile revisionist power has indeed arrived on the scene, but it sits in the Oval Office, the beating heart of the free world. Across ancient and modern eras, orders built by great powers have come and gone—but they have usually ended in murder, not suicide.[25]

The fading of liberalism is not necessarily coterminous with the fading of democratization, however. Democracies of a kind have come and gone and returned again in the macro-region since they were left behind by the British Empire. As chapters 3, 4 and 6 by Shandana Khan Mohmand, Chua Beng Huat and Lamia Karim in this volume demonstrate, in most countries of the region outside the Gulf elections do play a major part in representing popular wishes to government and in extracting benefits from the state. They are valued by populations for those reasons.

Even in "theocratic" Iran or one-party Singapore, as in Putin's Russia, elections play an important role in signifying discontent and wise governments pay heed to their signals. However, while all these cases differ greatly from each other, they also differ enormously from standard versions of democracy set out in Western political science (which, as we now see from the growing differences among Western democracies, are not in fact "standard" even in the West).

Democracy is also not a linear picture of progress, either in the sense that, once established, it cannot be overthrown (as Bangladesh, Thailand and the Maldives have repeatedly demonstrated) or that it proceeds along a set, Western-defined path. This path supposedly leads away from the politics of "big men", offering patronage and protection and kinship groups voting collectively, towards individual citizens voting for mass political parties.

Instead, as Khan Mohmand's chapter 4 on the political dynamics of rural Pakistan illustrates, political change is not linear. In the

CONCLUSION

Punjabi countryside, the picture is neither one of the gradual but
steady consolidation of organized modern political parties nor of the
unchanging domination of so-called feudal local powerbrokers, but a
longstanding interaction—and, even within limits, a relatively stable
one—between the two. Over the past two generations, sometimes
the centralized political parties have had the upper hand, and local
powerbrokers have had to come to them seeking places, and sometimes it has been the other way around.

At no point, however, have the political parties been able to dis-
pense altogether with the local bosses and simply appoint their own
people, nor have the bosses managed to establish their own power
without support from political parties. The "decline" of local political
families, often presented as the product of modernization, has often
been no more than the continuation of an age-old process whereby
successful families become wealthy, decadent, and unwilling to do
the gruelling work of extracting patronage from the state and distrib-
uting it to followers, and defending those followers against the police
and the courts. In consequence, they are replaced by new, hungry
political families willing to do this work.[26]

In the Global Indian Ocean, as in parts of the West, the failure of
the democratizing dreams of liberal order is marked not only by the
persistence or return of openly authoritarian governments, or authoritarian systems embodying limited elements of democracy (as represented, in their very different ways, by Singapore, Thailand,
Myanmar, Iran and Ethiopia). It is also marked by the rise of "illiberal
democracies", genuinely elected and popular, but representing ideologies of ethno-religious domination and exclusivity, with a marked
tendency to ferocious and extra-judicial forms of policing—to which
large parts of the population give enthusiastic support, out of their
fear for the growth of criminal gangs and the spread of drugs. Owing
to this development, not one of the Indian Ocean states (except for
Australia, Mauritius, and her French-ruled neighbour Réunion) can
be seen as a liberal democracy today.

In some respects, these forms of illiberal democracy are an even
graver disappointment and challenge for the Western liberal project
than the dictatorial systems are.[27] For the sins of dictators can be
blamed on the dictators and ruling elites, but when democratic

majorities elect undemocratic governments, liberals themselves have to break a fundamental democratic taboo and question the will and wisdom of the sovereign people.

In the Global Indian Ocean, while the most important development of this kind has been in India, the most bitter disappointment has been in Myanmar since the beginning of the pogroms against the Rohingya Bengali Muslim minority. Cheerleaders of liberal order built up an ideal image of Aung San Suu Kyi as a beacon of democracy, humanitarianism and feminism, completely forgetting that her political prestige came originally from the legacy of her father, Aung San, the leader of ethnic Burmese nationalism against British rule.[28] As Karim argues in her poignant chapter on gender, liberal order and development, such wishful thinking has a long genealogy and an equally long history of disenchantment.

The Burmese paranoia about the Rohingya—a population seen as growing steeply because of migration from Bangladesh—forms part of backlashes against migration and globalization in many parts of the world, including prominently in South Africa.[29] It is not just therefore that the states of the Indian Ocean are not aiming to "get to Denmark", and could not get there even if they wanted to. It is also that Denmark itself is no longer Denmark. The economic recession beginning in 2008, the economic crisis stemming from the pandemic of 2020, and the problems of "turbo-charged" free-market capitalism which they have yet again demonstrated, have dealt that model blows from which it may never recover.

In the Global Indian Ocean, however, the first blow to the Washington Consensus was dealt by the Asian financial crisis of 1997–8 (which also ushered in the end of the "democratic" experiment in Russia). World Bank and International Monetary Fund advice worsened the recession by enabling US banks to be bailed out, rather than protecting the working and middle classes of South East Asia. Consequently, regional states became determined to preserve their economic sovereignty and independence,[30] above all, whenever they had the means to do so, by accumulating the largest possible sovereign wealth funds and shunning practically all Washington Consensus prescriptions.

Since then, Indian Ocean states have also maintained or imposed, as far as state weakness and elite corruption would allow, limits on

CONCLUSION

financial inflows and outflows, to reduce both capital flight and the speculation which contributed so much to the 1998 crisis. Ever since then, in aspiration at least, most of the states of the region have been closer to Beijing's model in this regard than they have been to Washington's; and the even worse meltdown of 2008 amply confirmed the Chinese Communist Party in this view, as Mitter's chapter 9 underlines. What effect the pandemic crisis of 2020 will have remains to be seen, but it is highly unlikely to lead to any reduction in the desire for state controls. The official slogan adopted by the Malaysian hosts of the December 2019 summit of leaders of Muslim states in Kuala Lumpur was very indicative of this approach, and of how far it diverges from Western conceptualizations of economic development over the past generation: "The role of development *in achieving national sovereignty*" (my italics). Not development for its own sake, or even for the sake of the well-being of populations, but to strengthen national power and independence.

Varieties of statehood and nationalism

The reasons for the variety of state forms and political orders in the Indian Ocean highlighted above are themselves various.[31] Compared with Africa and Latin America, more semi-independent states managed to survive through the colonial period, with their very different state traditions. Unlike Europe and, to a lesser extent, East Asia, the states of the macro-region were historically less subjected to shaping by US hegemony and US-sponsored regional organizations.

But, above all, this pluriformity stems from much older patterns. In the Indian Ocean there was no one universal religion to create over hundreds of years certain basic common patterns, even if through much of the region Islam was a powerful unifying and cosmopolitan factors among political and intellectual elites and in commerce, as Verhoeven argues in his introduction. Unlike in East Asia, there was no Chinese regional cultural and economic hegemon to exercise political dominance and shape common cultural patterns. The states and cultures of India always exerted a major influence, both through trade and, in earlier times, through the export of syncretic versions of Hinduism and Buddhism. This ancient Indian religious and cultural influence is visible in actual and former temples from Thailand to Indonesia, and helps to mark southeast Asia as a cultural zone of transition between the Indian Ocean and East Asia. However, being divided and pluriform themselves, these Indian states never achieved anything like the Chinese Empire's combination of political, economic and cultural influence in East Asia.

Today, the Republic of India would dearly love to achieve something like this, but the obstacles to regional hegemony are enormous—not least the fact that the subcontinent is not controlled by one Indian state but is divided into different, mutually hostile states. Pakistan in particular is a formidable barrier to Indian regional power, not only in terms of its military challenge and political influence, but because its geographical location makes it impossible for India to imitate China's Belt and Road (see Mitter's chapter 9) and create overland routes for Indian trade with the Middle East and Europe. Militarily, India also has to reckon with the looking presence of Chinese forces on its northern Himalayan borders, and with memories of India's defeat by China in that region in 1962. So while the lands bordering the Ocean have been linked together for millennia by trading communities and cultural interchange, this region has also always been marked out by its vastly different traditions,: as has been a key proposition of the book, it has lacked a strong regional hegemon—with the relatively brief exception of British imperial domination from the late 18th to the mid-20th centuries and the thin hegemony of liberal international order under US leadership after 1980.

Where the Indian subcontinent has echoed the role of China in East Asia has been in its generation of tremendously successful regional networks of commerce and finance. However, as outlined in Blom Hansen's chapter, this was due originally neither to the initial initiative of states (as Verhoeven too emphasizes in the introduction, the Pax Britannica later provided the political frame and the guaranteed regional peace that allowed these connections to expand vastly) nor to the actions of free-ranging capitalist entrepreneurs, as imagined by liberal internationalists.

On the contrary, many of the most successful capitalists have been members of exceptionally closely knit and closed ethno-religious groups with strong commercial traditions, and their success has been in large part due to trust and mutual support (in effective, a collective insurance policy). In other words, just as the success or failure of modern state systems often has roots in the distant past, so the bases for the achievements of these groups in circumstances of globalization were laid down not by modern capitalism, let alone democracy, but by ethno-cultural patterns established centuries earlier. Not that this should surprise us, since this phenomenon was observable in Europe centuries ago, among Jews, dissenting Protestants and others. The economic success of highly visible transnational minorities, enormously increased by capitalist globalization, has made them the targets of hatred by less successful "indigenous" majorities.

This is a feature of the Global Indian Ocean today which links it—sometimes in sinister ways—to previous patterns of nation-building in Europe. For while the regional states, and the macro-region as a whole, have specific features, a central theme of this book has been that this is also a *global* region, deeply impacted by patterns of neoliberalism which affect the region as a whole just as a previous era of laissez-faire globalization affected most of the world in the generations before 1914.

As Marx and Engels noted, central to globalized capital has been its intensely disruptive character. Shaking up traditional societies in order to make them more open and receptive to "development" has been essential to the capitalist process.[32] Some social groups benefited greatly as a result, while others suffered severely. All, however, saw their inherited traditions, forms of behaviour and, above all, status radically changed as a result, leading to deep insecurity even among the relative victors of the process. W.H. Auden dubbed the modern era the "age of anxiety".[33] That is quintessentially true of large parts of the Global Indian Ocean today.

The search for effective statehood

The societies around the Indian Ocean are all in their different ways engaged in a search for the preservation or restoration of *order*—political, economic, cultural and psychological. This means above all order in the most basic sense of physical security, rather than more expansive liberal visions, as Reno and Woldemariam show in chapters

7 and 8. All too often in this region, civil war and famine are recent historical memories, close neighbours, or both. Societies are also in the grip of the revolutionary economic, cultural and sometimes demographic changes brought on by globalization.

Not surprisingly, therefore, populations in the region have a much greater willingness than most Westerners to exchange freedom for stability and security. This sets them fundamentally at odds with some of the basic premises of contemporary Western liberalism—though 19th-century European liberal-nationalist state-builders would have understood their concerns well enough. In the Middle East, the old saying that one night of anarchy (*fitna*) is worse than a hundred years of tyranny has been given new force by the horrors of state collapse and civil war in Libya, Syria, Iraq and Yemen; but it is not too far from the consciousness or at least the subconsciousness of people all over the region.

As Khan Mohmand shows in chapter 4, if we are to think in more meaningful ways about what democracy amounts to in contexts like that of Pakistan, we must understand its practice as substantially different from that of Western-style liberal orders. Middle-class fears of anarchy or revolution from below help to explain why, contrary to standard neo-Whig expectations, the growth of economic middle classes in the region has by no means necessarily led to strong demands for democracy—let alone a willingness to let democracy take its course once achieved.[34]

This pattern has been visible in recent decades in Thailand, where the failure even of successful export-led growth to benefit much of the population (especially in provinces relatively remote from Bangkok) led first to a populist movement based on the provincial masses, and then to that government being ousted from power when the elites and the middle classes swung back behind authoritarian rule by the army, in defence of their economic privileges and in the name of loyalty to monarch and nation.

These fears have deeply affected the process of building modern states, which differ from their predecessors in that, to be successful, they have to promote successful economic development, as Steffen Hertog illustrates in this volume with the case of the Gulf. To secure the acceptance of society for the disruptions involved, these states also need to gain some form of legitimacy. This most vital of all state assets derives from a difficult and apparently contradictory combination of success in radical economic *change* with a reasonably successful claim to the preservation of essential and supposedly *unchanging* core traditions. The struggle to mix this elixir is central to modernity, and its name is nationalism.

Alongside this political-cultural process runs that of creating the modern state itself; and every modern state—whether democratic, authoritarian, or somewhere in-between—requires a sovereign people as its base. Throughout the Global Indian Ocean, states and regimes are attempting, with greater or lesser success, to build nationalisms and to draw legitimacy from them.

Only Singapore, of all the macro-region's states, has been able to side-step these conflicting pressures. And, as chapter 3 emphasizes, Singapore is genuinely unique, as a pure creation of Pax Britannica strategy and commerce without an ethno-religious hinterland, sustained today by the US Navy to reap the benefits of liberal order. All the same, one would have expected Singapore to become a society and state openly dominated by the Cantonese and Fukienese traditions to which it owes both most of its population and its immense commercial success.

The fact that, instead, it has chosen English as its official language and multi-ethnicity as its official identity says a great deal for the power, the driving modernist vision, and the British education of its semi-elected ruler Lee Kuan Yew, his party and dynasty. Also important in this regard is the fact that though the Cantonese language has great cultural and economic vitality, it has never been a language of state—while Mandarin, in its spoken version, is in effect a foreign language for most of Singapore's Chinese population.

Beng Huat's chapter 3 provides a fascinating exposition of how four very different traditions—two Western, two Eastern—came together to foster Singapore's extraordinary success: the commercial traditions of the Cantonese and Fukienese Chinese diaspora and the South Indian diaspora; the authoritarian, paternalist and technocratic tradition of the British imperial civil service; and the British tradition of social solidarity and the welfare state, encouraged by the experience of World War I and II. Few people would have predicted in advance that this combination could work, let alone work brilliantly—an example of the tendency of historical change to defy ideological paradigms.

Through Singapore the Global Indian Ocean demonstrates a wider insight about states and economic development. Contrary to the belief of naive advocates of a borderless "connected world", strong states are essential to economic development, both because only they can mobilize the resources and public support necessary to create great infrastructure projects, and because only they can enforce the legal frameworks under which the contracts on which successful capitalism depends can be assured. Where states are weak (in Pakistan for example), we have long been able to observe a pattern whereby the World Bank pressures the state to adopt strong investment laws, and international NGOs pressure the state to adopt strong human rights laws—and both sets of laws are meaningless because they are ignored or subverted by predatory courts and police.

But in Singapore, as everywhere else, as Hertog emphasizes in chapter 5, even those few states which still attribute sovereignty to God and the monarch need to define and therefore limit their citizen body in order to decide who enjoys the full benefits of the welfare state and subsidized state employment. Where elements of democracy exist, then obviously the sovereign body is the voting citizen body.

At a deeper level, however, in periods of state-building, state transformation or state insecurity, the question is also which part of the population forms (in the German 19th-century phrase) the *Staatsvolk* or "people of state" and defines (in a term coined by Bassam Tibi) the country's *Leitkultur*;[35] which people gives its cultural colour to the state as a whole, and can expect that people of other backgrounds who wish to have rights and influence within the state either assimilate themselves to this People, or at the very least actively or tacitly recognize its predominance? Which people are to be subordinated, excluded and, in the worst cases, expelled or killed?[36]

Everywhere, there is an awareness among elites that states cannot maintain themselves where the sovereign people itself is divided concerning the issues of the basic ethnic, religious or cultural identity of the country and of who makes up its sovereign people. The terrifying examples of the collapsed states of the Middle East have rubbed this lesson home.

Certainly, open democracy is virtually impossible under these circumstances, as the melancholy example of Egypt during the Arab Spring demonstrates. Because of the strong legitimacy accorded by the population's recognition of "procedural justice", democracy has been very good at overcoming differences over secondary issues of policy, and gaining acceptance of majority decisions on such issues.[37] It cannot, however, resolve issues which transcend policy and touch on basic questions of identity and control; for how can a system, or country, survive if the essential character of its state changes to and fro with every election? Here, in the end, only a declaration from above can settle the matter, appealing with more or less conviction to certain a priori assumptions about the nature of the society concerned.

This was true in the creation of the secular ethnic-nationalist Turkish Republic by Kemal Ataturk and the army—and it is important to note that although more than 80 years later Recep Tayyip Erdoğan and the Justice Party moved Turkey some distance from Kemalist secularism, they were allowed to do so by the army only because they eventually accepted in full centralizing Kemalist ethnic nationalism. In Iran after the revolution, Ayatollah Khomeini and the clerical establishment created a system which allowed a constrained form of democracy, but only within the frame of Shia values and traditions, as formally interpreted by that establishment. The role of such figures recalls that of Rousseau's Lawgiver in the *Social Contract*—but, of course, not only does the role of such a figure contradict basic assumptions of liberal democracy, but finding him or her is easier said than done.[38]

The confidence of the proponents of liberal order in the strength and longevity of pluralism was unconsciously based on an assumption that while subordinate cultural identities might exist, liberal values would in any case hold hegemonic sway over all of them[39]—somewhat as previous political orders, like that of the Ottoman Empire, tolerated extensive cultural autonomy for minority groups on the clear understanding that one group alone would rule the state and set its official cultural identity. This—rather than the physical extermination of minority groups—is what ethno-religious forces in India, Myanmar and elsewhere hope to establish.

Nationalism, religion and the state

As the examples of India and Myanmar demonstrate, a religiously infused nationalism can be a powerful force for majoritarian tyranny and the exclusion of minorities. But by way of illustrating the variety and contradictions of the Global Indian Ocean, other examples demonstrate that a strong imperial and religious tradition can be a force for ethnic (though not cultural) inclusion and pluralism. This is visible in Iran, where the combination of near-universal Shi'ism, the ancient prestige of Persian, and equally ancient traditions of unified imperial statehood has created an exceptional nationalism but has also made possible the full integration of other ethnicities (though only as long as they are Shia). The fact that the Supreme Jurist, Ayatollah Khamenei, is an Azeri Turk by origin, as are a high proportion of the rest of Iran's religious, political and military leadership, follows a pattern which began a thousand years ago with Iran's conquest by, but assimilation of, the Seljuk Turks.[40]

As noted in Woldemariam's chapter and Verhoeven's introduction, the Ethiopian state too marries an imperial tradition to a strong religious identity particular to that state, allowing a remarkable degree of ethnic pluralism within the state elites. As Christopher Clapham observed:

> A multiethnic state from the earliest times, it [Ethiopia] gave relatively little weight to issues of ethnic origin, and individuals from peripheral areas as well as humble social backgrounds could reach positions not simply of power, but equally of authority and prestige. The price of this was, however, assimilation to a national political culture, which was largely (though not exclusively) defined in terms of the language, religion and values of the Amharic core, and was therefore liable to induce revolt from those who were not prepared to accept the terms on which incorporation into the national political system were offered.[41]

Under the communist Derg, Ethiopia went through the stages of Soviet policy under Lenin and Stalin: an initial offer of full autonomy to all national groups, followed by savage centralization and homogenization. Since 1991, the EPRDF regime has sought to combine an imperious one-party state (under the facade of democracy) with real ethnic autonomy not only in the cultural and linguistic but also the territorial sphere.[42] This, too, could be seen as echoing Moscow's policy both under Stalin's successors and (on a much-reduced scale) under Vladimir Putin.[43] The post-2015 upsurge in violence and inter-communitarian tensions in Ethiopia are pushing the federal project to its very limits—and what the EPRDF carefully built is acutely at risk of breaking.

Thailand—generally seen as a mono-ethnic state though it is in fact anything but—has benefited from a combination of old statehood over a multi-ethnic population, intense monarchical loyalty (with the monarch, as in Japan but not imperial Ethiopia, playing the role of a quasi-religious symbol strictly removed from the unpopular business of actual government) and the integrating role of Buddhism. This has allowed the successful integration—albeit not without considerable difficulty—of the Chinese population at both the mass and elite level, in part through emphasis on strong loyalty to the crown; and it has ensured that hostility to the largely Chinese business elites—as expressed for example by Thaksin Shinawatra's Redshirt movement—has remained of the "dog whistle" variety.[44]

This picture of ethnic integration has been very different, alas, in Myanmar, Malaysia, Indonesia and Sri Lanka. The divide-and-rule policies of British and Dutch colonial administrators are in part to blame, along with economic strategies of facilitating the movement of large numbers of workers from one part of their empire to another.[45] Of even greater long-term importance has been the fact that while Thailand has always been multi-ethnic, it has in effect been mono-religious—and, in addition, Buddhism, in contrast to the more modernistic versions of Islam and Christianity, has a strong capacity to incorporate and tolerate elements of older animist traditions. Chinese immigrants could assimilate into Thai Buddhism in ways that were not possible for Hindus or Muslims, and still less for Chinese Buddhists in Muslim Malaysia or Indonesia. Moreover, while both Myanmar and Java had ancient traditions of statehood, owing to colonial conquest they no longer possess monarchies that can act as integrating forces of loyalty.

At the heart of the Global Indian Ocean lies the most significant attempt to combine religion and nationalism. Hinduism was always much more important to the identity of independent India and the behaviour of the state than liberal propaganda alleged (it is notable that all attempts at outright secession from India have been on the part of non-Hindu ethno-religious populations). Nonetheless, the attempt by Modi's government and party to redefine India as an explicitly Hindu state does mark something new, both for India and for Hinduism.[46]

This attempt is particularly striking because it flies in the face of what many had assumed to be innate features of Hinduism: its diffuse, decentralized, pluralistic and open character as a religion. As Blom Hansen has written, the paradox of the anti-Muslim and anti-Christian ideology of the Hindu nationalists is that their project involves turning Hinduism into something much more like branches of Islam or Christianity: a monolithic faith with a strictly limited character associated with a particular set of ethno-cultural characteristics and allegiances.[47]

Whether the Hindu nationalists' version of Hinduism is seen as exclusive or inclusive depends on whom they are trying to include. The key to understanding this question lies in the nature and impact of the caste system. This system was always integral to Hindu society and, indeed to a lesser extent, to Muslim, Sikh and Christian society in the subcontinent as well.

Politically conscious Hindu movements in the late 19th century were directed against the British Raj and the Muslim population, but in the specific context of threats to Hindu dominance stemming from the caste system. First, there was the threat that Muslim and Christian missionaries might convert a majority of Untouchables, former tribals, and other Hindu lower castes, thereby reducing Hindus from a religious majority to a plurality in British India. Second, by creating reserved parliamentary seats for the lower castes, the British rulers might achieve the same result in political terms.[48] The Untouchable leader B.R. Ambedkar's later advocacy of conversion to Buddhism was seen as a variant of the same threat.[49]

Since 1947, the manipulation of these fears by Hindu chauvinists has been largely either cynical or delusional, but anti-Muslim sentiment has gained extra strength from mobilization against Pakistan. On the other hand, the threat of caste loyalty to Hindu and Indian unity has gained force from the creation of caste-based parties across

North India, often violently at odds with each other and the national parties. Meanwhile, the Congress Party's creation of reserved sectors of education and bureaucracy for lower and backward castes has led to ferocious resentment among the higher castes.

From their inception, Hindu nationalist movements aimed to reduce these threats not only by raising up the lower castes, but by incorporating them in a new form of Hinduism in which every Hindu Indian would be essentially equal. Gandhi's concern for the Untouchables—"Children of God", as he called them—was one version of this. Nor was this simply upper-caste hypocrisy. Hindu nationalist and reformist movements like the Arya Samaj made an explicit point of encouraging inter-caste marriages among its members.[50] Modi, like many of his followers, comes from a lower caste, and his movement has done its best to appeal to the lowest castes and the tribals, including by turning them against the Muslim "Other" and sometimes by encouraging them to attack, loot and kill their Muslim neighbours.

Social, economic and cultural developments in recent decades have given a tremendous impetus to political Hinduism. Rapid urbanization means that traditional caste ties and restrictions are ever harder to maintain, at least with the old strictness.[51] Together with free-market capitalism and mass and social media, this transforms traditional society at its very core, introducing individualism where it has been historically almost unknown. The extraordinary social and psychological tensions produced by these changes find solace in nationalism—as in 19th-century Europe—but since this is the religiously soaked subcontinent, also in religion, but an old–new religion reshaped along new lines—spontaneously from below as much as by influence from above—to suit new classes and a new society, and intrinsically linked to nationalism. This is the combination that Modi and his followers hope will give hegemony in India to themselves and to their version of Hindutva.[52]

In the past, any such attempt would have been seen as doomed to fail and as tremendously dangerous to the national unity of an India that has often been seen to be held together precisely by its diversity and the consequent inability of any group to aim at the sort of hegemony that would terrify other groups into secession. But although the

BJP and RSS are overwhelmingly concentrated in the Hindi- and Marathi-speaking "cow belt" of northern and central India, compared with certain predecessors Modi has been extremely careful not to present their appeal in ethno-linguistic terms.

If BJP hegemony survives the economic crisis resulting from the pandemic, and if Modi can continue to combine emphasizing Hindu unity with accommodating ethno-religious Hindu minorities, then he may realistically hope to reshape India as something more like Iran. The chief sufferers of course will be the Muslims.

US hegemony: From thin to emaciated?

The enduring power of nationalism has profound repercussions not only for state-building but also for the geopolitics of the region. Despite a relative US "retreat", these geopolitics are still heavily influenced by Washington.[53] As Verhoeven's introduction highlights, the US attempt at "thick hegemony" in the Indian Ocean in the wake of the Cold War was both historically quite new for the US and of short duration. A scaling down of these ambitions does not in itself denote "retreat".[54]

Militarily, the US maintains the strongest naval and air forces and is the only country that can project military power far beyond its own borders. As demonstrated by the assassination of Iranian Revolutionary Guards commander Qasem Soleimani in Iraq in January 2020, the US can fire missiles across the region if it feels the need to do so. In Yemen and Somalia, the US has conducted sustained drone and special forces campaigns for a number of years, as detailed by Reno in his essay in this collection. In Afghanistan, of course, it has conducted the longest war in US history.

With its bases at Diego Garcia, in Qatar and Bahrain, and at Djibouti, and its capacity to massively reinforce these bases by sea and air, the US retains the ability, if necessary, to deny naval access to the region by any other great power. With the exception of Iran and the shadow al-Shabaab and Taliban authorities in Somalia and Afghanistan (see chapter 8), no regional power opposes the US militarily—and even the Taliban are now seeking agreement with Washington.

In terms of economic power, US investment in (in terms of both business and infrastructure) and trade with the region are now greatly surpassed by China. However, many states are still periodically forced to look for assistance to the World Bank and the IMF and are highly susceptible to US pressure. As Karim showed in her chapter on the neoliberal development regime shows, even without overt coercion or geopolitical manipulation, developing countries like Bangladesh continue to slavishly implement the latest fads of globalization and development policy communities in Brussels and Washington. The interest rate policy of the Federal Reserve, moreover, still for the moment at least, acts as a metronome for credit conditions from the Cape to Indonesia.

The ideological hegemony of US capitalist democracy is also formally unchallenged except by the Islamists. All the states of the region espouse capitalism, and outside the Persian Gulf almost all of them claim to be democracies of some kind. Unlike in the Cold War, there is therefore no rival overarching and unified political, social and economic ideology of modernization to challenge that of the US and the West. The Chinese example of authoritarian state-led capitalism is certainly attractive to many of the elites of countries around the Indian Ocean, but China has not yet sought to turn this into a formal model for export, and (unlike the US or the USSR) has indeed stressed repeatedly that every country must develop its own particular form of state and government. The Covid-19 pandemic has done little to endear the world to Chinese Communist Party-style secrecy.

Everywhere in the region, American *liberal* democracy is challenged by *local* populist nationalisms (which however, as in India, generally claim to be democratic); but, then, this is also increasingly true within the US itself. Nationalism is also by its nature largely particular to the nation concerned. One can speak of a certain community of sentiment growing up between authoritarian nationalists in various parts of the world, but this is still very far from the Fascist Axis of the 1930s or the "alliance of dictatorships" which neo-conservatives and liberal imperialists like to conjure up as an ideal excuse for their own attempts to strengthen US hegemony.[55] As demonstrated by India and Pakistan and by Vietnam and China, authoritarian nationalist regimes are likely to be hostile to each other on grounds of nationalism and national interest.

American hegemony in Global Indian Ocean is, however, distinctly on the slender side,[56] as Verhoeven notes in chapter 1. Unlike in

Europe, it is not embedded in a formal security alliance led by the US, in genuine affinity between liberal democracies (though this took a beating from Trump's election), or in the close ethno-cultural relationship between the US and Britain. Unlike in Central America, it is not backed by a US military, political and economic hegemony so overwhelming that it allows the US to intervene in countries and overthrow governments that it dislikes. Washington can influence the foreign policy choices of states, but it has very little ability to influence the nature of their domestic political system. Nor for that matter does China yet possess this power. No country or regime in the region is pursuing the standard Westernizing liberal strategy of unequivocal alignment with America and the EU, laissez-faire capitalism, pluralistic governance and electoral democracy.

It is important to re-emphasize, however, as chapters 1, 3, 7 and 9 do, that if US hegemony is now thin, it was never in reality all that thick, with the exception of a brief, exceptional and somewhat illusory period from the collapse of the USSR to the financial crash of 2008. We should not be misled into taking the Wolfowitz Memo of 1992[57]—which proposed, in effect, the expansion of the Monroe Doctrine to the entire planet—as a longstanding historical norm, deviations from which constitute "revisionism"[58] and "threats to the global liberal order".[59] This memo was indeed taken by both the Clinton and Bush administrations from 1992 to 2008 as their standard operating procedure; but 16 years is not a long time in historical terms, and this kind of thick US planetary hegemony was neither accepted by other great powers nor in fact seriously enforced across most of the globe.

Throughout the Cold War, India, though much more of a liberal democracy (at least in appearance) than it is today, pursued a foreign policy that was often aligned with the USSR and was detested by elites in Washington. The Soviet Union sustained communist regimes in Ethiopia and Mozambique. States like Tanzania and Burma, though not formally aligned against the US, pursued economic and political strategies completely opposed to democratic capitalism. And, just as today, close US strategic allies felt under no compulsion at all to introduce liberal democracy at home. This was true of the Shah and General Suharto of Indonesia during the Cold War, and it remains true of Saudi Arabia and the other Gulf monarchies today.

The increasingly chauvinist and authoritarian nature of Hindu nationalism in India does, however, present a special problem for American liberal hegemony. Dictatorship in the Middle East can be explained away as the legacy of continuing pre-modern social structures. In Africa, it can be attributed to poverty. India has, however, been presented as the "largest democracy in the world", and the linchpin of the idea (common to both neo-conservatives and liberal internationalists) of a global "league of democracies" directed against China and Russia.[60] If Indian democracy has taken a form that by no stretch of the imagination can be called liberal, and is openly hostile to freedom of speech and human rights, then a linchpin of this ideological project disappears.[61]

A new Cold War?

While political developments in India are a severe blow to US liberal-internationalist beliefs, they need not seriously constrain US strategic and economic ties to India. As the Saudi–American alliance and many other Middle Eastern (see Hertog's chapter 5) and African examples (see chapter 7 on Ethiopia and Eritrea) demonstrate, Washington's democratic conscience is eminently flexible in this regard,[62] as it has been throughout liberal order's history. Outside Europe, the protection of the US and its way of life has never really prioritised "the spread of liberal democracy", and "security cooperation among nations" has in practice been defined as a subordinate alliance with the US.[63]

Both the Republican and Democratic elites want to make the US-India relationship the key element in an "Indo-Pacific" order containing China in "East Asia" as Mitter shows in his chapter. This neologism has however been generated purely for contemporary US geopolitical purposes: to create one strategic and political space under US leadership from the US military bases at San Diego and Pearl Harbor to those at Diego Garcia and Bahrain. As Rana Mitter shows in his chapter, such attempts to thereby contain or roll back China's deepening ties in the Global Indian Ocean are unlikely to succeed. Furthermore, the concept of an "Indo-Pacific" is highly questionable in terms of both historical trajectory and contemporary connections.

Historically, while the two regions have obviously overlapped in myriad ways (like the Islamic world and that of China), their core trajectories have been very different. The Confucian tradition, so central to the cultures of East Asia, has had a negligeable impact on the countries of the Indian Ocean. Chinese geopolitical power, which for most of the past 2,000 years overshadowed East Asia, was also almost entirely absent from the Indian Ocean; liberal order, even in its thin forms, has been much more consequential to the region than Chinese understandings of hierarchy and authority. Today, one could argue that the situation is more complex. Unlike the USSR during the Cold War, China today poses no threat of communist revolution to the developmentalist elites of Asia and Africa and can build on meaningful historical party-to-party ties.[64] On the contrary, as Mitter underlines in chapter 9, many see Chinese-style state-led authoritarian capitalism as vastly preferable to democratic populism and anarchy; such illiberal foundations under the thin hegemony of liberal international order seem quite attractive to many sovereigns. The US therefore does not possess automatic allies in these classes; quite the contrary, as Chua Beng Huat stresses in chapter 3: liberalism itself is still often considered a proxy for Western racial or civilizational supremacy. At the same time, this seems unlikely to spell a "New Cold War" in what is troublingly called the Indo-Pacific in Washington. Despite much closer economic and political ties between the two regions, China has only a minimal military presence in the Indian Ocean, as Mitter in chapter 9 reminds the reader, and India has no permanent military presence at all in the Far East. Militarily, China in future is likely to be able to dominate militarily in the East and South China Seas, but can hardly dominate the Indian Ocean. Even a relatively weak India can project naval power in the Ocean by virtue of its geographical position alone—but that is obviously not the case for India in the Far East.

In contemporary East Asia, Chinese hegemonic ambitions are obvious and historically determined. Territorial claims in the South China Sea have alarmed China's neighbours and helped to produce a degree of "balancing" against her (see chapter 3 for Singapore's charting of a careful course), which the US has sought to exploit. In the Indian Ocean, by contrast, Beijing has proceeded with great caution, expanding its commercial presence but limiting its military role. Contrary to alarmist reporting, China's development of ports (the so-called string of pearls) is not at present a military strategy.[65] The Chinese naval "station" in Djibouti does not begin to compare with the huge US air and naval bases in Bahrain, Qatar and Diego Garcia, or with the Indian and Australian naval presence. There are good reasons for Chinese caution.[66] Militarily, any Chinese squadron in the Indian Ocean would be hopelessly vulnerable in the case of war, surrounded and outnumbered by US and Indian forces. By virtue of its geographical position, any Indian government with reasonable air and naval forces would be in a position to interdict Chinese trade across the Ocean. That is in part the reason for creating Belt and Road overland routes to Europe and the Middle East, which would be safe from US blockade.

China's only reliable overland route to the Indian Ocean lies through Pakistan; and while Beijing has promised (but mostly not yet delivered) $52 billion of investment for the China–Pakistan Economic Corridor (CPEC), the Communist Party appears wary of making the sort of security commitments to Islamabad that could be seen as giving it a green light for action against India, and risk nuclear war.[67] As of 2021, Gwadar, the Pakistani port on the Arabian Sea and the projected terminus of the CPEC is not a Chinese naval base, and there seem to be no plans to make it one in the near future (for that matter, it is as yet hardly even a viable commercial port). Rather than an active Chinese strategic asset, the military development of Gwadar should rather be seen as a card that China wishes to keep up its sleeve, and that it will only play if it feels it really has to, in response to Indian actions directed against China.

While developing its overland energy routes to Iran, and opposing US sanctions, China has also avoided following Tehran and Moscow into a stronger anti-US position in the Middle East despite many opportunities to exploit US difficulties and mistakes in the region. To date, China's strategy in the Indian Ocean can therefore be seen as one of developing actual economic assets but only potential military assets, which will not be realized unless China feels absolutely compelled to do so. In the Middle East and the Gulf, despite Chinese promises of huge investments in Iran and growing ties with the UAE and Saudi Arabia, it remains to be seen whether these commitments will be fulfilled, or whether they are more in the nature of a warning to Washington not to push China too hard in the Far East. If the Chinese-Iranian relationship does in fact become a close partnership, this would mark an important step towards dividing parts of the Global Indian Ocean into opposing geopolitical camps—and one that risks breaking its "global" and increasingly (re-)integrated character. Pakistan in particular would face an extremely difficult and dangerous choice between its security partnership with China, and the dependence of many Pakistani families on remittances from relatives working in the (bitterly anti-Iranian) Saudi Arabia and UAE. Pakistan would also have to fear increased Saudi sponsorship of anti-Shia Sunni extremist groups in Pakistan, as part of Riyadh's proxy war with Tehran.

China's economic superiority over India and its tremendous role in global trade mean that its economic role and influence around the Indian Ocean considerably outweigh those of India, despite India's vast population and geographical location at the heart of the Ocean. Even Chinese economic investment needs to be exercised with caution, however, as in several countries it has led to fears of excessive indebtedness and economic domination. Part of the story behind Sri Lanka's 2018 political crisis was the swing of the Sirisena–Wickremesinghe government towards Delhi because of just these fears, and then back again when India failed to come anywhere near matching China's investments.[68] As the Sri Lankan case illustrates, India's great power ambitions are also limited not only by its lack of financial resources compared with those of China, but also by the fact that as the local power, India has inherited tensions with several of its neighbours, which the US and China, being distant powers, both lack.

India's diaspora, like that of China, is a major source of influence but, as an often visible and prosperous minority amidst poorer majorities, risks becoming a target of local hostility. This happened in the past in South Africa, and could well happen again, given the political role of Indian businessmen there, as Blom Hansen's chapter reminds us. Anti-Chinese feeling may grow steeply as a result of the pandemic. Chinese workers in Africa are also widely unpopular. If these people come under attack, then both Delhi and Beijing will face dilemmas over whether to court local unpopularity by defending their overseas communities or abandoning them and losing legitimacy at home.

China's greatest strategic leverage by far lies not in the Indian Ocean but the eastern Himalayas, where China defeated India crushingly in 1962, retains military superiority, and has maintained a territorial claim on Arunachal Pradesh, with a view to increasing pressure in this sector if India takes a stronger anti-Chinese stance elsewhere (for example, in the South China Sea).[69] This is a threat which helps explain Delhi's caution in confronting China.

Arunachal Pradesh also illustrates the limits to any US–Indian alliance. For unless US–Chinese relations were to suffer a truly catastrophic deterioration, it seems very unlikely that Washington would commit itself to fight for India in the Himalayas, any more than India would commit itself to fight with the US in the South China Sea. Rather than an alliance (implying a formal security guarantee, like the US alliance with Japan), the US relationship with India is better seen as an evolving and cooperative but also limited relationship.

From Washington's point of view, its relationship with Delhi is limited not only by Indian weakness but also by India's self-perceived strength. Jawaharlal Nehru was mocked by nationalist realists for his naive support for "non-alignment", rather than seeking an alliance with the US.[70] Yet, given India's weakness, any alliance with Washington during the Cold War was going to place India in the position of a very junior partner; and even when India was vastly poorer and weaker than she is today, it was an absolute principle of the Indian elites that India was a great power in her own right and a pole of a multipolar world, and nobody's subordinate.[71]

This resembles the Russian elite's view of their country's role, and is seen as mandated by the immense size of India's population and the grandeur of her cultural tradition. This feeling was reflected in the strong opposition to the US–India nuclear deal, which in America's view gave India everything it could realistically want, but which was seen by many Indians as giving Americans intolerable rights of intervention in Indian nuclear policy.

But while the risks of a Cold War in the Global Indian Ocean are limited, they are nonetheless dangerous. The danger stems, above all, from the way in which US administrations have maintained ideological hostility to the Chinese Communist Party (including the new Biden Administration), apparently in the hope of weakening it from within, as the USSR was weakened and eventually destroyed. This strategy is highly unlikely to succeed and may actually strengthen the party (by allowing it to portray liberal critics as US agents), but the question is what the Chinese leadership's view will be of this strategy. For while on most issues China and the US threaten only each other's secondary interests, state survival is by definition a vital interest. If the Chinese see the US as deliberately threatening this, then they will be tempted to hit back wherever they can do so with reasonable safety, and relations will spiral rapidly downward.[72] The danger of this development has been greatly increased by the pandemic crisis, in which both Washington and Beijing have engaged in bitter recriminations accompanied by baseless conspiracy theories.

The danger for Indian Ocean states is that this superpower rivalry will feed into their own internal divisions and, in some cases, point towards new civil wars. The present era lacks the absolute ideological confrontation of bipolarity—but, then, the Cold War on the ground was often as much about local ethnic, kinship and political rivalry as it was about communism and anti-communism. India and the US may support certain political parties and factions against others backed by China. Even more dangerously, the great powers might back different ethnic groups against each other. The possibilities of such splits became apparent, at the time of writing, in the internal travails of Sri Lanka in 2018. In Pakistan, it is easy to imagine a situation in which Washington would back certain political parties against others backed by the army and aligned with Chinese interests.

The local divisions between and within Indian Ocean states, and the tenuous, contested and uncompleted progress of their nation-building efforts, therefore lay them and the region open to superpower interference. As several of the chapters in this book (4, 5, 7) have sought to indicate, most of the nation-states of the Global Indian Ocean are stronger than they sometimes appear to Western observers, but they still cannot afford to be exposed to this kind of added pressure. The consequences of the Covid-19 pandemic may also greatly increase these pressures and give new opportunities for outside manipulation.

CONCLUSION

So, as the Global Indian Ocean shows us, what we are left with after the supposed "end of history" is in fact just history—an open-ended process of the development of the human species as worked upon by local and planetary forces of climate and ecology. In future, it seems probable that it will be, above all, by their response to climate change that states will stand or fall; and this is most especially true in the Indian Ocean, which, for reasons of population, heavily populated low-lying areas, water shortages, and vulnerability to changes in rainfall patterns, is the most threatened region of the globe. Starting with the pandemic, the state orders of the Global Indian Ocean will also therefore be a critical laboratory for humanity's capacity to respond—or not—to the challenges that will face us all in future.

NOTES

1. ORDERING THE GLOBAL INDIAN OCEAN: THE ENDURING CONDITION OF THIN HEGEMONY

1. Francis Fukuyama, *The End of History and the Last Man* (New York: Perennial, 1992).
2. Dipesh Chakrabarty, *Provincializing Europe: Postcolonial Thought and Historical Difference* (Princeton: Princeton University Press, 2000).
3. Kishore Mahbubani, *The New Asian Hemisphere* (New York: Public Affairs, 2008), 43–8.
4. Amitav Acharya and Barry Buzan, *The Making of Global International Relations: Origins and Evolution of IR at Its Centenary* (Cambridge: Cambridge University Press, 2019).
5. Meles Zenawi, "African Development: Dead Ends and New Beginnings", Master's diss., Erasmus University, Rotterdam, n.d.; Lee Kuan Yew, *The Singapore Story* (Englewood Cliffs: Prentice Hall, 1998).
6. Gaurav Desai, *Commerce with the Universe: Africa, India and the Afrasian Imagination* (New York: Columbia University Press, 2013).
7. Robert Kaplan, *Monsoon: The Indian Ocean and the Future of American Power* (New York: Random House, 2010); Harry Verhoeven, "The Gulf and the Horn: Changing Geographies of Security Interdependence and Competing Visions of Regional Order", *Civil Wars* 20, no. 3 (2018): 333–57.
8. Amitav Acharya, "Global International Relations (IR) and Regional Worlds: A New Agenda for International Studies", *International Studies Quarterly* 58, no. 4 (2014): 647–59.
9. Sebastian Conrad, *What is Global History?* (Princeton: Princeton University Press, 2016).
10. Wang Hui, "The Idea of Asia and Its Ambiguities", *Journal of Asian Studies* 69, no. 4 (2010): 985–9.
11. Edward A. Alpers, *The Indian Ocean in World History* (Oxford: Oxford University Press, 2014).
12. For an (Indian Ocean) exemplar of how fruitful such an approach can be, see

Engseng Ho, *The Graves of Tarim: Genealogy and Mobility across the Indian Ocean* (Berkeley: University of California Press, 2006).

13. Michael E. Bonine, Abbas Amanat and Michael Ezekiel Gasper, eds., *Is There a Middle East? The Evolution of a Geopolitical Concept* (Stanford: Stanford University Press, 2012).

14. Fernand Braudel, *The Mediterranean and the Mediterranean World in the Age of Philip II*, 2 vols. (Berkeley: University of California Press, 1949 and 1996).

15. Thomas Benjamin, *The Atlantic World in the Age of Empire* (London: Wadsworth Publishing, 2000); John K. Thornton, *A Cultural History of the Atlantic World, 1250– 1820* (Cambridge: Cambridge University Press, 2012).

16. Philip Steinberg, *The Social Construction of the Ocean* (Cambridge: Cambridge University Press, 2001).

17. Janice Thomson, *Mercenaries, Pirates and Sovereigns: State-Building and Extraterritorial Violence in Early Modern Europe* (Princeton: Princeton University Press, 1994).

18. Edward Said, *Culture and Imperialism* (New York: Vintage, 1993).

19. Andrew Hurrell, "One World? Many Worlds? The Place of Regions in the Study of International Society", *International Affairs* 83, no. 1 (2007), 127–46; Amitav Acharya, "How Ideas Spread: Whose Norms Matter?", *International Organization* 58, no. 2 (2004): 239–75.

20. Prasenjit Duara, "Asia Redux: Conceptualizing a Region for Our Times", *Journal of Asian Studies* 69, no. 4 (2010): 963–83; Jean Comaroff and John L. Comaroff, *Theory from the South, or How Euro-America Is Evolving toward Africa* (London: Paradigm Publishers, 2012).

21. Kuan-hsing Chen, *Asia as Method: Toward Deimperialization* (Durham: Duke University Press, 2010).

22. Karl Polanyi, *The Great Transformation* (Cambridge: Beacon Press, 1944).

23. This paragraph paraphrases excerpts of Thomas Blom Hansen's 2017 keynote at the Doha conference on "The Liberal State and Its Alternatives in the Indian Ocean World".

24. John M. Steadman, *The Myth of Asia* (London: Macmillan, 1969).

25. David Scott, *Conscripts of Modernity: The Tragedy of Colonial Enlightenment* (Durham: Duke University Press, 2004), 8.

26. Isabel Hofmeyr, "The Black Atlantic Meets the Indian Ocean: Forging New Paradigms of Transnationalism for the Global South; Literary and Cultural Perspectives", *Social Dynamics* 33, no. 2 (2007): 3–32.

27. Moradewun Adejunmobi, "Claiming the Field: Africa and the Space of Indian Ocean Literature", *Callaloo* 32, no. 4 (2009): 1247–61.

28. Paul Gilroy, *The Black Atlantic: Modernity and Double Consciousness* (Cambridge, MA: Harvard University Press, 1993); Marcus Rediker, *The Slave Ship: A Human History* (Harmondsworth: Penguin, 2008).

29. Amitav Ghosh, *In an Antique Land* (London: Vintage, 1992); Sugata Bose and Kris Manjapra, eds., *Cosmopolitan Thought Zones: South Asia and the Global Circulation of Ideas* (London: Palgrave, 2010).

30. Robert Gilpin, *War and Change in World Politics* (Cambridge: Cambridge University Press, 1981).

31. Charles P. Kindleberger, *The World in Depression, 1929–1939* (Berkeley: University of California Press, 1973).

32. A.F.K. Organski and Jacek Kugler, *The War Ledger* (Chicago: Chicago University Press, 1980).

33. Abdul Sheriff, "Globalisation with a Difference", in *The Indian Ocean: Oceanic Connection and the Creation of New Societies*, ed. Abdul Sheriff and Engseng Ho (London: Hurst, 2014), 11–41.

34. Himanshu Prabha Ray and Edward A. Alpers, eds., *Cross Currents and Community Networks: The History of the Indian Ocean World* (New Delhi: Oxford University Press, 2007).

35. Andrew Philips and J.C. Sharman, *International Order in Diversity: War, Trade and Rule in the Indian Ocean* (Cambridge: Cambridge University Press, 2015).

36. K.N. Chaudhuri, *Trade and Civilisation in the Indian Ocean* (Cambridge: Cambridge University Press, 1985).

37. Andre Gunder Frank, *Reorient: Global Economy in the Asian Age* (Berkeley: University of California Press, 1998).

38. Michael Pearson, *The Indian Ocean* (Abingdon: Routledge, 2003), 62–80.

39. Ross Dunn, *Adventures of Ibn Battuta* (Berkeley: University of California Press, 1986), 116.

40. Christopher A. Bayly, "'Archaic' and 'Modern' Globalization in the Eurasian and African Arena, c.1750–1850", in *Globalization in World History*, ed. A.G. Hopkins (London: Random House, 2002), 47–73.

41. Janet Abu Lughod, *Before European Hegemony: The World System AD 1250–1350* (Oxford: Oxford University Press, 1991).

42. Rene Barendse, *Arabian Seas: The Indian Ocean World of the Seventeenth Century* (Armonk, NY: M.E. Sharpe, 2002), 88–91.

43. Fahad Ahmad Bishara, *A Sea of Debt: Law and Economic Life in the Western Indian Ocean, 1780–1950* (Cambridge: Cambridge University Press, 2017).

44. Sanjay Subrahmanyam, *Explorations in Connected History: From the Tagus to the Ganges* (Oxford: Oxford University Press, 2005).

45. Gwyn Campbell, *The Structure of Slavery in Indian Ocean Africa and Asia* (London: Frank Cass, 2004).

46. William Gervase Clarence-Smith, ed., *Abolition and Its Aftermath in Indian Ocean Africa and Asia* (London: Routledge, 2005).

47. Mark Cohen, "Islam and the Jews: Myth, Counter-myth, History", in *Jews among Muslims*, ed. Shlomo Deshen and Walter P. Zenner (London: Palgrave Macmillan, 1996), 50–63.

48. Niels Steensgaard, "The Indian Ocean Network and the Emerging World Economy c.1500–c.1750", in *The Indian Ocean: Explorations in History, Commerce and Politics*, ed. Satish Chandra (New Delhi: Sage Publications, 1987), 127–9.

49. John M. Hobson and Jason C. Sharman, "The Enduring Place of Hierarchy in World

Politics: Tracing the Social Logics of Hierarchy and Political Change", *European Journal of International Relations* 11, no. 1 (2005): 63–98.

50. Hedley Bull, *The Anarchical Society: A Study of Order in World Politics* (London: Macmillan, 1977).

51. Ian Clark, *Hegemony in International Society* (Oxford: Oxford University Press, 2011).

52. G. John Ikenberry, *After Victory: Institutions, Strategic Restraint, and the Building of Order after Major Wars* (Princeton: Princeton University Press, 2001).

53. Tony Smith, "Democracy Promotion from Wilson to Obama", in *US Foreign Policy and Democracy Promotion*, ed. Michael Cox, Timothy J. Lynch and Nicolas Bouchet (Abingdon: Routledge, 2013), 13–36.

54. Niall Ferguson, *Empire: The Rise and Demise of the British World Order and the Lessons for Global Power* (London: Allen Lane, 2002).

55. Duncan Bell, *Reordering the World: Essays on Liberalism and Empire* (Princeton: Princeton University Press, 2016).

56. Mark Mazower, *No Enchanted Palace: The End of Empire and the Ideological Origins of the United Nations* (Princeton: Princeton University Press, 2009).

57. Naazneen Barma, Giacomo Chiozza, Ely Ratner and Steven Weber, "A World without the West? Empirical Patterns and Theoretical Implications", *Chinese Journal of International Politics* 2, no. 4 (2009): 525–44.

58. G. John Ikenberry, *Liberal Leviathan* (Princeton: Princeton University Press, 2011), 26.

59. Harry Verhoeven, "The Self-fulfilling Prophecy of Failed States: Somalia, State Collapse and the Global War on Terror", *Journal of Eastern African Studies* 3, no. 3 (2009): 405–25.

60. Michael Ignatieff, *Empire Lite: Nation-Building in Bosnia, Kosovo and Afghanistan* (London: Vintage, 2003).

61. Stephen D. Krasner, "Building Democracy after Conflict: The Case for Shared Sovereignty", *Journal of Democracy* 16, no. 1 (2005): 69–83.

62. James Mayall and Ricardo Soares de Oliveira, eds., *The New Protectorates: International Tutelage and the Making of Liberal States* (London: Hurst, 2011).

63. Chua Beng Huat, *Liberalism Disavowed: Communitarianism and State Capitalism in Singapore* (Ithaca: Cornell University Press, 2017), 125.

64. Uday Singh Mehta, *Liberalism and Empire* (Chicago: University of Chicago Press, 1999).

65. Jason C. Sharman, *Empires of the Weak: The Real Story of European Expansion and the Creation of the New World Order* (Princeton: Princeton University Press, 2019).

66. Jane Burbank and Frederick Cooper, *Empires in World History: Power and the Politics of Difference* (Princeton: Princeton University Press, 2010).

67. John Darwin, *The Empire Project: The Rise and Fall of the British World-System, 1830–1970* (Cambridge: Cambridge University Press, 2009), 1.

68. Frederick Cooper, "Empire Multiplied. A Review Essay", *Comparative Studies in Society and History* 46, no. 2 (2004): 258–9.

69. George Curzon, *Persia and the Persian Question*, vol. 2 (London: Longmans, Green & Co., 1892), 450–1.

70. John Darwin, *Unfinished Empire: The Global Expansion of Britain* (Cambridge: Cambridge University Press, 2009).

71. Kaushik Roy, *The Army in British India: From Colonial Warfare to Total War, 1857–1947* (London: Bloomsbury, 2012).

72. Christopher A. Bayly, *The Birth of the Modern World, 1780–1914* (Oxford: Blackwell, 2004).

73. Fahad Ahmad Bishara, "Mapping the Indian Ocean World of Gulf Merchants, c.1870–1960", in *The Indian Ocean: Oceanic Connection and the Creation of New Societies*, ed. Abdul Sheriff and Engseng Ho (London: Hurst, 2014), 69–93.

74. Samson A. Bezabeh, *Subjects of Empires/Citizens of States: Yemenis in Djibouti and Ethiopia* (Cairo: American University in Cairo Press, 2016).

75. Marcello de Cecco, *Money and Empire: The International Gold Standard, 1890–1914* (Oxford: Oxford University Press, 1974), 122.

76. Lance E. Davis and Robert A. Huttenback, *Mammon and the Pursuit of Empire: The Political Economy of British Imperialism, 1860–1912* (Cambridge: Cambridge University Press, 1986).

77. Andrew Walter, *World Power and World Money: The Role of Hegemony and International Monetary Order* (New York: St Martin's Press, 1991).

78. Mike Davis, *Late Victorian Holocausts: El Niño Famines and the Making of the Third World* (London: Verso, 2002).

79. John C. Caldwell, "Malthus and the Less Developed World: The Pivotal Role of India", *Population and Development Review* 24, no. 4 (1998): 675–96.

80. Mahmood Mamdani, *Citizen and Subject: Contemporary Africa and the Legacy of Late Colonialism* (Princeton: Princeton University Press, 1996).

81. McCourt, David M. "What was Britain's 'East of Suez role'? Reassessing the withdrawal, 1964–1968." *Diplomacy & Statecraft* 20, no. 3 (2009): 453–472.

82. John Gerard Ruggie, "International Regimes, Transactions, and Change: Embedded Liberalism in the Postwar Economic Order", *International Organization* 36, no. 2 (1982): 379–415.

83. Joseph S. Nye, "Will the Liberal Order Survive: The History of an Idea", *Foreign Affairs* 96, no. 1 (2017): 11.

84. G. John Ikenberry, "The Logic of Order: Westphalia, Liberalism, and the Evolution of International Order in the Modern Era", in *Power, Order and Change in World Politics*, ed. G. John Ikenberry (Cambridge: Cambridge University Press, 2014), 83–106.

85. Niall Ferguson, "Hegemony or Empire?", *Foreign Affairs* 82, no. 5 (2003): 160.

86. Hannes Lacher and Julian Germann, "Before Hegemony: Britain, Free Trade, and Nineteenth-Century World Order Revisited", *International Studies Review* 14, no. 1 (2012): 99–124.

87. Timothy J. McKeown, "Hegemonic Stability Theory and 19th Century Tariff Levels in Europe", *International Organization* 37, no. 1 (1983): 73–91.

88. Stephen D. Krasner, *Structural Conflict: The Third World against Global Liberalism* (Berkeley: University of California Press, 1985).

89. Waltraud Queiser Morales, "US Intervention and the New World Order: Lessons from Cold War and Post-Cold War Cases", *Third World Quarterly* 15, no. 1 (1994): 77–101.

90. Ryan M. Irwin, *Gordian Knot: Apartheid and the Unmaking of the Liberal World Order* (Oxford: Oxford University Press, 2012).

91. Harry Verhoeven, "The Party and the Gun: African Liberation, Asian Comrades and Socialist Political Technologies", *Third World Quarterly* 41, no. 3 (2020), 560–581.

92. Getachew, Adom. *Worldmaking after Empire*. Princeton University Press, 2019.

93. Christopher J. Lee, ed., *Making a World after Empire: The Bandung Moment and Its Political Afterlives* (Athens, OH: Ohio University Press, 2010).

94. Vijay Prashad, *The Darker Nations: A People's History of the Third World* (New York: New Press, 2007).

95. Frederick Cooper, *Africa in the World* (Cambridge, MA: Harvard University Press, 2014).

96. Bradley R. Simpson, *Economists with Guns: Authoritarian Development and US–Indonesian Relations, 1960–1968* (Stanford: Stanford University Press, 2008).

97. Simon Bromley, *American Hegemony and World Oil: The Industry, the State System and the World Economy* (University Park, PA: Penn State Press, 1991).

98. Engseng Ho, "Empire through Diasporic Eyes: A View from the Other Boat", *Comparative Studies in Society and History* 46, no. 2 (2004): 210–46.

99. Thandika Mkandawire and Adebayo Olukoshi, eds., *Between Liberalisation and Oppression: The Politics of Structural Adjustment in Africa* (Dakar: Codesria, 1995).

100. James Ferguson, "Formalities of Poverty: Thinking about Social Assistance in Neoliberal South Africa", *African Studies Review* 50, no. 2 (2007): 71–86.

101. Joe Studwell, *How Asia Works: Success and Failure in the World's Most Dynamic Region* (New York: Grove Press, 2013), 209–13.

102. https://www.trumanlibrary.org/whistlestop/50yr_archive/inagural20jan1949.htm.

103. Michael E. Latham, *The Right Kind of Revolution: Modernization, Development, and US Foreign Policy from the Cold War to the Present* (Ithaca: Cornell University Press, 2010).

104. Sengupta, Mitu. "Making the State Change Its Mind—the IMF, the World Bank and the Politics of India's Market Reforms." *New Political Economy* 14, no. 2 (2009): 181–210.

105. Atul Kohli, *Poverty amid Plenty in the New India* (Cambridge: Cambridge University Press, 2012).

106. Abdi Ismail Samatar, "Structural Adjustment as Development Strategy? Bananas, Boom, and Poverty in Somalia", *Economic Geography* 69, no. 1 (1993): 25–43.

107. Cf. the optimistic argument in Emmanuel Gyimah-Boadi, "African Ambiguities: The Rebirth of African Liberalism", *Journal of Democracy* 9, no. 2 (1998): 18–31.

108. John L. Comaroff and Jean Comaroff. "Criminal Justice, Cultural Justice: The Limits of Liberalism and the Pragmatics of Difference in the New South Africa", *American Ethnologist* 31, no. 2 (2004): 188–204.

109. Eric Hobsbawm and Terence Ranger, eds., *The Invention of Tradition* (Cambridge: Cambridge University Press, 1983); Anthony Reid, *Imperial Alchemy: Nationalism and Political Identity in Southeast Asia* (Cambridge: Cambridge University Press, 2010).

110. Amy Chua, *World on Fire: How Exporting Free Market Democracy Breeds Ethnic Hatred and Global Instability* (New York: Anchor, 2004).

111. Amartya Kumar Sen, "Democracy as a Universal Value", *Journal of Democracy* 10, no. 3 (1999): 3–17.

112. Andrew Sartori, *Liberalism in Empire: An Alternative History* (Berkeley: University of California Press, 2014); John Njenga Karugia, "Connective Afrasian Sea Memories: Transregional Imaginaries, Memory Politics, and Complexities of National 'Belonging'", *Memory Studies* 11, no. 3 (2018): 328–41; Samadia Sadouni, *Muslims in Southern Africa: Johannesburg's Somali Diaspora* (London: Palgrave Macmillan, 2019).

113. Arjun Appadurai, *Modernity at Large: Cultural Dimensions of Globalization* (Minneapolis: University of Minnesota Press, 1996).

114. Colin Dueck, *Reluctant Crusaders: Power, Culture and Change in American Grand Strategy* (Princeton: Princeton University Press, 2006).

115. Charles Lipson, *Reliable Partners: How Democracies Have Made a Separate Peace* (Princeton: Princeton University Press, 2003).

116. Ikenberry, *Liberal Leviathan*, xi.

117. Gilbert Rist, *The History of Development: From Western Origins to Global Faith* (London: Zed Books, 1997), 69.

118. Tim Dunne and Trine Flockhart, eds., *Liberal World Orders* (New York: Oxford University Press, 2013).

119. Choong, William. "The return of the Indo-Pacific strategy: an assessment." *Australian Journal of International Affairs* 73, no. 5 (2019): 415–430.

120. Naazneen Barma, Ely Ratner and Steven Weber, "The Mythical World Order", *National Interest*, no. 124 (March/April 2013): 56–67.

121. Ivo H. Daalder and James M. Lindsay, *The Empty Throne: America's Abdication of Global Leadership* (New York: Public Affairs, 2018).

122. John J. Mearsheimer, "Bound to Fail: The Rise and Fall of the Liberal International Order", *International Security* 43, no. 4 (2019): 7–50.

123. Robert Keohane, *After Hegemony* (Princeton: Princeton University Press, 1984).

124. Phillips and Sharman, *International Order in Diversity*, 6.

2. A HISTORY OF DISTRIBUTED SOVEREIGNTY: TRADE, MIGRATION AND RULE IN THE GLOBAL INDIAN OCEAN

1. Janet Ewald, "Crossers of the Sea: Slaves, Freedmen and Other Migrants in the Northwestern Indian Ocean, c.1750–1914", *American Historical Review* 105, no. 1

(2010): 68–91. See also A. Stanziani, *Sailors, Slaves and Immigrants: Bondage in the Indian Ocean World, 1750–1914* (London: Palgrave, 2014).

2. Gwynn Campbell, *Structure of Slavery in Indian Ocean Africa and Asia* (London: Routledge, 2004).

3. Thomas M. Ricks, "Slaves and Slave Traders in the Persian Gulf, 18th and 19th Centuries: An Assessment", *Slavery and Abolition* 9, no. 3 (1988): 60–70.

4. Joseph E. Harris, *The African Presence in Asia: Consequences of the East African Slave Trade* (Evanston: Northwestern University Press, 1971).

5. Omar H. Ali, *Malik Ambar: Power and Slavery across the Indian Ocean* (New York: Oxford University Press, 2016); Edward A. Alpers and Amy Catlin-Jhairazbhoy, *Sidis and Scholars: Essays on African Indians* (Trenton: Red Sea Press, 2005).

6. These communities in Pakistan, at times also referred to as the *makran* caste, have not received much serious scholarly attention, despite the work of activists such as Sylvianie Diouf (http://thesidiproject.com/) and a recent exhibition at the New York Public Library (http://exhibitions.nypl.org/africansindianocean/index2.php).

7. C.R. Boxer, *The Portuguese Seaborne Empire, 1415–1825* (London: Hutchinson and Co., 1969).

8. L. Benton and L. Ford, *The Rage for Order: The British Empire and the Origins of International Law* (Cambridge, MA: Harvard University Press, 2016). See also A. Anghie, *Imperialism, Sovereignty and the Making of International Law* (Cambridge: Cambridge University Press, 2007).

9. Eric L. Beverley, *Hyderabad, British India, and the World: Muslim Networks and Minor Sovereignty, c.1850–1950* (New York: Cambridge University Press, 2015).

10. Barbara Ramusack, *The Princes and Their States* (Cambridge: Cambridge University Press, 2007); Beverley, *Hyderabad, British India and the World*.

11. Ajay Skaria, *Hybrid Histories: Forests, Frontiers and Wildness in Western India*, Studies in Social Ecology and Environmental History (Oxford: Oxford University Press, 2001); Sanjib Baruah, *Durable Disorder: Understanding the Politics of Northeast India* (Oxford: Oxford University Press, 2007).

12. See David Commins, *The Gulf States: A Modern History* (London: I.B. Tauris, 2009); James Onley, *Britain and the Gulf Shaikhdoms, 1820–1971: The Politics of Protection.* (Qatar: CIRS, Georgetown University in Qatar, 2009).

13. A. Sheriff, *Slaves, Spices, and Ivory: Integration of an East African Commercial Empire into the World Economy* (Athens, OH: Ohio University Press, 1987); F. Cooper, *Plantation Slavery on the East Coast of Africa* (Charlottesville: University of Virginia Press, 1980).

14. Fred Morton, *Children of Ham: Freed Slaves and Fugitive Slaves on the Kenya Coast* (Boulder, CO: Westview Press, 1990); Saada O. Wahab, "Emancipation and Post-emancipation in Zanzibar", in *Transition from Slavery in Zanzibar and Mauritius*, ed. A. Sheriff, V. Teelock, S.O. Wahab and S. Peerthum (Dakar: Codesria, 2016), 45–68. Fahad Bishara's recent study explores the economic relations and dependencies of this region through the lens of Islamic law. Fahad Bishara, *A Sea of Debt: Law and Economic Life in the Western Indian Ocean* (Cambridge: Cambridge University Press, 2017).

15. Andrew Gardner, *City of Strangers: Gulf Migration and the Indian Community in Bahrain* (Ithaca: Cornell University Press, 2010).

16. A.R. Disney, *History of Portugal and the Portuguese Empire*, 2 vols. (Cambridge: Cambridge University Press, 2009); Sanjay Subrahmanyam, *The Portuguese Empire in Asia, 1500–1700: A Political and Economic History* (London: Wiley-Blackwell, 2012).

17. For an interesting account of Portuguese rule in Goa and the mobilization of both theological and cosmopolitan resources to justify empire, see Boxer, *The Portuguese Seaborne Empire*, and Pamila Gupta, "The Disquieting of History: Portuguese Decolonization and Goan Migration in the Indian Ocean", *Journal of Asian and African Studies* 44, no. 1 (2009): 19–47.

18. Crispin Bates and Marina Carter, *Mutiny at the Margins: New Perspectives on the Uprising of 1857* (Delhi: Sage Publications, 2017).

19. The Indian Penal Code was promulgated in 1860 and forms to this day the backbone of criminal law in India, Pakistan and Bangladesh. On the gradual expansion of British law, see Radhika Singha, *A Despotism of Law: Crime and Justice in Early Colonial India* (Delhi: Oxford University Press, 1998). For an account of how a dispersed colonial economy turns into a more unified "national economy" in the 20th century in India, see Manu Goswami, *Producing India: From Colonial Economy to National Space* (Chicago: University of Chicago Press, 2004). Goswami shows how India's extensive rail network helped the colonial state exercise territorial control but how it also unleashed unprecedented movement of migrants to fast-growing cities and populations fleeing conflicts, droughts and famines.

20. Sugata Bose, *A Hundred Horizons: The Indian Ocean in the Age of Global Empire* (Cambridge, MA: Harvard University Press, 2006).

21. See, for instance, Abdul Sheriff, *Dhow Cultures and the Indian Ocean: Cosmopolitanism, Commerce, and Islam* (Amsterdam: KIT Publishers, 2010).

22. David Cannadine, *Ornamentalism: How the British Saw Their Empire* (Oxford: Oxford University Press, 2002).

23. Ronen Palan, *The Offshore World: Sovereign Markets, Virtual Places, and Nomad Millionaires* (Ithaca: Cornell University Press, 2006).

24. See L. Benton, *A Search for Sovereignty: Law and Geography in European Empires, 1400–1900* (Cambridge: Cambridge University Press, 2010). Benton points out that in the colonies, sovereignty was regarded as "divisible", and thus *distributed* in my terminology, as opposed to the enormous emphasis on the indivisibility and integrity of sovereignty in the European tradition (for the origin of the doctrine of indivisibility, see Ernst Kantorowich's classic study, *The King's Two Bodies: A Study in Mediaeval Political Theology* (Princeton: Princeton University Press, 1957)), a legal bedrock supposedly enshrined and codified by the 1648 Treaty of Westphalia. For a re-evaluation of this treaty, see Stephane Beaulac, "The Westphalian Model in Defining International Law: Challenging the Myth", *Australian Journal of Legal History* 8 (2004): 181–213.

25. Michel Foucault, *Discipline and Punish: The Birth of the Prison* (Harmondsworth: Penguin, 1980).

26. Clifford Geertz, *Negara: The Theatre State in Nineteenth Century Bali* (Princeton: Princeton University Press, 1980).

27. Bernard Cohen, *Colonialism and Its Forms of Knowledge* (Princeton: Princeton University Press, 1996); Sudipta Sen, *Distant Sovereignty: National Imperialism and the Origins of British India* (London: Routledge, 2002).

28. Arjun Appadurai, *Worship and Conflict under Colonial Rule: A South Indian Case* (Delhi: Orient Blackswan, 1981).

29. Angma Dey Jhala, *Royal Patronage, Power and Aesthetics in Princely India* (London: Routledge, 2016); Cannadine, *Ornamentalism*.

30. Peter van der Veer, *Imperial Encounters: Religion and Modernity in India and Britain* (Princeton: Princeton University Press, 2002).

31. John Torpey, *The Invention of the Passport: Surveillance, Citizenship and the State* (Cambridge: Cambridge University Press, 2000).

32. In India, even after the promulgation of the Indian Penal Code in 1860, legal regulation of property, inheritance and family law was relegated to discrete community institutions. Other legal systems, many based on Islamic law and customary law, governed the populations in the princely states and other territories across the Indian Ocean world under indirect rule or bound by treaties to the British Empire, such as the sultanates of Malaya, the Persian Gulf or the Swahili coast

33. Singha explores this problem of legibility, jurisdiction and care in a fascinating analysis of poor haj pilgrims from India and elsewhere in the Indian Ocean space who found themselves stranded in Mecca and Medina. Radhika Singha, "Passport, Ticket, and India-Rubber Stamp: 'The Problem of the Pauper Pilgrim' in Colonial India ca. 1882–1925", in *The Limits of British Colonial Control in South Asia: Spaces of Disorder in the Indian Ocean Region*, ed. Harald Fischer-Tine and Ashwini Tambe (London: Routledge, 2008).

34. Claude Markovits, *The Global World of Indian Merchants, 1750–1947: Traders of Sind from Bukhara to Panama* (Cambridge: Cambridge University Press, 2000).

35. Jonah Blank, *Mullahs on the Mainframe: Islam and Modernity among the Daudi Bohras* (Chicago: University of Chicago Press, 2002).

36. Farhad Daftary, *A Modern History of the Ismailis: Continuity and Change in a Muslim Community* (London: I.B. Tauris, 2010); Teena Purohit, *The Aga Khan Case: Religion and Identity in Colonial India* (Cambridge, MA: Harvard University Press, 2012).

37. John McLeod, *Sovereignty, Power, Control: Politics in the States of Western India, 1916–1947* (Leiden: Brill, 1999).

38. Douglas Haynes, *Rhetoric and Ritual in Colonial India: The Shaping of a Public Culture in Surat City, 1852–1928* (Berkeley: University of California Press, 1991); Douglas Haynes, "From Avoidance to Confrontation? A Contestatory History of Merchant–State Relations in Surat, 1600–1924", in *Contesting Power: Resistance and Everyday Social Relations in South Asia*, ed. Douglas Haynes and Gyan Prakash (Berkeley: University of California Press, 1992).

39. Edward Simpson, *Muslim Society and the Western Indian Ocean: The Seafarers of Kachchh* (London: Routledge, 2006); Edward Simpson and Kai Kresse, eds., *Struggling with History: Islam and Cosmopolitanism in the Western Indian Ocean* (London: Hurst, 2007); Edward Simpson, "Why Bhatiyas Are Not 'Banias' and Why This Matters: Economic Success and Religious Worldview among a Mercantile Community of Western India", in *Divines richesses: religion et économie en monde marchand indien*, ed. Pierre Lachaier and Catherine Clémentin-Ojha (Paris: École français d'Extrême-Orient, 2008), 91–111.

40. http://memoncommunity.blogspot.in/2007/10/following-is-list-of-top-40-richest.html.

41. The late Asghar Ali Engineer, tireless campaigner against communal violence in India, was born into the Bohra community. He broke with the community's orthodoxy and devoted considerable energy to research and expose poverty and inequalities within the Muslim Gujarati trading communities. See, for instance, *Islamic Perspective: A Biannual Journal; A Special Issue on Bohras, Khojas and Memons*, ed. by Asghar Ali Engineer (Bombay: Institute of Islamic Studies), 1 (January 1988): 192–211.

42. For a comprehensive overview of the commercial networks of Gujarati and Sindhi trading communities and their alliances and intersections, see Claude Markovits, "Indian Merchant Networks outside India in the Nineteenth and Twentieth Centuries: A Preliminary Survey", in *Connecting Seas and Connected Ocean Rims: Indian, Atlantic, and Pacific and China Seas Migrations from the 1830s to the 1930s*, ed. Donna Gabaccia and Dirk Hoerder (Leiden: Brill, 2011), 79–107.

43. Vahed Goolam, "'Unhappily Torn by Dissensions and Litigations': Durban's 'Memon' Mosque, 1880–1930", *Journal of Religion in Africa* 36 (2006): 23–49.

44. Umrah is a non-mandatory visit to Mecca in addition to the haj. Many wealthy Muslims go for umrah many times in their lives, trips that are often combined with business or leisure activities for their families.

45. Hugh Tinker, *A New System of Slavery and Export of Indian Labor Overseas, 1830–1920* (Oxford: Oxford University Press, 1974).

46. Mabel Palmer, *The History of the Indians in Natal*, Natal Regional Survey, vol. 10 (Cape Town: Oxford University Press, 1957).

47. *Documents Relating to the New Asiatic Bill*, 13–14, quoted in ibid., 94.

48. This was to replace an older system encouraging repatriation created in 1895 when the government began to tax labourers who did not return to India. In 1914 the Indians Relief Act encouraged voluntary repatriation supervised by the Protector of Indian Immigrants in Natal, an office created in the 1860s to supervise the administration of indentured labour. The scheme had had a certain effect, several thousands of Indians did return in each of the following years (Palmer reports a figure of 3,199 in 1920 and 2,699 in 1921 (ibid., 78)), but the birth rate among Indians was so high that it had little effect on the overall size of the Indian population in South Africa. The annual increase in the Indian population was about 3 per cent a year up to 1911. Between 1911 and 1921 it was reduced to 0.73 per cent in spite of constant and high birth rates. Between 1921 and 1936 it increased up to

1.90 per cent and stabilized in the following decades around 2.8–3.0 per cent. See P. Brijlal, "Demographic Profile", in *Indian South Africans*, ed. A.J. Arkin, K.P. Maygar and G.J. Pillay (Pinetown: Owen Burgess, 1989), 123–40.

49. http://mea.gov.in/protector-general-emigrants.htm.

50. Singha, "Passport, Ticket, and India-Rubber Stamp".

51. The Government of India discontinued the haj subsidy in 2017. Many Muslims supported this move and preferred to purchase a ticket in an open market rather than through the artificially inflated prices offered by the Haj Committee.

52. *Social, Economic and Educational Status of the Muslim Community in India: A Report*, by Justice Sachar (The Prime Minister's High Level Committee, Government of India, November 2006); The Mehmoodur Rehman Committee Report, *The Socio-economic and Educational Backwardness of Muslims in Maharashtra* (Mumbai: Government of Maharashtra, 2013).

53. This section summarizes more detailed material I have published elsewhere. See T.B. Hansen, "Bridging the Gulf: Migration and Modernity among Muslims in Mumbai", in *Empire, Migration, Community*, ed. Crispin Bates (London: Macmillan, 2000).

54. Nile Greene, *Bombay Islam: The Religious Economy of the West Indian Ocean, 1840–1915* (Cambridge: Cambridge University Press, 2012).

55. K. Ballhatchet, *Race, Sex, and Class under the Raj: Imperial Attitudes and Policies and Their Critics, 1793–1905* (London: Weidenfeld and Nicholson, 1980).

56. See *Social, Economic and Educational Status of the Muslim Community in India: A Report*. For Mumbai and the state of Maharashtra, see *The Socio-economic and Educational Backwardness of Muslims in Maharashtra*. See also Abdul Shaban, *Mumbai: Political Economy of Crime and Space* (Hyderabad: Orient Blackswan, 2010); and https://www.newsclick.in/over-55-undertrials-are-muslims-dalits-or-tribes-says-ncrb-prison-statistics-report.

57. Sunil Amrith, *Crossing the Bay of Bengal: The Furies of Nature and the Fortunes of Migrants* (Cambridge, MA: Harvard University Press, 2015); Andrew Willford, *The Cage of Freedom: Tamils and the Ethnic Fetish in Malaysia* (Ann Arbor: University of Michigan Press, 2006); Sankaran Krishna, *Postcolonial Insecurities: India, Sri Lanka and the Question of Nationhood* (Minneapolis: University of Minnesota Press, 1999).

58. Bakirathi Mani and Latha Varadarajan, "'The Largest Gathering of the Global Indian Family': Neoliberalism, Nationalism and Diaspora at the Pravasi Bharatiya Divas", *Diaspora* 14, no. 1 (2005): 45–74.

59. See Ashwin Desai, "The Zuma Moment: Between Tender-Based Capitalists and Radical Economic Transformation", *Journal of Contemporary African Studies* (2018): 1–15.

3. LIBERAL ORDER'S ILLIBERAL PRODIGY: SINGAPORE AS A NON-LIBERAL ELECTORAL DEMOCRATIC STATE

1. Partha Chatterjee, *Lineages of Political Society: Studies in Postcolonial Democracy* (New York: Columbia University Press, 2011), 2–3.

2. Francis Fukuyama, *The End of History and the Last Man* (New York: Perennial, 1992).

3. Larry Diamond, ed., *Political Culture and Democracy in Developing Countries* (Boulder, CO: Lynne Rienner Publications, 1993).

4. Muthiah Alagappa, ed., *Taiwan's Presidential Politics: Democratization and Cross-Straits Relations in the Twentieth-First Century* (Armonk, NY: M.E. Sharpe, 2001).

5. David J. Steinberg, *The Philippines: A Singular and a Plural Place* (Boulder, CO: Westview Press, 2000), 121.

6. Paul Hutchcroft and Joel Rocamora, "Strong Demands and Weak Institutions: The Origins and Evolution of the Democratic Deficit in the Philippines", *Journal of East Asian Studies* 3, no. 2 (2003): 259–92.

7. Garry Rodan and Caroline Hughes, *The Politics of Accountability in Southeast Asia: The Dominance of Moral Ideologies* (Oxford: Oxford University Press, 2014).

8. Ibid., 12–13.

9. John Bowen, "On the Political Construction of Tradition: *Gotong Royong* in Indonesia", *Journal of Asian Studies* 45, no. 3 (1986): 545–61.

10. Chua Beng Huat, "'Asian Values' Discourse and the Resurrection of the Social", *Positions: East Asian Culture Critiques* 7, no. 2 (1999): 573–92.

11. Ariel Heryanto, "Pop Culture and Competing Identities", in *Popular Culture in Indonesia*, ed. Ariel Heryanto (London: Routledge, 2008), 20.

12. Richard Robison, "The Politics of Asian Values", *Pacific Review* 9, no. 3 (1996): 309–27.

13. Jothie Rajah, *Authoritarian Rule of Law: Legislation, Discourse and Legitimacy in Singapore* (Cambridge: Cambridge University Press, 2012).

14. Chua Beng Huat, "Singapore as Model", in *Worlding Cities: Asian Experiments and the Art of Being Global*, ed. Ananya Roy and Aihwa Ong (Chichester: Wiley-Blackwell, 2011), 29–54.

15. These racial categories are established purely for administrative convenience as ethnic, linguistic and religious differences within each category are intentionally ignored to produce a "homogenized" racial group.

16. Poh Soo Kai, Tan Kong Fang and Hong Lysa, eds., *The 1963 Operation Coldstore in Singapore* (Kuala Lumpur: Strategic Information and Research Development Centre, 2013).

17. Cherian George, "Consolidating Authoritarian Rule: Calibrated Coercion in Singapore", *Pacific Review* 20, no. 2 (2007): 127–45.

18. Chua Beng Huat, *Communitarian Ideology and Democracy in Singapore* (London: Routledge, 1995), 5–78.

19. Significantly, from independence onwards, every generation of PAP cabinet ministers has counted a few who have taken significant reductions on their private sector salaries when assuming ministerial responsibilities in response to the nation's "call".

20. Chua Beng Huat, *Liberalism Disavowed: Communitarianism and State Capitalism in Singapore* (Singpaore: NUS Press; Ithaca: Cornell University Press, 2017).

21. Minxin Pei, "The Real Singapore Model", *Straits Times*, 31 March 2015.

22. Lee Kuan Yew, "Why Singapore Is What It Is", keynote address to the International Bar Association, *Straits Times*, 15 October 2007.

23. Kelvin Tan and Cherian George, "Civil Society and the Societies Act", *Straits Times*, 27 March 2001.

24. In 2000, a small public park in the city has been designated a "free speech space", which the LGBTs use to hold the annual Pink Dot Day, a festival of love. See Lynette Chua, *Mobilizing Gay Singapore: Rights and Resistance in an Authoritarian State* (Singapore: NUS Press, 2014), 119–22.

25. Rajah, *Authoritarian Rule of Law*.

26. Zakir Hussain, "Raffles, MM Lee and the Rule of Law", *Straits Times*, 28 October 2008.

27. Kanishka Jayasuriya, "The Rule of Law and Capitalism in Asia", *Pacific Review* 9, no. 3 (2007): 367–88.

28. Laurent Pech, "Rule of Law in France", in *Asian Discourses of Rule of Law: Theories and Implementation of Rule of Law in Twelve Asian Countries, France and the US*, ed. Randall Peerenboom (London: Routledge, 2004), 87.

29. Chakrabarty, Bidyut. *Forging power: Coalition politics in India*. Oxford University Press, 2005.

30. Goh Chok Tong, "Singapore: Global City of Buzz, Home for Us", 2010, http://www.news.gov.sg/public/sgpc/en/media_release/agencies/micacsd/speech/S-20.

31. *Straits Times*, 9 September 2015. However, not without slippage into partisanship in government; throughout the 1990s, it had punished residents in public housing estates in constituencies that had elected non-PAP MPs by denying the estates funds for upgrading facilities and amenities.

32. Barrington Kaye, *Upper Nanking Street* (Singapore: University of Malaya Press, 1960).

33. Loh Kah Seng, *Squatters into Citizens: The 1961 Bukit Ho Swee Fire and the Making of Modern Singapore* (Singapore: NUS Press, 2013).

34. For details on the national public housing programme, see Chua Beng Huat, *Political Legitimacy and Housing: Stakeholding in Singapore* (London: Routledge, 1997).

35. T.T.B. Koh, "The Law of Compulsory Land Acquisition in Singapore", *Malayan Law Journal* 35 (1967): 9–22.

36. Aline K. Wong and Stephen H.K. Yeh, eds., *Housing a Nation: 25 Years of Public Housing in Singapore* (Singapore: Housing and Development Board, 1985), 40–1.

37. *Straits Times*, 25 September 2015.

38. Chua, *Political Legitimacy and Housing*.

39. Leonard Seabrooke and Duncan Wigan, "Brexit and Global Wealth Chains", *Globalizations* 14, no. 6 (2017): 820–9.

40. Goh Keng Swee, "Social, Political and Institutional Aspects of Development Planning", in *The Economics of Modernization* (Singapore: Asia Pacific Press, 1972), 210.

41. For example, on 1 April 2014, 800,000 households who lived in public housing

flats received between S$45 and S$65 each from the government, totalling S$45 million (*Straits Times*, 1 April 2014), to defray their utility consumption.

42. Changes in banking regulations after the 1997 Asian regional financial crisis compelled DBS to relinquish its property business; DBS Land was merged with another state-owned property development company, Pidemco Land, in 2000, to form CapitaLand, now a global property company with vast investment in Singapore, China and, to a lesser extent, Australia and Europe. Its 2013 financial year revenue was more than S$3.9 billion and after-tax profit approximately $850 million.

43. V. Shih, "Tools of Survival: Sovereign Wealth Funds in Singapore and China", *Geopolitics* 14, no. 2 (2009): 328–44; Henry Wai-chung Yeung, "Strategic Governance and Economic Diplomacy in China: The Political Economy of Government-Linked Companies from Singapore", *East Asia* 21, no. 1 (2004): 40–64.

44. G.L. Clark and A. Monk, "Government of Singapore Investment Corporation (GIC): Insurer of Last Resort and Bulwark of Nation-State Legitimacy", *Pacific Review* 23, no. 4 (2010): 431.

45. Getachew, Adom. *Worldmaking after Empire*. Princeton University Press, 2019.

46. He was generally disappointed with what he saw in the then new postcolonial states in Africa; https://mothership.sg/2018/07/lee-kuan-yew-in-africa/ (accessed 1 May 2020).

47. Quoted in Katherine Enright, "A Historical Perspective on Singapore–China Relations: 1965–1975", *Singapore Policy Journal*, a Harvard Kennedy School Student Publication, 29 October 2019, https://spj.hkspublications.org/2019/10/25/a-historical-perspective-on-singapore-china-relations-1965–1975/ (accessed 2 May 2020).

48. Tommy T.B. Koh, Li Lin Chang and Joanna Koh, eds., *The Little Red Dot*, vol. 3: *Reflections of Foreign Ambassadors of Singapore* (Singapore: World Scientific Publishers, 2015).

49. https://www.straitstimes.com/asia/se-asia/pm-lee-urges-small-nations-to-team-up-to-amplify-their-influence (accessed 1 May 2020).

50. S. Jayakumar, *Be at the Table or Be on the Menu: A Singapore Memoir* (Singapore: Straits Times Press, 2015). The author, a law professor, was minister of foreign affairs from 1994 to 2004 and deputy prime minister, 2004–9.

51. Daniel Wei Boon Chua, *US–Singapore Relations, 1965–1975: Strategic Non-alignment in the Cold War* (Singapore: NUS Press, 2017).

52. https://www.cia.gov/library/readingroom/docs/CIA-RDP67B00446R000500010022–2.pdf (accessed 2 May 2020).

53. Quoted in Enright, "A Historical Perspective on Singapore–China Relations: 1965–1975".

54. Alexius A. Pereira, *State Collaboration and Development Strategies in China: The Case of China–Singapore Souzhou Industrial Park 1992–2002* (London: Routledge, 2003).

55. Stephan Ortmann and Mark R. Thompson, "China's Obsession with Singapore: Learning Authoritarian Modernity", *Pacific Review* 27, no. 3 (2014): 433–55.

56. https://www.scmp.com/week-asia/politics/article/2051322/how-singapores-military-vehicles-became-beijings-diplomatic (accessed 6 May 2020).

57. For example, Janaki Nair, *The Promise of the Metropolis: Bangalore's Twentieth Century* (Oxford: Oxford University Press, 2005); M.W. Bowman, "Imagining a Modern Rwanda: Sociotechnological Imaginaries, Information Technology, and the Postgenocide State", in *Dreamscapes of Modernity: Sociotechnical Imaginaries and the Fabrication of Power*, ed. Sheila Jasanoff and Sang-Hyun Kim (Chicago: University of Chicago Press, 2015), 79–102.

58. For example, Stephan Ortmann and Mark R. Thompson, "China and the Singapore Model", *Journal of Democracy* 27, no. 1 (2016): 39–48.

59. https://sinosphere.blogs.nytimes.com/2015/03/23/in-lee-kuan-yew-china-saw-a-leader-to-emulate/ (accessed 9 March 2018).

60. Pereira, *State Collaboration and Development Strategies in China*.

61. *Sunday Times*, 13 March 2016.

62. Michael H. Cognato, "China Investment Corporation: Threat or Opportunity?", *NBR Analysis* (Seattle) 19, no. 1 (2008): 9–36.

63. Ortmann and Thompson, "China's Obsession with Singapore".

4. HYBRID CLIENTELISM AS DEMOCRACY IN THE GLOBAL INDIAN OCEAN

1. Barrington Moore, *Social Origins of Dictatorship and Democracy: Lord and Peasant in the Making of the Modern World* (Boston: Beacon Press, 1993); Ruth Berins Collier, *Paths toward Democracy: The Working Class and Elites in Western Europe and South America* (Cambridge: Cambridge University Press, 1999); Charles Boix, *Democracy and Redistribution* (Cambridge: Cambridge University Press, 2003); Charles Tilly, *Contention and Democracy in Europe, 1650–2000* (Cambridge: Cambridge University Press, 2004); Daron Acemoglu and James A. Robinson, *The Economic Origins of Dictatorship and Democracy* (Cambridge: Cambridge University Press, 2006).

2. Martin Shefter, *Political Parties and the State: The American Historical Experience* (Princeton: Princeton University Press, 1993); Francis Fukuyama, *Political Order and Political Decay: From the Industrial Revolution to the Globalization of Democracy* (New York: Farrar, Straus and Giroux, 2014).

3. Guillermo A. O'Donnell, "Illusions about Consolidation", *Journal of Democracy* 7, no. 2 (1996): 34–51; Patrick Chabal and Jean-Pascal Daloz, *Africa Works: Disorder as Political Instrument* (Oxford: James Currey Publishers, 1999).

4. Herbert Kitschelt and Steven I. Wilkinson, *Patrons, Clients and Policies: Patterns of Democratic Accountability and Political Competition* (Cambridge: Cambridge University Press, 2007); Susan Stokes, "Pork, by Any Other Name …: Building a Conceptual Scheme of Distributive Politics", paper presented to APSA, 2009, Toronto; Susan C. Stokes, Thad Dunning, Marcelo Nazareno and Valeria Brusco, *Brokers, Voters, and Clientelism: The Puzzle of Distributive Politics* (Cambridge: Cambridge University Press, 2013).

5. Javier Auyero, "The Logic of Clientelism in Argentina: An Ethnographic Account",

Latin American Research Review 35, no. 3 (2000): 55–81; Kanchan Chandra, *Why Ethnic Parties Succeed: Patronage and Ethnic Head Counts in India*, Cambridge Studies in Comparative Politics (New York: Cambridge University Press, 2004); Benjamin A. Olken, "Direct Democracy and Local Public Goods: Evidence from a Field Experiment in Indonesia", *American Political Science Review* 104, no. 2 (2010): 243–67; Kitschelt and Wilkinson, *Patrons, Clients and Policies*; Simeon Nichter, "Vote Buying or Turnout Buying? Machine Politics and the Secret Ballot", *American Political Science Review* 102, no. 1 (2008): 19–31; Stokes et al., *Brokers, Voters, and Clientelism*.

6. John D. Powell, "Peasant Society and Clientelist Politics", *American Political Science Review* 64, no. 2 (1970): 411–25; James C. Scott, "Patron–Client Politics and Political Change in Southeast Asia", *American Political Science Review* 66, no. 1 (1972): 91–113.

7. Ineke van Kessel and Barbara Oomen, "'One Chief, One Vote': The Revival of Traditional Authorities in Post-Apartheid South Africa", *African Affairs* 96, no. 385 (1997): 561–85; Carolyn Logan, "Selected Chiefs, Elected Councilors and Hybrid Democrats: Popular Perspectives on the Co-existence of Democracy and Traditional Authority", *Journal of Modern African Studies* 47, no. 1 (2009): 101–28; Tim Kelsall, *Business, Politics, and the State in Africa* (London: Zed Books, 2003); J.B. Murtazashvili, "Informal Federalism: Self-Governance and Power Sharing in Afghanistan", *Publius: The Journal of Federalism* 44, no. 2 (2014): 324–43; Siwan Anderson, Patrick Francois and Ashok Kotwal, "Clientelism in Indian Villages", *American Economic Review* 105, no. 6 (2015): 1780–816; Shandana Khan Mohmand, *Crafty Oligarchs, Savvy Voters: Democracy under Inequality in Rural Pakistan* (Cambridge: Cambridge University Press, 2019).

8. Lucas M. Novaes, "Disloyal Brokers and Weak Parties", *American Journal of Political Science* 62, no. 1 (2018): 84–98.

9. Anirudh Krishna, ed., *Poverty, Participation, and Democracy: A Global Perspective* (New York: Cambridge University Press, 2008); Amit Ahuja and Pradeep Chhibber, "Why the Poor Vote in India: 'If I Don't Vote, I Am Dead to the State'", *Studies in Comparative International Development* 47 (2012): 389–410.

10. A term that is used in public rhetoric in Pakistan not to signify a system of rural production but to refer to a multifaceted relationship of extreme social, political and economic inequality between landlords and other rural classes.

11. Andrew Wilder, *The Pakistani Voter: Electoral Politics and Voting Behaviour in the Punjab* (Oxford: Oxford University Press, 1999); Philip Keefer, Ambar Narayan and Tara Vishwanath, "The Political Economy of Decentralization in Pakistan", World Bank, Policy Research Group, Washington, 2003; Herbert Kitschelt, "Expert Survey on Citizen–Politician Linkages: Initial Findings for Pakistan in Comparative Context", Duke University, 2009.

12. Ali Cheema and Shandana Khan Mohmand, "Local Government Reforms in Pakistan: Legitimising Centralisation or a Driver for Pro-Poor Change", Institute of Development Studies and Collective for Social Science Research, 2003; Akbar Zaidi, "State Military and Social Transition", *Economic and Political Weekly*,

3 December 2005: 5173–81; Shandana Khan Mohmand, "Losing the Connection: Party–Voter Linkages in Pakistan", *Commonwealth and Comparative Politics* 52, no. 1 (2014): 7–31.

13. Wilder *The Pakistani Voter*; Ali Cheema, Asim Ijaz Khwaja and Adnan Qadir, "Local Government Reform in Pakistan: Context, Content and Causes", in *Decentralization and Local Governance in Developing Countries: A Comparative Perspective*, ed. Pranab Bardhan and Dilip Mookherjee (Cambridge: MIT Press, 2006), 257–84.

14. Khan Mohmand, *Crafty Oligarchs, Savvy Voters*.

15. Powell, "Peasant Society and Clientelist Politics"; John Gaventa, *Power and Powerlessness: Quiescence and Rebellion in an Appalachian Valley* (Urbana: University of Illinois Press, 1982).

16. Caste in Pakistan does not look like caste in India, but it exists nevertheless, and divides especially its rural population into hierarchically organized status groups.

17. These quite obviously match Dahl's dimensions of polyarchy. See Robert A. Dahl, *Polyarchy: Participation and Opposition* (New Haven: Yale University Press, 1971).

18. These are all pseudonyms.

19. The three main *quoms* or caste groups in rural Punjab, in order of rank, are *zamindar* (agricultural), *kammi* (artisanal), and *muslim sheikh* (labour). Within each *quom*, there are *biradaris* (kinship groups) that are also, often, ranked hierarchically.

20. A large landowner whose family was given land at the time of the original settlement of the village.

21. The person appointed by the colonial state as responsible for revenue collection and regulation of village affairs and to act as the main intermediary between the state and the village. Very often this was the largest landowner in a village. In most villages the position has become hereditary.

22. Shahnaz Rouse, "Agrarian Transformation in a Punjabi Village: Structural Change and Its Consequences", PhD diss., University of Wisconsin-Madison, 1988; Saghir Ahmad and Hamza Alavi, "A Village in Pakistani Panjab: Jalpana", in *South Asia: Seven Community Profiles*, ed. Clarence Maloney (New York: Holt, Rinehart and Winston, 1974), 131–72.

23. *Maalik* literally means "lord".

24. Ian Talbot, *Khizr Tiwana: The Punjab Unionist Party and the Partition of India* (Karachi: Oxford University Press, 2002).

25. Literally, "mother and father".

26. Interview with vote bloc leader's brother, Chak 2, May 2013.

27. Interview with colony leader, Chak 1, May 2013.

28. Member of the Provincial Assembly.

29. Interview with vote bloc leader, Chak 1, May 2013.

30. Interview with vote bloc leader, Chak 2, May 2013.

31. Both candidates were still going to run—the Mekan candidate as an independent, and Qureshi, the landed elite, as the PML-N candidate, on the understanding that the winner would get the PML-N seat in the provincial assembly.

32. Interview with Mekan leader, Sahiwal, May 2013.

33. Interview with independent landowner, Tiwanabad, May 2013.
34. Michelle D'Arcy and Agnes Cornell, "Devolution and Corruption in Kenya: Everyone's Turn to Eat?", *African Affairs* 115, no. 459 (2016): 246–73; Fiona Anciano, "Clientelism as Civil Society? Unpacking the Relationship between Clientelism and Democracy at the Local Level in South Africa", *Journal of Asian and African Studies* 53, no. 4 (2018): 593–611.
35. Stokes et al., *Brokers, Voters, and Clientelism*; James A. Robinson and Thierry Verdier, "The Political Economy of Clientelism", *Scandinavian Journal of Economics* 115, no. 2 (2013): 260–91.
36. Thad Dunning and Janhavi Nilekani, "Ethnic Quotas and Political Mobilization: Caste, Parties, and Distribution in Indian Village Councils", *American Political Science Review* 107 (2013): 35–56; Pradeep. K. Chhibber and Rahul Verma, *Ideology and Identity: The Changing Party Systems of India* (New York: Oxford University Press, 2018); Jennifer Bussell, *Clients and Constituents: Political Responsiveness in Patronage Democracies* (New York: Oxford University Press, 2019).
37. Haseeb Bajwa, Ali Cheema, Shandana Khan Mohmand and Asad Liaqat, "Party over Person: Voter Preferences for Leaders in a Pakistani Megacity", Working paper, Institute of Development and Economic Alternatives, 2020.

5. THE ARABIAN OIL STATE: INFRASTRUCTURAL POWER AND SOCIAL SEGMENTATION

1. J. Davis, *Libyan Politics: Tribe and Revolution* (London: I.B. Tauris, 1987).
2. S. Hertog, *Princes, Brokers, and Bureaucrats: Oil and the State in Saudi Arabia* (Ithaca: Cornell University Press, 2010).
3. Karen Barkey, *Empire of Difference: The Ottomans in Comparative Perspective* (Cambridge: Cambridge University Press, 2008).
4. Johnson Chun-Sing Cheung, "Rentier Welfare States in Hydrocarbon-Based Economies: Brunei Darussalam and Islamic Republic of Iran in Comparative Context", *Journal of Asian Public Policy* 10, no. 3 (2017): 287–301.
5. Laura El-Katiri, "The Guardian State and Its Economic Development Model", *Journal of Development Studies* 50, no. 1 (2014): 22–34.
6. Toby Craig Jones, "America, Oil, and War in the Middle East", *Journal of American History* 99, no. 1 (2012): 208–18; Robert Vitalis, *America's Kingdom: Mythmaking on the Saudi Oil Frontier* (Stanford: Stanford University Press, 2007).
7. Robert Keohane, *After Hegemony* (Princeton: Princeton University Press, 1984).
8. Giacomo Luciani, "Allocation vs. Production States", in *The Rentier State*, ed. Hazem Beblawi and Giacomo Luciani (London: Croom Helm, 1987); Hootan Shambayati, "The Rentier State, Interest Groups, and the Paradox of Autonomy: State and Business in Turkey and Iran", *Comparative Politics* 26, no. 3 (1994): 307–31, https://doi.org/10.2307/422114.
9. S. Hertog, "The Post-WWII Consolidation of Gulf Nation-States: Particularities of

Oil-Based Nation-Building", in *The Emergence of the Gulf States*, ed. J.E. Peterson (London: Bloomsbury Press, 2016).

10. Hertog, *Princes, Brokers, and Bureaucrats*.

11. Justin J. Gengler, "Royal Factionalism, the Khawalid, and the Securitization of 'the Shi'a Problem' in Bahrain", *Journal of Arabian Studies* 3, no. 1 (2013): 53–79.

12. Mehran Kamrava, *Qatar: Small State, Big Politics* (Ithaca: Cornell University Press, 2013).

13. Christopher Davidson, *Abu Dhabi: Oil and Beyond* (London: Hurst, 2011), 75ff.

14. John Peterson, *Oman in the Twentieth Century* (London: Croom Helm, 1978).

15. Michael Herb, *The Wages of Oil: Parliaments and Economic Development in Kuwait and the UAE* (Ithaca: Cornell University Press, 2014). There are many theories to explain the Kuwaiti (semi-)democratic exception, but Herb convincingly links it to the need for international support in face of repeated Iraqi threats to Kuwait's survival as an independent state.

16. S. Hertog, "Shaping the Saudi State: Human Agency's Shifting Role in Rentier-State Formation", *International Journal of Middle East Studies* 39, no. 4 (2007): 539–63.

17. Barbara Geddes, *Politician's Dilemma: Building State Capacity in Latin America*, new edn (Berkeley: University of California Press, 1996).

18. Ahmed Banafe and Rory Macleod, *The Saudi Arabian Monetary Agency, 1952–2016: Central Bank of Oil* (New York: Palgrave Macmillan, 2017); Arthur N. Young, *Saudi Arabia: The Making of a Financial Giant* (New York: New York University Press, 1983).

19. S. Hertog, "Petromin: The Slow Death of Statist Oil Development in Saudi Arabia", *Business History* 50, no. 5 (2008): 645–67.

20. S. Hertog, "Defying the Resource Curse: Explaining Successful State-Owned Enterprises in Rentier States", *World Politics* 62, no. 2 (2010): 261–301, https://doi.org/10.1017/S0043887110000055.

21. Herb, *The Wages of Oil*.

22. Michael Roll, ed., *The Politics of Public Sector Performance: Pockets of Effectiveness in Developing Countries* (London: Routledge, 2015).

23. S. Hertog, "A Quest for Significance: Gulf Oil Monarchies' International Soft Power Strategies and Their Urban Dimensions", in *Learning from Gulf Cities*, ed. Harvey Molotch and Davide Ponzini (New York: NYU Press, 2018).

24. One partial exception to this is the UAE, which has recently emerged as a significant regional military power—but without reducing its civilian state-building ambitions in any way.

25. Ricardo Soares de Oliviera, *Oil and Politics in the Gulf of Guinea* (London: Hurst, 2007); Geoffrey Wood, "Business and Politics in a Criminal State: The Case of Equatorial Guinea", *African Affairs* 103, no. 413 (2004): 547–67, https://doi.org/10.1093/afraf/adh084; Douglas A. Yates, *The Rentier State in Africa: Oil Rent Dependency and Neocolonialism in the Republic of Gabon* (Trenton: Africa World Press, 1996).

26. Ferdinand Eibl and Steffen Hertog, "Political Subversion and Rentier State Building in the Gulf", draft paper, London, 2016.

27. This chapter does not discuss the role of religion in nation- or state-building in the Arabian Peninsula. The differences in terms of the political role of Islam between these states are more significant than their similarities. As such, they cannot account for the particular ideological hybrid I identify here in the context of investigating the liberal order and its transcendence in the Global Indian Ocean.

28. Jim Krane, "Stability versus Sustainability: Energy Policy in the Gulf Monarchies", PhD diss., Judge Business School, Cambridge University, 2013.

29. Ferdinand Eibl and Steffen Hertog, "Why Are Some Oil Dictators Nice to Their People?", draft paper, London, 2016; Farrukh Iqbal and Youssouf Kiendrebeogo, "Public Spending and Education Attainment in the Middle East and North Africa', *Review of Middle East Economics and Finance* 11, no. 2 (2015): 99–118.

30. Natalia Tamirisa and Christoph Duenwald, "Public Wage Bills in the Middle East and Central Asia", Fiscal Affairs Departmental Paper Series, International Monetary Fund, Washington, DC, 2017.

31. Hertog, "The Post-WWII Consolidation of Gulf Nation-States".

32. Seymour Martin Lipset, "Some Social Requisites of Democracy: Economic Development and Political Legitimacy", *American Political Science Review* 53, no. 1 (1959): 69–105, https://doi.org/10.2307/1951731.

33. Charles Tilly, *Coercion, Capital, and European States, A.D. 990–1992*, Studies in Social Discontinuity, rev edn (Cambridge, MA: Harvard University Press, 1992).

34. Pamela Erskine-Loftus, Victoria Penziner Hightower and Mariam Ibrahim Al-Mulla, *Representing the Nation: Heritage, Museums, National Narratives, and Identity in the Arab Gulf States* (Abingdon: Routledge, 2016); Calvert W. Jones, *Bedouins into Bourgeois: Remaking Citizens for Globalization* (New York: Cambridge University Press, 2017).

35. Nabil Mouline, *The Clerics of Islam: Religious Authority and Political Power in Saudi Arabia* (New Haven: Yale University Press, 2014).

36. Hertog, *Princes, Brokers, and Bureaucrats*.

37. Hertog, "A Quest for Significance".

38. Ibid.

39. Jonathan Miran, *Red Sea Citizens: Cosmopolitan Society and Cultural Change in Massawa* (Bloomington: Indiana University Press, 2009).

40. J. Peterson, *The Emergence of the Gulf States: Studies in Modern History* (London: Bloomsbury, 2016); Jonathan Miran, "Mapping Space and Mobility in the Red Sea Region, c.1500–1950", *History Compass* 12, no. 2 (2014): 197–216.

41. James Onley, "Transnational Merchant Families in the Nineteenth-and Twentieth-Century Gulf", in *The Gulf Family: Kinship Policies and Modernity*, ed. A. Al-Sharekh (London: Saqi Books, 2007), 36–57.

42. Noora Lori, "Unsettling State: Non-citizens, State Power, and Citizenship in the UAE", PhD diss., Johns Hopkins University, 2013.

43. Claire Beaugrand, *Stateless in the Gulf: Migration, Nationality and Society in Kuwait* (London: I.B. Tauris, 2018).

44. Engseng Ho, "Names beyond Nations: The Making of Local Cosmopolitans", *Études Rurales*, no. 163–164 (2002): 215–31.

45. Lori, "Unsettling State".

46. Suresh Naidu, Yaw Nyarko and Shing-Yi Wang, "Worker Mobility in a Global Labor Market: Evidence from the United Arab Emirates", New York University, 2014.

47. S. Hertog, "A Comparative Assessment of Labor Market Nationalization Policies in the GCC", in *National Employment, Migration and Education in the GCC*, ed. Steffen Hertog (Berlin: Gerlach Press, 2012), 75–116.

48. John Chalcraft, "Migration and Popular Protest in the Arabian Peninsula and the Gulf in the 1950s and 1960s", *International Labor and Working-Class History* 79, no. 1 (2011): 28–47; Vitalis, *America's Kingdom*.

49. Stéphane Lacroix, *Awakening Islam: The Politics of Religious Dissent in Contemporary Saudi Arabia* (Cambridge, MA: Harvard University Press, 2011).

50. Courtney Freer, "Rentier Islam: Muslim Brotherhood Affiliates in Kuwait, Qatar, and the United Arab Emirates", DPhil diss., Oxford University, 2016.

51. Tilly, *Coercion, Capital, and European States*.

52. Jeffrey Herbst, *States and Power in Africa: Comparative Lessons in Authority and Control* (Princeton: Princeton University Press, 2014).

53. Daron Acemoglu, Simon Johnson and James A. Robinson, "The Colonial Origins of Comparative Development: An Empirical Investigation", *American Economic Review* 91 (5 (2001): 1369–401; Crawford Young, *The African Colonial State in Comparative Perspective* (New Haven: Yale University Press, 1994).

54. Robert H. Jackson, *Quasi-States: Sovereignty, International Relations and the Third World* (Cambridge: Cambridge University Press, 1993).

55. Chalmers A. Johnson, *MITI and the Japanese Miracle: The Growth of Industrial Policy, 1925–1975* (Stanford: Stanford University Press, 1982); Peter B. Evans, *Embedded Autonomy* (Princeton: Princeton University Press, 1985); Robert Wade, *Governing the Market: Economic Theory and the Role of Government in East Asian Industrialization* (Princeton: Princeton University Press, 2003).

56. Joel S. Migdal, *State in Society: Studying How States and Societies Transform and Constitute One Another* (Cambridge: Cambridge University Press, 2001).

57. Herb, *The Wages of Oil*.

58. Jill Crystal, "The Scuritization of Oil and Its Ramifications in the GCC States", in *Environmental Politics in the Middle East: Local Struggles, Global Connections*, ed. Harry Verhoeven (London: Hurst, 2018), 75–97.

6. WOMEN AS OBJECTS OF DEVELOPMENT: NEOLIBERALISM IN BANGLADESH

1. Sanchita Banerjee Saxena, *Made in Bangladesh, Cambodia and Sri Lanka: The Labor behind the Global Garments and Textiles Industries* (Amherst, NY: Cambria Press, 2014). Sandya Hewamanne, *Stitching Identities in a Free Trade Zone: Gender and Politics in Sri Lanka*

(Philadelphia: University of Pennsylvania Press, 2007); Vincent Hardy and Jostein Hauge, "Labour Challenges in Ethiopia's Textile and Leather Industries: No Voice, No Loyalty, No Exit?", *African Affairs* 118, no. 473 (2019): 712–36.

2. The Norwegian Nobel Committee gave the 2006 Peace Prize to Yunus and the women of the Grameen Bank. The United Kingdom knighted Fazle Abed in 2010 in recognition of his work with rural poverty. The third most influential NGO leader is Dr Zafrullah Chowdhury, who founded the Maoist-style people's health-care centre, Gonoshasthaya Kendro. Zafrullah's socialist ideas of free and afford-able health care for all received less attention both at the global and national levels.

3. Leila Abu-Lughod, "Do Muslim Women Really Need Saving? Anthropological Reflections on Cultural Relativism and Its Others", *American Anthropologist*, 104, no. 3 (2002): 783–90.

4. Bjorke S. Risager, "Neoliberalism Is a Political Project: An Interview with David Harvey", *Jacobin Magazine*, 23 July 2016, 3, https://www.jacobinmag.com/2016/07/david-harvey-neoliberalism-capitalism-labor-crisis-resistance/.

5. Ibid, 5.

6. David Harvey, *The Condition of Postmodernity* (Oxford: Blackwell, 1992), 147.

7. Ibid., 147.

8. Joseph E. Stiglitz, "Capital-Market Liberalization, Globalization, and the IMF", *Oxford Review of Economic Policy* 20, no. 1 (2004): 57–71.

9. Leela Fernandes, "Introduction", in *Feminists Rethink the Neoliberal State: Inequality, Exclusion, and Change*, ed. Leela Fernandes (New York: New York University Press, 2018), 3.

10. Irene Tinker and Michele Bo Bramson, *Women and World Development* (Washington, DC: Overseas Development Council, 1976); Caroline Moser, *Gender Planning and Development: Theory, Practice and Training* (London: Routledge, 1993); Naila Kabeer, *Reversed Realities: Gender Hierarchy in Development Thought* (London: Verso, 1994).

11. Debika Jain, *Women, Development and the United Nations; A Sixty Year Quest for Justice* (Bloomington: Indiana Press University, 2005).

12. Ritu Sharma, "Women and Development Aid", *Foreign Policy in Focus*, 5 October 2005, http://fpif.org/women_development_aid/.

13. Adrienne Germain, "A Major Resource Awaiting Development", *New York Times*, 26 August 1975.

14. Ibid.

15. Kabeer, *Reversed Realities*.

16. Linda Mayoux, "Questioning Virtual Spirals: Microfinance and Women's Empowerment in Africa", *Journal of International Development* 11, no. 7 (1999): 957–84.

17. Meena Khandewal and Carla Freeman, "Pop Development and the Uses of Feminism", in *Seduced and Betrayed: Exposing the Contemporary Microfinance Phenomenon*, ed. Milford Bateman and Kate Maclean (Albuquerque, NM: SAR Press, 2017), 57.

18. Lamia Karim, *Microfinance and Its Discontents: Women in Debt in Bangladesh*

(Minneapolis: University of Minnesota Press, 2011); Jude Fernando, *Microfinance: Perils and Prospects* (London: Routledge, 1996); Milford Bateman and Sonja Novkovic, "Muhammad Yunus's Model of Social Business: A New, More Humane Form of Capitalism or a Failed 'Next Big Idea'?", in *Seduced and Betrayed: Exposing the Contemporary Microfinance Phenomenon*, ed. Milford Bateman and Kate Maclean (Albuquerque, NM: SAR Press, 2017), 103–26.

19. Sandra Harding, "Just Add Women and Stir?" in *Missing Links: Gender Equity in Science and Technology for Development*, ed. Gender Working Group, United Nations Commission for Science and Technology for Development (New York: UNIFEM, 1995), 295.

20. Just Faaland and John Parkinson, *Bangladesh: The Test Case for Development* (Boulder, CO: Westview Press, 1976), 5.

21. Fahimul Quadir, "The Political Economy of Pro-market Reforms In Bangladesh: Regime Consolidation through Economic Liberalization", *Contemporary South Asia* 2, no. 4 (2000): 197–212.

22. Ibid.

23. Ibid.

24. Lamia Karim, "Resistance and Its Pitfalls: Analyzing NGO and Civil Society Politics in Bangladesh", in *Sage Handbook of Resistance*, ed. David Courpasson and Steven Vallas (London: Sage Publications, 2016), 461–75.

25. Yasmin Saikia, *Women, War and the Making of Bangladesh: Remembering 1971* (Durham, NC: Duke University Press, 2010).

26. Abm Ziaur Rahman, "Correlations between Green Revolution and Population Growth: Revisited in the Context of Bangladesh and India", *Asian Affairs* 26, no. 3 (2004): 41–60.

27. Farida Akhter, *Depopulating Bangladesh: Essays on the Politics of Fertility* (Dhaka: Narigrantha Prabartana, 1992).

28. Richard Eaton, *The Rise of Islam and the Bengal Frontier, 1204–1760* (Berkeley: University of California Press, 1996).

29. Lamia Karim, "Democratizing Bangladesh: State, NGOs and Militant Islam", *Cultural Dynamics* 16, nos. 2 & 3 (2004): 291–318.

30. Mayoux, "Questioning Virtual Spirals".

31. Karim, *Microfinance and Its Discontents*; Bateman and Novkovic, "Muhammad Yunus's Model of Social Business".

32. Jonathan Sterne and Carol Stabile, "Using Women as Middle Men: The Real Power of ICTs", *Feminist Studies* 3, no. 3 (2004): 364.

33. Achim Berg, Saskia Hedrich and Thomas Tochtermann, *Bangladesh's Ready-Made Garments Industry: The Challenge of Growth* (Frankfurt: McKinsey Consulting, Inc., 2011), 11.

34. Bangladesh Garment Manufacturers and Exporters Association (BGMEA), http://www.bgmea.com.bd/.

35. Ibrahim Hossain Ovi, "RMG Exports Saw 8.7% Growth in Last Fiscal Year", *Dhaka*

Tribune, 5 July 2018, https://www.dhakatribune.com/business/2018/07/05/rmg-exports-saw-8–76-growth-last-fiscal-year (accessed 29 October 2018).

36. http://www.bgmea.com.bd/.

37. Gunseli Berik, "Revisiting the Feminist Debates on the International Labor Standards in the Aftermath of Rana Plaza", *Studies in Comparative International Development* 52, no. 2 (2017): 3.

38. Ibid.

39. Naila Kabeer and Simeen Mahmud, "Globalization, Gender and Poverty: Bangladeshi Women Workers in Export and Local Markets", *Journal of International Development* 16, no. 1 (2004).

40. "Mastercard Foundation, BRAC Launch Microfinance Program in Uganda", 26 November 2008, https://philanthropynewsdigest.org/news/mastercard-foundation-brac-launch-microfinance-program-in-uganda.

41. Muhammad Yunus, "Sacrificing Microcredit for Megaprofits", *New York Times*, 14 January 2011, https://www.nytimes.com/2011/01/15/opinion/15yunus.html.

7. DIVIDE AND RULE: PARTITION AND ILLIBERAL STATE-BUILDING IN THE HORN OF AFRICA

1. Michael Woldemariam, "Partition Problems: Historical Memory, Relative Power, and the Origins of the Eritrean-Ethiopian War", *Nationalism and Ethnic Politics* 21, no. 2 (2015): 166–90.

2. Penderel Moon, *Divide and Quit* (Berkeley: University of California Press, 1962).

3. Chaim Kaufmann, "Possible and Impossible Solutions to Ethnic Conflict", *International Security* 20, no. 4 (1996): 136–75; Chaim Kaufmann, "When All Else Fails: Ethnic Population Transfers and Partitions in the Twentieth Century", *International Security* 23, no. 2 (1998): 129–56. For other work along these lines, see Alexander Downes, "The Holy Land Divided: Defending Partition as a Solution to Ethnic Wars", *Security Studies* 10, no. 4 (2001): 58–116; Donald Horowitz, "The Cracked Foundations of the Right to Secede", *Journal of Democracy* 14, no. 2 (2003): 5–17; Alexander Downes, "The Problem with Negotiated Settlements to Ethnic Civil Wars", *Security Studies* 13, no. 4 (2004): 230–79; Brendan O'Leary and Nicholas Sambanis, "Nationalism and International Security", in *The Oxford Handbook of International Security*, ed. A. Gheciu and W. Wohlforth (Oxford: Oxford University Press, 2018), 415–31. Some argue that partition, when it is sanctioned by international interventions, might prompt other groups to deploy violence to achieve such an outcome: Alan Kuperman, "The Moral Hazard of Humanitarian Intervention: Lessons from the Balkans", *International Studies Quarterly* 52, no. 1 (2008): 49–80.

4. For a well-conceptualized depiction of the "illiberal" state in Africa, see Will Jones, Ricardo Soares de Olivera and Harry Verhoeven, "Africa's Illiberal State Builders", University of Oxford, Refugee Centre Working Paper Series 89, 2013, 1–25. They argue that "These states are ruled by unified and well-organized movements that

have, in the aftermath of conflict, captured the state and established durable political order, building a core of functional institutions. Their aspirations go beyond a
short-term resource grab, as they use the state to centralize resources and create
and/or strengthen a robust edifice of control ... [they] rule in defiance of liberal
peace precepts, having first used war and then the post-conflict political order to
establish a hegemonic order and stranglehold over the political economy."

5. The Mereb is a seasonal river that defines much of the border between Eritrea and
Ethiopia, particularly on the Tigrinya-speaking highland plateau.

6. Sumit Ganguly, "A Tale of Two Trajectories: Civil–Military Relations in Pakistan
and India", *Journal of Strategic Studies* 39, no. 1 (2015): 142–57; Kunal Mukherjee,
"Why Has Democracy Been Less Successful in Pakistan than India?", *Asian Affairs*
41, no. 1 (2010): 67–77.

7. Maya Tudor, "Explaining Democracy's Origins: Lessons from South Asia",
Comparative Politics 45, no. 3 (2013): 253–72; Maya Tudor, *The Promise of Power:
The Origins of Democracy in India and Autocracy in Pakistan* (Cambridge: Cambridge
University Press, 2013).

8. Ayesha Jalal, *Democracy and Authoritarianism in South Asia* (Cambridge: Cambridge
University Press, 1995); Ayesha Jalal, *The State of Martial Rule: The Origins of
Pakistan's Political Economy of Defence* (Cambridge: Cambridge University Press,
2007).

9. J. Di John and J. Putzel, "Political Settlements: Issues Paper", Governance and
Social Development Resource Centre, June 2009, 4.

10. Mushtaq Khan, "State Failure in Weak States: A Critique of the New Institutionalist
Explanations", in *New Institutional Economics and Third World Development*, ed.
J. Harris, Janet Hunter and Colin M. Lewis (London: Routledge, 1995), 71–86.

11. Ruth Collier and David Collier, *Shaping the Political Arena: Critical Junctures, the Labor
Movement, and Regime Dynamics in Latin America* (South Bend: Notre Dame University
Press, 2002).

12. Obviously, another layer of explanation is necessary to explain why the absence of
a pact of domination leads to the different outcomes of democratization and democratic consolidation, on the one hand, and state weakness and collapse, on the
other.

13. Michael Woldemariam, "The Making of an African 'Pariah': Eritrea in the
International System", in *Post-Liberation Eritrea*, ed. Tekle Woldemikael
(Bloomington: Indiana University Press, 2018).

14. John Markakis, *Ethiopia: The Last Two Frontiers* (Oxford: James Currey, 2011);
Martin Plaut, *Understanding Eritrea: Inside Africa's Most Repressive State* (London: Hurst
Publishers, 2016).

15. For a complete account of the 1941 "Woyane" rebellion, see Gebru Tareke,
Ethiopia: Power and Protest: Peasant Revolts in the 20th Century (Cambridge: Cambridge
University Press, 1991).

16. John Young, "The Tigray and Eritrean People's Liberation Fronts: A History of
Tensions and Pragmatism", *Journal of Modern African Studies* 34, no. 1 (1996): 105–

20; Richard Trivelli, "Divided Histories, Opportunistic Alliances: Background Notes on the Eritrean-Ethiopian War", *Africa Spectrum* 33, no. 3 (1998): 257–89.

17. The previous nine paragraphs are drawn from Woldemariam, "Partition Problems". Also see Michael Woldemariam, "After the Split: Partition, Successor States, and the Dynamics of War in the Horn of Africa", *Journal of Strategic Studies* 41, no. 5 (2016): 1–37.

18. Amare Tekle, *Eritrea and Ethiopia: From Conflict to Cooperation* (Trenton: Red Sea Press, 1994).

19. Author's interview with a prominent Ethiopia elder who participated in the July 1991 transition conference, March 2009; Getachew Metaferia, *Ethiopia and the United States* (New York: Algora Publishing, 2009), 77–8.

20. Metaferia, *Ethiopia and the United States*, 78 writes that "some believed that the TPLF, under Meles Zenawi, was not willing to agree to a competing organization, the EPLF, gaining leadership within Ethiopia's framework and assiduously worked for the secession of Eritrea".

21. Markakis, *Ethiopia*, 230.

22. Author's interview with senior OLF commander and politburo member, April 2011.

23. Fantahun Ayele, *The Ethiopian Army: From Victory to Collapse, 1977–1991* (Evanston: Northwestern University Press, 2014), 202; Markakis, *Ethiopia*, 231.

24. In the Council of Representatives (Ethiopia's transitional parliament), the OLF occupied 12 seats while the TPLF-led EPRDF occupied 32 (making it the largest bloc). In the 17-member Council of Ministers, the OLF only held 4 seats. The critical portfolios of president, prime minister, foreign minister, and defence and internal affairs were all occupied by the EPRDF. Also, EPRDF forces were designated as the interim army of Ethiopia.

25. Information on TPLF–OLF–EPLF relations is drawn from the author's interview with a senior OLF commander and politburo member, April 2011, and confirmed by Leenco Lata, "The Making and Unmaking of Ethiopia's Transitional Charter", in *Oromo Nationalism and the Ethiopian Discourse*, ed. Asafa Jalata (Trenton: Red Sea Press, 1998): 65–7. Leenco Lata was OLF chairman during the transition.

26. See Howard Whitt, "Angry Ethiopians Protest US Role", *Chicago Tribune*, 30 May 1991, http://articles.chicagotribune.com/1991–05–30/news/9102180242_1_rebel-led-rebel-soldiers-ethiopian.

27. The author's review of the "Collected Papers of Paul Henze", which can be found at the Institute of Ethiopian Studies in Addis; Jane Perlez, "Ethiopians to Discuss a New Regime", *New York Times*, 1 July 1991, https://www.nytimes.com/1991/07/01/world/ethiopians-to-discuss-a-new-regime.html.

28. "Eritrea: Opposition Members Held in Ethiopia", *Indian Ocean Newsletter*, 14 May 1994.

29. See ELF-RC, "Statement Issued by the International Relations Office of the ELF-RC, January 30, 1997", https://fas.org/irp/world/para/docs/humanr~2.htm (accessed 5 March 2018).

30. Tesfatsion Medhanie, *Eritrea and Its Neighbors in the 'New World Order': Geopolitics, Democracy, and 'Islamic Fundamentalism'* (Bremen: Lit Verlag, 1994), 119–20.

31. "Collected Papers of Paul Henze", Institute of Ethiopian Studies archives, Addis Ababa.

32. "Prime Minister Meles Zenawi on Record about Ethiopians Deported From Eritrea", 22 August 1991, http://dehai.org/conflict/speeches/meles-1991.htm

33. Direct quote was relayed to author by an Ethiopian academic via email in December 2014.

34. Author's interview with TPLF politburo member, 6 May 2015. This informant also noted that the TPLF worried that the alternative to deportation was massacres.

35. Jeffrey Lefebvre, "Post-Cold War Clouds on the Horn of Africa", *Middle East Policy Council*, September 1995, https://mepc.org/node/4859.

36. Harry Verhoeven, *Water, Civilization, and Power in Sudan: The Political Economy of Military-Islamist State Building* (Cambridge: Cambridge University Press, 2015), 118–19.

37. "Ethiopia Accuses Sudan of Destabilising Neighbours", Agence France Press, 19 January 1994.

38. Author's interview with former minister, Transitional Government of Ethiopia, April 2011.

39. Medhanie, *Eritrea and Its Neighbors in the 'New World Order'*, 118.

40. Bradley Simpson, *Economists with Guns: Authoritarian Development and US–Indonesian Relations, 1960–1968* (Stanford: Stanford University Press, 2008).

41. Elsje Fourie, "China's Example for Meles' Ethiopia: When Development 'Models' Land", *Journal of Modern African Studies* 53, no. 3 (2016): 289–316; Denis Tull, "China's Engagement in Africa: Scope, Significance, and Consequences", *Journal of Modern African Studies* 44, no. 3 (2006): 459–79.

8. INTERVENTION AND ORDER IN FAILED STATES

1. "Remarks by President Trump at Working Lunch with African Leaders", 10 September 2018, https://www.whitehouse.gov/briefings-statements/remarks-president-trump-working-lunch-african-leaders/.

2. Carla Babb, "VOA Exclusive: Dozens More US Troops Deployed to Somalia", 14 April 2017, https://www.voanews.com/a/dozens-more-us-troops-deployed-somalia-voa-exclusive/3809351.html. Later estimates put the deployment at around 500 US troops. Caroline Houck, "'We're Finding It Difficult to Hold' Territory in Somalia: Senator", *Defense One*, 2 March 2018, http://www.defenseone.com/threats/2018/03/were-finding-it-difficult-hold-territory-somalia-senator/146376/.

3. Claire Lockhart and Ashraf Ghani, *Fixing Failed States: A Framework for Rebuilding a Fractured World* (New York: Oxford University Press, 2008).

4. G. John Ikenberry, *After Victory: Institutions, Strategic Restraint, and the Rebuilding of Order after Major Wars* (Princeton: Princeton University Press, 2001), 23.

5. The latter include Benjamin Powell, Ryan Ford and Alex Nowrasteh, "Somalia after

State Collapse: Chaos or Improvement?", *Journal of Economic Behavior and Organization* 67 (2008): 657–70; Peter Leeson, "Better Off Stateless: Somalia Before and after Government Collapse", *Journal of Comparative Economics* 35, no. 4 (2007): 689–710; Kenneth Menkhaus, "State Failure, State-Building, and Prospects for a 'Functional Failed State' in Somalia", *Annals of the American Academy of Political and Social Science* 656 (Fall 2014): 154–72.

6. Stig Jarle Hansen, *Al Shabaab in Somalia: The History and Ideology of a Militant Islamist Group, 2005–2012* (London: Hurst & Co., 2013); Harry Verhoeven, "The Self-fulfilling Prophecy of Failed States: Somalia, State Collapse and the Global War on Terror", *Journal of Eastern African Studies* 3, no. 3 (2009): 405–25.

7. Ashley Jackson, *Life under the Taliban Shadow Government* (London: Overseas Development Institute, 2018).

8. Stephen Krasner and Jeremy Weinstein, "Improving Governance from the Outside In", *Annual Review of Political Science* 17 (May 2014): 123–45. Krasner served as director of the policy planning at the US State Department from 2005 to 2007.

9. Ian Clark, *Hegemony in International Society* (New York: Oxford University Press, 2011).

10. Harry Verhoeven, "The Gulf and the Horn: Changing Geographies of Security Interdependence and Competing Visions of Regional Order", *Civil Wars* 20, no. 3 (2018): 333–57.

11. Department of State, *Outlaw Regime: A Chronicle of Iran's Destructive Activities* (Washington, DC: Department of State, 2018), https://www.state.gov/documents/organization/286410.pdf.

12. Amin Saikal, "Afghanistan on the Edge of a Political Abyss", *International Studies* 47, no. 1 (2010): 36; Dexter Filkins, "Death of an Afghan Godfather", *New Yorker*, 12 July 2011, https://www.newyorker.com/news/news-desk/death-of-an-afghan-godfather.

13. Anders Themnér, ed., *Warlord Democrats in Africa: Ex-military Leaders and Electoral Politics* (London: Zed Books, 2017).

14. Aisha Ahmed, *Jihad & Co.: Black Markets and Islamist Power* (New York: Oxford University Press, 2017).

15. Karl Eikenberry, "The Limits of Counterinsurgency Doctrine in Afghanistan", *Foreign Affairs*, 59, no. 18 (2013): 67.

16. US Government Accountability Office, *Afghanistan: Oversight and Accountability of U.S. Assistance* (Washington, DC: GAO, 2014), 5, https://www.gao.gov/assets/670/664034.pdf.

17. Government of Somalia, *Aid Flows in Somalia: An Analysis of Aid Flow Data* (Mogadishu: World Bank, 2017), 4, https://reliefweb.int/sites/reliefweb.int/files/resources/Aid%20Flows%20Booklet%20-%202017.pdf.

18. Federal Government of Somalia, "The Somali Compact", March 2013, http://eeas.europa.eu/archives/new-deal-for-somalia-conference/sites/default/files/the_somali_compact.pdf.

19. United Kingdom, "London Conference on Somalia Communique", 23 February

2012; United Nations, "UN and Partners Issue Warning against Somali Peace Process Spoilers", News Release, 1 May 2012, http://www.un.org/apps/news/story.asp?NewsID=41890#.WiR9nUqnGCg.

20. AMISOM, "Somali Women Agree on Model to Improve Gender Parity in 2016 Elections", News Release, 20 June 2016.

21. United Nations Security Council, "Report of the Secretary-General on Somalia", New York, 12 May 2015, http://www.un.org/ga/search/view_doc.asp?symbol=s/2015/331.

22. Center for International Policy, "4 Charts on Spike in U.S. Military and Police Aid to Africa", *Security Assistance Monitor*, 3 June 2015, http://securityassistance.org/blog/4-charts-spike-us-military-and-police-aid-africa.

23. European Commission, "African Peace Facility Annual Report 2016", Brussels, 2017, 15, http://www.africa-eu-partnership.org/sites/default/files/documents/apf_ar2016_en_v1_web.pdf.

24. Helen Epstein, *Another Fine Mess: America, Uganda and the War on Terror* (New York: Columbia Global Reports, 2017); "It's Time for the U.S. to Rethink Its Approach to Uganda", *Washington Post*, 8 April 2016, https://www.washingtonpost.com/opinions/its-time-for-the-us-to-rethink-its-approach-to-uganda/2016/04/08/1b1d80ae-fce1–11e5–80e4-c381214de1a3_story.html?utm_term=.c345f44011c2.

25. Marc Lacey, "Efforts by C.I.A. Fail in Somalia, Officials Charge", *New York Times*, 8 June 2006, http://www.nytimes.com/2006/06/08/world/africa/08intel.html?_r=0; Abdi Ismael Samatar, "Ethiopian Invasion of Somalia, US Warlordism and AU Shame", *Review of African Political Economy* 34, no. 111 (2007): 155–65.

26. "Ethiopia Base in Somalia Attacked by al-Shabab", BBC News, 9 June 2016, http://www.bbc.com/news/world-africa-36487435.

27. "Somalia Al-Shabab: Deadly Double Car Bombing near Presidential Palace", BBC News, 24 February 2018, http://www.bbc.com/news/world-africa-43177348; Jason Burke, "Militants Who Killed 23 at Mogadishu Hotel Used Intelligence Service ID Cards", *The Guardian*, 29 October, 2017, https://www.theguardian.com/world/2017/oct/29/somalia-fires-security-officials-after-bomb-attack.

28. Elements of the story were recounted to the author by the hotel's owner, Mogadishu, July 2013 and August 2014. The owner was killed in an October 2015 al-Shabaab attack on the hotel. "Somalia: Al-Shabab Attack Kills 15 in Mogadishu Hotel", BBC News, 1 November 2015, http://www.bbc.com/news/world-asia-34691602.

29. Jeffrey Gettleman, Mark Mazzetti and Eric Schmitt, "US Relies on Contractors in Somalia Conflict", *New York Times*, 10 August 2011, http://www.nytimes.com/2011/08/11/world/africa/11somalia.html.

30. "French Somalia Raid 'Was a Trap'", *Africa Confidential* 54, no. 2 (18 January 2013): 11; AFP, "France Defends Failed Somali Raid as Toll Mounts", 14 January 2013, https://www.news24.com/Africa/News/France-defends-failed-Somali-raid-20130114.

31. United Nations Security Council, "Report of the Monitoring Group on Somalia and Eritrea Pursuant to Security-Council Resolution 2111 (2013): Somalia", 13 October 2014, 64, https://www.un.org/ga/search/view_doc.asp?symbol=S/2014/726.

32. Since 2014 the Somali government has announced annual amnesty programmes: http://www.bbc.com/news/world-africa-39513909, https://www.thestar.com/news/atkinsonseries/generation911/2016/06/25/inside-the-secret-somalia-rehab-camp-for-former-shabab-members.html, https://www.voanews.com/a/former-al-shabab-commander-urges-others-to-surrender/2616855.html, and http://www.bbc.com/news/world-africa-29044368.

33. Javid Ahmad, *Dress Like Allies, Kill Like Enemies: An Analysis of 'Insider Attacks' in Afghanistan* (New York: West Point, Modern War Institute, 2017).

34. United Nations Security Council, "Report of the Monitoring Group on Somalia and Eritrea Pursuant to Security-Council Resolution 2182 (2014): Somalia", 19 October 2015, 185, https://www.un.org/ga/search/view_doc.asp?symbol=S/2015/801; "Somalia: AMISOM Struggles", *Africa Confidential* 57, no. 5 (4 March 2016): 9–10.

35. US World News Report, "Somali Plane Bomber Was a Teacher at an Islamic School, Known as a Talkative, Religious Man with a Sense of Humor", 16 February 2016, http://www.usnews.com/news/world/articles/2016–02–16/somali-plane-bomber-was-known-as-religious-but-not-extremist.

36. United Nations Security Council, "Report of the Monitoring Group on Somalia and Eritrea Pursuant to Security Council Resolution 2002 (2011)", 13 July 2012, 12, http://www.un.org/ga/search/view_doc.asp?symbol=S/2012/545.

37. United Nations Security Council, "Report of the Monitoring Group on Somalia and Eritrea, Pursuant to Security Council Resolution 2111 (2013): Somalia", 13 October 2014, 28–30, http://www.un.org/ga/search/view_doc.asp?symbol=S/2014/726.

38. World Bank, "World Bank Summary of Financial Diagnostic Assessment", 30 May 2012, iv; Legacy Center, *Overview of Corruption, Underlying Causes, and Its Impacts on Somalia* (Legacy Center for Peace and Transparency, Mogadishu, 2016), 8.

39. United Nations Security Council, 8165th Meeting, 24 January 2018, http://www.un.org/en/ga/search/view_doc.asp?symbol=S/PV.8165.

40. Jeffrey Gettleman, "Fueled by Bribes, Somalia's Election Seen as Milestone of Corruption", *New York Times*, 7 February 2017, https://www.nytimes.com/2017/02/07/world/africa/somalia-election-corruption.html.

41. United Nations Security Council, "Report of the Secretary-General on Somalia", 8 January 2016, http://undocs.org/S/2016/27; Katharine Houreld, "Exclusive: U.S. Suspends Aid to Somalia's Battered Military over Graft", Reuters, 14 December 2017, https://www.reuters.com/article/us-somalia-military-exclusive/exclusive-u-s-suspends-aid-to-somalias-battered-military-over-graft-idUSKBN1E81XF.

42. "AMISOM Loses Friends", *Africa Confidential* 56, no. 20 (20 October 2015): 11.

43. Colin Robinson, "The Somali National Army: An Assessment", *Small Wars and Insurgencies*, 2018, forthcoming.

44. Shabelle Media Network, "Four Killed as Army Forces Exchange Gunfire in Adado", 14 August 2016, http://www.shabellenews.com/2016/08/four-dead-as-military-forces-exchange-gunfire-in-adado/.

45. United Nations Security Council, "Report of the Monitoring Group on Somalia and Eritrea Pursuant to Security Council Resolution 2244 (2015): Somalia", 31 October 2016, 160–3, http://www.un.org/ga/search/view_doc.asp?symbol=S/2016/919.

46. Drazen Jorgic, "Failure to Pay Soldiers Threatens Somalia's War on Islamists", Reuters, 8 October 2015, https://www.reuters.com/article/us-somalia-security-insight/failure-to-pay-soldiers-threatens-somalias-war-on-islamists-idUSKCN0S-21GP20151008.

47. Hosham Dawod, "Iraqi Tribes in the Land of Jihad", in *Tribes and Global Jihadism*, ed. Virginie Collombier and Olivier Roy (London: Hurst & Co., 2018), 15–32; Amatzia Baram, "Neo-Tribalism in Iraq: Saddam Hussein's Tribal Policies, 1991–1996", *International Journal of Middle East Studies* 29, no. 1 (1997): 1–31.

48. This perspective emerged during author's discussions with a Somali official, 4 July 2012; Farah Ahmed Mohamed, "Somalia: The Abduction of French Agents Well Planned, Sources", *Mareeg*, http://www.mareeg.com/fidsan.php?sid=12959&tirsan=3.

49. Some TFG officials and militia leaders revealed in discussions with the author their personal concerns about security due to perceived al-Shabaab infiltration of security services, Mogadishu, June–July 2012.

50. Jean-Pierre Filiu, "Lesson from Kismayo", *Jihadica*, 6 October 2009, http://www.jihadica.com/lesson-from-kismayo/.

51. Matthew Campbell, "French Agent Marc Aubriere's Amazing Barefoot Escape through Mogadishu", *The Australian*, 31 August 2016, http://www.theaustralian.com.au/news/world/french-agent-marc-aubrieres-amazing-barefoot-escape-through-mogadishu/story-e6frg6so-1225767742461.

52. Discussions with a loquacious hotel owner in Mogadishu, August 2013 and August 2014; Abdiaziz Hassan and Abdi Sheikheuters, "Qaeda Linked Somali Group Takes One of French Hostages", Reuters, 16 July 2009, https://uk.reuters.com/article/uk-somalia-conflict/qaeda-linked-somali-group-takes-one-of-french-hostages-idUKTRE56F2T920090716.

53. Anne-Marie Slaughter, "Mercy Killings", *Foreign Policy* 136 (2003): 72.

54. G. John Ikenberry, *Liberal Leviathan: The Origins, Crisis, and Transformation of the American World Order* (Princeton: Princeton University Press, 2011).

55. Rita Abrahamsen and Michael Williams, "Security beyond the State: Global Security Assemblages in International Politics", *International Political Sociology* 3, no. 1 (2009): 1–17.

56. David Kilcullen, *The Accidental Guerrilla: Fighting Small Wars in the Midst of a Big One* (New York: Oxford University Press, 2009); James Scott, "Revolution in the Revolution: Peasants and Commissars", *Theory and Society* 7, no. 1 (1979): 97–134.

57. This framing of the idea of global security professionals is drawn from Adam Sandor,

"Border Security and Drug Trafficking in Senegal: AIRCOP and Global Security Assemblages", *Journal of Intervention and Statebuilding* 10, no. 4 (2016): 490–512.

58. Mark Mazetti, "Efforts by C.I.A. Fail in Somalia, Officials Charge", *New York Times*, 8 June 2006, http://www.nytimes.com/2006/06/08/world/africa/08intel.html; author discussion with one such businessman in Mogadishu, 19 August 2013.

59. "Foreign Funds", *Africa Confidential* 47, no. 8 (14 April 2006): 8; "Terror in Mogadishu", *Africa Confidential* 47, no. 11 (16 May 2006): 3–4.

60. Jeffrey Gettleman, Mark Mazzetti and Eric Schmitt, "U.S. Relies on Contractors in Somalia Conflict", *New York Times*, 10 August 2011, http://www.nytimes.com/2011/08/11/world/africa/11somalia.html.

61. Interview, Dagmada Shangaani, Mogadishu, 1 July 2012.

62. Department of State, "U.S. Foreign Policy in Somalia", Remarks by Under Secretary for Political Affairs Wendy Sherman, 3 June 2014, http://iipdigital.usembassy.gov/st/english/texttrans/2014/06/20140612301214.html#ixzz47M0V1HgZ.

63. Ty McCormick, "U.S. Operates Drones from Secret Bases in Somalia", *Foreign Policy*, 2 July 2015, http://foreignpolicy.com/2015/07/02/exclusive-u-s-operates-drones-from-secret-bases-in-somalia-special-operations-jsoc-black-hawk-down/.

64. Interview and discussion, Dagmada Waaberi, Mogadishu, 17 August 2013.

65. Interview, Villa Somalia, 13 August 2014.

66. Joseph Steigman, "Logistics at the Edge of the Empire: US Army Logistics Trainers in Somalia", *Small Wars Journal*, 7 February 2018, http://smallwarsjournal.com/print/85241. (The article's author reported that the article was removed from that website after objections from the US embassy in Mogadishu.)

67. Author's personal observations, Iraq and Afghanistan.

68. United Nations General Assembly, "Report of the Working Group on the Use of Mercenaries as a Means of Violating Human Rights and Impeding the Exercise of the Rights of Peoples to Self-determination", 1 July 2013, 11–14, https://documents-dds-ny.un.org/doc/UNDOC/GEN/G13/153/79/PDF/G1315379.pdf?OpenElement.

69. "American Airlift", *Africa Confidential* 50, no. 19 (25 September 2009): 2. For drone attacks, see "Drone Wars Somalia: Analysis", New America Foundation, http://securitydata.newamerica.net/drones/somalia-analysis.html.

70. Interviews, UPDF personnel and AMISOM officials, 2012 through 2015; United Nations Security Council, "Report on Somalia of the Monitoring Group on Somalia and Eritrea Submitted in Accordance with Resolution 2317 (2016)", 2 November 2017, 83, http://www.securitycouncilreport.org/atf/cf/%7B65BFCF9B-6D27-4E9C-8CD3-CF6E4FF96FF9%7D/s_2017_924.pdf.

71. *Contra* John Gerard Ruggie, "International Regimes, Transactions and Change: Embedded Liberalism in the Postwar Economic Order", *International Organization* 36, no. 2 (1982): 379–415.

72. Tanja Borzel and Thomas Risse, *Effective Governance under Anarchy: Institutions,*

Legitimacy, and Social Trust in Areas of Limited Statehood (New York: Cambridge University Press, forthcoming).

73. Seyoum Mesfin and Abdeta Dribssa Beyene, "The Practicalities of Living with Failed States", *Daedalus* 147, no. 3 (Winter 2018): 128–40.
74. Kevin Sieff, "Exclusive: U.S.-Funded Somali Intelligence Agency Has Been Using Kids as Spies", *Washington Post*, 7 May 2016, https://www.washingtonpost.com/world/africa/exclusive-us-funded-somali-intelligence-agency-has-been-using-kids-as-spies/2016/05/06/974c9144-0ce3-11e6-a6b6-2e6de3695b0e_story.html.
75. David Cannadine, *Ornamentalism: How the British Saw Their Empire* (New York: Oxford University Press, 2002).
76. As in Robert Gilpin, *War and Change in World Politics* (New York: Cambridge University Press, 1981).

9. CHINA IN THE INDIAN OCEAN: THE SEARCH FOR A NEW HEGEMON?

1. There is an immense range of work on the relationship between the US and China. Rosemary Foot and Andrew Walter, *China, the United States and Global Order* (Cambridge: Cambridge University Press, 2010), is an excellent starting point.
2. See https://chinapower.csis.org/energy-footprint/ and https://www.chathamhouse.org/expert/comment/middle-east-s-shifting-energy-politics.
3. David L. Shambaugh, *China Goes Global: The Partial Power* (Oxford: Oxford University Press, 2013), 7.
4. Alastair Iain Johnston, "How New and Assertive Is China's New Assertiveness?", *Quarterly Journal: International Security* 37, no. 4 (2013): 7–48, and "China in a World of Orders: Rethinking Compliance and Challenge in Beijing's International Relations", *International Security* 44, no. 2 (2019): 9–60.
5. Yan Xuetong, *Leadership and the Rise of Great Powers* (Princeton: Princeton University Press, 2019), 203.
6. On the way that China is doing this in international organizations, see Rosemary Foot, *China, the UN, and Human Protection* (Oxford: Oxford University Press, 2020).
7. John Chaffee, "Diasporic Identities in the Historical Development of the Maritime Muslim Communities of Song-Yuan China", *Journal of the Economic and Social History of the Orient* 49, no. 4 (2006): 395–420; Tansen Sen, "The Formation of Chinese Maritime Networks to Southern Asia, 1200–1450", *Journal of the Economic and Social History of the Orient* 49, no. 4 (2006): 421–53.
8. Robert Finlay, "The Voyages of Zheng He: Ideology, State Power, and Maritime Trade in Ming China", *Journal of the Historical Society* 8, no. 3 (2008): 327–47.
9. Julia Lovell, *The Opium War: Drugs, Dreams and the Making of China* (London: Picador, 2012).
10. Xiaoyuan Liu, *A Partnership for Disorder: China, the United States, and their Policies for the Postwar Disposition of the Japanese Empire, 1941–1945* (Cambridge: Cambridge University Press, 1996).
11. Rana Mitter, *China's War with Japan: The Struggle for Survival, 1937–1945* [US title: *Forgotten Ally*] (London: Allen Lane, 2013), 246–7.

12. Naoko Shimazu, "Diplomacy as Theatre: Staging the Bandung Conference of 1955", *Modern Asian Studies* 48, no. 1 (2014): 225–52.

13. Philip Roessler and Harry Verhoeven, *Why Comrades Go to War: Liberation Politics and the Outbreak of Africa's Deadliest Conflict* (London: Hurst, 2016), 98–104.

14. For a remarkable Chinese–Zimbabwean personal memoir, see Chung, Fay, *Re-living the Second Chimurenga: Memories from the Liberation Struggle in Zimbabwe* (London: African Books Collective, 2006).

15. W. Edmund Clark, *Socialist Development and Public Investment in Tanzania, 1964–73* (Toronto: University of Toronto Press, 1978).

16. On Deng's priorities, Ezra Vogel, *Deng Xiaoping and the Transformation of China* (Cambridge MA: Harvard University Press, 2011).

17. See, for example, Yan, *Leadership and the Rise of Great Powers*.

18. https://chinapower.csis.org/china-naval-modernization/.

19. Jonathan Ward, https://www.eastwestcenter.org/system/tdf/private/apb386. pdf?file=1&type=node&id=36149.

20. Jonathan Dixon, "From 'Pearls' to 'Arrows': Rethinking the 'String of Pearls' Theory of China's Naval Ambitions", *Comparative Strategy* 33, no. 4 (2014): 389–400, doi: 10.1080/01495933.2014.941730.

21. Seifudein Adem, "China in Ethiopia: Diplomacy and Economics of Sino-Optimism", *African Studies Review* 55, no. 1 (2012): 143–60; Maddalena Procopio, "Kenyan Agency in Kenya–China Relations: Contestation, Cooperation and Passivity", in *New Directions in Africa–China Studies*, ed. Chris Alden and Daniel Large (London: Routledge, 2018), 193–208.

22. Andrew Small, *The China Pakistan Axis: Asia's New Geopolitics* (New Delhi: Random House, 2015).

23. Harry Verhoeven, "Is Beijing's Non-Interference Policy History? How Africa Is Changing China", *Washington Quarterly* 37, no. 2 (2014): 55–70, doi: 10.1080/016 3660X.2014.926209.

24. Hend Elmahly and Degang Sun, "China's Military Diplomacy towards Arab Countries in Africa's Peace and Security: The Case of Djibouti", *Contemporary Arab Affairs* 11, no. 4 (2018): 111–34.

25. https://www.stripes.com/news/africom-chief-expect-more-chinese-bases-in-africa-1.515263.

26. Note, however, the debate between scholars such as John Ikenberry in *Liberal Leviathan: The Origins, Crisis and Transformation of the American World Order* (Princeton: Princeton University Press, 2011) who argue that a liberal order can contain China, and John Mearsheimer, *The Tragedy of Great Power Politics* (New York: W.W. Norton, 2014), who argues that it cannot.

27. http://www.xinhuanet.com/english/special/2017-11/03/c_136725942.htm; http://www.chinadaily.com.cn/china/19thcpcnationalcongress/2017-11/04/content_34115212.htm.

28. Daniel A. Bell, *The China Model: Political Meritocracy and the Limits of Democracy* (Princeton: Princeton University Press, 2015).

29. https://thediplomat.com/2017/10/the-community-of-common-destiny-in-xi-jinpings-new-era/.

30. On an early example of China's engagement with developmentalist discourse, see Rana Mitter, "State-Building after Disaster: Jiang Tingfu and the Reconstruction of Post-World War II China, 1943–1949", *Comparative Studies in Society and History* 61, no. 1 (2019): 176–206.

31. This topic has been widely debated. Evelyn Goh gives a thoughtful overview of the changing dynamics in the region in *The Struggle for Order: Hegemony, Hierarchy and Transition in Post-Cold War East Asia* (Oxford: Oxford University Press, 2013)

32. https://thediplomat.com/tag/china-marshall-plan/.

33. https://www.economist.com/leaders/2018/07/26/chinas-belt-and-road-plans-are-to-be-welcomed-and-worried-about.

34. Laleh Khalili, "The Infrastructural Power of the Military: The Geoeconomic Role of the US Army Corps of Engineers in the Arabian Peninsula", *European Journal of International Relations* 24, no. 4 (2018): 911–33.

35. Odd Arne Westad, *The Global Cold War: Third World Interventions and the Making of Our Time*s (Cambridge: Cambridge University Press, 2011).

36. https://timesofindia.indiatimes.com/blogs/toi-edit-page/the-new-colonialism-chinas-bri-or-silk-road-project-is-coming-to-be-seen-across-asia-as-the-road-to-ruin/.

37. See https://www.thenational.ae/opinion/comment/the-example-of-sri-lanka-handing-over-a-port-to-china-shows-the-belt-and-road-initiative-was-never-meant-to-be-pure-altruism-1.768918.

38. Michael Auslin, *The End of the Asian Century* (New Haven: Yale University Press, 2016).

39. https://www.voanews.com/a/china-welcomes-saudi-plans-invest-cpec-project-with-pakistan/4604946.html.

40. https://www.theguardian.com/world/2017/jun/07/china-to-set-up-military-bases-in-pakistan-pentagon-report.

41. https://www.newstatesman.com/halford-mackinder-father-geopolitics.

42. Gary Bass, *The Blood Telegram: Nixon, Kissinger, and a Forgotten Genocide* (New York: Alfred A. Knopf, 2014).

43. Ikenberry, *Liberal Leviathan*.

44. Graham Allison, *Destined for War: Can America and China Escape Thucydides' Trap?* (Boston: Houghton Mifflin Harcourt, 2017).

45. Odd Arne Westad, "Can China Lead?", in *The China Questions: Critical Insights into a Rising Power*, ed. Jennifer Rudolph and Michael Szonyi (Cambridge, MA: Harvard University Press, 2018), 71.

10. CONCLUSION: THE INDIAN OCEAN AND GLOBAL PATTERNS OF ORDER AND DISORDER

1. Stephen Hopgood, *The Endtimes of Human Rights* (Ithaca: Cornell University Press, 2013), 167.

2. Andrew Philips and J.C. Sharman. *International Order in Diversity: War, Trade and Rule in the Indian Ocean* (Cambridge: Cambridge University Press, 2015).

3. C. Roe Goddard, Patrick Cronin and Kishore C. Dash, eds., *International Political Economy: State–Market Relations in the Changing Global Order* (Boulder, CO: Lynne Rienner, 2003).

4. Odd Arne Westad, *The Global Cold War* (Cambridge: Cambridge University Press, 2005).

5. Isabel Hofmeyr, "The Black Atlantic Meets the Indian Ocean: Forging New Paradigms of Transnationalism for the Global South; Literary and Cultural Perspectives", *Social Dynamics* 33, no. 2 (2007): 3–32; Uma Kothari and Rorden Wilkinson, "Colonial Imaginaries and Postcolonial Transformations: Exiles, Bases, Beaches", *Third World Quarterly* 31, no. 8 (2010): 1395–412.

6. Tobias Hagmann and Filip Reyntjens, eds., *Aid and Authoritarianism in Africa: Development without Democracy* (London: Zed Books, 2016).

7. Thomas Minadoi and Rudi Matthee, *War between the Turks and the Persians: Conflict and Religion in the Safavid and Ottoman Worlds* (London: I.B. Tauris, 2018).

8. See Anatol Lieven, "Hindu Nationalism: A Reality Check for Liberalism and Globalisation", The Valdai Club, 23 May 2017, http://valdaiclub.com/search/?q=Anatol+Lieven+India#result.

9. Manmohan Singh, "Of Oxford, Economics, Empire and Freedom", *The Hindu*, 10 July 2005, https://www.thehindu.com/2005/07/10/stories/2005071002301000.htm.

10. Achin Vanaik, "India's Two Hegemonies", *New Left Review* 112 (July–August 2018).

11. Thomas Blom Hansen, *The Saffron Wave: Democracy and Hindu Nationalism in Modern India* (Princeton: Princeton University Press, 1999); Walter Andersen and Sridhar D. Damle, *Messengers of Hindu Nationalism: How the RSS Reshaped India* (London: C. Hurst, 2019).

12. John J. Mearsheimer "Bound to Fail: The Rise and Fall of the Liberal International Order", *International Security* 43, no. 4 (Spring 2019): 7–50.

13. David D. Laitin, "The Political Economy of Military Rule in Somalia", *Journal of Modern African Studies* 14, no. 3 (1976): 449–68.

14. Thomas L. Friedman, *The Earth Is Flat: A Brief History of the 21st Century* (New York: Farrar, Straus and Giroux, 2006). For a classic statement of America's right and duty to create and dominate this liberal internationalist order, see Secretary of State Madeleine K. Albright, Commencement Address, Harvard University, Cambridge, Massachusetts, 5 June 1997.

15. Francis Fukuyama, *The End of History and the Last Man* (New York: Free Press, 2006). For a more nationalist portrayal of the role of Britain and America in creating this universal new order, see Walter Russell Mead, *God and Gold: Britain, America and the Making of the Modern World* (New York: Alfred A Knopf, 2007).

16. Michael Tomasky, "Between Cheney and Chomsky", in *The Fight Is for Democracy: Winning the War of Ideas in America and the World*, ed. George Packer (New York:

HarperCollins, 2003), 41. See also Paul Berman, *Terror and Liberalism* (New York: W.W. Norton, 2003).

17. Immanuel Kant, *Project for a Perpetual Peace*. For a classic contemporary academic statement of this belief, see Michael Doyle, *Ways of War and Peace: Realism, Liberalism and Socialism* (New York: W.W. Norton, 1997).

18. Alexander Zevin, *Liberalism at Large: The World according to the Economist* (London: Verso Books, 2019).

19. John Ikenberry, "The Future of the Liberal World Order", *Foreign Affairs* 90, no. 3 (2011).

20. See for example Hillary Clinton, "We Are on the Right Side of History", remarks to the Growth Faculty, 12 September 2018, https://www.thegrowthfaculty.com/onDemand/.

21. Minxin Pei, "Is China Democratizing?", *Foreign Affairs* 77, no. 1 (1998): 68–82.

22. Andrew Hurrell, "Beyond the BRICS: Power, Pluralism, and the Future of Global Order", *Ethics and International Affairs* 32, no. 1 (2018): 89–101.

23. William A. Callahan, "China's 'Asia Dream': The Belt Road Initiative and the New Regional Order", *Asian Journal of Comparative Politics* 1, no. 3 (2016): 226–43.

24. Michael H. Smith and Richard Youngs, "The EU and the Global Order: Contingent Liberalism", *International Spectator* 53, no. 1 (2018): 45–56.

25. G. John Ikenberry, "The Plot against American Foreign Policy: Can the Liberal Order Survive", *Foreign Affairs* 96, no. 3 (2017): 1.

26. Anatol Lieven, *Pakistan: A Hard Country* (New York: Oxford University Press, 2011).

27. Fareed Zakaria, *The Future of Freedom: Illiberal Democracy at Home and Abroad*, rev. edn (New York: W.W. Norton, 2007).

28. Headlines about Benazir Bhutto—like "Benazir's tender democracy"—were an earlier version of Western liberals' Pygmalion-like tendency to fall in love with images that they themselves have created.

29. Jonathan Crush, "The Dark Side of Democracy: Migration, Xenophobia and Human Rights in South Africa", *International Migration* 38, no. 6 (2001): 103–33.

30. Amitav Acharya, "After Liberal Hegemony: The Advent of a Multiplex World Order", *Ethics and international Affairs* 31, no. 3 (2017): 271–85.

31. Andrew Phillips and Jason C. Sharman, "Explaining Durable Diversity in International Systems: State, Company, and Empire in the Indian Ocean", *International Studies Quarterly* 59, no. 3 (2015): 436–48.

32. Karl Marx and Friedrich Engels, *The Communist Manifesto* (London: Penguin Classics, 2012).

33. W.H. Auden, *The Age of Anxiety: A Baroque Eclogue* (Princeton: Princeton University Press, 2011).

34. Ammara Maqsood, *The New Pakistani Middle Class* (Cambridge, MA: Harvard University Press, 2017).

35. Bassam Tibi, *Europa ohne Identitaet? Die Krise der multikulturellen Gesellschaft* (Munich: Bertelsmann, 1998).

36. Michael Mann, *The Dark Side of Democracy: Explaining Ethnic Cleansing* (Cambridge: Cambridge University Press, 2005).

37. James L. Gibson, "Understandings of Justice: Institutional Legitimacy, Procedural Justice, and Political Tolerance", *Law and Society Review* (1989): 469–96.

38. Jean-Jacques Rousseau, *The Social Contract* (London: Penguin, 1978), book II, chapter 7. Emphasising the authoritarian and even potentially totalitarian aspects of Rousseau's thinking on the lawgiver, this idea had considerable impact on the thought of Carl Schmitt, and in particular aspects of his "decisionism" and concept of the "commissarial dictator". See Carl Schmitt, *The Concept of the Political*, translated with an introduction by George Schwab (Chicago: University of Chicago Press, 2007), 37–45.

39. Georg Sørensen, "Liberalism of Restraint and Liberalism of Imposition: Liberal Values and World Order in the New Millennium", *International Relations* 20, no. 3 (2006): 251–72.

40. John Murphy, *Ali Khamenei* (New York: Chelsea House Publications, 2007); Ali M. Ansari, *The Politics of Nationalism in Modern Iran* (New York: Cambridge University Press, 2012).

41. Christopher Clapham, *Transformation and Continuity in Revolutionary Ethiopia* (Cambridge: Cambridge University Press, 1988), 195; see also Sarah Vaughan and Kjetil Tronvoll, *The Culture of Power in Contemporary Ethiopian Political Life* (Stockholm: Swedish International Cooperation Agency, 2003).

42. Jon Abbink, "Ethnic-Based Federalism and Ethnicity in Ethiopia: Reassessing the Experiment after 20 Years", in *Reconfiguring Ethiopia: The Politics of Authoritarian Reform*, ed. Jon Abbink and Tobias Hagmann (New York: Routledge, 2013).

43. As Putin has written, "Historically, Russia has been neither a mono-ethnic state nor a US-style 'melting pot', where most people are, in some way, migrants. Russia developed over centuries as a multinational state, in which different ethnic groups have had to mingle, interact and connect with each other—in domestic and professional environments, and in society as friends. Hundreds of ethnic groups live in their native lands alongside Russians. The development of vast land areas throughout Russia's history has been a joint affair between many different peoples. Suffice it to say that ethnic Ukrainians live in an area stretching from the Carpathian Mountains to Kamchatka, and the same is true of ethnic Tartars, Jews and Byelorussians." Vladimir Putin, "Russia: The Ethnicity Issue", *Nezavisimaya Gazeta*, 23 January 2012, http://archive.premier.gov.ru/eng/events/news/17831/. In this essay, Putin also, however, writes firmly that the central guiding culture of this multi-ethnic state must be the Russian tradition.

44. Chris Baker and Pasuk Phongpaichit, *A History of Thailand* (Cambridge: Cambridge University Press, 2011); Michael Kelly Connors, *Democracy and National Identity in Thailand* (New York: Routledge, 2002), 128–52; Frank E. Reynolds, "Civic Religion and National Community in Thailand", *Journal of Asian Studies* 36, no. 2 (1977): 267–82.

45. R.E. Elson, *The Idea of Indonesia: A History* (New York: Cambridge University Press,

2009); Pramoedya Ananta Toer, *The Chinese in Indonesia* (Singapore: Select Publishing, 2008); Wu-ling Chong, *Chinese Indonesians in Post-Suharto Indonesia: Democratisation and Ethnic Minorities* (Hong Kong: Hong Kong University Press, 2018); Lian Kwen Fee, *Race, Ethnicity and the State in Malaysia and Singapore* (Boston: Brill, 2006); Anoma Pieris, *Sovereignty, Space and Civil War in Sri Lanka: Porous Nation* (New York: Routledge, 2018).

46. Achin Vanaik, "India's Two Hegemonies", *New Left Review* 112 (July–August 2018); Prashant Jha, *How the BJP Wins: Inside India's Greatest Election Machine* (New Delhi: Juggernaut, 2017).

47. Thomas Blom Hansen, "The Vernacularisation of Hindutva", *Contributions to Indian Sociology* 30, no. 2 (1996); Romila Thapar, "Syndicated Hinduism", in *The Historian and Her Craft: Collected Essays and Lectures*, ed. Romila Thapar, vol. 4 (New Delhi: Oxford University Press, 2018).

48. Susan Bayly, *Caste, Society and Politics in India from the 18th Century to the Modern Age* (New York: Cambridge University Press, 2001); Christophe Jaffrelot, *Religion, Caste and Politics in India* (New York: Oxford University Press, 2011).

49. Krithika Varagur, "Converting to Buddhism as a Form of Political Protest", *The Atlantic*, 11 April 2018, https://www.theatlantic.com/international/archive/2018/04/dalit-buddhism-conversion-india-modi/557570/.

50. Dattatrey Vable, *The Arya Samaj: Hindu without Hinduism* (New Delhi: Vikas, 1983).

51. Divya Vaid, "Caste in Contemporary India: Flexibility and Persistence", *Annual Review of Sociology* 40 (2014): 391–410.

52. By comparison with Ethiopia or Iran, the Hindu nationalists do suffer from the severe problem that the greatest pre-colonial Indian empire, that of the Mughals, was a Muslim empire, and India's most famous architectural monuments date from that era. This has required a degree of historiographical amnesia and falsification on the part of Modi's followers that is extreme even in the annals of nationalism.

53. Robert J. Lieber, *Retreat and Its Consequences: American Foreign Policy and the Problem of World Order* (Cambridge: Cambridge University Press, 2016).

54. Erik Jones, "From the End of History to the Retreat of Liberalism", *Survival* 59, no. 6 (2017): 165–74.

55. Larry Diamond, Marc F. Plattner and Christopher Walker, eds., *Authoritarianism Goes Global: The Challenge to Democracy* (Baltimore: Johns Hopkins University Press, 2016); Azar Gat, "The Return of Authoritarian Great Powers", *Foreign Affairs* 86 (2007): 59–65.

56. Beate Jahn et al., *Journal of International Relations and Development*, Special Issue Critiquing Liberalism, 15, no. 12 (April 2012).

57. See "Defense Planning Guidance 1994–1999", US National Security Council, 16 April 1992, https://www.archives.gov/files/declassification/iscap/pdf/2008-003-docs1–12.pdf.

58. Walter Russell Mead, "The Return of Geopolitics: The Revenge of the Revisionist Powers", *Foreign Affairs* 93 (2014): 69–75.

59. Mauro F. Guillén, *Rude Awakening: Threats to the Global Liberal Order* (Philadelphia: University of Pennsylvania Press, 2018).
60. Jarrod Hayes, *Constructing National Security: US Relations with India and China* (Cambridge: Cambridge University Press, 2013).
61. For example, Vice President Mike Pence's speech to the Hudson Institute on 4 October 2018, https://www.hudson.org/events/1610-vice-president-mike-pence-s-remarks-on-the-administration-s-policy-towards-china102018.
62. Katerina Dalacoura, "US Democracy Promotion in the Arab Middle East since 11 September 2001: A Critique", *International Affairs* 81, no. 5 (2005): 963–79.
63. John Ikenberry and Anne-Marie Slaughter, *Forging a World of Liberty under Law* (Princeton: Princeton University Press, 2006), 6.
64. Harry Verhoeven, "The Party and the Gun: African Liberation, Asian Comrades and Socialist Political Technologies", *Third World Quarterly* 41, no. 3 (2020), 560–581.
65. David Brewster, "Beyond the 'String of Pearls': Is There Really a Sino-Indian Security Dilemma in the Indian Ocean?", *Journal of the Indian Ocean Region* 10, no. 2 (2014): 133–49.
66. Lee Jones and Jinghan Zeng, "Understanding China's 'Belt and Road Initiative': Beyond 'Grand Strategy' to a State Transformation Analysis", *Third World Quarterly* 40, no. 8 (2019): 1415–39.
67. Andrew Small, *The China–Pakistan Axis: Asia's New Geopolitics* (New York: Oxford University Press, 2015).
68. Darren J. Lim and Rohan Mukherjee, "What Money Can't Buy: The Security Externalities of Chinese Economic Statecraft in Post-war Sri Lanka", *Asian Security* 15, no. 2 (2019): 73–92.
69. Hongzhou Zhang and Mingjiang Li, "Sino-Indian Border Disputes", ISPI Analysis no. 181, 2013, https://www.ispionline.it/sites/default/files/pubblicazioni/analysis_181_2013.pdf.
70. The failure of the Non-Aligned Movement has been replicated since the end of the Cold War by that of regional organizations in Asia, as discussed briefly in chapter 1. The hope that regional organizations would be able to create new regionally generated political orders that would exclude outside great power interference has so far proved empty. The Association of Southeast Asian Nations remains a forum for limited cooperation, deeply divided over the issue of Chinese expansionism and rival claims to the South China Sea. The South Asian Association for Regional Cooperation is paralysed by Indian hopes of regional hegemony and the opposition of other South Asian states to this. Most dramatic of all has been the collapse of the Gulf Cooperation Council (GCC). The strong resemblance of the autocratic Sunni monarchies seemed to give it a chance of becoming something like the European Union, but the GCC too has foundered on internal divisions.
71. For the realist and nationalist character of Nehru's policy towards the US, see Rudra Chaudhuri, *Forged in Crisis: India and the USA since 1947* (London: Hurst and Co., 2013).
72. Hugh White, *The China Choice: Why We Should Share Power* (New York: Oxford University Press, 2013).

INDEX

Note: Page numbers followed by "*f*" refer to figures.

307

INDEX

INDEX

INDEX

INDEX

Nakfa, 173
Napoleonic Wars, 42, 44
Nasser, Gamal Abdel, 215
Natal (South Africa), 20, 55
Natal Indian Congress, 57
Natal Porbandar Trust, 54
National Committee, 151
"National Day of Prayer", 57
National Guard, 127, 128
National Intelligence and Security
Agency (NISA), 194, 201, 202,
205
National Party–Labour Party
government, 56
National Trades Union Congress,
82
Nationalism, 255
"nations and nationalities", 173
natios, 13
NATO (North Atlantic Treaty
Organization), 194, 239
Navy SEALs, 205
Naxalite movement, 151
Nazism, 23
NCO, 202
Neguse, Zecharias, 180
Nehru, Jawaharlal, 25, 214, 215,
233, 235, 261
Nehruvian liberal social democ-
racy, 69
Neoliberal ideas, 162
neoliberalism, 27, 29, 142, 143
Nepal, 148, 231
New York Times, 146, 154
New York, 29, 200
Niger, 206
NISA. *See* National Intelligence
and Security Agency (NISA)
Nobel Peace Prize, 153
non-governmental organizations
(NGOs), 128, 142, 145, 148,
151, 156, 157, 248

North African, 119
North America, 19, 63, 231, 232,
239
North Atlantic, 27, 34, 96, 114,
216
North India, 46, 253
Norway, 232
Novaes, Lucas, 95
Nyerere, Julius, 25, 215
NYU Abu Dhabi, 129

OAU. *See* Organization of African
Unity (OAU)
Obama, Barack, 31, 79
Occupational Safety, 143
"oceanic histories", 9
OCI. *See* Overseas Citizens of
India (OCI)
odious native customs", 205
OECD countries, 124
"Office of the Protector of
Immigrants", 56
oil state, 117–39
OLF. *See* Oromo Liberation Front
(OLF)
Oman Airways, 121
Oman, 11, 15, 25, 44, 48, 117,
121, 123, 124, 138, 215
OPDO. *See* Oromo People's
Democratic Organization
(OPDO)
Operation Restore Hope, 27
Opium Wars, 213
Orban, Viktor, 236
Organization of African Unity
(OAU), 181
Oromo Liberation Front (OLF),
176, 177, 178
Oromo People's Democratic
Organization (OPDO), 177
Oromo territories, 177
Orthodox Christians, 172

INDEX

Ottoman Empire, 118, 135, 234, 249

Outlaw Regime, 190

Overseas Citizens of India (OCI), 64

Pacific, 27, 36, 210

"pact of domination", 175, 179, 181

Pakistan Muslim League-Nawaz (PML-N), 99, 106, 109

Pakistan People's Party (PPP), 69, 98, 99, 106, 107, 110

Pakistan Tehreek-e-Insaf (PTI), 99

Pakistan, 26, 27, 31, 36, 44, 48, 52, 53, 54, 68, 69, 70, 71, 84, 94, 95, 97, 98–9, 100, 101, 106, 108, 113, 115, 149, 152, 163, 164, 166–8, 210, 218, 225, 226, 229, 231, 232, 237, 240, 244, 246, 248, 252, 255, 259, 260, 262

Pakistani Kashmir, 225

Pakistani Punjab, 31

panchayat, 103

pandemic crisis, 243

pan-Islamic nationalism, 153

PAP. *See* People's Action Party (PAP)

"parallel Somalia policy", 200, 201

Parkinson, John, 150

parochial identity, 135

Parsis, 52

Partition (1947), 2, 98, 163–71, 174, 175, 178, 179, 182, 183, 184, 185, 225

Party Congress, 219

Patel, 52

Pax Americana, 3, 4, 5, 15, 16, 23, 26, 28, 33, 34, 67, 87, 119, 143, 165, 184, 188, 189, 191, 204, 221, 232, 234

Pax Britannica, 5, 11, 15, 16, 17, 18, 20, 21, 22, 23, 24, 25, 26, 32, 33, 34, 37, 38, 41, 88, 122, 200, 205, 213, 231, 244, 247

Pax Romana-style, 14

PELU. *See* Public Entertainment Licensing Unit (PELU)

Penang, 19

Pentagon, 9, 225

People of Indian Origin (PIO), 64

People's Action Party (PAP), 72

People's Front for Democracy and Justice (PFDJ), 170

People's Liberation Army Navy, 6

Percy Amendment, 146

Persia, 43, 49, 52

Persian Gulf, 18, 27, 42

petro-monarchy, 118

PFDJ. *See* People's Front for Democracy and Justice (PFDJ)

PGE. *See* Provisional Government of Eritrea (PGE)

Philippines, 26, 27, 69, 217

Philpot, Daniel, 165

"phone ladies", 154, 155

phone purchase loan, 156

PIO. *See* People of Indian Origin (PIO)

PLA Navy, 217, 226

PML-N. *See* Pakistan Muslim League-Nawaz (PML-N)

PML-Q, 106

"political settlement", 165, 168

Porbandar, 52, 53, 54

Portugal, 25, 46

Portuguese, 13, 15, 43, 44, 46, 233, 234

post-Cold War, 226

post-colonial, 113, 214, 215, 222, 229, 232, 233, 235, 236, 237

post-Derg transitional arrangements, 174

INDEX